# ƒrench
## CIVILIZATION
### AND ITS DISCONTENTS

# After the Empire:
# The Francophone World and
# Postcolonial France

### Series Editor

Valérie Orlando, Illinois Wesleyan University

### Advisory Board

Robert Bernasconi, Memphis University
Alec Hargreaves, Florida State University
Chima Korieh, Central Michigan University
Françoise Lionnet, UCLA
Obioma Nnaemeka, Indiana University
Kamal Salhi, University of Leeds
Tracy D. Sharpley-Whiting, Hamilton College
Frank Ukadike, Tulane University

This series is dedicated to the promotion of intellectual thought on and about the Francophone world. *After the Empire* provides a forum for the publication of original works that explore Francophone literature and cinema, politics, history, and culture. The series problematizes notions of identity and exile and includes the study of the Francophone world's relationship to France as an integral part of Francophone expression.

*Of Suffocated Hearts and Tortured Souls: Seeking Subjecthood through Madness in Francophone Women's Writing of Africa and the Caribbean*, by Valérie Orlando

*Francophone Post-Colonial Cultures: Critical Essays*, edited by Kamal Salhi

*In Search of Shelter: Subjectivity and Spaces of Loss in the Fiction of Paule Constant*, by Margot Miller

*French Civilization and Its Discontents: Nationalism, Colonialism, Race*, edited by Tyler Stovall and Georges Van Den Abbeele

# *french* CIVILIZATION
# AND ITS DISCONTENTS

## *nationalism, colonialism, race*

EDITED BY TYLER STOVALL
GEORGES VAN DEN ABBEELE

LEXINGTON BOOKS

Lanham • Boulder • New York • Oxford

Back cover poster courtesy of the National Archives, Overseas Section, Aix-en-Provence (France), all rights reserved.

This poster was one of many created to advertise the 1931 Colonial World's Fair in Paris. The fair was one of the largest ever held in Paris, and it sought to give the French a better appreciation for the nation's colonies and their contributions to national life. The poster, which emphasizes French dominance of a variety of exotic peoples, illustrates nicely the tension between French ideas of universalism and the logic of imperial expansion.

LEXINGTON BOOKS

Published in the United States of America
by Lexington Books
An imprint of the Rowman & Littlefield Publishing Group, Inc.
4501 Forbes Boulevard, Suite 200, Lanham, Maryland 20706

PO Box 317
Oxford
OX2 9RU, UK

Copyright © 2003 by Lexington Books

British Library Cataloguing in Publication Information Available

**Library of Congress Cataloging-in-Publication Data**

French civilization and its discontents : nationalism, colonialism, race
/ edited by Tyler Stovall and Georges Van Den Abbeele.
    p. cm.
Includes bibliographical references and index.
 ISBN 0-7391-0646-5 (hardcover : alk. paper)—ISBN 0-7391-0647-3
(pbk. : alk. paper)
  1. France—Civilization. 2. France—Relations—French-speaking
countries. 3. French-speaking countries—Relations—France. 4.
France—Race relations. I. Stovall, Tyler Edward. II. Van Den Abbeele,
Georges.
 DC33.F777 2003
 944.08—dc21
                                                          2003009223
Printed in the United States of America

⊚™ The paper used in this publication meets the minimum requirements of
  American National Standard for Information Sciences—Permanence of Paper
for Printed Library Materials, ANSI/NISO Z39.48–1992.

# CONTENTS

# ACKNOWLEDGMENTS

We would like to thank the University of California Humanities Research Institute for its initial support in funding a resident research group (winter 1996) and ensuing conference on the topic of "French Identity in Question" (held at the University of California, Santa Cruz, April 18–19, 1997). Further support to develop this volume of essays came from the Davis Humanities Institute, the UC-Davis Committee on Research, the UC-Santa Cruz Center for Cultural Studies, and the France/Berkeley Fund of UC-Berkeley. We would like to thank Sharon O'Toole Dubois, Erica Johnson, Kristin Koster, John Van Den Heuvel, Michael G. Vann, Jason Proetorius, and Maureen Morasch for their dedicated and timely material assistance at various stages of this project. We are very grateful to Serena Krombach, Senior Editor at Lexington Books, for her encouragement and patient support of the publication of this book. Finally, we would like to thank the contributors to this volume for their creativity, expertise, and patience.

# INTRODUCTION

*Tyler Stovall and Georges Van Den Abbeele*

This volume is about the state of France, its language and culture in the world today. France is, of course, not what it used to be.

A century ago, two European powers appeared infallibly dominant in world affairs: Great Britain and France. The history of the subsequent decades would, however, be marked by the unanticipatedly swift decline of these powers. On the one hand, the rival nation-states of Germany, Russia, and the United States directly challenged their supremacy in various ways, most spectacularly during the course of the two world wars. On the other hand, in a perhaps less dramatic but ultimately more decisive way, they lost their vast empires as former colonies demanded their independence, sometimes through successful petition, at other times by long and bloody struggle. What the arduous process of decolonization revealed, in any case, was the manifest dependence of the formerly great powers on their colonial possessions as a source of unparalleled commercial wealth (agricultural and mineral resources as well as massive, cheap labor) and geopolitical reach. At mid-century, following the end of World War II but just prior to decolonization, no one questioned that Britain and France should hold permanent seats on the Security Council of the newly created United Nations along with the other indisputable superpowers—the United States, China, and the Soviet Union. Today, it seems strange and anachronistic that the two European nations should continue to exert veto power in that venue when larger, more powerful countries such as Germany, India, or Japan do not.

   While the pull of a common language and cultural heritage slowly led the
English to the current melding of their geopolitical interests and policies
with their now supremely dominant ex-colony, the United States, France
has trod a less clearly determined path, one whose *apparent* vagaries and
inconsistencies—alternating between strongly pro-American and intensely
anti-American attitudes, dropping in and out of NATO, promoting neocolonialist ventures and claiming to speak on behalf of the "third world,"
etc.—is best understood as the persistent assertion, since the time of
Charles de Gaulle, of an independence and exceptionalism that retains at
least the illusion if not the reality of a continuing importance in world affairs. For most of the twentieth century, though, the political decline of
France remained successfully masked or compensated by the enduring
worldwide prestige of its culture and intellectual life—rather vaingloriously
referred to by the French as their "civilization." From surrealism and exis-
tentialism through the various strands of structuralism and poststructuralism, French thought reigned supreme with parallel sway in literature,
painting, architecture, and the cinema. The names of Jean-Paul Sartre, Simone de Beauvoir, Michel Foucault, Le Corbusier, François Truffaut, and
Jean-Luc Godard dot the intellectual landscape of the last century and define Paris, to follow Walter Benjamin's magnificent expression, not just as
the "capital of the nineteenth century" but that of the twentieth century
as well.[1] More importantly, Paris served as an intellectual "mecca" throughout this time as the adopted home of innumerable writers and artists from
throughout the world: Gertrude Stein, Djuna Barnes, Ernest Hemingway,
Walter Benjamin himself, Carl Dreyer, Pablo Picasso, Richard Wright, Paul
Robeson, James Joyce, Samuel Beckett, Vasili Kandinsky, Max Ernst, and so
on. As the place where Aimé Césaire, Léon Damas, and Léopold Sédar
Senghor first met and studied together, Paris served as the seedbed for the
Negritude movement. And Parisian presses (Présence Africaine and L'Har-
mattan, among others) have disseminated the works of such renowned
Francophone postcolonial writers as Frantz Fanon, Camara Laye, Jacques
Rabemananjara, Kateb Yacine, Rachid Boudjedra, Tahar Ben Jelloun, Assia
Djebar, Édouard Glissant, Maryse Condé, Patrick Chamoiseau, and Linda
Lê, many of whom have lived or still live in the French metropolis. Traditionally, this impressive internationalism of the French cultural scene was
nurtured and sustained by the cosmopolitan aspirations of the French Enlightenment and the universalist ideals of the 1789 Revolution, defining *la
patrie* as the home of liberty, equality, and fraternity for all.
   And yet . . . and yet those republican virtues that made France and its
"civilization" so inviting a place and so cosmopolitan an abode seem in-

creasingly suspect as historical research and current circumstances bring the limits of French identity increasingly to the fore. While the world-renowned Francophone authors just mentioned may be published in Paris, their works remain surprisingly ignored by the French academic establishment, which remains content to study the masterpieces of the classic metropolitan writers while consigning the most vibrant strand of contemporary thought and literature written in French to the specialty venues of "local" or even "foreign" literature. Gone too seem to be the heydays of French thought as French university life reasserts its return to normalcy after sweeping away the last vestiges of "la pensée 68."

For scholars of French studies abroad, the metropolitan drift back to traditionalism and rigid disciplinarity appears decidedly at odds with what has and still does fuel interest in things French outside France, namely the interdisciplinary progressivism of French "theory" and the pluricultural dynamism of Francophone letters. The widely read and translated works of Michel Foucault, Jacques Derrida, Jacques Lacan, and other French "critical theorists" have in turn propelled the international development of various new, interdisciplinary fields of study, including postcolonialism, cultural studies, gender studies, queer theory, and the like. Yet, increasingly, the inspiration and sphere of references in these fields derive more apparently from the complex legacy of the British Imperium and its American continuation than from any continental context, much less what is happening in Paris. The irony here is that even those who continue to do classical French theory in an American context find themselves increasingly alienated from, if not utterly at odds with, the prevailing academic trends in France itself.

Compounding the issue of French studies as practiced *outside* of France is that of the study of French literature and culture that has arisen outside of France and indeed throughout the French-speaking world in spite of metropolitan French indifference and hostility. The study of what has come to be called "Francophone" literature and cultural history (including the critical study of the French colonial administration and its aftermaths) is incontestably the fastest growing subfield of French studies worldwide today. Yet this exhilarating expansion of the corpus of French studies finds few approving echoes in the metropolis, and this despite the sudden development of something like a global Francophone consciousness with an almost dizzying array of lateral contacts all around the periphery as Anglo-American scholars circumvent Paris to interact with their Caribbean, Canadian, African, and Pacific counterparts. Of course, such a decentering of France in French studies also means the increasing development of research projects and activities that cannot and indeed could never be funded by traditional arms of the French government per se, such as the Ministry of Culture. What happens, then, when the study of French is no longer coterminous with the study of France? Such is indeed the question that has guided the collaborators to this volume. Oddly, the situation that would gloomily seem to describe a general crisis of French studies in a downturn turns out to designate a vertiginous expansion whose main threat is the very erosion of the category of French identity that holds the field together. As such, the project contained in this volume is not simply a French version of Anglo postcoloniality, and certainly not an attempt to restore the French colonial empire at the expense of the British. Rather, the contributors to this collection are both elaborating models of the new French studies *and* engaging in a risky struggle with those who would still hope to see the study of French safely brought back within the confines of the hexagon and who yearn for a renewed emphasis on the cultural retransmission by non-French scholars of the state of thought in the metropolitan capital in accordance with the longstanding republican ideal of *la mission civilisatrice*. A sign of sorts made this dissonance overt in 1993 when the revisionist *New History of French Literature* was translated into the language of Racine and Voltaire. Originally published in English by Harvard University Press with entries written primarily by Anglo-American scholars, though headed by Dénis Hollier (a French native) as its editor in chief, the volume was quickly denounced in the French press as so much graffiti irreverently scrawled on the literary monuments of French civilization by uncouth agents of the *politiquement correct*.[2] Few foresaw the icy Gallic response to the reimportation of French thought in the hands of its foreign admirers back to its homeland.

The exportation of French cultural values and intellectual traditions was first institutionalized by the colonial school systems seeking to advance France's "civilizing mission" throughout its empire, then aggressively developed worldwide through the establishment of the Alliance Française institutes and the dedicated work in every country by that peculiarly French diplomatic officer, the "attaché culturel." But clearly no proponents of these missions of French civilization ever expected that cultural exchange to be in any way bidirectional. France's "missions," forged by the Jacobin heritage of the Revolution, have seemingly always understood its "universalism" to be coterminous with the assimilation of a specifically French identity and its republican values. The very word *civilization*, first coined in the eighteenth century by the philosopher Mirabeau to indicate both the reality of organized society and the ideal of human progress, took on what Jean Starobinski has termed a "sacred authority" during the period of the French

Revolution and afterwards: "Postrevolutionary language naturally identified the sacred values of the Revolution with those of civilization and therefore claimed for France, the fatherland of revolution, the privilege of leading civilization's advance guard, of serving as its beacon."[3] First the revolutionary armies and then those of Napoleon found justification for their aggressive incursions abroad in this ideology of spreading civilization (i.e., the current French version of it) to others, willing or not, and "liberating" them from barbarity and superstition. The quasi-religious zeal of this policy led no less than Victor Hugo triumphantly to proclaim that "the French people have been the missionary of civilization in Europe."[4] In the next few decades, French colonialism and imperialism aggressively expanded this "civilizing mission" to the rest of the world.

In practice, though, especially that concretized under colonial rule, limits were drawn with some folks considered worthy of being civilized while others were termed "unassimilable" and doomed to never-ending barbarism. The ideological presupposition being that France epitomized civilization as no other nation did and that to be French was synonymous with being civilized, all non-French peoples were under the burden of having to prove their being civilized while struggling to shed recurring suspicions of their barbarism. Consequently, full assimilation with French identity and (its) civilization would always remain a kind of unreachable asymptote, even for the "évolués" and no matter how long they slaved in French schools, perfected their language skills, or lived in Paris itself. There would remain, for instance, the enduring anxiety of never speaking French well enough or being quite cultured enough in one's appreciation of French theater, cuisine, or wine, though in actuality there are no greater French purists than Belgian grammarians, Senegalese diplomats, or American professors of French. As for those not included in such francophilic games, "inassimilability" has long operated as a covert term for religious, racial, or national exclusion. In the colonies, there thus obtained a two-tiered system of education and administration: one for the "indigènes" and another for "assimilés." These assimilationist ideals of the French colonial project are, of course, very different from the British policy of "indirect rule" and difficult to evaluate in the contemporary context of global multiculturality. For if the worst excesses of French colonialism predicated a sweeping denial of cultural particularism and indeed of any possible non-French identity (emblematized by such absurdities as the erection of statues to Joan of Arc in the Mauritanian desert or the forcible recantation by African and Asian schoolchildren of "nos ancêtres les Gaulois"), on the other hand, the concomitant universalist ideals of the French Revolution also legitimated and encouraged the very struggle against that colonialist oppression. Resistance to the Jacobin paradigm thus often takes the form of its radical reappropriation, as differently described in chapters in this volume by Donna Hunter, Hafid Gafaiti, and Édouard Glissant. Moreover, the French concept of a civic rather than an ethnic nationalism wreaks further havoc with any easy extension of the postcolonial theory of hybridity to a Francophone context just as it highlights the particular scandal of current French attitudes against immigrants—given France's historic acceptance and absorption of foreigners, closer to the United States in this regard than to most other European countries.

A good example of the particular tension between French cultural imperialism, on the one hand, and universalism, on the other, can be found in the proposal the French government, after the end of World War II, made to its colonies for the establishment of a single *Union française* in the hope they could all join together in one vast nation with equal rights and representation for all. Some, like Martinique and Guadaloupe, found this option appealing and chose to become full-fledged departments within the French metropolitan state. Others read this expansive gesture as precisely the epitome of French colonialist ideology and rejected the proposal outright, preferring instead to become independent states. The stakes involved were perhaps most tragically revealed in the Algerian situation, involving a long, bloody struggle for independence made worse by the fact that the former colony had already long been incorporated into the French republic as three separate departments. Far from accrediting the Algerian resistance as in any way anticolonial, the French could only see the uprising as an illegitimately secessionist civil disturbance, given that Algeria already was officially "part" of France. "L'Algérie c'est la France," declared François Mitterand himself in 1954 by way of dismissing the claims of the FLN rebels. As for those colonies that opted for deparmentalization, the ambiguous legacy of that choice has become increasingly apparent in their continuing economic and administrative dependency on Paris, while many of the officially independent former colonies remain financially, commercially, or even militarily indebted to France.

As for the metropole itself, one result of the decolonization has been that the already rather limited (and manifestly ethnocentric) concept of assimilation has become increasingly circumscribed by a France whose current intellectual energies have turned inward by a tremendous concern, at times even an obsession with its own historical memory. On the one hand, this development has certainly issued forth in such masterpieces as Pierre Nora's multivolume *Realms of Memory* and in the important critical work to reveal the extent of collaborationism under the Vichy Régime.[5] On the other hand,

despite such self-critical achievements, the turn to memory is also a reaffir-
mation of and harkening back to traditional French values and identity, manifest in such sentimental nostalgia films as *Manon des sources* and *Jean de
Florette*, or the return to filmic adaptations of classic novels such as *Le
colonel Chabert* (precisely the kind of "cinéma de papa" decried by the
champions of the French New Wave back in the 1950s). In the area of literary criticism, the theoretical adventurism of structuralism, which garnered
such international attention and controversy, has given way to the more empirical and archival approach of *la critique génétique* that elucidates the specific, "generative" procedures by which individual authors have come to
write their works. More generally, the awakening of French memory has
tended to remain rather selective (the crimes of Vichy, yes, but not so much
about those of French imperialism in North Africa or Southeast Asia).

Most alarming is the forgetting of France's long and remarkable history
of immigration (comparable only to the United States) with the recent attention to the so-called immigrant problem, spectacularly exploited by the
xenophobic likes of Jean-Marie Le Pen and his far-right National Front
Party.[6] Here, the tensions between the high-minded proclamations of the
universal "rights of man and citizen" and the bitter reality of identity politics have issued into a full-blown crisis of French republican values. In
many respects, contemporary France is a land of vibrant multiculturalism,
symbolized most publicly by the European and World Cup champion
French soccer team led by its powerful forward, Zinedine Zidane, himself
a Beur of Algerian descent, and teammates of African, Latin American, and
Eastern European origin. But like the treasure of contemporary Francophone literature, traces of French multiculturalism are all too quickly dis-
missed as ethnic exceptionalism or cases of exemplary assimilation while
panic before the demographic rise of Islam to surpass both Judaism and
Protestantism as France's second most practiced religion has led to increasing restrictions on French identity in defiance of the nation's tradition
(or at least traditional rhetoric) of civic nationalism. The most outrageous of
these restrictions, the infamous Pasqua legislation of 1993, denied automatic citizenship to children *born in France* of immigrant parents, a move
that very specifically targeted the Beurs, or French native population of
Maghrebin descent, effectively disenfranchising this significant community
*within* France. Such departures from legal precedent mark the increasing
anxiety of the French over who they are or have become as well as offering
an ironic testimony to the changed reality of contemporary France.

Regardless or in spite of such aggressive disavowals of the changing multicultural, multiracial identity of France today matched by an

overcompensatory need to demonstrate technological advancement (through nuclear testing in the South Pacific, atomic power plants along the Rhine, the Concorde, the TGV, even the Minitel)—both of which tend nonetheless to underscore French decline and the loss of political/ military clout and cultural prestige—there is no question that there has arisen in the last few decades something like a "Francophone" culture on a worldwide scale. We use the word here, in quotation marks, to highlight the immense heterogeneity of the phenomenon. To be precise, the so-called Francophone world is a far-flung composite of many cultures/ nations whose common attachment to the use of the French language belies amazingly different histories and cultural trajectories. Many but not all are former colonies, with or without French settler communities. Some Francophone locations—such as Martinique, Tahiti, or Réunion— are still technically part of France, included in the metropole as "overseas departments." For some, French is the official language of the nation; for others, French is one of several languages used; and in still other cases, French remains important in a more localized sphere such as commerce, civil administration, or education.

And while the perfect grammar and style of *les assimilés* may have been the ideal for earlier generations of Francophone writers, increasingly they have chosen to express themselves in the dialects, creoles, or hybrid tongues of their scattered communities. This linguistic license taken in the face of what is historically the most rigidified and tightly policed of languages has profound implications for the central role of France and the standard norm of French. The traditional bulwark of French nationalism since the era of absolutism, safeguarded in its "purity" and authenticity by that special institution known as the *Académie française*, the French language is an especially regulated and homogenized tongue. More than the prestige dialect of the Île-de-France that has managed to impose itself over all others, standard French has become thanks to its overtly political manipulation since the seventeenth century both a powerful discriminatory apparatus in the creation of administrative elites (the correct use of standard French is the sine qua non of legal authority and bureaucratic power) *and*, through the school system and other cultural institutions, the very condition of French identity itself as the ability to speak a single, tightly standardized language no matter what one's region, social class, or ethnic identity: to be French means to speak standard French and a fortiori if you are Belgian or Québécois or Haitian or Senegalese or Tunisian. Not only has the politics of the French language meant the virtual eradication of regionalist dialects within France itself (from Breton to Provençal) but in its

colonial manifestation it has aimed at the suppression of indigenous languages as well as their cultures. Indeed, no picture of French colonialism
is more arresting than that of the *assimilés* who speak an impeccable
French and evince all the trappings of Parisian *mondanéité* while having
lost all sense of their own language and culture. The integrity of the French
language, in sum, is at the very core of the concept of universalism.

Ironically, though, and as Édouard Glissant eloquently argues, the very
extent of the Francophone world and the sheer diversity of peoples to assimilate have in fact spawned an intense unraveling of French linguistic purity and universalism in the phenomenon known as "creolization." The
word *créole* refers of course to those "composite languages" that arose primarily in the islands and other enclosed colonized spaces of the New World
inhabited by large, transplanted African populations whose use of language
had to be flexible and subtle enough to work through the unparalled
plurilingualism of the Caribbean (including colonial European languages,
diverse African tongues, and the remnants of indigenous American speech).
For Glissant, the concept of creolization speaks not just to such localized
*linguae francae* but to a generalized phenomenon of heterogeneity in cultural as well as linguistic practices. The specific fate of French, often cited
as the key pan-African language of commerce and diplomacy, is to achieve
perhaps its universalist aspirations but only at the cost of its becoming
something very other than the preserved and controlled language of the
*Académie française*—something much more protean, changeable, and diverse, something able to cross linguistic and cultural boundaries precisely
because of *its* ability to assimilate an ever-increasing diversity of speakers.
Only such an "assimilation" that in fact leaves the identity of French in
question is capable of achieving the kind of multicultural reach universalism so egregiously failed to do and of keeping the French language alive
and compelling to some 113 million native speakers worldwide and another
61 million second language or occasional speakers.[7] Whereas English may
boast many more speakers around the world, its increasing state as a kind
of international lingua franca appears to be impoverishing it through sim-
plification and the normalizing effect of global media. French, on the other
hand, outside France (but also to a lesser extent within it as the provincial
dialects of areas like Brittany, Provence, and Alsace are reasserted) everywhere betrays the traces of its local history and customs. This rootedness of
the French language in the specific human expression of its different location is at least partially a result of its *non*-hegemonic status in most Francophone countries. In Africa and Southeast Asia, the use of French occurs
within or despite a long conflictual history with the indigenous languages of

former colonies. In the Caribbean and Indian Ocean archipelagoes, the creole languages have arisen borrowing from the diverse languages of their transplanted occupants: French, African, South Asian. Even in noncolonial locations such as Canada, Belgium, or Switzerland, French exists in competition not only with competing national languages (English, Dutch, German) but also with its dialectal variants (Joual in Quebec, Walloon and Marollien in Belgium, various forms of Rheto-Romance in Switzerland). The survival of French in all these locations has historically depended upon its creative mixing with other languages and consequent departures from the hexagonal norms of *français standard*.[8]

The contemporary development of something like a "global" French has been spurred by an increasing level of interchange between Francophone locations that bypasses Paris entirely. These exchanges are aided by contemporary advances in telecommunications, jet travel, and educational exchanges. While Haitian writers publish in Montreal, films are coproduced in Belgium, Tunisia, and Burkina Faso, and the international Francophone studies council (CIEF), headquartered in Louisiana, holds its annual meeting just about anywhere but France: Dakar, Tunis, Abidjan, Hanoi, etc. The rise of such an autonomous and vibrant "francophonie" is again viewed rather ambiguously in France. Certainly, there is a sense of renewed opportunity for France and French to maintain a semblance of internationalism. On the one hand, the French government supports an annual "sommet de la francophonie" to discuss issues of mutual interest, has instituted a ministry of Francophone affairs, and the Académie has even eased some orthographic strictures. On the other hand, though, the annual summit of Francophone nations is clearly understood to be under French leadership and its "haut conseil" by the president of France. The French university continues to ignore the contributions of Francophone authors, and in the face of perceived threats to linguistic purity, the French government most peculiarly amended the constitution in 1992 to extend "protection" to the French language itself. The reaction to a globalized Francophone language and culture is thus not unlike that before the changing demography of the hexagon itself. To lose control of the French language is perhaps the ultimate indignity for the metropole, the final revenge of the *inassimilés* as they finally lay claim to the full legacy of republican values, but also the greatest hope for French *and* Francophone salvation from the Anglo-American global imperium.

As for the state of French studies, the lesson of creolization is that France itself is no longer as French as it once seemed. The future of French civilization would thus seem to lie in the hands of its most ostensive "discontents." Our reprise of Sigmund Freud's title to his famous study of cultural behavior, *Civilization and Its Discontents*, where he extended his model of the individual psyche to the level of society itself as a repressive structure (with the rule of law incarnating the parental superego), pays homage to the impressive impact the father of psychoanalysis has had on French critical thought from surrealism up through Jacques Lacan. More generally, though, without subscribing to a Freudian viewpoint, the contributors to this volume all see the primary value of studying the "discontents" to a societal (imperial?) norm that constructs itself as a "civilization" while remaining blind (or "unconscious") to its own particular modes of repression. "French Civilization" also recalls the specific pedagogical subject matter designed to supplement and reward the grueling study of the French language. The historical and cultural materials that traditionally made up coursework in French "Civ" were clearly celebratory if not wholly laudatory in nature. As far as we can tell, however, French Civ has always been designed exclusively for exportation (or for the teaching of *foreign* students *in* France, such as at the well-established Cours de Civilisation Française program of studies at the Sorbonne). Although French students are certainly not immune from the triumphalist ideology of French Civilization, their exposure comes indirectly through disciplinary coursework in grammar, literature, history, and so forth. And since they are French already, there is no need to study what it might mean to be French. Indeed, the subtext of the traditional French Civ course was always about learning what one needed to know in order to *be* French, a pedagogical exercise thoroughly in the service of assimilationist colonialism. The contemporary wave of critical French and Francophone cultural studies represents another decentering of metropolitan influence as those discontents with French Civilization tell their versions of the story, one that most pointedly does *not* begin with "nos ancêtres les Gaulois."

It is to further these alternative, "discontented" versions of French identity and its reputed "civilization" that this collection of essays is dedicated. And first and foremost we begin by questioning the very Frenchness of French thought itself, a question that leads to the discovery that its most cutting-edge intellectuals and artists have found their inspiration far outside the hallowed confines of the hexagon. For Richard Terdiman, the famous concepts of "marginality" and "heterology" that mark the influential thought of Michel de Certeau are themselves rehearsed in this key intellectual's long sojourn and *Bildungsweg* outside France, most especially in North and South America. Patricia Morton analyzes the particularity of Le Corbusier's relation to an exoticized eastern Europe and Middle East as a foundational moment in the development of his revolutionary architectural style, one that has without exaggeration incarnated the very essence of modernity in the built environment. In the world of the cinema, Winifred Woodhull demonstrates the central importance in 1930s French film of exotic landscapes (both provincial and colonial) for the nostalgic recovery of a France thought to be lost to the "decadence" of urban modernity, while Janet Bergstrom reveals the cinematic innovations of France's most controversial contemporary filmmaker, Claire Denis, whose childhood experience in colonial Africa continues to motivate and frame her relentless, irreverent treatment of race and gender roles.

The African diaspora intersects powerfully and in many ways with the Francophone world and our second series of essays addresses that area. Édouard Glissant, as already indicated, eloquently argues on behalf of the creolization of the French language as its best hope. For Glissant, though, the concept of creolization speaks not just to localized *linguae francae* but to a generalized phenomenon of heterogeneity in cultural as well as linguistic practices. Such a refractory heterogeneity can also be found on the intellectual level, as Donna Hunter explains in her discussion of two non-French black thinkers, C. L. R. James and Anna Julia Cooper, whose activism on behalf of racial equality was spurred by the emancipatory and egalitarian ideals of the French revolution as well as by the example of the so-called "Black Jacobins" who led Haiti to its independence from France in 1802 as the first and for long decades the only independent black republic in the world. A later moment in Haitian history is visited by Valerie Kaussen in her treatment of *noirisme*, a fascist ideology that sprang up under the U.S. occupation of the country (1915–1934) in reaction not only to white imperialism but also to the "mulatto" Francophone elite of the island and their common oppression of the black Haitian masses. A more progressive treatment of the "fact of blackness" is found in the Martinican philosopher Frantz Fanon, traditionally viewed as influenced by Hegelian Marxist thought in a Negritude context. Ethan Kleinberg demonstrates, on the contrary, how Fanon's profound *critique* of Hegel directly contests the then reigning interpretation *in France* of the German philosopher, specifically that interpretation put forward by the Russian immigré Alexandre Kojève, whose foregrounding of the master/slave dialectic was popularly espoused by contemporary French intellectuals, such as Jean-Paul Sartre, Raymond Queneau, and Jean Hyppolite. Finally, in his analysis of Nobel laureate Maryse Condé's novel, *Crossing the Mangrove*, Jean Jonassaint forcefully questions the ethnocentrism of major critics who fail to see or recognize an important antecedent in Jacques Roumain's *Masters of the Dew*. That a Guadeloupean writer should be influenced by a Haitian novelist only appears strange in a context where all Francophone writers are viewed as derivative of metropolitan French, European, or Anglo-American models rather than as perceptive and inspired readers of each other. That such a blindness to the Caribbean and Francophone intertexts remains prevalent even among many critics of Francophone and postcolonial literature suggests the extent to which literary criticism itself is not yet postcolonial in its thinking. We can only wonder at the way such literary critical blindness itself mirrors the unique economic dependence of Martinique and Guadaloupe as overseas departments of a France whose trade policies facilitate direct trade (even for foodstuffs and other necessities) between the islands and the distant metropole while setting powerful barriers between them and adjacent Caribbean nations, including Cuba and Haiti.

A third group of essays addresses the other major cultural interface between France and former members of its empire, namely the Maghreb but also the Islamic world in general. Indeed, the confusion between the two is the source of a whole host of problems, as Hafid Gafaiti and Driss Maghraoui elucidate, through precise analyses of the French conquest of Algeria in the nineteenth century. Both manipulating and disavowing the multicultural complexity of Algeria, the French authorities soon pegged the devout Muslim as the epitome of the unassimilable who could never legitimately enter the secular republic. Gafaiti and Maghraoui cite the ways this colonial doctrine carries over into the France of today, characterized by intense intolerance and racism toward its Maghrebian inhabitants. And as previously mentioned, that racism seems all the more striking given the prominence of Islam as the second most common religion in France and by the significant Beur population of French nationals born of North African  immigrant parents or grandparents. Yet the Beurs in the aftermath of the Pasqua and similar legislation continue to be considered "immigrants" in their own country of birth, thus begging the question of what it means to be an immigrant. The result is nothing less than a crisis in French identity, its universalist values, and the status of citizenship in a supposedly civic republic. For Gafaiti, this crisis is marked not just by the colonial past but also by France's ongoing neocolonial relations with Algeria itself. While no less realist in his appraisal of this situation, Maghraoui does see some hopeful signs in the emergence of new political forms in France built around alternative associations like the "organisation politique." Ali Yedes examines another legacy of the French involvement in North Africa, namely the conflicted identity of the so-called "Pieds-Noirs" or European settlers in colonial Algeria, virtually all of whom were "repatriated" to France after Algerian independence in 1962. The experience of that relocation has been

lived, however, as a permanent exile for a community that, even in the heyday of colonial occupation, felt inferior to the French of the metropole and
culturally closer to the indigenous Algerians they themselves looked down
upon. Finally, Nancy Wood considers still another category of Maghrebins,
the Jews of Algeria. Their history, marked by the ebb and flow of anti-
semitism in metropolitan *and* colonial France, is one that alternates between legally imposed French citizenship in a still colonial context (the
Crémieux Decree of 1870) and its cynical retraction under Vichy, before
the mass departure of the Jewish population in the immediate aftermath of
Algeria's independence in 1962. The history of this conflicted status becomes a particularly poignant *lieu de mémoire* for Algerian Jews living in
France today, many of whom in the prevalent climate of anti-Maghrebin
intolerance emphasize the amicable relations between Jews and Muslims in
the face of French colonial policies of selective assimilation. Finally, as she
points out through the evocation of this specific community residing in
France, which includes such eminent figures as philosopher Jacques Derrida and writer Hélène Cixous, some of France's leading contemporary
thinkers are not really so very French after all, even as they indubitably incarnate the most progressive spirit of French thought far beyond the confines of the hexagon.

Once we have taken the point of view, then, of such Francophone "discontents" with French Civilization, we find the lines between France and
its colonies blurring in strange and suggestive ways. Yet, one should caution
against too readily assuming that the tension between cross-cultural euphoria and metropolitan anxieties is only a contemporary phenomenon, as Lyn
Thompson demonstrates with reference to the links between fin de siècle
decadent literature and the creole as figure of racial and sexual transgression. With reference to the Great War, Tyler Stovall examines the policing
of racial and sexual boundaries in the context of the massive importation of
colonial laborers, especially from North Africa and Southeast Asia, to work
alongside French women in businesses and factories while French men
went off to fight in the trenches. Moving again outside of France to nearby
Belgium, Georges Van Den Abbeele examines that country's conflicted relation to French identity in terms of a nationalist iconography of Belgium as
child, most recently resurgent in the aftermath of the pedophile scandals,
at a moment when that nation verges on dissolution.

The strength of these essays no doubt lies in their assertive ability to
change perspective as need be to question the fundamental categories and
terms of French identity, looking both within France and outside of it for
answers. Far from focusing on Francophone culture in isolation and as a po-

tential ghetto for scholars of French, this volume insists on the necessity of studying France and the Francophone world together, on recognizing not only the presence of France in the Francophone world but also the central place occupied by the Francophone world within the very heart of the metropole. That such a new approach to French studies should emanate from an American context need hardly surprise anyone, given that American scholars may in fact be in the best geographic and intellectual position to reconfigure the study of French within this larger frame based no longer centrally in Paris but in Montreal, Brussels, Ifrane, Dakar, Port-au-Prince, New York, California . . . and, yes, in Paris too.

Work on this volume was complete before the events of 2003 put French foreign policy overtly at odds with that of the United States, not only over the invasion of Iraq but also with regards to the consolidation of various EU policies, such as the ban on genetically modified food, farm subsidies, or the proposal to develop a common European defense force. The same period saw President Jacques Chirac's historic first state visit to Algeria, while former President Valéry Giscard d'Estaing chaired the commission that drafted a European constitution, signaling once again the French embrace of the EU as an alternative to American economic and military predominance. Time and space do not allow us to comment on these recent developments as their manifold complexities surely deserve, save to offer a caveat against uncritically viewing these developments, most especially in the American context, as harbingers of some newly-enlightened French state forgoing its old dreams of empire to embrace the new postcolonial reality. It is certainly too early as we write in the summer of 2003 to see where these new directions will lead the French, but the "independent" policies of the French state, including its currently pro-European and anti-American attitude, remain consistent with what we described at the beginning of this introduction as the French search for a new global identity in the aftermath of its loss of both power and prestige subsequent to the loss of its colonial empire.

## NOTES

1. Benjamin used this expression to title two different short essays in 1935 and 1939 that provide overviews of his massive and ultimately unfinished masterwork, posthumously published as *Das Passagen-Werk*, ed. Rolf Tiedemann (Frankfurt: Suhrkamp, 1982). A French translation by Jean Lacoste exists under the title *Paris:*

*capitale du XIXe siècle* (Paris: Editions du Cerf, 1989). In English, the book has been published as *The Arcades Project*, trans. Howard Eiland and Kevin McLaughlin (Cambridge, Mass.: Belknap Press, 1999).

2. See, among others, the review by Angelo Rinaldi, "Tagueurs," *L'Express*, March 25, 1993.

3. Jean Starobinski, *Blessings in Disguise; or, the Morality of Evil*, trans. Arthur Goldhammer (Cambridge, Mass.: Harvard University Press, 1993), 17, 19–20.

4. Cited in Starobinski, *Blessings in Disguise*, 20.

5. See especially, in this regard, Henri Rousso, *The Vichy Syndrome: History and Memory in France since 1944*, trans. Arthur Goldhammer (Cambridge, Mass.: Harvard University Press, 1991).

6. On the history of immigration in France, the work of Gérard Noiriel has become the essential point of reference, most especially *The French Melting Pot: Immigration, Citizenship, and National Identity*, trans. Geoffroy de Laforcade (Minneapolis: University of Minnesota Press, 1996).

7. These statistics are based on the 1999 *Rapport sur l'état de la francophonie dans le monde* put out by the Haut Conseil de la Francophonie and published on an occasional basis in Paris by La documentation française. An excellent discussion of the problems in producing such a census can be found in the 1990 edition, pp. 17–38. As for the tremendous controversies and anxieties triggered by the issue of creolization, a historical process in any case well under way, they have not yet hit the Anglophone world with the exception of a few isolated cases (the American debate over Ebonics and bilingual education, for example), primarily because of the current global hegemony of English achieved through the postwar American domination of the world's politics, economics, and information networks. One wonders when creolization will begin to be felt in the Anglo-American context. At that time, what will have happened to the Francophone world should prove most instructive.

8. "Departure" may not be the right word here since it connotes both a chronological and cultural deviance from some preexisting French "norm." In many cases, nonhexagonal French retains archaisms or elements of competing dialects such as Breton or Picard, which were *never* included in the standardized French officially sanctioned by the *Académie française* since its inception in the seventeenth century.

# PART I

# THE INTELLIGENTSIA AND NEW CONCEPTIONS OF FRENCH IDENTITY

It is only fitting that we begin this study of changing conceptions of France with a section on the intelligentsia, a group that has, from the era of the Enlightenment to the present day, played a central role in defining what (and who) is French. The four chapters in this section consider cultural figures whose work calls into question ideas of French universalism and a cultural master narrative. Together they depict an intellectual tradition characterized by richness, multilayered levels of complexity, and influences from a wide variety of sources and traditions.

In chapter 1, Richard Terdiman discusses how one of the key French exponents of poststructuralism, Michel de Certeau, developed his own concept of marginality. Showing how both de Certeau's life and work lay *outside* the mainstream of French intellectual life, Terdiman argues that he laid the basis for a new, alternative vision of difference, distinct from both French universalism and "Anglo-Saxon" multiculturalism. The work of de Certeau thus demonstrates the diversity of French thought, and one way in which a thinker at the same time marginal and central can transcend traditional limits, laying the ground for a more inclusive intellectual practice. In a very different sense, chapter 2 by Patricia Morton demonstrates the influence of marginality on a seminal French thinker, Le Corbusier. In her analysis of the great architect's 1911 trip to the Balkans, Morton challenges traditional conceptions of his thought as Orientalist, arguing that primitivism is a more accurate way of understanding Le Corbusier's reaction to

this trip. She thus situates his work in the context of the vogue for the primitive in early twentieth-century France, demonstrating how Le Corbusier's
notion of what it meant to be French depended upon a non-French Other.

The remaining two chapters explore the ways in which filmmakers have
used their medium both to create and to deconstruct traditional ideas of
France. In chapter 3, which is centered on French cinema in the 1920s,
Winifred Woodhull notes the preference of realist filmmakers during that
era for exotic locales, be they rural and provincial or colonial, as a way of
implicitly critiquing a metropolitan urban civilization centered in Paris. She
analyzes four films, three set in Provence and one in Quebec, demonstrating how romanticization of the margins of French life served to rebuke the
decadence of the center, setting the stage for the reactionary cultural politics of Vichy. At the same time, however, Woodhull demonstrates that two
of these films, *Toni* and *Maria Chapdelaine*, use modernist cinematic styles
to undermine the traditional polarity between tradition and modernity, and
between metropolitan France and the exotic Francophone world. In an
even more explicit manner, chapter 4 by Janet Bergstrom explores a French
aesthetic in which the margin has become the center. In her study of the innovative French filmmaker Claire Denis, Bergstrom illustrates the operation of marginality at both thematic and stylistic levels. Denis, who grew up
in colonial Francophone Africa, portrays in her films a France where racial
diversity and the legacies of colonialism are ever-present, unquestioned
facts. At the same time, her emphasis on the opacity of her characters and
the fragmentation of their stories calls into question linear narratives of
French life.

These four chapters show to what extent French intellectual production,
usually considered to lie at the heart of national identity, draws upon both
canonical and marginal influences. In these cases, to be French is to be not
just conscious of the Other, but to be, to an important extent, part of it.

●

# THE MARGINALITY OF
# MICHEL DE CERTEAU

*Richard Terdiman*

The resistance of others is the condition of our own development [*progrès*].

—Michel de Certeau, *L'Étranger, ou l'union dans la différence*

Out of the endless and overwhelming flux, we conjure epiphanies as if by miracle. We make meanings. But the condition for our doing so is an experience of ends. For meaning is the consequence of a limit, meaning is an effect of margins. The border where we materialize such meaning is what makes meanings possible. We perceive and conceive and construct and learn on this frontier.

The margin or frontier or border is where something is divided from something else. The *something* could be anything; but the margin makes it what it is. On the border, through separation, its definition, and its relation to what differs from it, become conceivable. Heraclitean projections of ceaseless change then metamorphose into a topology, and begin to frame a temporality. In this sense, continuities are meaningless. Out of the flux, it is difference that crystallizes signification.

This paradigm has a fundamental seduction for historical and interpretive sensibility. In contemporary understanding, it is only through the marking of a difference, through the projection of a border, that the notions of history or of interpretation make sense. This power of the liminary thus resituates the margin as cardinal. We navigate our meanings across these borders. They always materialize from elsewhere.

Michel de Certeau made this principle fundamental in his understanding of history as of culture. Consider his 1980 preface to *The Writing of History*. It begins this way: "Amerigo Vespucci the Discoverer arrives from the sea" (xxv).[1] This narrative is not innocent. Geographically and temporally, it enfolds and exposes the mystery by which meanings arise and interpretations become possible. Politically it projects the potential for violence—or at least the constituting incursion—that accompanies the framing of any signification.

It would be difficult to write an account in which de Certeau's thinking about borders was not powerfully overdetermined by the circumstances of his own biography. Repeatedly, regularly, he sought the margin. It was a distinctive feature of his life as of his thinking. By way of comparison, we might consider the series of eminent figures from Paris who, during the 1970s and 1980s, repeatedly visited the United States—colonizing America for theory, as we might say. Nearly every one of them remained firmly based in Paris. Among this remarkable group of the theory jet-setters of the period, the lone geographic exception was de Certeau. He was the only one who left Paris to accept a full-time position teaching in the United States (at the University of California, San Diego, for six years after 1978). Before this time he had regularly traveled to South America, Mexico, and Canada for teaching and research.[2] In part these displacements reflected a native sense of adventure; in part, however, they translated the fact that, for a long period, de Certeau was in effect an outsider in Paris. As an ordained Jesuit in a resolutely secularized academy—one whose anticlericalism has long been a fundamental ideological tenet—de Certeau did not have, and at the time he accepted his position in the United States he could not have had, a regular post in the French university.[3] It is difficult to imagine that this form of professional disqualification (to consider just one resonance of marginality arising in his own biography) had no relation to de Certeau's sensitivity to problems of difference, disadvantage, and subordination.

Translated onto the level of theory and methodology, the forms and the logic of this sensitivity to the marginal is the problem I analyze here. I want to examine the forms and modes of social understanding that de Certeau rooted in heterology, in what we could call the constancy of difference, or the centrality of the marginal. But we need to remember that while theory informs practice, the two registers cannot simply be conflated. *Language* and *bodies* diverge in fundamental ways. Consequently the reality of marginalization is not just a theoretical counter or an intellectual effect. Marginalization's roots are always political, it always embodies the cruel reality of power. Theorize about marginalization as much as you like, you *know* the threat, the weight of it when—as happened to de Certeau during his time at UCSD—the *Migra*, the U.S. immigration authorities, serve notice that you may be thrown out of the country.[4] As I examine the bases and structure of de Certeau's relation to marginality, it will be important not to forget that, underlying the euphoria of high-theoretical elucubration, the problem under analysis always implicates real bodies, always discloses the affliction of real human lives.

In de Certeau's representations, things always appear intricately modulated. At times this makes him hard to understand.[5] This is a margin effect, in the sense that the difficulty of his writing can be interpreted as an effect of the pressure put on language when its objective is framing and representing the border phenomena de Certeau termed "heterology."[6] Meaning arises on this margin. But capturing that incipience powerfully stresses language's capacity for expression and self-reflection. The discourse of heterology strives to seize its own medium, to express the possibility of its own saying. This is like trying to see vision. Speaking on the margin, speaking about marginality, are constitutively arduous. When we attempt to talk about that protean and ungraspable non-place where everything passes over, we learn how frustratingly experience can wriggle away from words.

Today marginality has become fashionable. But while acknowledging this, I want to suggest an aspect of our understanding of marginality that— in the United States at least—has itself been subtly marginalized. Through his work starting in the 1960s, Michel de Certeau located himself near the beginnings of our contemporary fascination with the margin. And he remains one of its most provocative and insightful theorists. His reflection upon the modes and the significance of difference was extraordinarily diverse. It is central to a remarkable series of his books, stretching from *The Capture of Speech* (1968), through *Culture in the Plural* (1974), *The Writing of History* (1975), and on to *The Practice of Everyday Life* (1980) and *The Mystic Fable* (1982). Now that all of these have appeared in English, it becomes clear how the reflection upon difference that has occupied us for more than two decades now converges with and has found inspiration in de Certeau's work. But what seems most important here is not to award him any prize of intellectual priority, but to recover some resonances of his understanding of marginality that our own uptake has tended to shadow or sideline.

In our multicultural world, "marginality" has most often been construed along lines of race, class, gender, and ethnicity. I do not wish to repudiate that construction. De Certeau was framing it himself as early as 1974, in a portion of *Culture in the Plural* that he called "New Marginalisms." But his work gives us a powerful impetus to *extend* the list. For him the state of marginality is common to a great variety of social and cultural situations. His notion of heterology, and the diverse forms of otherness it projects and encompasses, conceives experiential connections and similarities between many diverse varieties of otherness. The project of heterology imagines *regularities of difference* that many prominent strains of theorizing have tended to veil or even explicitly to deny.

In an important moment of his analysis in *Culture in the Plural*, de Certeau wrote: "The difficulty of a certain number of minority movements is to have begun by defining themselves *negatively*. Cultural, social or ethnic autonomy has always manifested itself in saying 'no.'"[7] Thus more than twenty years ago, de Certeau anticipated our sometimes bitter debate today concerning identity politics. His critique still has political and analytical force. What is powerful about it is that he takes a *tactical and historical* view of the tension between the various forms of essentialism and their theoretical antagonists. Long before Gayatri Spivak legitimized the notion of "strategic essentialism,"[8] de Certeau was arguing for a fundamental *situatedness* of theoretical or political conceptions of these issues, and a pattern of connection between marginal positions that helps to make them comprehensible even in their diversity and their difference.

The implications of such an analysis are striking. They invoke and they project the sorts of effects that we frequently ignore when theory travels, when it crosses the borders marked by geography, race, class, gender, ethnicity, religion, or other social markers.[9] Theory always carries political stakes, and in our selection of the interpretive model we bring to bear, these are never neutral. Theories are always site- and time-sensitive. So as a disadvantaged group seeks to define itself culturally, or socially, or economically, or politically, the negativity that de Certeau identified he conceives not as a transhistorical necessity, but as an evolving moment in such a group's self-constitution. Then the antagonism between essentialism and universalism—one of the recurrent and, regularly, most sterile debates within multiculturalism today—ceases to be a fruitless binary contention, and can be reconceived as a productive pressure developing in the history of each group and in their relations with others against whom they initially assert their negativity.

In the face of the insistent claims of identity politics that still powerfully influence conceptions of social life in our multicultural world, I want to underline the issue of social understanding, of interpretive epistemology, that such essentialist framings of marginality render opaque, and that de Certeau's analysis was reconceiving as early as 1974. I seek to recover some resonances of the figure of *difference* that can broaden the thematics of marginality that has been the major preoccupation of this discourse, in the United States at least. To do so, I will focus upon the bases de Certeau projected for an understanding of the marginal. How does his conception diverge from what I might term mainstream constructions of marginality?

Like the negations by which groups initially counterpose themselves against dominant social forces and discourses, these latter proto-theoretical constructions are typically based upon a figure of reversal. In them, subordination and domination invert themselves. But I will argue that there are several versions of such reversal—some more thoughtful and useful to our analyses, some less. Still, the paradigm is familiar, and it is sustained on the part both of numerous minority rhetorics, and also in influential segments of the majority. Its political objective is to stigmatize the prejudice that projects categorial inferiority. Surely this repudiation of intolerance is salutary. But in the process, it often happens that the mechanisms of inequality themselves become invisible. As we censure marginalization, we ought to remember the means by which it is produced in social life, to uncover and articulate the conditions of marginalization's possibility. Our solidarity with the victims of inequality will be more credible and effective if our critique reveals not only the moral but the *material* bases which sustain it.[10]

We are familiar with the formation that results when this latter element is overlooked. Then rhetorics of victimization and compensation tend to prevail. Under their influence, in certain parts of the developed world to be on the margin has come to mean occupying a rhetorical *center*. Some early versions of Cultural Studies that concentrated upon a multitude of marginalisms in effect institutionalized this reversal. But while such strategies might resolve inequalities in an imaginative realm, they do very little to help in the material or the political one. So however progressive these paradigms were at an earlier moment of uncovering and valorizing the experience of disadvantaged groups, this effect can no longer entirely compensate for a certain static, even rigidifying idealization of marginality that results from such projections of its paradoxical benefit. It would be a very restricted revolution if such a turnaround, such a valorization of disadvantage, amounted to nothing more than a shift of arithmetic sign, a reflexive substitution of *plus* for *minus*. I will return to this issue in a consideration of de Certeau's understanding of the "privilege of marginality."

What is missing in the paradigms of victimization is analysis of the epistemological opportunities and consequences of difference and of marginality. Our understanding of marginality needs to integrate as deeply as it can the role of borders and differences in creating the conditions of possibility of *any* understanding. This is where de Certeau's insights about marginality and difference of all sorts can be most useful. For his focus upon the ubiquity and productivity of difference urges us beyond any paradigm of *victimization, compensation,* or *reversal,* and toward a reflection upon the material and political mechanisms by which the guilty hierarchies marking social existence and cultural meaning are constructed and sustained.

Consider the relations between two of de Certeau's own analyses: *The Capture of Speech,* his 1968 account of the May student uprising in France;[11] and his 1976 essay "The Politics of Silence: The Long March of the Indians," republished in *Heterologies.*[12] *The Capture of Speech* foregrounds the problem of the possession (or the conquest) of language—not in the psychoanalytic but in the sociopolitical sense. De Certeau identifies communication as the irreducible element in the politics of modern societies. Who has the *effective* right to speak? how is it acquired? what happens when it is inhibited or denied? These problems de Certeau believed were central to the frustrations that led to the May 1968 uprising in France. The problem of substantive marginalization, of denial of access to communication and hence of exclusion from politics, of suppression of diversity— these remain active issues despite the passage of more than three decades since May 1968. At that time, de Certeau's analysis brilliantly outflanked the liberalism of the period of its composition—or even of our own period. What he examined was not the formalism of rights—to speak, to vote, to publish—which were secured for all French citizens in a long and often bloody campaign since the 1789 Revolution. What concerned him were the acquisition and the exercise of political expression and participation. To "communicate" in a modern political system means not only having the right to speak, but *possessing the conditions that allow being heard.* For the revolutionaries of May 1968, society seemed to function to inhibit them from communication. No one listened to them until the eruption of May. But de Certeau's conception of the crisis has implications well beyond the May revolt. His analysis foregrounded the conditions of political and social marginalization, inferiority, or silencing for *any* disadvantaged group.

An operational definition of marginalization flows from de Certeau's analysis. "Marginalization" results from the blockage of any group's ability to *participate* in the social exchanges that constitute a society's politics. *How* these blockages occur is at the heart of the analysis. While some inhibitions of this capacity to participate are enforced by what Althusser termed the "repressive apparatuses" of the state—it was these that had had to be overturned for the *formal* rights of French citizens to be established—the more daunting case that has increasingly confronted us in liberal societies since the French Revolution arises in the operation of the *other* apparatuses that regulate social existence, what Althusser termed the "ideological" ones.[13] Repression at the point of the gun is clear and, if you accept the inevitable violence, it can be combated through the same mechanism. But the injuries of contemporary racism—in modern societies decreed by no one and denied by many—are not symmetrically contestable. White people are not much disadvantaged by the contempt that blacks may feel for them. As the practices which cause the injuries that one group can inflict upon another are maddeningly diffuse and insidious, so the struggle against them is maddeningly difficult to mount. Culture is astonishingly refractory. As the United States learned in Vietnam, changing "hearts and minds" is arduous. Such transformation is not notably fostered even when one party to a conflict controls the exercise of violence. And even that condition is contravened in the case of marginalized groups, against whom both ideological *and* repressive apparatuses are systematically deployed.

Such a conception illuminates the conditions of marginalization, inferiority, or silencing that regularly (if mystifyingly) de-privilege social groups even in the absence of any "legal" basis for their disqualification. The problem then turns out to be that of maintaining political process in a situation of social diversity. The notion of "communication" at the heart of *The Capture of Speech* itself captures what is analytically knotty about marginalization in contemporary societies. Through its emphasis on *reciprocal* exchange, it insists upon examining, not the abstract realm of legal rights and claims, but the empirical and material space of a society's effective practices. It argues that the determinations upon behavior are more subtle and elusive than any analysis of formal rights can seize. And perhaps most significantly, it focuses attention upon the diffuse and seemingly immaterial realm of *language* whose determinations of social conduct are as mystifying as they are powerful.[14]

The situation of the Indian tribes of South America would seem to be very different. But in "The Politics of Silence" (subtitled "The Long March of the Indians," 1976), de Certeau shows how the notion of *communication* proves effective in the analysis of political situations quite diverse from the one that had led him to the formulations of *The Capture of Speech*. In "The Long March," he considers the entry into politics of the indigenous tribes of the region North Americans would call "South of the Border." More than twenty years after he wrote the essay, the news from Chiapas tells us how prescient his analysis has proven. "The Long March" projects a mode of difference that interrogates dominant white power in what de Certeau ironically reminds us we still call "Latin" America (*Heterologies*, 227). It is this very power to ask a question about something that typically does not question it-self that makes the argument that the Indians have in fact *established com-munication* and entered politics.[15]

In de Certeau's solicitation and citation of an indigenous voice, his work converges—before the letter, as we might say—with the concerns of post-modern anthropology from James Clifford and George Marcus to Johannes Fabian. We could reinterpret this disciplinary evolution in just the terms that de Certeau defined in *The Capture of Speech*. Its concern is to estab-lish the possibility of effective *communication* between groups and cultures. The etymology of the term "communication"—related to English "com-mon" and German *gemein*—carries the root notion of "exchanging with." Across the borders that divide cultures, in this movement at the margin, epistemology becomes *bidirectional*. Then those whom we call the "others" draw us toward them, and make meanings we can neither predict nor con-strain. This is how a specific experience of marginality begins to refigure the paradigm of social and cultural discourses, and to restore a register of ex-perience that had been made inaudible and unavailable—had been *mar-ginalized*. In *L'Étranger*, de Certeau put this in the resonant formula I've already quoted as the epigraph to this essay: "The resistance of others is the condition of our own development [*progrès*]."[16] I want to consider the model of social practice and understanding that he projects in such a sen-tence.

Leaving aside liberal guilt, and thinking only of the methodological moves these insights suggest, we could say that de Certeau's conception of communication with others foregrounded the production of "knowledge" in *bidirectional and mutual* implication and determination between social groups. Gayatri Spivak's question—can the subaltern speak?—thereby re-ceived a practical and insistent answer: all of us, subaltern and guild cultural scientist, must *insist* that she do so. This is not a matter of generosity or of noblesse oblige. Even in domination we are victimized if we are too free to speak about others not free to answer. To enable our own discourse, it is necessary to enable the discourse of those who are nominally its object of study. Beyond the salutary sociopolitical consequences that our multicul-tural world is seeking to realize, the transfer to the "other" not only of the power of expression and inscription, but of *power itself* has fundamental *epistemological* consequences. Indeed, de Certeau suggests that these could be construed as the most significant motivation for the ethics and pol-itics which our practices of difference are attempting to project.

Thus, while every marginality remains different, our mode of awareness and openness to the claims of what is different from us along any number of dimensions is an inquiry that de Certeau's work urges us to deepen. From this point of view, *marginality* and *critique* inevitably converge— indeed they turn out to be alternative modes of existence of the same set of epistemological potentials and cultural realities. This convergence becomes both a scholarly resource and a political imperative in a world that a certain pessimistic common wisdom tends to portray as increasingly massified, cen- tralized, and univocal, dominated by a dominant discourse that at times seems simply to have exhausted the field of utterance.[17]

Against such projections, heterology or the discipline of the margin tells us that no single formulation, no monothetic conception, can ever ade- quately understand or express the complication of our lives—a complication that arises not only on account of empirical profusion or plethora, of the multiplicity and scattering of facts, but more importantly from an authentic and multivalent diversity of interests that can never be subsumed, never be reduced, to a single hegemony. Heterology then becomes a fundamental in- tellectual discipline for a multifarious world, and allows us to relate struc- tures of difference ranging over the whole realm of social and cultural—but also temporal, and geographic, and even theological—difference.

But there remains a puzzle in the perceptions of de Certeau's heterolo- gies, as in a broad variety of political, social, and cultural theories that seek to rectify or refigure the *silencing* that, according to the argument I have been making, defines the existence of marginalized groups. A fundamental ethic underlies this effort, the uncompromising commitment to an egalitar- ianism whose parameters we would have to go on to specify. The old—now sadly suspect—name for this ethic was "humanism," the belief in the irre- ducible value of every human life and of all human experience.

However, accepting this ethical foundation, what I want to consider here is the *epistemological* consequences of taking heterology seriously. What happens to our knowledge when we seek to ascertain and to assimilate the knowledge of the other? Heterology projects an epistemological advantage in disadvantage itself. We could frame it with this question: what is the priv- ilege of marginality?

In response, I will attempt some conceptual archaeology and analysis. We need to distinguish several senses in which one could argue the epistemolog- ical value of "otherness." The first of these derives directly from the human- ist ethic to which I just referred. It posits an a priori advantage in difference or in diversity, analogous to the biological advantage in species differentiation: a salutary richness in the primary material of existence. This view maintains that it is better for there to be multiple sites, sources, and options in any ele- ment of human existence. This is the point of view of most cultural pluralists.

This position can be distinguished from, but leads easily to, another. Here the emphasis shifts to a proto-*critical* potentiality in difference, manifested in a multiplicity of perspectives that de-center the authority and self-evidence of any dominant position. Heterology deterritorializes hegemony. It posits the indispensable founding condition for ideological critique. We could see it in the image of Montaigne's Cannibals or Montesquieu's Persians, posed through their authors' deliciously duplicitous assumptions of naïveté as marveling over the odd and incomprehensible practices of the French. What Roger Caillois termed the "sociological revolution" by which, in confrontation with an *other*, it becomes possible to dishabituate and de-privilege one's own ideologies and practices, then produces a fundamental instrument for reforming them.[18]

On this view, to remain vital, discourses need regeneration by exposure to difference. My use of the word "reform" was meant to invoke not only the advantages but also the limitations of the heterological processing by which such regeneration is imagined to occur. But we need to look more directly at the incompleteness inherent in this formulation of heterology itself. This shortcoming arises when, in the confrontation of positions that the encounter with difference mediates, we ignore or forget the issue of differential *power* that underlies such situations. For paralleling—and most often outflanking—the engagement of any two positions or practices on terms of logical or propositional equality is the verticality that frames them, regularly inscribing the material superiority of one, the subordination of the other.

Consider the following perception from a 1997 study of race attitudes in America: "A black person [in the United States] cannot go very long without thinking about race."[19] It's obvious that this preoccupation does not function the same way for whites. Such asymmetries are the registers of hierarchy. They inscribe the capacity of domination to determine what might seem an irresistible flow of power (exercised from the side of the hegemonic) and, reciprocally, of preoccupation (running, predictably, in the reverse direction). Any heterology needs to be acutely aware of such effects.

I am moving here toward a projection of the heterological that would be inflected by—and conscious of—an older model of the dialectic. Some further elements of such a model arise from a perhaps unexpected source in feminist theory. Consider the following, drawn from Drucilla Cornell's and Adam Thurschwell's essay "Feminism, Negativity, Subjectivity": "Many theorists, both feminist and nonfeminist, have identified negativity as the feminine. Each has done so in her or his own way, but all locate in 'woman' that which eludes representation and other forms of categorial confinement."[20]

What does this association of difference with negativity mean? The notion evokes twin dynamics that seem to me crucial in understanding how any form of marginality, or disadvantage, or difference from some supposed norm, could produce a communication (in the strong sense I have been evoking), and generate a politics. These dynamics are, first, *the inscription of hierarchy*, and second, *critical potential*. Difference here invokes not only the diversity of perspective that most models appeal to, but also the material power-differentials to which I have been referring. As it enters the circuit of communication, "negativity" thus figures a perspectival displacement, but one that we need to understand as offset in *two* directions: marking differences both in *position* and in *power*. It is this double displacement that makes heterology not just the study of abstract propositional heterogeneity, but the register of material politics.

Any functioning practical, ideological, or conceptual system has a repertoire of elements that appear licit and admissible within it. Elements extrinsic to these—any heteronomous factors—then appear, initially, as incomprehensible or meaningless. If the process of understanding stopped at this point, we could say that there was no process at all. For something that is really *meaningless* simply drops out of any social or imaginative transaction and disappears. The border projected in such a situation would then remain as uncrossable, as hermetic, as some in the United States would like our national borders to become.

But in real social experience almost nothing falls into that category of absolute and unbridgeable difference. In social existence, borders are never airtight. Rather, what cannot be immediately accommodated by or integrated into a system appears as a challenge to it. It both works upon it and gets worked on in its turn. This processing continues until some sort of negotiation—whether violent or peaceful—allows it to be assimilated. So "negativity" in this construction never figures a fixed state, nor can it stand in static opposition to a dominant system. Rather negativity injects into any system a perturbing—and potentially a transforming—impulse. Negativity propels systems out of *logic* and into *history*. Heteronomy is not only the register of difference, but the determinant of change.

Consequently this second formulation of marginality's privilege does not simply celebrate diversity in the way that a zoo might value increasing the number of species in its collection. Rather, it draws attention to the *system-altering potentiality of difference*. This figuration is homologous with accounts of the effects of more traditional forms of disadvantage. Groups formerly silenced begin to express themselves, their competing perspectives, and their needs or demands. Dominant structures adjust to provide some proportion of what is demanded by those they dominate. This scenario corresponds to a model of liberal politics in which the objective is accommodation of diverse interests toward the end of reducing friction and optimizing social benefit. Optimists or apologists for liberal regimes will praise the capacity of such systems for adjustment to the expression of new needs. Pessimists or opponents of the status quo will speak about "repressive tolerance," and remind us (with cogent historical examples) that the State's potential for violence always cohabits with that of benign accommodation.

But beyond these two conceptions there is a third—and much stronger—form of the claim of marginality's epistemological privilege. Although the methodological roots of this final avatar have been established for nearly two centuries, its influence on contemporary models of marginality has not been sufficiently registered. We need therefore to reexamine the relationship between de Certeau's heterology and Hegel's account of the dialectic. In a period as reflexively anti-Hegelian as ours, such a convergence risks seeming a provocation. For it is true that one powerful way of defining post-structuralisms, with which de Certeau's work has often been associated, is to see them as a systematic attempt to purge the memory of Hegel from methodology and from representation.

I believe, however, that our blindness to Hegel's presence in contemporary models is itself an effect of ideological repulsion—in part, of the intergenerational kind that Harold Bloom has termed the "anxiety of influence." In France the material basis for this anxiety, or at least this influence, was strong. Beginning in the 1930s, the so-called Hegel revival involved important French figures. Between 1934 and 1938, Bataille and Lacan, Queneau and Merleau-Ponty were members of Kojève's seminars at the École Pratique des Hautes Études.[21] Indeed, the echoes of Kojève's and Hyppolite's seminars, and of the latter's translation of the *Phenomenology*, were still so strong when I was an undergraduate in Paris in the 1960s that the buzz concerning them sounded very similar to what we were later to experience concerning Lacan's legendary seminars.

De Certeau had done his own systematic study of Hegel around 1954—particularly, a careful reading of the *Phenomenology* in the original German—during the period of his Jesuit training at the Scolasticate of Chantilly. He worked there with Joseph Gauvin, and in later years he spoke of the extraordinary influence of this reading of Hegel upon his intellectual and political development.[22] There are few explicit references to Hegel in de Certeau's published work. But in some of its most important aspects, a deep atmospheric and conceptual filiation links the project of his heterology to Hegel, and particularly to the famous account of the dialectic in the second part of the *Phenomenology of Spirit*.[23]

I suggested that we need to distinguish several senses in which we might understand the epistemological status of alterity. The first of those I traced celebrates diversity, but ignores the differentials of power that inevitably mark it. The second position then restores the registration of this power verticality or hierarchy. What I want to suggest now is a third alternative concerning marginality's privilege. This third model or conception functions powerfully, if silently, within de Certeau's heterology. And it recapitulates a fundamental move in Hegel.

Since Foucault, we have internalized the power differentials that seem inherent in any social or cultural difference. The distinguishing element of the third position that I now want to consider is a startling *inversion* of such differentials. Its image arises in Hegel's analysis of consciousness and recognition in the *Phenomenology* (particularly Part B, Section IV-A). We are not obliged to accept all of the details of Hegel's analysis to see the unexpected innovation that it authorizes and, indeed, mandates.[24]

From the point of view of the inquiry into marginality, the essence of Hegel's assertion in the "Lordship and Bondage" section of the *Phenomenology* is this. Common sense attributes relative impotence to the subordinate member of any relationship defined by differential power. But in the practice of social life, an epistemological advantage constitutively (if counterintuitively) accompanies this sociopolitical inferiority. Conversely the position of nominal superiority occupied by the dominant member of a social relationship turns out to carry an intrinsic handicap. These unexpected entailments of any structure characterized by social differential *invert the disadvantage of disadvantage*, and make the consciousness of social existence available from positions of inferiority or marginality an indispensable element in our potential for understanding the world.[25]

In most accounts of the "Lordship and Bondage" (or the "Master-Slave") allegory in Hegel, the emphasis falls on the actors' stakes in the symbolic combat modeled by the dialectic: upon the readiness (or lack of it) on the part of the dramatis personae in this elemental playlet to frame the definition of existence through their willingness to transgress existence itself: in other words, through the risk of death. This risk, of course, itself ultimately figures the difference indispensable to any meaning—which is why in the *Phenomenology* preface Hegel speaks so movingly of knowledge's necessary acceptance of this threat. He evokes

the tremendous power [*Macht*] of the negative. . . . Death, if that is what we want to call this non-actuality, is of all things the most dreadful, and to hold

fast to what is dead requires the greatest strength. . . . But the life of *Geist* does
not shrink from death or prevent itself from being touched by devastation, but
rather endures it and maintains itself in it. . . . It wins its truth only when, in
absolute dismemberment [*Zerrissenheit*], it finds itself. *Geist* has this power
only by looking the negative in the face, and enduring it. This enduring the
negative is the magical power [*Zauberkraft*] that converts it into being.[26]

This evocation and promotion of the negative is very powerful. But my emphasis is on a *different* difference. I want to take a closer look at how, in the
*Phenomenology*'s dialectic of consciousness and recognition, Hegel re-
conceives the link between individuals and redefines their relationship.
What happens is a surprising reversal of consciousness. This is the deep secret and the startling innovation at the heart of the dialectic in this part of
the *Phenomenology*. A clear social hierarchy nominally orders the positions
of the Lord and of the Bondsman. But Hegel projects overturning it
through the differential possibility of knowledge.[27]

In Hegel's allegory, the Lord achieves control over the Bondsman through
his acceptance of the risk of death. Whatever we might think of Hegel's myth
about the origin of this authority in their allegorical combat, its structure corresponds to our everyday experience of power relations and domination. We
internalize such structures almost before we have language to describe them,
and we live them in every moment of our lives. The existence of such structures of domination is the point that most ordinary understandings of marginality reach. And we have indeed grown skillful at detecting the determinants
that enforce domination and subservience, and the patterns of experience that
enact it and that consequently map marginality as a site of determined disadvantage. Whole narratives of victimization are written in this key.

But thinking about de Certeau's reflection upon marginality, I want to
bring Hegel's notion of epistemological reversal into contact with de
Certeau's representations of subordinated individuals and groups. In Hegel,
as the dialectic proceeds, the subservience of the Bondsman unexpectedly
flips over to reveal itself as the determining condition of a privilege of understanding. For the Bondsman, the inferior, turns out to have a gift of vision that propels him into a position of epistemological advantage.

For Hegel this potentiality is determined by the structure that dictates
the Bondsman's experience of subordination, and stems from the forms of
labor that social inferiority imposes upon his existence. Inferiority then becomes the paradoxical condition of possibility for a special form of insight.
In Part VI of the *Phenomenology*, on Self-Alienated Spirit, Hegel invokes a
concrete example of this sort of surprising reversal drawn from Diderot's

*Rameau's Nephew.* Basing himself upon insights already present in Diderot's dialogue, Hegel construes the ignominy and baseness of Rameau as paradoxically *enabling* perception of crucial truths concerning society and human existence: "The shamelessness which gives utterance to this deception [the content of what *Geist* says about itself] is just for that reason the greatest truth. This kind of talk is the madness of [Diderot's Rameau]" (*Phenomenology*, 317)—in other words, it comes from and articulates a perspective that in truth is not mad at all.

The energy that drives this inversion, and that destabilizes the hierarchy that initially figures the domination of Hegel's Lord, emerges from and is based upon the inferior position occupied by figures like Hegel's Bondsman and Diderot's Rameau. "Through this rediscovery of himself by himself, the bondsman realizes that it is precisely in his work in which he seemed to have only an alienated existence that he acquires a mind of his own" (*Phenomenology*, 118–19; translation modified). The Bondsman in fact turns out to be in much fuller contact with the world and its oppositions than the Lord.[28]

This reversal powerfully inflects the notion of marginality. I should say immediately that in tracing this pattern of reversal, I don't want to be understood as apologizing for domination, still less as somehow celebrating it. Nor do I want to associate myself with some perverse "nostalgie de la boue," or the sort of ethnic chic that attracts suburban white kids to become gangsta rappers. But our task is to understand what is the case. Domination exists, and it bears heavily upon lives all over the world. Then the move that construes the state of oppression or of subservience—with its undoubted and ethically intolerable suffering—as comporting an opportunity for insight may help us to understand the full set and breadth of human relations that are determined by the reality of inequality and disadvantage. I think this is one of the most powerful perceptions in de Certeau's heterology, and particularly in his thinking about the condition of marginality.

De Certeau is surely not the only thinker to have had an insight about such reversals. To illustrate, let me begin by offering a case that may seem less ethically troubling than those that invoke groups whose oppression is more brutal and brutalizing. I'm thinking of Proust's account of the paradoxical advantages of neurosis in *Remembrance of Things Past*. Neurotics suffer greatly, but their pain also functions to create opportunity. Thus one of Proust's physicians, clearly ventriloquizing for the author, says this to the narrator's neurotic grandmother:

You must accept being a neurotic [*une nerveuse*]. You belong to that magnificent and pitiable family which is the salt of the earth. Everything great that we have comes from neurotics. It is they, and no one else, who found religions and create masterpieces. The world will never know how much it owes them, and above all how much neurotics have suffered to provide it.[29]

We can find versions of such an epistemology in a large number of places. Feminist theory offers analogous models that (in "standpoint theory" and other paradigms) argue the singular perspective that women's consciousness provides on social existence; or that seek to reclaim the supposed diagnoses of "hysteria" that have been directed against women throughout history (and particularly since the nineteenth century) by rewriting such phenomena as an epistemological or affective advantage.[30] A similar reversal arguably occurs in Marx's account in "On the Jewish Question" of the relation of Jews to the larger society, and particularly to the problem of global emancipation. Marx maintains that the supposedly marginalized Jews in fact stand for—and implicitly understand—*everyone*, that Jews have realized in their own consciousness and identity truths that remain veiled in majoritarian, "Christian," existence.[31] In *History and Class Consciousness* Lukács, following Marx, attributes a corresponding privilege of insight to the working class, a privilege structurally denied to their capitalist oppressors.[32] And postcolonial theory offers analogous models of such reversals.[33]

The general paradigm for these diverse but convergent reconceptualizations of disadvantage is the notion of *critique* as it has developed in strains of progressive thought from German Idealism to our own day. This is why it finds such a natural home in the models we associate with contemporary poststructuralism, and in the kinds of reversals we have become familiar with in deconstruction. The existence of the exercise of *critique* always implies some form of perspectival externality and some perception of social disadvantage. The power of critique arises in this disempowerment. Now I want to conclude by bringing this perspective into contact with de Certeau's own theoretical and analytical work.

Heterology is the term that increasingly we associate with de Certeau's theory of social difference. But in the light of this paradigm of epistemological and experiential reversal from Hegel to our own day, now heterology turns bidirectional. To know and to respect the other is an ethical responsibility that we all bear. But in the image of de Certeau's analysis in "The Long March of the Indians," the situated knowledge of those who are dominated turns domination inside-out to constitute a site of knowledge that intrinsically *we cannot achieve on our own*.[34] This limitation on our understanding—in the image of the one that paradoxically constrains the domination of domination in Hegel's astonishing allegory—changes the modalities of any possible knowledge.

We could take as the emblem of this perception in the work of Michel de Certeau two linked passages near the end of his introduction to *The Mystic Fable*:

> The mystics . . . translated [their] situation into their texts . . . in the social figures that dominate their discourse, those of the madman, the child, the illiterate. It is as if, in our own day, the eponymous heroes of knowledge were the fallen members of our society—old people, immigrants, or the "village idiot," who, says Simone Weil, "truly loves truth," because instead of "talents" favored by education, he has this "genius" that "is nothing but the supernatural virtue of humility in the realm of thought." (24–25)

> "The deciphering of history," as Albert Béguin was wont to say, "is reserved for certain begins of pain and suffering." One must connect with this religious and social experience the movement that led "spiritual" learned men and theologians toward witnesses who humbled their competency: maids, cowherds, villagers and so on. These characters, real or fictitious, were like pilgrimages to an alternative "illumination." . . . These intellectual converts to "barbarism" testify to the disarray of their knowledge confronted with the misfortune that had stricken a system of reference. (26)

The integration of two linked factors already evoked in my discussion is what makes de Certeau's heterology a powerful model of marginality, analytically richer than many others. The first of these factors is the bidirectionality of communication that he argues can function even in situations of subordination or oppression. He recovers unexpected resonances of the effectiveness even of the powerless.[35] At the model's ethical and political center, this structure inscribes an injunction to look for *capability* on the margins, where ordinarily ideology suggests we will find only dependency and subservience.

Second, de Certeau's heterology makes the potentiality for material *reversal* of epistemological privilege a fundamental methodological principle based upon the very existence of subordination. This element at the heart of his theory reanimates the conception of difference, which heterology conceives not in some static simplicity, but rather as including within itself all the ambiguity and complexity of social life, and all its intrinsic propensity for change.

We *need others* for many reasons. However, in the quasi-Hegelian—or the deeply *Christian*—move that in my interpretation of de Certeau's work powerfully extends the force and scope of heterological understanding, what comes to light is the theory of an inadequacy that makes the other's knowledge not just an indispensable complement for but a constitutive metadiscourse of our own. The sorts of ties that bind human individuals and groups are deepened and complicated in such an epistemological extremity, as a result of the combined opportunity and necessity of extending the grasp of our knowledge through *authentically* honoring the knowledge of others.

This primordial reversal situates heterology as the most general form of any epistemology. Then all social knowledge is enabled from the margin, and all understanding arises in difference—not only in the abstract sense that I suggested at the opening of this chapter, but as a consequence of the privilege of comprehension that can arise in any situation of social inferiority, exclusion, or disadvantage. Such situations of inequality and marginalization lamentably define our existence. Thinking alone cannot conjure them away. But in the face of these imperfections, de Certeau's insights about alterity join with his luminous humanism to provide a powerful model for conceiving social relationships in an increasingly diverse and differential world.

## NOTES

1. All translations in this essay are mine, although I have consulted published English versions.

2. See the "Biobibliographie" of de Certeau by Luce Giard, in Giard, ed., *Michel de Certeau: Cahiers pour un temps* (Paris: Centre Georges Pompidou, 1987), 248.

3. De Certeau's candidacy had been proposed for a position in the Cinquième Section of the École Pratique des Hautes Études, which specializes in religious studies. Predictably, the anticlerical faculty there opposed him because of his ordination. At the same time, however, the more clerically inclined also voted against him because of his heterodox position within the Church. Consequently his candidacy failed completely. (Personal communication from Jacques Le Brun.)

4. When he came to UCSD, de Certeau's U.S. visa had to be renewed every year. Without it, he had no job. The Immigration and Naturalization Service (INS) summoned him for what the bureaucracy terms an examination of his immigration status. His association with the Socialist Party in France was no help in those Cold War Reagan years. The INS threatened to cancel his visa. Eventually, after vigorous efforts by university colleagues and officials, it was renewed and his immigration status was regularized. In 1981, Mitterand won the presidency in France, the French university got some new blood at the top, and in 1984, having been elected to a position as Directeur d'Études at the École des Hautes Études, de Certeau returned to Paris. Unfortunately this was just a year and a half before he died.

5. In connection with the determined difficulty of de Certeau's writing, there is a history to be written about his work's reception. I have given the beginning of such

a history in a short essay on him written for Lawrence Kritzman, ed., *Columbia History of Twentieth-Century French Thought* (New York: Columbia University Press, forthcoming).

6. On his adoption of this term, see Luce Giard, "Mystique et politique, ou l'institution comme objet second," in *Histoire, mystique et politique: Michel de Certeau*, ed. Luce Giard, Hervé Martin, and Jacques Revel (Grenoble: Jérôme Millon, 1991), 34.

7. Michel de Certeau, *Culture in the Plural*, trans. Tom Conley (Minneapolis: University of Minnesota Press, 1997), 125; my emphasis.

8. Spivak, "Criticism, Feminism, and the Institution," an interview with Elizabeth Grosz, in Gayatri Chakravorty Spivak, *The Postcolonial Critic: Interviews, Strategies, Dialogues*, ed. Sarah Harasym (New York: Routledge, 1990), 11. See Tan See Kam, "Making Space for Heterologies," *Social Semiotics* 6, no. 1 (1996): 40 (special issue on de Certeau). Tan rightly points out that what Spivak terms "strategic" is what de Certeau, in *Practice of Everyday Life*, rather called "tactical."

9. See *Traveling Theory, Traveling Theorists*; *Inscriptions* 5, special number, ed. James Clifford and Vivek Dhareshwar (Santa Cruz, Calif.: Group for the Critical Study of Colonial Discourse, 1989).

10. In this regard, we might fruitfully look again at a classic and brilliant account of one register of such socially imposed exclusion, Albert Memmi's *Le Racisme* (Paris: Gallimard, 1982; a new edition appeared in 1994). Memmi's courageous and insightful discussion of the *benefits* that racism's adherents derive from their bigotry is remarkable. It distances analysis from the false and facile idealism of purely ethical conceptions to demonstrate how racism *performs*, how it pays off for those practicing it. Memmi develops a concept he terms "heterophobia" that could be useful in understanding the ubiquity and persistence of marginalizing ideologies and practices throughout the world. Memmi's book has appeared in English: *Racism*, trans. Steve Martinot (Minneapolis: University of Minnesota Press, 2000).

11. In *The Capture of Speech and Other Political Writings*, trans. Tom Conley (Minneapolis: University of Minnesota Press, 1997), part I.

12. The essay was published in *Le Monde Diplomatique*, no. 273 (décembre 1976) and in *La Prise de parole*, ed. Luce Giard, 2d ed. (Paris: Seuil coll. Points, 1994), 147–61. It appears in English translation in de Certeau's *Heterologies: Discourse on the Other* (Minneapolis: University of Minnesota Press, 1986), 225–33.

13. Althusser's distinction was elaborated in "Ideology and Ideological State Apparatuses (Notes towards an Investigation)," in *Lenin and Philosophy and Other Essays*, trans. Ben Brewster (New York: Monthly Review Press, 1971), 127–86. De Certeau always used the term "ideological" in a much more restricted sense than the one Althusser defines. I consider the passage in modern societies from repressive to ideological determination of disadvantage in *Present Past: Modernity and the Memory Crisis* (Ithaca, N.Y.: Cornell University Press, 1993), 92–93.

14. Here a convergence with Habermas's notion of the "ideal speech situation" becomes clear. De Certeau was already referring to Habermas in *The Capture of Speech*.

15. We might think that in writing about (and seemingly "for") the Indians in this essay, de Certeau—perhaps unwittingly—assumes a position of paternalistic hegemony that only displaces in a more benign direction the ongoing political domination of the Indians by the descendants of Europeans. For de Certeau wrote his essay in *French,* and it appeared initially in the most highbrow of Paris's newspapers. But as the note at the beginning of the essay in *Heterologies* reminds us, and as Luce Giard's preface to *La Prise de Parole* explains in more detail, "The Long March of the Indians" was written to serve as postface to a collection of political texts, manifestos written *by and for* indigenous Indians from Mexico, Colombia, Panama, Venezuela, and other countries of Central and South America. And the very texture of de Certeau's essay, beginning with a long extract from, and throughout extensively quoting the manifestos themselves, at least complicates the issue of hegemonic voicing in the space of politics defined at once by the Indians' confrontation with the dominant power in their own countries and by the resonances of this contention in the developed West. The texts in the collection were published by the "Association pour la Diffusion de l'Information sur L'Amérique Latine" which de Certeau had cofounded. See Luce Giard's preface to her edition of *La Prise de Parole,* 23. The reference in the title of the essay to the classic and most consequential instance of the seizure of political power from white Westerners by a nonwhite people—the Chinese revolution—sufficiently suggests that de Certeau was aware of the ideological and political complications of Western solidarity with the struggles of the Indians.

16. *L'Étranger, ou l'union dans la différence* (Paris: Desclée de Brouwer, 1968), 217.

17. This is why it is so important to recover the manifold modes in which, in one of his most fundamental insights, de Certeau demonstrated this reality's secret internal multivalence, its non-self-identity, and the consequent richness of its potential. Consider in this regard the complex of marginal experiences that he and his collaborators brought to light in *The Practice of Everyday Life.* These revealed as a variegated and rich positivity forms of practice that a number of analyses from Max Weber to the Frankfurt School had simply consigned to a dead and uncommunicative absence.

18. Caillois, preface to Montesquieu, *Oeuvres complètes* (Paris: Gallimard-Pléiade, 1949–1958), 1:5.

19. David K. Shipler, *A Country of Strangers: Blacks and Whites in America* (New York: Knopf, 1997), quoted in K. Anthony Appiah's review, *New York Times Book Review,* November 16, 1997, 11.

20. In *Feminism as Critique: On the Politics of Gender,* ed. Seyla Benhabib and Drucilla Cornell (Minneapolis: University of Minnesota Press, 1987), 145.

21. See Michael S. Roth, *Knowing and History: Appropriations of Hegel in Twentieth-Century France* (Ithaca, N.Y.: Cornell University Press, 1988), appendix. On the general phenomenon of Hegel's influence on French thought in the period since the 1930s, see also Judith P. Butler, *Subjects of Desire: Hegelian Reflections in*

*Twentieth-Century France* (New York: Columbia University Press, 1987). The major figures in the "Hegel revival"—Jean Hyppolite, Alexandre Kojève, Alexandre Koyré, and Eric Weil—have all now been widely studied and/or translated into English.

22. Giard, "Biobibliographie," 246. Some of this information is based upon personal communication with de Certeau during his time in California. Luce Giard has provided the most thoughtful reflection on Hegel's importance for de Certeau. See her "Mystique et politique," cited earlier, particularly "La Matrice Hégélienne," 27–36. Giard, de Certeau's literary executor and closest collaborator during the last decade and a half of his life, calls de Certeau "the most Hegelian of Gauvin's students," and speaks about the "decisive role" of Hegel in de Certeau's intellectual development, and the "structuring presence" of Hegel's thought in de Certeau's own work; "Mystique et politique," 28–29.

23. I quote here from Hegel, *Phenomenology of Spirit*, trans. A. V. Miller (Oxford: Clarendon Press, 1977).

24. It has become commonplace to point out that the French "Hegel revival" in the 1930s and after tended to focus selectively on certain aspects of Hegel's work—particularly the "Master-Slave dialectic"—to the exclusion or at least the minimization of other strands. Even though de Certeau read Hegel in the 1950s in the original German, inevitably his reading was inflected by the modes of understanding that dominated in France during the period, reflecting the cultural prestige of the interpretations stemming from Kojève and Hyppolite particularly. This "French" Hegel is still Hegel. It would be a mistake to reject or to "other" it.

25. Among many other discussions relevant to this point, see most recently Fredric Jameson, "Marxism and Postmodernism," in *The Cultural Turn: Selected Writings on the Postmodern, 1983–1998* (London: Verso, 1998), 43.

26. *Phenomenology*, "Preface," 19; translation modified.

27. Concerning the reversal in Hegel's Master-Slave dialectic, see most recently Fredric Jameson, "Transformations of the Image in Postmodernity," in *The Cultural Turn*, 104.

28. On this point, see Christopher Gosden, *Social Being and Time* (Oxford: Blackwell, 1994), 65–66.

29. *À la recherche du temps perdu*, ed. Jean-Yves Tadié (Paris: Gallimard-Pléiade, 1988), 2: 601; my translation.

30. On "standpoint theory" see particularly *Feminism and Science*, ed. Evelyn Fox Keller and Helen E. Longino, particularly the essays by Sandra Harding, "Rethinking Standpoint Epistemology," 235–48; Donna Haraway, "Situated Knowledges," 249–63; and Helen Longino, "Subjects, Power, and Knowledge: Description and Prescription in Feminist Philosophies of Science," 264–79. Harding's essay is particularly apposite to my concerns here. She writes: "The standpoint epistemologists . . . have claimed to provide a fundamental map [for analysis]: 'start thought from marginalized lives' and 'take everyday life as problematic'" (236). These two tenets converge remarkably with those that we might conceive as the overarching

program for de Certeau's theoretical and analytic work. For one feminist rewriting of "hysteria" in terms of epistemological privilege, see Jane Gallop, "Keys to Dora," in *In Dora's Case: Freud-Hysteria-Feminism*, ed. Charles Bernheimer and Claire Kahane (New York: Columbia University Press, 1985), 200–220. Gallop considers the volume by Hélène Cixous and Catherine Clément, *The Newly Born Woman*, which raises the question of whether the female hysteric is a victim or, rather, a hero-ine. Gallop's (and Clément's) point is that Freud's Dora does not just give in to hys-teria, she makes visible and herself "sees" the rejection of bodies and the consequent humiliation traditionally inflicted upon women. I'm grateful to Julia Simon for the reference to Gallop's work.

31. In *Karl Marx: Early Writings*, ed. T. B. Bottomore (New York: McGraw-Hill, 1963), 36–40, particularly 39. The question of the rhetoric and diction of "On the Jewish Question" is controversial. At times Marx has been taken as overtly anti-Semitic in this work. I rather read his seemingly repugnant statements about the Jews as inflected by a powerful sarcasm, and by the trope (analogous to a more re-cent example in the work of Lyotard; see *Heidegger et "les juifs"*) of projecting out of general consciousness an ironically seen archetypal "Jew" which it is the func-tion of Marx's writing not to reinforce but rather ironically to undermine.

32. "This same reality deploys the motor of class interests to keep the bour-geoisie imprisoned within this immediacy while forcing the proletariat to go beyond it. . . . For the proletariat to become aware of the dialectical nature of its existence is a matter of life and death. . . . " "Reification and the Consciousness of the Prole-tariat," in *History and Class Consciousness: Studies in Marxist Dialectics*, trans. Rodney Livingston (Cambridge, Mass.: MIT Press, 1971), 164, 181.

33. See C. L. R. James, "The Black Jacobins" (play), in *The C. L. R. James Reader*, ed. Anna Grimshaw (Oxford: Blackwell, 1992), particularly the brilliant speech James composed for his protagonist Toussaint L'Ouverture, 77; or Frantz Fanon, *The Wretched of the Earth*, trans. Constance Farrington (New York: Grove Press, 1968); or Bill Ashcroft, Gareth Griffiths, and Helen Tiffin, *The Empire Writes Back: The-ory and Practice in Post-Colonial Literatures* (London: Routledge, 1989).

34. Luce Giard, developing what she believes is the fundamental bearing of de Certeau's own work, puts it this way: "The presence of the other, of the multiplicity of others, sustains the requirement of radicality, for no one can conduct the eluci-dation of meaning alone; the contribution of critique, the diversity of perspectives and the difference of positions held by others are indispensable: 'Communication is necessary for the recognition of radicality.'" "Mystique et politique, ou l'institu-tion comme objet second," in *Histoire, Mystique et Politique*, ed. Luce Giard and Pierre-Jean Labarrière (Paris: Jérome Millon, 1991), 25. Giard's concluding citation is from de Certeau, *Le christianisme éclaté* (Paris: Seuil, 1974), 38.

35. To many of his readers these will seem analogous to the surprising depths and complexities that in *The Practice of Everyday Life* he and his collaborators dis-covered in seemingly banal quotidian usages.

## 2

# DISORIENTING LE CORBUSIER: CHARLES-EDOUARD JEANNERET'S 1911 *VOYAGE D'ORIENT*

*Patricia A. Morton*

This journey to the East, far from the gossamer architecture of the North, a response to the persistent call of the sun, the wide expanses of blue seas and the great white walls of temples—Constantinople, Asia Minor, Greece, Southern Italy—will be like an ideally shaped vase, from which the heart's most profound feelings will flow.

—Le Corbusier, *Le Voyage d'Orient*

In 1911, Charles-Edouard Jeanneret, later known as Le Corbusier, made a *Voyage d'Orient* from Germany to the Balkans, Turkey, and Greece. Jeanneret traveled with his Swiss friend, Auguste Klipstein, an art historian who lived in Berlin at the time. In 1910, Jeanneret had received a grant from the Art School in his hometown, La-Chaux-de-Fonds, Switzerland, to write an account of the industrial and decorative arts in Germany, for which task he spent a year in Munich, Berlin, Nuremberg, Würzberg, and Halle.[1] Klipstein proposed that they travel together to Eastern Europe, particularly Budapest and Bucharest where he intended to look at paintings by El Greco.[2] Under the impetus of a recent interest in classicism, Jeanneret suggested that they extend the trip to Constantinople and Greece.[3] Klipstein and Jeanneret debarked from Dresden for Prague on May 25, 1911. After traveling through Prague, Vienna, Hungary, the Balkans, Romania, Bulgaria, Turkey, Greece, and Italy, Jeanneret ended his *Voyage* when he returned to La-Chaux-de-Fonds in November. Contradictory purposes and motivations compelled Jeanneret to take this journey.

His expedition to the East provided Jeanneret with a period in which he syn-thesized the diverse experiences and influences of the previous four years. It was, sequentially, an expedition to the wilds of Eastern Europe, an experiment in exoticism, and a pilgrimage to the monuments of classical civilization.

This journey is one of the best documented, most scrutinized periods of Jeanneret's life. His articles on the journey, published serially in the La-Chaux-de-Fonds newspaper *La Feuille d'Avis* in 1911, were published posthumously as a book in 1966; his sketchbooks from the journey have been issued in facsimile edition; and the book has been translated into Chinese, Italian, Japanese, Russian, and English.[4] This comprehensive information gives a detailed picture of his immediate impressions of the places visited and his larger concerns at the time. Most studies give the *Voyage* a prominent place in Jeanneret's creative development and his subsequent work as Le Corbusier. Following Le Corbusier's own assertions, historians agree that this journey was a pivotal, "decisive" event in his formation: it was a rite of pas-sage and the culmination of his four-year self-education program, according to H. Allen Brooks.[5] Giuliano Gresleri, who has published comprehensive documentation of the *Voyage*, called it "the most convincing insight yet into the emotional and intellectual situation which enabled the architect Le Cor-busier to reach full development. . . . What made Jeanneret an exceptional architect . . . is this very collision with a different type of reality which other-wise immediately remains essentially alien, is pushed aside."[6]

Some authors distinguish Jeanneret's *Voyage d'Orient* from the Grand Tour taken by educated northern Europeans in the seventeenth and eigh-teenth centuries, or from Orientalist travel to exotic locales. Gresleri sees the *Voyage* as the antithesis of the Grand Tour to Italy, which confirmed for the traveler "what he already knew"; for Gresleri, Jeanneret's journey was an encounter with the unexpected. The cities of Berlin and Vienna "were cities which were entirely identified with the Occident and represented nothing except known and normal reality."[7] In the view of Max Adolf Vogt, following Gresleri's suggestion, it was a "reversed" Grand Tour that took Jeanneret to Eastern Europe and Greece rather than to Rome via the Alps.[8] Timothy Benton, however, notes that the itinerary to Athens by way of the Balkans was a standard one: "Jeanneret's motivation was partly the classic one of test-ing his taste against the great monuments of antiquity. A literary tradition, stemming from at least the eighteenth century, combined the pursuit of an-tique perfection with a romantic observation of the primitive and the deca-dent."[9] Sibel Bozdogan views the *Voyage* as a counter-Orientalist trip on which Jeanneret entered the Orient with a spirit of discovery and dialog rather than self-affirmation and the objectification of the Oriental subject.

Richard Ingersoll, in response to Bozdogan, refutes her interpretation of Jeanneret's *Voyage* as a postcolonial experience. Ingersoll points out that this trip was grounded in Orientalist preconceptions acquired from such thinkers as his mentor William Ritter, novelist and amateur of Eastern European culture, and Ernest Renan, archetypal Orientalist. Ingersoll asserts that "Like most Orientalists he had a sincere respect for the culture of the Other, but never intended to reverse the position of domination."[10]

While the apologetics for Jeanneret/Le Corbusier's Orientalism efface the role colonial discourse played in shaping his view of non-European cultures and peoples, his critics characterize the *Voyage* in reductive terms that gloss over the complexities of his thinking and experiences. Jeanneret was indoctrinated in colonial discourse by his mentors, living and literary, and absorbed from them the implicit hierarchies and power relations of the imperial worldview. Rather than demonize Jeanneret/Le Corbusier as an unreconstructed colonialist or Orientalist, however, this article places the *Voyage* within a more ambivalent constellation of discourses. Specifically, this journey belongs to the discourse of "primitivism," the preference for societies, cultures, and art from simpler times, states of evolution, or mentalities.[11] Nineteenth-century cultural relativism and the quest for a world art history, as well as Orientalism and colonial discourse, form the background for Jeanneret's reception of the East.

Jeanneret pursued "primitive" artistic and architectural sources not regulated by the norms of academic, European culture that might serve as the means for a more spontaneous, expressive architecture. His itinerary and purpose followed the two primary tendencies in modern primitivism: the valorization of peasant, vernacular, or nonliterate culture as a means for producing a more primal art or architecture, and a search for origins in the classical, exemplified by the primitive hut of Enlightenment theories. Robert Goldwater defined "primitivism" in modern art as a search among Western artists for something below the surface of things—farther back in time, psychology, or geography—that is simpler and more profound, valuable, or powerful because of its simplicity.[12] The primitivists assumed that delving beneath the surface would reveal this basic quality. This search for a simplicity unites the disparate primitivist movements in literature, art, and architecture, but the nature of "simplicity" varies with the goals of the seeker.

The *Voyage* began as the search for authentic folk art created by cultures untouched by corrupt, industrialized Europe. The map of Jeanneret's itinerary published in *The Decorative Art of Today*, Le Corbusier's treatise on the decorative arts, labels each location either Industry, Folklore, or Culture: Germany was the locus of Industry, Eastern Europe that of Folklore, and Turkey and Greece of Culture.[13] Jeanneret had gone to Germany to confirm

what Gresleri calls "certitudes:" his faith in German efficiency, the leadership
of architects such as Thomas Fischer and Peter Behrens, the superiority of
German art.[14] His stay in Germany and his research into its decorative arts
had left him disillusioned with northern culture and ready to find alternatives
in Eastern folk art or classical antiquity. As Baker notes, "These doubts about
modern civilized existence form a major theme of his writings on the journey,
and just as their origin seems to have been in northern climates where man
is too rational and not sufficiently relaxed, Jeanneret found himself searching
for the antidote in the peasant cultures of southern lands, where ancient customs had not been eroded by modern life."[15] His interest in Eastern European folklore was stimulated by William Ritter, with whom he had a intense
correspondence throughout 1910–1911.[16] Ritter gave him a copy of his book,
*L'entêtement Slovaque*, in which he described peasant life in vivid, Romantic
passages; Ritter's picturesque account of and his enthusiasm for the culture
of the region influenced Jeanneret to study its folk art.[17] Goldwater has identified folk art as one of the roots of modern primitivism: "In the twentieth-
century movements, exotic arts were valued, in which it is imagined that technique has been kept properly subordinate by the intensity of the emotion
expressed, or indigenous arts (folk, children, and madmen) where, ideally, the
medium would be obliterated in favor of a direct conveying of emotion."[18]
According to Barbara Maria Stafford, "What the eighteenth-century traveler
in search of fact sought in a mineral and vegetable primitivism and attained
through a science of nature, the nineteenth-century archaeologist of popular
sentiment discovered in folk art and a science of man."[19] Jeanneret followed
the example of these nineteenth-century travelers in search of folklore and
primitive art in nearby locales. Paul Gauguin, for example, went to Brittany
before he went to Tahiti to find a primitive landscape and culture.[20]

Folk art served Jeanneret as a means for accessing primitive emotions
and sensory responses to aesthetic form:

> The art of the peasant is a striking creation of aesthetic sensuality. If art elevates
> itself above the sciences, it is precisely because, in opposition to them, it stim-
> ulates sensuality, awakening profound echoes in the physical being. It gives to
> the body—to the animal—its fair share and then, upon this healthy base con-
> ducive to the expansion of joy, it knows how to erect the noblest columns.[21]

As a demonstration of the sensuality provoked by folk art, Jeanneret described his encounter with a vase, a recurring motif in his early articles for
*La Feuille d'Avis*:

> You recognize these joys: to feel the generous belly of a vase, caress its slender
> neck, and then explore the subtleties of its contours. Hands thrust into the deep-

est part of your pockets and eyes half-closed, to give way slowly to the fantasy of glazes, the burst of yellows, the velvet tone of the blues; to be involved in the animated struggle between brutal black masses and victorious white elements.[22]

Jeanneret and Klipstein made it their mission to find a perfect vase, an exemplar of peasant production that had evaded the insidious effects of Western European fashion. They trekked deep into Hungary, to the small city of Baja, where they located the archetypal vase in a potter's attic "out of *A Thousand and One Nights*":

> The jars were there, in their joyous dazzle and clean vigor, and their beauty was consoling. To unearth them, we had to search through all the sad bric-a-brac without country or family that inundates all of Europe: and even here in Hungary, where the peasant knows how to create like a great artist, we found the offerings of the merchants even more embarrassing and the sway of fashion over still-naive souls, more disastrously effective. There was too much multicolored glassware with golden floral designs, too much china spotted with a shameful ornamentation of Louis XV seashells or with flowerets dressed in last year's taste. We had to flee from the invading and filthy "Europeanization" to the tranquil refuges where survives—abating and soon to be submerged—the great popular tradition.[23]

This attitude is consistent with "primitivism" as a search for a simpler, less sophisticated culture. Jeanneret saw folk art as the root of ancient civilization, preserving primal values and forms. "Considered from a certain point of view, folk art outlives the highest civilizations. It remains a norm, a sort of measure whose model is ancestral man—the savage, if you will."[24] Like the Pre-Raphaelites, who preferred the "primitive" Renaissance painters to mannerists like Michelangelo, Jeanneret looked for simpler, primitive forms that were throwbacks to a preindustrial aesthetic and technique, which he situated in Eastern Europe. Although he uncovered the archetypal vase, Jeanneret seems to have been dissatisfied with his discoveries, since he later disallowed folk as the best source for modern architecture.

That he went to rural Hungary is consistent with Western European conceptions of Eastern Europe as a repository for such backward culture. As Larry Wolff has demonstrated, the Enlightenment "invented" Eastern Europe as its complement, its first "Other" and locus for the primitive, defined by opposition and adjacency. Eighteenth-century travelers from Western Europe freely "annotated, embellished, refined, or refolded" a mental map of Eastern Europe, intellectually combining its countries into a coherent whole, comparing them with Western Europe, and establishing the developmental division of the continent. In Wolff's view, Eastern Europe's ambiguous location, within

Europe but not fully European, made it a location for backwardness, which al-
lowed it to mediate between the poles of civilization and barbarism.[25] In his
*Voyage*, thus, Jeanneret traveled from the oversophisticated styles of Western
Europe and the primitive peasant art of Eastern Europe, retracing the journeys taken by his predecessors. He further emulated them by continuing to
Constantinople, the "trinity" of Stamboul, Pera, and Scutari, where he arrived
on July 5, 1911; he and Klipstein rented a room in the European district of
Pera, where Loti had also lived.[26] Wolff has noted that Enlightenment travelers discovered Eastern Europe on the way to Constantinople or St. Peters-
burg, the two extremities at the circumference of Europe.[27]

Like Loti and others before him, Jeanneret availed himself of the opportunity to "go native" and dabble in ambiguous sexual and creative roles while
in Istanbul. One of the most notorious documents of the *Voyage* consists of
a photograph, posed and taken in Istanbul, of Jeanneret and Klipstein in Oriental garb, perhaps reenacting a scene from Pierre Loti's novel, *Aziyadé*.[28]
Jeanneret played the title role, dressed in drag as the Circassian slave, and
Klipstein, seated on a carpeted divan, wore a turban and took Loti's place.
Jeanneret sent the photograph to his brother, Albert, with a joking note pre-
tending to be offended that Klipstein had resisted his charms.[29] The photograph appears to be part of an experimentation with identities and disguises
on the *Voyage*.[30] Disguise, masquerade, and cross-dressing were an important part of Orientalist travel; Lamartine, Nerval, and Eberhardt all "went
native" to immerse themselves in local life. According to Emily Apter, this
performance had precedents: "*Aziyadé* functioned as an underground script
for the initiate, interpreted provisionally in salon skits and 'real life,' as when
two Western-educated Turkish women, Nouryé and Zennour Noury-Bey,
purportedly snared Loti in his own sequel by posing as Aziyadé reincarna-
tions, returned in the flesh from a fictional tomb."[31]

Giuliano Gresleri believes that Jeanneret's desire to "penetrate the au-
tochthonic sphere" compelled him to wear disguise, so that he could enter
the unique realm of "being adrift" as Barthes characterized Loti's peregri-
nations.[32] Gresleri contends that Jeanneret's readings, often recommended
by Ritter, were the frame that allowed him to "become part of the picture,"
and that they triggered a psychological shift in Jeanneret, from spectator to
protagonist of events and things, so that he belonged physically to the
place.[33] Ali Behdad has theorized "going native" on the Orientalist journey
as a loss of self and ontological control:

> Far from being an egoistic drive for knowledge, the desire for the Orient is the
> return of a repressed fascination with the Other, through whose differentiat-

ing function European subjectivity has often defined itself since the Crusades. Beyond their interests in self-realization through their journeys to the Orient, travelers such as Nerval, Eberhardt, and Flaubert had a great desire to understand and even become part of the Oriental culture. Such a desire . . . makes the orientalist subject surrender his or her power of representation and pursuit of knowledge by becoming a hedonistic participant in the "immediate" reality of the Oriental culture.[34]

His Istanbul sojourn allowed Jeanneret to lose himself partially and absorb himself in the quotidian life and architecture of the city. Influenced by Orientalist travel narratives, this segment of the *Voyage* was an excursion in self-discovery and an adventure in the realm of the alien, scripted by Loti and Claude Farrère. As an upper-class, white male, Jeanneret, like Loti, was able to experience the Orient within the gendered power regime of imperialism, as Apter observes:

> The art of cultural camouflage was important to Loti's self-fashioning as both textual and (auto)biographical figure. A naval officer from Brittany, he was famous for having himself photographed in the local costumes, both masculine and feminine, of the foreign territories he visited, including China, Japan, the South Sea Islands, North Africa, West Africa, and the Middle East. He even extended this fascination with exoticist drag to the Moorish interior of his own home at Rochefort, transformed into a kind of domestic stage-set modeled after the Turkish apartment that *Aziyadé*'s central character appoints for himself in the Istanbul Casbah.[35]

Jeanneret masqueraded "en travesti" as Loti, but only in private. To be "en travesti" is to take on disguise, wear fancy dress, cross-dress. "Travestir" means to falsify, deform. Contrary to Gresleri's assertions, there is no evidence that Jeanneret ever displayed his Oriental persona in public; he never surrendered himself to the Orientalist experience to this degree. The ability to dress up and down is temporary and untruthful, a function of the mutability of gender identity. Although Jeanneret and Klipstein played at transvestism in the privacy of their room, they did not give up their distance from Turkish life. A hesitancy to lose identity and ontological self-fashioning kept Jeanneret from "going native" all the way.

According to Behdad, the Orientalist narrative is not, and cannot be, a translation of the traveler's experience, but is a rewriting of a precursor's text. "As a result, the subject's desire for the Orient is not the desire for the Other; rather, it is a desire defined for him by the orientalist intertext."[36] As Gresleri put it: "Like the characters in the novels of Loti and Farrère which accompany Jeanneret on his travels, these men have but one aim in view, self-discovery."[37] Jeanneret acknowledged his sources in a letter to Ritter:

> To conclude my life of study I am preparing a great journey. The Slovakian land, the plain of Hungary, the Bulgarian, Romanian nations, which I don't know how to describe. You have made them so dear to me that I want to go there. . . . Claude Farrère, in *L'Homme qui assassina*, made me love in advance, for these many years, the dead city, the Muslim city [Constantinople]. . . . Books, books! . . . these are my rare and intimate initiators in this long journey of reverie.[38]

Jeanneret's choice of destinations, and the style he used in describing these places, was influenced by his intertexts, such as Farrère and Loti's novels, both set in Istanbul, Ritter's *L'entêtement Slovaque*, and Renan's *Prière sur l'Acropole*, all of which were in his library.[39] The title itself derives from numerous travel narratives published in the eighteenth and nineteenth centuries. Benton and Turner assert that he tried to imitate the florid language and colorful imagery that Ritter and Farrère employed in their descriptions of Eastern Europe and Istanbul, and that his reception of the Acropolis was based on Renan's pamphlet.[40]

In the course of the *Voyage*, Jeanneret struggled to integrate new influences into his views on architecture and culture. While he pursued the ideal peasant vase and performed as an Oriental, he was increasingly under the sway of theories that linked modern architecture to the classical tradition. His employment in the offices of Auguste Perret (Paris, 1908) and Peter Behrens (Berlin, 1910–1911) exposed him to classicizing architecture in the modern materials of reinforced concrete, steel, and glass. During this period, he read a text, recommended by Ritter, that affected profoundly his attitude toward classical civilization: Alexandre Cingria-Vaneyre's *Les Entretiens de la Villa du Rouet*.[41] Cingria-Vaneyre posited a connection between the Suisse-romande region, the French-speaking area of Switzerland that included the Jura and La-Chaux-de-Fonds, and Greco-Latin civilization. Drawing on Gobineau's theories of race, according to H. Allen Brooks, Cingria believed that the people of the Suisse-romande were descended from the Greeks and Romans, and their folk art preserved ancient classical values.[42] He maintained that there should be a new Suisse-romande identity and culture, and that the true spirit of the region was Mediterranean, not northern (Germanic). For Cingria-Vaneyre, Suisse-romande art and architecture should look for inspiration to the classical tradition and the "classical" landscape of the region, which he likened to Greece and Constantinople, two highlights on Jeanneret's *Voyage*.[43] According to Paul V.

Turner, Cingria was a reactionary, "dreaming of escaping from the vulgarity of modern industrial life by recreating the calm beauty and elegance which he finds in the Classical art of the South," a primitivist vision shared by Jeanneret.[44]

The second side of Jeanneret's primitivism, his quest for an original architectural source, may have been initiated by Cingria's text and Ritter's reverence for antiquity. Before he left Germany, he wrote to Ritter:

> Recently, you have evoked majestically, the great attraction of the Latin and classical light. . . . My spirit has been, during these months, as open to comprehending the classical genius as my dreams, which have carried me there obstinately. The whole current era looks, doesn't it, more than ever to the happy lands where grow white rectilinear marbles, vertical columns and entablatures parallel to the line of the seas.[45]

This primitivism was motivated by a search for origins, a "higher" source, and a belief in the superiority of a simple life close to nature, based on Montaigne's and Rousseau's valorization of the savage in a more natural, less corrupt state of being. Peter Collins traces modern ideals of honesty in architecture to "those notions of Greek Revivalism which can also claim Rousseau as their ancestor, and which were responsible, two centuries ago, for a type of Primitivism which sought for new architectural roots in the remote past."[46] Enlightenment theories of architecture posited a primal architectonic form, the primitive hut, from which all forms of architecture derived. Alan Colquhoun has placed Le Corbusier among Enlightenment thinkers, such as Rousseau and Laugier, who sought the origins of society in the primitive past, and theorized the beginning of architecture as the primitive hut. Colquhoun notes that Laugier's search was not for a vernacular architecture, but a pure classicism, the "pure sources of classical architecture." In the Enlightenment, "primitivism" was very different from the Romantic approach to vernacular architecture: "It was a 'return' not to a particular, idiosyncratic culture, based on local craft traditions, but to the sources of architecture as a universal language obeying the necessities of natural law."[47]

Jeanneret left Germany disappointed in the medieval and modern decorative arts of Western Europe and primed to appreciate antique classicism. In a letter to Charles L'Eplattenier, his former teacher in La-Chaux-de-Fonds, he expressed deep disappointment with the German arts and a preference for Greek and Roman culture: "And now, at present, I have much enthusiasm for Greece and Rome, and only an eclectic interest in those arts which make me uneasy—northern Gothic, Russian barbarisms, German torments."[48] The

worth Cingria gave to southern classicism intersected with Jeanneret's latent
classical tendencies, which were reinforced by another text he took on the
*Voyage*, Ernest Renan's poetic paean to Athens, *Prière sur l'Acropole*.[49] As
Richard Etlin has demonstrated, Jeanneret was influenced by French Hellenism as formulated by Viollet-le-Duc and Auguste Choisy; *Prière sur
l'Acropole* belongs to this tradition.[50] Etlin places Jeanneret's reception of the
Acropolis within a strand of French architectural Hellenism, including Renan, that perceived it as a sublime aesthetic icon, "a creation so perfect that
it transcends the limitations of the mortals who fashioned it and that places
the view in the presence of divinity made manifest. . . . "[51] Jeanneret understood the Parthenon as the repository of a "sacred standard, the basis for all
measurement in art."[52] Later, as Le Corbusier, he considered the Parthenon
an ideal, crystalline form: "There has been nothing like it anywhere or at any
period. It happened at a moment when things were at their keenest, when a
man, stirred by the noblest thoughts, crystallized them in a plastic work of
light and shade."[53] This interpretation is indebted deeply to Renan's description of the temple as an "ideal crystallized in marble."

In the typical trajectory of such Orientalist journeys, Jeanneret left Western Europe in search of the exotic, found it in Eastern Europe and Istanbul,
and took on the trappings of Orientalist disguise. But he was repelled, ultimately, by its corruption and hybridity and returned to his "true" roots in classicism and Western European culture.[54] At the end of his journey, Jeanneret
rejected folk culture as a source for modern art and architecture. He found a
hybrid, compromised by metropolitan fashions: "I am about to contradict myself, or make myself clear: peasant art proceeds from the art of the city. It belongs to it as one of its by-products. It is a cross-breed, but still beautiful, with
interesting characteristics and, in any case, showing powerful strength."[55]
Rather than an unadulterated source of primitive art, the folk culture he discovered in Eastern Europe was tainted by contact with and influence from
metropolitan culture. Even after his disillusionment with the corrupt peasant
art he found in Eastern Europe, however, Jeanneret/Le Corbusier continued
to value folk culture as a primitive equivalent to machine form. In his treatise
on decorative art, published as Le Corbusier, he glorified folk art and its capacity to evoke a universal, spontaneous impression:

> Folk culture is a magnificent creation. An achievement purified by time and
> number. . . . Folk culture is so powerful that we all immediately respond to it;
> it offers the broadest channel for the expression of the mind and the heart.
> Whether Tartar, Romanian, Scandinavian, Negro, or Bavarian, it holds past
> ages within itself.[56]

Despite his admiration for folk art, Jeanneret could not use it as the basis for modern architecture because of its lack of the "eternal" values of universal classicism, as he made clear in *The Decorative Art of Today:*

> Equally the time is past when we—men of vigour in an age of heroic reawakening from the powers of the spirit, in an epoch which rings out with a tragic thunder not far from Doric—can lounge on ottomans and divans among orchids in the scented atmosphere of the seraglio and behave like so many ornamental animals or hummingbirds in impeccable evening dress, pinned through the trunk like a collection of butterflies to the swathes of gold, lacquer or brocade on our wall-paneling and hangings.[57]

Repudiating Jeanneret's pretend experience in the "scented atmosphere of the seraglio," Le Corbusier championed the virile virtues of archaic classicism as a primitive source for modern architecture. The primitive must be pure to serve as the complement, the "other," of metropolitan civilization. Greek antiquity provided a better source for Jeanneret's primitivism since it was distant in time and space from Western art and architecture and yet was its ostensible origin. His shift to universalism was part of the logic of primitivism: the dearth of a pure vernacular primitive in Eastern Europe and Turkey necessitated a turn to the internalized primitive of antiquity. By contrast with the decadence and hybridity of Oriental or folk art, the Parthenon offered truth and enduring values: "For two thousand years, those who have seen the Parthenon have felt that here was a decisive moment in Architecture. We are at a decisive moment. At the present time when the arts are feeling their way . . . the Parthenon gives us sure truths and emotions of a superior, mathematical order."[58]

According to Goldwater, primitive art is usually a stimulus or catalyst to modern art, not directly borrowed from or the direct cause of primitive qualities in that art. The primitive helped Western artists and architects formulate their own goals and methods and served as a referent, not a direct source.[59] Colin Rhodes, historian of primitivism in modern art, points to an equivocal issue at the heart of primitivism: although artists used the primitive as a support and justification for cultural or social change, their efforts were directed toward change expected to emerge within the West. There was no question of the comprehensive substitution of Western culture, or its unacceptable aspects, by the primitive.[60] The schism between folk culture and universal classicism was a central problem for Jeanneret's thinking from the start of the *Voyage*. Unable to reconcile himself to the mixed vernacular of Eastern Europe or "go native" with abandon, Jeanneret jettisoned his affiliation with folklore, ornament, and primitive art, and attached himself to universalism.

At the end of his *Voyage*, Jeanneret found himself and his Western roots. Alain Grosrichard has identified this rebound to the same as the recurrent culmination of Western fantasies of the East. Jeanneret completed his adventure with the affirmation of self essential to any European's journey:

> This gaze, which to me is other, knows more about me than I do myself. And when I attempt to go and look behind what I believe to be the point from which, over there in that other world, it looks at me, it is myself and our world that I find in the end.[61]

## NOTES

1. See Giuliano Gresleri, "Home Ties Adrift Abroad: The Oriental Journey of Ch. E. Jeanneret," *Daidalos* 19 (March 1986): 102–11; and H. Allen Brooks, *Le Corbusier's Formative Years* (Chicago: University of Chicago Press, 1997). Jeanneret's research in Germany resulted in his first book, *Étude sur le mouvement d'art décoratif en Allemagne* (La-Chaux-de-Fonds: Haefeli, 1912).

2. Letter from Jeanneret to Ritter, March 1, 1911, Fondation Le Corbusier. Klipstein wrote his doctoral dissertation on El Greco.

3. Geoffrey H. Baker, *Le Corbusier: The Creative Search* (New York: Van Nostrand Reinhold, 1996), 138.

4. Le Corbusier, *Le Voyage d'Orient* (Paris: Forces Vives, 1966), 11–12; Le Corbusier, *Voyage d'Orient: Sketchbooks*, trans. Mayta Munson and Meg Shore (New York: Rizzoli, 1987); Le Corbusier, *Journey to the East*, trans. and ed. Ivan Zaknic (Cambridge, Mass.: MIT Press, 1987). The only philological edition of the *Voyage*, including his photographs, sketches, and letters, was published in Italian translation, rather than the original French: Giuliano Gresleri, ed., *Le Corbusier Viaggio in Oriente (gli inediti di Ch. E. Jeanneret fotographo e reporter)* (Venice: Fondation Le Corbusier and Marsilio, 1984).

5. Le Corbusier, *The Decorative Art of Today*, trans. James Dunnett (Cambridge, Mass.: MIT Press, 1987), 206; Brooks, 95 and 256.

6. Gresleri, "Home Ties Adrift Abroad," 107–8.

7. Gresleri, "Home Ties Adrift Abroad," 108.

8. Adolf Max Vogt, "Remarks on the 'Reversed' Grand Tour of Le Corbusier and Auguste Klipstein," *Assemblage* 4 (1987): 40.

9. Timothy Benton, "Voyage d'Orient," in *Le Corbusier: Architect of the Century* (London: Arts Council of Great Britain, 1987), 56.

10. Sibel Bozdogan, "Journey to the East: Ways of Looking at the Orient and the Question of Representation," *Journal of Architectural Education* 41, no. 1 (1988): 38–45; Richard Ingersoll, Letter to the Editor, *Journal of Architectural Education* 42, no. 4 (1989): 61.

11. On primitivism in modern architecture, see my entry "Primitivism," in Stephen Sennott, ed., *Encyclopedia of Twentieth-Century Architecture* (New York: Fitzroy Dearborn, 2004).

12. Robert Goldwater, *Primitivism in Modern Art* (Cambridge, Mass.: Belknap Press, 1986), 251.

13. Le Corbusier, *The Decorative Arts of Today*, trans. James Dunnett (Cambridge, Mass.: MIT Press, 1987), 212.

14. Gresleri, "Home Ties Adrift Abroad," 105.

15. Baker, *Le Corbusier*, 143.

16. Ritter's work includes *Algyptiaque* (1891); *Le royaume de Carmen Sylva: de Bucarest à Sinaia* (1894); *Pierre Loti aux Lieux-Saints* (1895); and *Prague nocturne* (1896).

17. Turner, *The Education of Le Corbusier*, 92. William Ritter, *L'entêtement Slovaque* (Paris: Bibliothèque de l'Occident, 1910). On Jeanneret's relationship with Ritter, see Brooks, *Le Corbusier's Formative Years*, 216–18.

18. Goldwater, *Primitivism in Modern Art*, 254.

19. Barbara Maria Stafford, *Voyage into Substance: Art, Science, Nature, and the Illustrated Travel Account, 1760–1840* (Cambridge, Mass.: MIT Press, 1984), 472.

20. See Fred Orton and Griselda Pollock, "Les Données bretonnantes: La prairie de répresentation," *Art History* (September 1980): 314–44; Griselda Pollock, *Avant-garde Gambits, 1888–1893: Gender and the Colour of Art History* (London: Thames and Hudson, 1992); Stephen Eisenman, *Gauguin's Skirt* (New York : Thames and Hudson, 1997).

21. Le Corbusier, *Le Voyage d'Orient*, 15.

22. Le Corbusier, *Le Voyage d'Orient*, 13–14.

23. Le Corbusier, *Le Voyage d'Orient*, 14–15.

24. Le Corbusier, *Le Voyage d'Orient*, 15.

25. Larry Wolff, *Inventing Eastern Europe: The Map of Civilization on the Mind of the Enlightenment* (Stanford, Calif.: Stanford University Press, 1994), 6 and 9.

26. Brooks, *Le Corbusier's Formative Years*, 271.

27. Wolff, *Inventing Eastern Europe*, 43–44.

28. Pierre Loti, *Aziyadé* (Paris: Calmann-Lévy, 1879). Gresleri asserts that the scene derived from *Aziyadé*, but none of Jeanneret's letters, articles, or books mention the novel in this context. This seems to be speculation on Gresleri's part, although not acknowledged as such.

29. Letter from Jeanneret to Albert Jeanneret, September 1911, Athens, published in Gresleri, *Viaggio in Oriente*, 387–88; Benton, "Voyage d'Orient," 56.

30. Gresleri claims that while in Istanbul Jeanneret adopted Turkish garb and drifted through the city as "a Turk among the Turks." Gresleri, "Home Ties Adrift Abroad," 107.

31. Emily Apter, *Continental Drift: From National Characters to Virtual Subjects* (Chicago: University of Chicago Press, 1999), 136.

32. Apter, *Continental Drift*, 136.

33. Gresleri, "The Rediscovered Sketchbooks," in *Voyage d'Orient: Sketchbooks*, 13.

34. Ali Behdad, *Belated Travelers: Orientalism in the Age of Colonial Dissolution* (Durham, N.C.: Duke University Press, 1994), 21.

35. Apter, *Continental Drift*, 137.

36. Behdad, *Belated Travelers*, 26.

37. Gresleri, "Home Ties Adrift Abroad," 105.

38. Letter from Jeanneret to Ritter, March 1, 1911, Fondation Le Corbusier.

39. Claude Farrère, *L'Homme qui Assassina* (Paris: 1907); Ritter, *L'entêtement Slovague*. See Paul V. Turner, *The Education of Le Corbusier* (New York: Garland, 1977) on Jeanneret's reading and library.

40. Benton, "Voyage d'Orient," 56–57.

41. Alexandre Cingria-Vaneyre, *Les Entretiens de la Villa du Rouet. Essais dialogués sur les arts plastiques en Suisse romande* (Genève: Jullien, 1908).

42. Brooks, *Le Corbusier's Formative Years*, 237.

43. Turner, *The Education of Le Corbusier*, 86.

44. Turner, *The Education of Le Corbusier*, 89. Turner attributes Cingria's influence to Jeanneret's return to La-Chaux-de-Fonds at the end of the *Voyage* and his subsequent classical works, such the Villa Favre-Jacot.

45. Letter from Jeanneret to Ritter, March 1, 1911, Fondation Le Corbusier.

46. Peter Collins, *Changing Ideals in Modern Architecture, 1750–1950* (Montreal: McGill University Press, 1965), 253.

47. Alan Colquhoun, *Modernity and the Classical Tradition: Architectural Essays, 1980–1987* (Cambridge, Mass.: MIT Press, 1989), 28 and 30.

48. Letter from Jeanneret to Charles L'Eplattenier, January 16, 1911, quoted in Brooks, 244.

49. Ernest Renan, *Prière sur l'Acropole* (Athens: Eleftheroudakis & Barth, n.d).

50. Richard Etlin, "Le Corbusier, Choisy, and French Hellenism: The Search for a New Architecture," *Art Bulletin* 69, no. 2: 264–78. In a detailed analysis of Renan's text, Henriette Psichari has traced its sources and inspirations, including Michelet, Guigniaut, Beulé, and Lamartine. Henriette Psichari, *La Prière sur l'Acropole et ses mystères* (Paris: Editions du Centre National de la Recherche Scientifique, 1956), 109–23.

51. Etlin, "Le Corbusier, Choisy, and French Hellenism," 274.

52. Le Corbusier, *Voyage d'Orient*, 158.

53. Renan, *Prière sur l'Acropole*, 1; Le Corbusier, *Towards a New Architecture*, trans. Frederick Etchells (New York: Praeger, 1960), 203–4.

54. It is beyond the scope of this article to examine Jeanneret and Klipstein's stay on Mount Athos. See Ivan Zaknic, "Le Corbusier's Epiphany on Mount Athos," *Journal of Architectural Education* 43, no. 4: 27–36.

55. Le Corbusier, *Le Voyage d'Orient*, 116.

56. Le Corbusier, *The Decorative Art of Today*, 36.

57. Le Corbusier, *The Decorative Art of Today*, 192.

58. Le Corbusier, *Towards a New Architecture*, 205.

59. Goldwater, *Primitivism in Modern Art*, 252–53.

60. Colin Rhodes, *Primitivism and Modern Art* (New York : Thames and Hudson, 1994), 13.

61. Alain Grosrichard, *The Sultan's Court: European Fantasies of the East*, trans. Liz Heron (London: Verso, 1998), 25.

# 3

# FRANCE IN THE WILDERNESS

*Winifred Woodhull*

French cinema of the 1930s is best known for the poetic realist films of directors such as Jean Renoir, Julien Duvivier, and Marcel Carné, many of which are centered on beleaguered working-class men whose dramas unfold in urban settings, and who usually succumb to a terrible destiny. One thinks of Jean Gabin, the eponymous hero of Duvivier's 1937 film *Pépé le Moko*, who plays a Parisian thief hiding from the French police in the Casbah of Algiers. Pépé's fatal descent from the Casbah to the port, his capture, and ultimate suicide result from his fascination with a beautiful French tourist played by Mireille Balin, who embodies the irresistible, unattainable potency and glamor that Pépé associates with the city of Paris.

Yet a number of films in this period, including some by the directors just named, focus not on urban existence but on rural or small-town life in various regions of France or other Francophone spaces. And hundreds of 1930s movies, whether Foreign Legion dramas such as Duvivier's *La Bandera* or military comedies such as Christian-Jaque's *Un de la légion*, are set in France's colonies, the majority of them in North Africa. These films bear witness to a struggle that had been waged throughout the nineteenth and twentieth centuries, but that acquires particular force during the Third Republic and the Vichy Régime: the struggle to define the relation of regional cultures to the nation as a whole, and to define French national identity through figurations of its difference from cultures that are seen as alien and primitive. At stake in the struggle is the determination of that which constitutes "true

France," as well as the possibilities for restructuring the relation between the "pays réel" and the "pays légal," to use the terms coined by Charles Maurras at the time of the Dreyfus Affair.[1] As the forces of modernization and centralization gain ascendancy, regional languages and social practices either erode or adapt to changing circumstances and take on new forms. Aspects of regional culture that seem to be in danger of disappearing are recorded by ethnographers, enshrined in museums, photographed and circulated on postcards, celebrated by writers, and projected onto the silver screen. In some cases the regional cultures acquire new life; in others, they are nostalgically kept on life support. Either way, their singularity is defended, usually with an eye to critiquing some of the adverse effects of urbanization and industrialization, and sometimes with the goal of making a frontal attack on republican institutions and values.

In the cinema of the 1930s, regional cultures, notably those of Brittany and Provence, often appear as enclaves of tradition in which rural or small-town communal life, patriarchal authority, and an idealized, "authentic" Frenchness are contrasted with the evils of urban life, which include economic exploitation and social anonymity as well as dangerous forms of female emancipation and cultural mixing. In this chapter, I discuss four films, three of which deal with Provence: Jean Renoir's *Toni* (1934), Marcel Pagnol's *Angèle* (1936), and Jean Grémillon's *Gueule d'amour* (1937). The fourth, to which I devote the greatest attention, is Julien Duvivier's *Maria Chapdelaine* (1934). The latter film is not about a French region per se, but about French Canada, which, in many respects, is treated like a region of France both in Duvivier's film and in the 1912 novel on which it is based.

The novel, *Maria Chapdelaine: Récit du Canada Français*, was written by Louis Hémon, a young Breton who was educated in Paris, where he studied law and modern oriental languages.[2] Hémon began publishing in sports magazines in Paris, then moved to England where he wrote fiction before spending eighteen months in Quebec working on farms and writing *Maria Chapdelaine*. It is tempting to speculate that Hémon's interest in French Canada, specifically his view that a certain authentic Frenchness survives there, is tied to the fact that he comes from the province of Brittany, whose own culture was being eroded, to some extent, and brought into the new national mainstream at the turn of the century in a process that, according to Eugen Weber, turned "peasants into Frenchmen."[3] However, certain passages in Hémon's novel display a keen awareness of the ways in which the French idealize Canada. For example, he stages a meeting between Quebeckers and a Frenchman and his two sons who have come to Quebec to escape the constraints of urban existence, only to discover that life in northern Canada is almost unbearably harsh. The Frenchmen had been spurred to leave France by "la lassitude du trottoir et du pavé, l'air pauvre des villes; la révolte contre la perspective sans fin d'une existence asservie. . . . Maintenant ils ne pouvaient guère s'esquisser une moue évasive et chercher laquelle de leurs illusions leur restait encore" (weariness of the footway and the pavement, of the town's sullied air; revolt against the prospect of lifelong slavery. . . . Now their best was a sorry effort to evade the question, as they groped for any of the illusions that remained to them), p. 132/191. Moreover, Hémon presents to his readers the Canadians' view of these strange Frenchmen, their astonishment that the father could have made a living in France as a piano tuner. Still, this becomes the occasion for the Canadians to acknowledge good-naturedly their cultural inferiority. Says Samuel Chapdelaine: "Et moi qui ne sais seulement pas lire. —Ni moi! ajouta promptement Ephrem Surprenant. Conrad Néron et Egide Racicot firent chorus: —Ni moi! —Ni moi! Et tous se mirent à rire" ("And here I am, not even able to read!" "Nor I!" struck in Ehphrem Surprenant. Conrad Neron et Egide Racicot added: "Nor I!" "Nor I!" in chorus, whereupon the whole of them broke out laughing), pp. 131–32/189–90. Hémon's novel, which was initially received in Quebec as a "model" of French Canadian literature, has been the subject of much critical debate in the past few decades, as Quebec writers and intellectuals have challenged the understanding of their culture as a pale, distorted, or archaic reflection of French culture.[4] Moreover, Hémon's *Maria Chapdelaine* has inspired other films in the wake of Duvivier's: Marc Allégret's *The Naked Heart*, produced in the United Kingdom in 1949, and a more recent *Maria Chapdelaine* produced in Quebec by Gilles Carle in 1983.[5]

Basically, I want to argue that, to a certain extent, Duvivier's film recolonizes the Quebec wilderness and idealizes it as a place where a supposedly authentic Frenchness is preserved, both "naturally" in the ice and snow of the Lake St. John area, where the action unfolds, and culturally in the life created by the valiant *défricheurs*, woodcutters who clear the land and farm it briefly before moving on to "faire de la terre" (make land) elsewhere. The film also exoticizes Quebec in various ways, just as Pagnol and Grémillon exoticize Provence, with a view toward establishing the superiority of the region, or former colony, over modern, industrialized areas in France, English Canada, and the United States. But I want to argue as well that the cinematic form of Duvivier's *Maria Chapdelaine*, unlike that of *La Bandera* and most other films set in the colonies or in a region of France, suggests new ways of conceiving the relation between tradition and modernity, and between various Francophone spaces. In its innovative breaks

with classic realist cinematic codes within a realist film, *Maria Chapdelaine* shares with Renoir's *Toni* an interest in exploring the fruitful interplay
of languages, cultures, and identities in modern societies of Europe and
North America.

## PROVENCE ON THE SCREEN

*Toni* is based on a true story involving an Italian immigrant laborer who was
killed by virtue of having been suspected of a crime he did not commit, that
is, the murder of a French foreman near the quarry where he worked. Toni's
conflict with the foreman, Albert, stems not only from class antagonism, but
from his passion for Josefa, a Spanish laundress who ended up marrying Albert after he forced her to have sex with him. A title at the beginning of the
film tells us that "l'action se passe dans le Midi de la France, en pays latin, là
où la nature, détruisant l'esprit de Babel, sait si bien opérer la fusion des
races" (the action takes place in the south of France, in Latin country, where
nature, destroying the spirit of Babel, is so effective at bringing about the fusion of races). The apparent essentialism of this statement is amply coun-
tered by the critical naturalism of Renoir's style in a film that is now regarded
as a precursor to Italian neorealism, in its exclusive location shooting in natural light, and its long takes and fluid camera work that have been said to so-
cialize the spaces depicted, for instance by encompassing in a single shot
Toni and Albert, immigrant worker and boss, on the lip of the quarry, the
workplace that shapes their adversarial relationship.[6]

The cinematic originality of *Toni* is evident, too, in Renoir's use of non-
professional actors, as well as professionals from the south of France, notably Charles Blavette in the title role, speaking in the accents and locutions
of workers from Italy, Spain, Corsica, and Provence. The fact that the actors speak French (the national language) rather than Provençal, as industrial and agricultural laborers did at that time, stems from the concurrent
emergence of synchronized sound and national cinema in the 1930s. But
the exclusive use of French does not prevent the film from designating social differences through language, for example, by contrasting Toni's southern accent with Albert's northern one, an accent that reinforces Albert's
association with industrial power and marks his social privilege. Despite the
film's financial backing and distribution by Marcel Pagnol's production
company, Renoir's *Toni* was a flop, both because of its disconcerting style
and because of its unorthodox subject matter. The plight of immigrant
workers was an unpopular subject in a historical period in which France was

being chauvinistically claimed for the French, due to the shortage of jobs during the Great Depression and to the widespread xenophobia fostered by the rise of fascism.

Other 1930s films dealing with life in Provence were big hits, however, the most famous ones being those of Pagnol. Adapted from his popular plays, these films attracted large audiences eager to see well-known stage actors on the screen. Like Renoir's *Toni*, Pagnol's cinema was filmed on location in Provence, used actors from the south of France who spoke with the local accent, and is now associated with Italian neorealism. But whereas Renoir used an innovative naturalistic style to present the world of industrial laborers in Provence as "foreign," that is, alienated both economically and culturally, Pagnol's filmed theater encouraged viewers to see Provence as a relatively unproblematic "home." As many critics have noted, Pagnol deliberately exoticized Provence—its landscapes, its buildings, its language—as a way of marking its social and cultural difference from, and its superiority to, northern and/or urban, industrial France. Echoing Laura Mulvey's comments on D. W. Griffith, Ginette Vincendeau notes that Pagnol's use of long takes rather than editing suggests a refusal to acknowledge the modernity of cinema and the aesthetics specific to it.[7] In addition, his style perhaps betrays nostalgia for certain antiquated aspects of Provençal culture that would best be consigned to the dustbin of history.

In this connection, I want to comment on Pagnol's *Angèle*, in which the title character is a farm girl who runs off with a city slicker. The city slicker promises to marry her, but in fact forces her to work for him in a Marseilles brothel once he has lured her away from the protective family circle. Angèle is cruelly punished for having succumbed to the charms of the city and for having borne an illegitimate child by the villain who seduced her: her father locks her up in an outbuilding when she returns to the family farm. The repentant fallen woman is reintegrated into the rural community through a marriage arranged, in consultation with her father, by a young mountain man who truly loves her and is willing to assume paternal responsibility for her child. The film's narrative relies heavily on outdated patriarchal discourses, which become the vehicle for figuring the city/country conflict in terms of heterosexual relationships: the corrupt, abusive, impersonal city is denounced, while Provence appears as the site of communal solidarity and legitimate masculine authority. Feminist critics have rightly signaled an important countercurrent in the film, that is, its implicit affirmation of Angèle's resourcefulness and independence in coping with her difficult situation, and the material and moral support provided by female relatives and friends as well as by the Fernandel character, a simpleminded farm hand who functions as a "proto-woman."[8] But by and large, *Angèle* is a classic "fallen woman" film in which the "fall" is a trope for the sleaze of modern life, and the redemption a trope for the goodness of rural Provence.

Grémillon's *Gueule d'amour*, released one year after *Angèle*, similarly pits the communal spirit of Provence against the cold calculation and self-interestedness of the city, albeit without making any use of local accents (all the actors speak with northern accents). A bizarre melodrama set in the garrison town of Orange, the film features Jean Gabin in the role of Lucien, a spahi whose good looks and lady-killing ways have earned him the nickname "Gueule d'amour." Lucien is laid low by Mireille Balin in the role of Madeleine, a heartless Parisian femme fatale who squanders her lover's money in the Cannes casino, then abandons him after he leaves the army and follows her to Paris. Madeleine's luxurious surroundings in the sixteenth arrondissement (her elegant apartment, her avant-garde art, her immense modern bathroom) contrast sharply with Lucien's in the print shop where he works as a typographer, in the bistrot where he dines, and in his working-class rooming house. Madeleine's brutal rejection of Lucien in favor of an aging sugar daddy points up the decadent immorality of Paris, just as Lucien's comical dismissal by Madeleine's mother, who condescendingly refers to him as "le genre costaud" (the muscular type) before sending him packing, underlines the snobbery of the Parisian ruling class.

When Lucien returns to Orange to open a modest bar and café, he must accept the fact that he has become a nobody in the town where he was once adored by young girls and mature (married or widowed) women, and where his sexploits were admired and envied by his commanding officers. At the café in Orange, there is a final confrontation between Lucien and Madeleine, in which Madeleine tries to regain her hold on Lucien, boasts of her power to enslave him emotionally, and threatens to seduce René, a doctor who had been Lucien's close friend in the army. After the inevitable "scène de rage," a hallmark of Jean Gabin's film performances, Lucien strangles Madeleine, then sinks into a state of tearful confusion before asking for help from René. The two men not only reaffirm their bond of friendship but display a strong homoerotic attraction to each other (sobs, clingy hugs, and kisses shown in medium close-ups usually reserved for heterosexual lovers) as René helps Lucien to escape by train in a third class car occupied by Italian immigrant laborers. The former spahi hopes to reach Marseille and then take a boat to Africa, where he will live in exile.

Although the film, like most others of its type in the 1930s, does little to disturb the opposition between the goodness of Provençal traditions and the evil of urban modernity, Grémillon's *Gueule d'amour* does not follow the pattern established in Pagnol's films, which is to designate Provence as the locus of legitimate and effective masculine authority. Instead, it leaves viewers with an image of French heterosexual masculinity on the run, rubbing elbows with European immigrant workers and potentially hiding out among the very Africans who were to have been subdued by the spahis.

A sequence from the beginning of the film illustrates the way in which Orange is doubly exoticized, both as a luminous southern locale with distinctive romanesque and contemporary architecture, and as the provisional home of the spahis, who, with much fanfare, parade into town on horseback. The film's exoticism functions to body forth the goodness and desirability of Orange, which is as much on display here as the film's star, Jean Gabin, the only spahi to be shown in isolation, in the center of the frame, and to be seen in medium shots rather than long shots. Admired by myriad young women who wave to him from their windows and balconies as he rides by in his "African" uniform (fez, *pantalon bouffant*), Gabin / "Gueule d'amour" is imbued with an erotic appeal that is enhanced by the visual and narrative associations between Orange and Africa.


## PROJECTIONS OF FRENCH CANADA

A similar exoticization is apparent in certain scenes from Duvivier's *Maria Chapdelaine*, which features Jean Gabin in the role of François Paradis, an adventurous trapper, fur trader, and woodcutter who lives a life of even greater isolation and mobility than that of the Chapdelaine family and their fellow *défricheurs*. True pioneers who continually push back the frontiers of the wilderness, François and the Chapdelaine family are contrasted with the sedentary strain of French peasants who have settled permanently near the parish churches and enjoy the limited comforts available in villages such as Peribonka, situated a considerable distance north of the city of Quebec.

François is one of three men courting Maria Chapdelaine, and the only one who inspires passion in the young woman. The other suiters are Eutrope Gagnon, a good-natured clod who has cleared the land adjacent to the Chapdelaine lot, and Lorenzo Surprenant, the son of a *défricheur*, who has moved to an unidentified big city and works in manufacturing. After François dies in a blizzard while trying to make his way to Maria at Christmas rather than waiting until spring as he had planned to do, and after her own mother, Laura, dies that same winter, Maria is momentarily tempted by Lorenzo's promise of a stimulating, comfortable, and relatively safe life in the city. But in the end, upon hearing the "voice of Quebec" enjoining all

French Canadians to carry on as they have supposedly been doing without the slightest change for hundreds of years, Maria decides to marry the boy next door and live the same life as her mother.

Duvivier's film features exotic views of François standing before an immense waterfall, shooting the rapids in a canoe, and acting as intermediary for a Belgian fur trader in his dealings with the Iroquois ("les sauvages"), a task that includes, implausibly, translation from the Iroquois language into French! These scenes were all shot in July 1934 when the French cast and film crew were working on location in Quebec. The film also features location footage of winter scenes shot in March 1934, when Duvivier went to Quebec with his cameraman, Armand Thirard. The ethnographic style of these scenes, in which we see vast snowy landscapes, sleighs, and even a dog sled, is reminiscent of Robert Flaherty's *Nanook of the North* and works to naturalize the film's depiction of the *défricheurs*. Other instances of exoticism and local color include Madeleine Renaud as Maria, frolicking with barnyard animals and driving an enormous haywagon, and the Indian and French people of Peribonka dancing in succession (not together) at the village festival to the beat of Iroquois drums and the strains of "Sur le Pont d'Avignon."

The film also exoticizes the language of the Quebeckers, devoting two entire scenes to a display of Canadianisms that the assumed French audience is invited to interpret as amusing archaisms (the Canadians' reference to the train as "le char"), strange anglicisms ("job," "foreman," etc.), and odd but comprehensible pronunciation ("touais" for "toi"). In this, the film does not follow the text of Louis Hémon's novel, but follows instead the altered form Hémon's manuscript was given when it was first published as a serial in 1912 in the Paris weekly *Le Temps*. As Nicole Deschamps points out, in the 1912 serial and in subsequent editions of the novel, Canadian terms, which Hémon had freely mixed in with the metropolitan French of his narration, were set off in quotation marks that had the effect of exoticizing Canadian French and recolonizing French Canada.[9]

Deschamps argues that Hémon's text is further colonized by the presentation of the 1916 edition published in Montreal by the LeFebvre press. Now classified as a rare book, this edition contains two prefaces by prestigious figures, one by Louvigny de Montigny of the Société Royale du Canada, and another by Émile Boutroux of the Académie française. This edition also features illustrations by a well-known local artist, Suzor-Côté. Deschamps comments that

> loin de révéler l'originalité du livre, proposé d'emblée comme un modèle à imiter, cet étalage dans la présentation détourne l'attention du texte lui-même

en la fixant sur des normes fictives: le chef-d'oeuvre idéal, le Canada français idéal. Parallèlement à l'initiative des rédacteurs du *Temps* qui soulignent l'exotisme du vocabulaire, les illustrations de Suzor-Côté sont des mises entre guillemets de la réalité québécoise décrite par Hémon. Personnages, objets, animaux, paysages, la première imagerie inspirée par *Maria Chapdelaine* appartient déjà au *folklore*. Ce ne sont plus des mots pittoresques qui sont isolés du contexte, c'est tout le "récit du Canada français" qui ne s'appartient plus. (pp. xi–xii)

far from revealing the originality of the book, presented from the start as a model to imitate, this display in the presentation distracts attention from the text itself and focuses it instead on fictive norms: the ideal masterpiece, the ideal French Canada. Parallel to the initiative of the editors of *Le Temps* who underscore the exoticism of the vocabulary, the illustrations of Suzor-Côté put into quotation marks the reality of Quebec described by Hémon. Characters, objects, animals, landscapes—the first imagery inspired by *Maria Chapdelaine* already belongs to folklore. It is no longer just a matter of picturesque words being isolated from their context, it is the entire "story of French Canada" that is no longer its own.

Introductions to various editions of the novel underscore the triumphalist note sounded in certain passages, effacing its aspect as a "conte de neige et d'absence" (story of snow and absence), in Deschamps's terms (p. vii). However, it must be acknowledged that Hémon's novel (and Duvivier's film as well) celebrates the Canadian *défricheurs* of the early twentieth century as hearty and loyal descendants of their French forebears. "Les colons de Champlain" (Champlain's colonists), as they are called by Louvigny de Montigny (p. iv), staunchly defend their language and traditions against the groups of "foreigners" who came to Canada after them and acquired most of the power and money but, in their view, lack a legitimate claim to authentic Canadian identity. Hémon writes:

Lorsque les Canadiens français parlent d'eux-mêmes, ils disent toujours "Canadiens," sans plus; et à toutes les autres races qui ont derrière eux peuplé le pays jusqu'au Pacifique, ils ont gardé pour parler d'elles leurs appellations d'origine: Anglais, Irlandais, Polonais ou Russes, sans admettre un seul instant que leurs fils, même nés dans le pays, puissent prétendre aussi au nom de "Canadiens." C'est là un titre qu'ils se réservent tout naturellement et sans intention d'offense, de par leur héroïque antériorité. (p. 60)

When French Canadians speak of themselves, it is invariably and simply as "Canadians"; whereas for all the other races that followed in their footsteps, and peopled the country across to the Pacific, they have kept the name of origin: English, Irish, Polish, or Russian; never admitting for a moment that their sons, albeit born in the country, have an equal claim to be called "Canadians." For that is a title that they reserve for themselves, quite naturally, and without thought of offending, by virtue of their heroic anteriority. (p. 89; translation modified)

The glorification of an immutable Frenchness finds expression in Duvivier's *Maria Chapdelaine* through the parish priest, a mouthpiece for the "voice of Quebec":

> Nous sommes venues ici il y a 300 ans. Nous sommes venus de France. Et nous sommes restés, et nous n'avons rien oublié, ni nos prières, ni nos chansons. . . . Au pays de Québec, rien n'a changé, et rien ne changera, parce que nous sommes un témoignage.

> We came here 300 years ago. We came from France. And we stayed, and we have forgotten nothing, neither our prayers nor our songs. . . . In Quebec, nothing has changed, and nothing will change, because we are testimony.

In the film, this is the only "voice" Maria hears, whereas in the novel, she hears three voices, none of which speak through a priest, and only one of which is the "la voix du pays de Québec, qui était à moitié un chant de femme et à moitié un sermon de prêtre" (the voice of Quebec, which was half the song of a woman, half the sermon of a priest), pp. 197/281; translation modified. That Hémon's Maria heeds the call of these voices with sad resignation rather than a triumphal spirit is evident in the following passage:

> Maria Chapdelaine sortit de son rêve et songea: "Alors je vais rester ici . . . de même!" car les voix avaient parlé clairement et elle sentait qu'il fallait obéir. Le souvenir de ses autres devoirs ne vint qu'ensuite, après qu'elle se fût résignée, avec un soupir. (p. 199)

> Maria Chapdelaine awaked from her dream to the thought: "So I shall stay—stay here after all!" For the voices had spoken clearly and she felt that she must obey. The memory of her other duties came only later, after she had resigned herself, with a sigh. (p. 284; translation modified)

In the film, on the other hand, the thundering voice of the priest more or less drowns out Maria's expressions of doubt, despondency, and resignation. In any case, Maria is finally convinced to sacrifice herself to a tradition that, the priest says, "nous devons transmettre . . . à de nombreux enfants" (we must transmit to numerous children).

Duvivier's film does more, though, than to sound a triumphalist note that resonates at the expense of a submissive young woman. While it is indisputable that *Maria Chapdelaine* conforms in many respects to the codes of melodrama and to the conventions of mainstream French realist cinema (including the practice of casting French actors in nearly all speaking parts), it makes some important departures from these conventions that emphasize the limitless desolation of the wilderness rather than its susceptibility to conquest, the uncertainty of the border between wilderness and civilization, and the marvellous possibilities for change that come into view on the frontiers of French and Quebec society. A striking example is the montage sequence that figures an array of subjective, social, and cultural positions whose relations to each other are posed as a question on Christmas Eve. The complicated junctures and disjunctures between Canada and France are figured in the montage, where French Christmas carols, such as "Il est né le divin enfant," are sung in the rustic Peribonka church by a children's chorus, and simultaneously in the Chapdelaine farmhouse by Gaby Triquet, the French child actress who plays the youngest Chapdelaine child, Alma-Rose, yet sings with an unmistakable Parisian accent. By juxtaposing shots of Maria Chapdelaine and her parents in their snowbound home, adults attending midnight mass in the Peribonka church, and François losing his way in the woods, the montage also draws attention to the possibilities for rethinking the relations between various psychic, social, and cultural spaces in Quebec—village, farmhouse, and forest; age and youth; men and women.

Another way in which Duvivier departs from realist conventions is through the use of subjective shots showing Maria's wishes for François's safe return in the spring. A superimposition conjures François's presence at Maria's side as she prays, blurring the boundary between wilderness and civilization, forest and farmhouse, woodsman and farm girl. Similarly, a dissolve gives expression to Maria's wishful thinking and conquers temporal barriers, transforming the harsh winter that marks the lovers' separation into the springtime that heralds their reunion. An unexpected cut from the spring landscape, as imagined by Maria, to a view of Maria veiled in black and silhouetted against the snow, brings Maria's reverie to an abrupt end.

In addition to unsettling the relation between wilderness and civilization, these cinematic processes emphasize a protean, surprising dimension of Maria's subjectivity, one that contradicts her aspect as a dutiful daughter of Quebec (and of France) whose only excitement stems from the inevitable melodramatic dream of finding true love that ends in marriage. Maria's love for François is not simply a domesticating force, figured poetically in the film by a series of small animals for which Maria displays a fondness after the woodsman wins her heart—chickens, goats, kittens, a chipmunk. Her love is also a wild, unpredictable force that extends into the wilderness, one that finds tragic but also fierce expression in the figure of the wolves that will eventually feed on François's corpse.[10] The stark gender opposition between François and Maria is undermined not only by the wildness attributed to Maria's love, but by the fact that it is François's excessive emotion, his boundless love for Maria, that causes him to undertake a foolish journey through the wilderness in the dead of winter. If he has gotten lost and succumbed to the elements, it is not just because he has come up against the limits of an experienced woodsman's ability to navigate in the wild under adverse conditions (as Hémon suggests in the novel); it is because he has been seized by an uncontrollable desire. No less than Maria, François is a subject of melodrama. The similarity between the two characters is thrown into relief by the use of cross-cutting and sound bridges (notably the traditional French song "Il y a longtemps que je t'aime") to link François's woodland journey to Maria's prayers for his safe return.

In Duvivier's figuration of François's growing disorientation and despair in his fatal trek through the woods, subjective shots play an important role. We see blinding snow and a landscape that teeters wildly as François staggers through the storm. These, together with the expressionistic lighting and set by Jacques Krauss, underscore the artifice of the relation to the wilderness and thus its susceptibility to radical change. Finally, there is an extraordinary use of subjective shots and other de-realizing devices in a sequence that cannot help but appear campy to today's audiences: famous French actors Jean-Pierre Aumont and Madeleine Renaud playing Canadians, Lorenzo and Maria, snowshoeing (in the Paris studio) along the banks of the Peribonka River (seen in rear-screen projection), in a scene where Lorenzo tries to persuade Maria to go with him to the city. Superimposed on a shot of the river are Montreal cityscapes that body forth Lorenzo's dazzling view of urban life, with its automobiles, busy streets, restaurants, and "vues animées" (moving pictures). The superimposition opens an imaginary cultural space that is at once distinctly modern and tenuously linked to the rural space figured by the river. The city, presented from Lorenzo's point of view, does not obliterate the countryside but takes up an unstable and mutable relation to it, not only by means of the superimposition, but also through cuts to close-ups of Maria gazing *in another direction*, unable or unwilling to participate in Lorenzo's vision. The startling views of Maria staring rather blankly at the wintry Canadian countryside do more than to evoke her despair at losing François and her uncertainty about leaving the land. They suggest a certain resistance to the colonization of her imagination by her suitor's vision, a refusal, perhaps, to accept the male city dweller's view as the only possible view of modernity. Lorenzo may be able to speak of all he has seen in Boston and Ottawa, but Maria, who has never been to a city, has nonetheless experienced her own version of modern life. I want to suggest that Duvivier's integration of techniques typical of French avant-garde filmmaking of the 1920s into mainstream melodrama of the 1930s, begins to undo the polarity between city and country, modernity and tradition, French and Francophone cultural spaces. Duvivier's "vues animées" unsettle the view of the wilderness as empty space to be conquered, making of it instead a site of cultural crossings and social invention, one where cinema can play a critical role. Moreover, they show that modernism in film—its presumed subversion of and superiority to realism— must be rethought by critics who are concerned with assessing the particular forms that modernity takes in non-European and/or rural cultural spaces.

## NOTES

1. See Herman Lebovics, *True France: The Wars Over Cultural Identity, 1900–1945* (Ithaca, N.Y.: Cornell University Press, 1992).

2. Louis Hémon, *Maria Chapdelaine: Récit du Canada Français* (Montreal: Boréal Express, 1980). Unlike previously published editions, this one, established by Nicole Deschamps, follows Hémon's original manuscript. Translations of the passages quoted are taken from Louis Hémon, *Maria Chapdelaine: A Tale of the Lake St. John Area*, trans. W. H. Blake (New York: Modern Library, 1934). Future references to these editions appear in parentheses in the text.

3. Eugen Weber, *Peasants into Frenchmen: The Modernization of Rural France* (Palo Alto, Calif.: Stanford University Press, 1976).

4. See Nicole Deschamps, Raymonde Héroux, and Normand Villeneuve, *Le Mythe de Maria Chapdelaine* (Montreal: Les Presses de l'Université de Montréal, 1980). This book comes in response, among other things, to the hunger for attention and approval from the French, expressed by Louvigny de Montigny in his preface to the first Canadian edition of Hémon's novel, published during World War I, where he writes of Hémon:

> il démontre encore l'affection que les écrivains de France, comme tous les Français, éprouvent à notre endroit lorsqu'ils nous étudient et nous regardent de près, et qu'il suffit d'un peu de sympathie et d'attention de part et d'autre pour que nous nous connaissions mieux, entre Canadiens et Français, ou plutôt que nous nous reconnaissions, de loin et de tout temps, aussi bien que Français et Canadiens se reconnaissent aujourd'hui dans les tranchées, face à l'ennemi commun. . . .
> *Maria Chapdelaine: Récit du Canada Français* (Montreal: J.-A.LeFebvre, 1916), vii.

he demonstrates once again the affection that French writers, like all Frenchmen, feel for us when they study us and look at us closely, and shows that all that is needed is a little sympathy on both sides so that we Canadians and French may know each other better, or rather so that we may recognize each other, from afar and for all time, just as French and Canadians recognize each other today in the trenches, facing a common enemy. . . .

5. See André Fortier, "Maria Chapdelaine à l'écran," *Séquences* 104 (avril 1981): 17–30.

6. For a detailed discussion of *Toni*, see Christopher Faulkner, *The Social Cinema of Jean Renoir* (Princeton, N.J.: Princeton University Press, 1986), 41–57.

7. Ginette Vincendeau, "Melodramatic Realism: On Some French Women's Films in the 1930s," *Screen* 3 (summer 1989): 58.

8. Vincendeau, "Melodramatic Realism," 57–59, and Susan Hayward, *French National Cinema* (London: Routledge, 1993), 168.

9. Nicole Deschamps, Preface to *Maria Chapdelaine* (Montreal: Boréal Express, 1980), ix–x. Future references to Deschamps are to this preface and will appear in parentheses in the text.

10. Duvivier's powerful (albeit momentary) disruption of melodramatic gender codes seems to echo a similar disruption in Hémon's novel, where the narrator remarks on the disturbing effects of language change in Quebec, fostered by vast open spaces and widespread illiteracy: "Des emprunts faits à d'autres langues ont encore accentué l'incertitude en ce qui concerne l'orthographe ou le sexe. . . . [D]es hommes s'appellent Herménégilde, Aglaé, Edwige" (Borrowings from other languages have added to the uncertainties of orthography and gender. . . . [M]en bear such names as Hermenegilde, Aglaë, Edwige), 43/63.

## 4

# OPACITY IN THE FILMS OF CLAIRE DENIS

Janet Bergstrom

My point of departure was an image:

Near the beginning of *Nénette and Boni*, we watch a young girl's face as it slowly passes across the screen, floating in water, calm, pensive, her eyes closed and then slowly opening, her long black hair trailing behind her. It's a beautiful shot, memorable. Anyway, it has never left me. When I try to understand the logic of Claire Denis's *mise en scène*, that image always returns to me as its emblem. Along with two brief shots that follow, separated from each other by marked shifts in camera angle, we are quickly and elliptically given the entire "narrative scene" that introduces one of the film's main char-. acters. Then space, time, and subject change abruptly.

For me, this face floating across the water is the very image of opacity. We can see that it is a girl, but what else? Is she a child or an adolescent? What is she thinking? The key element is her subjectivity, a sense of self hidden from any onlooker. She seems absorbed by inner thoughts, as if suspended in a moment of purity before voices from the outside break her solitude: a woman who calls "Antoinette!" rather harshly, several girls laughing as she gets out of the swimming pool.

We find out that Nénette has a lot on her mind, but it takes most of the movie to show that. In fact, she is both a child and an adult, or more accurately, she does not really fit either category, because although very young, she is pregnant. Troubled and withdrawn, Nénette rarely speaks more than a few words at a time. She refuses to the end to tell anyone how she feels about the problem that governs her existence, namely, her lack of control over her own body. We find out about the physical aspect of her predicament when she finally tells her brother, Boni, (it is not "visible"), but her pregnancy is the symptom of something more profound that she wants to repress. (Boni: "Who's the guy?" Nénette: "He doesn't exist.") She has attempted to ignore, and now wants to abort, the child inside her, but it is much too late in her pregnancy to be able to do that. The film's elliptical narration offers us Nénette's history in fragments, something that we can only guess about. We never have the impression of knowing her or the "story of her life" from her point of view. What we see in the film is one of the stories or histories that constitute Nénette, the one that intersects with her brother's daily routines and affective life: her need to become "unpregnant" again, which transforms, little by little, the nature of Boni's own desire.

Like many others in the film, Nénette appears to be of mixed ethnic origins. She doesn't even resemble her brother, although they have the same parents. However, métissage and the composite society of Marseilles, which have given rise to so many social conflicts, are never presented as "problems" or themes in the film, as is common in the new French versions of the social problem genre. We see a mixed society and we hear different accents and languages, but as part of the milieu the protagonists inhabit. Nobody talks about it. On the other hand, it is no accident that they figure so prominently in the film.

The hypothesis I would like to advance is that Claire Denis, increasingly in I Can't Sleep (1993), Nénette and Boni (1996), and Beau Travail (1999), is constructing a *mise en scène* of fragmentation that is related to the way in which she uses music and dance, and that in doing so, she is attempting to create a logic of narration in which "signification" can remain floating. I do not mean to suggest that her films are not rich in meaning. On the contrary, they raise questions that are precise, real, important, and contemporary. But in this character-driven (as opposed to action-driven) cinema, we frequently remain separated from the characters. We observe them, alone or with others, in settings that we see only partially, but that are much more significant for the density and texture of Denis's narrative proposals than backdrops. Claire Denis is working on a mode of enunciation dominated by the image, where there is little dialogue, and where the story progresses according to a fragmentary structure—fragments of what she terms the "unspoken" ["le non-dit"], which (one may realize sooner or later) belong to different pathways that form irregular, crisscrossing patterns (or filiations) within a carefully balanced narrative whole. This structure of fragments and filiation allows Denis to create what I call "narrative parentheses," in which music and sometimes dance seem to shift the narrative to another register, substituting for dialogue indirectly in a nonequivalent, nonreductive, and strongly expressive manner. Thus, Denis's conception of the "unspoken" is not a silent language of images. It is linked to opacity. Many "stories" within a given film (and each of them has many) are shown in bits and pieces, with important gaps in information that may never be filled in. We are often unsure, we even have the impression, sometimes, of being excluded. The problematic of the relationship between men and women, or as I prefer to call it, of sexual difference, plays an integral part in this narrative operation.

Claire Denis was born in Paris in 1948, but her family moved to Africa when she was only two months old. She grew up in several Francophone African countries (Cameroon, Somalia, Djibouti, Upper Volta [today, Burkina Faso]), where her father worked for the French colonial administration. When she was 14, she returned to France and lived with her grandfather in Sceaux, near Paris. After high school, she returned to Africa numerous times. She studied to be a filmmaker at IDHEC in Paris, and worked as an assistant to a number of important directors, among them, Dusan Makavejev (*Sweet Movie*, 1974), Jacques Rivette (*Duelle*, 1975; *Noroît*, 1976), Costa-Gavras (*Hannah K.*, 1983), Wim Wenders (*Paris, Texas*, 1983; *The Wings of Desire*, 1987), and Jim Jarmusch (*Down by Law*, 1986).

Her first feature, *Chocolat*, was selected for the official competition at the Cannes Film Festival in 1988, a major achievement. Claire Denis was then 39. The script, cowritten with Jean-Pol Fargeau like almost all her films, was based on her youth in Cameroon at the end of the 1950s. If the *mise en scène* and dialogue seem more traditional than her recent films (the scenography, for example, is more linear and classical), *Chocolat* engages with admirable clarity fundamental questions about differences in power between colonizers and colonized, and within this relationship of domination, about the conflicts of power between men and women as seen from the perspective of a young girl who tells us her story. Already, the sense of an "exterior look," the "unspoken," and opacity are in evidence. Among the feature films that followed are *Man No Run* (a documentary on the Cameroonian band Les Têtes brûlées, 1989), *Jacques Rivette: Le Veilleur* (part of the prestigious television series "Cinéma, de notre temps," 1989), *S'En Fout la Mort* (*No Fear, No Die*, 1990), *J'ai Pas Sommeil* (*I Can't Sleep*), *U.S. Go Home* (1994), *Nénette and Boni, Beau Travail, Trouble Every Day* (2001), and *Vendredi Soir* (*Friday Night*, 2002).[1]

*Jacques Rivette: Le Veilleur* is a two-hour discussion/interview between Rivette and film critic Serge Daney. Rather late in this film, we see its director briefly when Claire Denis joins the conversation to ask Rivette a question. I would like to underline three points about her appearance that pertain to her own films: (1) In response to Daney, who would like to talk to Rivette about his conception of narrative structure, Rivette continues a rather long discussion of Corneille by turning to the scenographic or dramaturgic structure of his plays; (2) The theme of dramaturgic strategy leads to another subject that is closely related for Rivette, namely the spectator's curiosity: how, on the formal level, to sustain the audience's interest in moving from one scene to the next, how to build a connection, how to advance the story?; and (3) At this point, we see Claire Denis (it is the only time in the film that she is on camera) who asks Rivette a question: curious, attentive, she advances her own perspective. Her entry reconfigures the dramatic scene before us from the couple Rivette–Daney into a triangle, a figure underscored by the panning movement of the camera that gradually reveals that Denis is sitting at the same table with them.

At the end of this part of the discussion, Rivette turns to address her as he makes reference to Scheherazade (the definitive figure, according to him, of the curiosity he was just describing), but the camera has reframed the image and Claire Denis is no longer visible. Rivette, therefore, looks off-screen toward the space where we know she is sitting. This little scene makes explicit how she had been there since the beginning, a narrator hidden from view, but with her own, independent look and intellectual position, absent from the frame but director of the discussion.

I mention this brief moment from a long interview because Claire Denis will develop these three elements in her own films, in her own way:

1. A scenography of filiation and fragmentation that is increasingly radical and disjunctive, yet strongly anchored in classic, balanced structures.
2. Curiosity, in league with visual attentiveness, absorption, and investigation. This goes hand in hand with opacity: bodies can be studied, but Claire Denis presents them in a way that seems to emphasize that they hide more than they reveal. She uses the possibilities of cinematic opacity to delay meaning, as if to prevent quick and obvious conclusions; for instance, the identification of gender (man/woman) is not particularly telling in her films, but it is an essential structural stepping-stone to other problems and complexities that are developed over the course of the narrative. So in that sense, sexual difference—similar to immigrant/non-immigrant or supposedly "pure French" identity—enables the indirect and usually unresolved constellation of problems in her films.
3. The indirect presentation of the questions these films turn on is often accomplished through a doubling or triangulation of vision. We may find out that someone is watching someone else rather late in a scene, and even then, the meaning of that character's look, which is often held rather long to indicate that it is significant, may not be evident or may become important only later in terms of the plot. This floating kind of meaning (floating since we can never guess which of these looks will lead to an explanation or a narrative development) is linked to the way Claire Denis often uses music and sometimes dance, in that music allows her characters to express an aspect of their interiority— what seems to be "real" emotion—obliquely. Most of the musical sequences in her films let meaning drift, inaccessible. They function as narrative parentheses, allowing for a protective, intimate, and imaginary space/time. As in Scheherazade's tales, meaning is not absent, but it is deferred within a network of other stories.

Claire Denis emphasizes that she is a filmmaker of the image. People speak less and less in her films, *Beau Travail* being the most radical example to date. In Stéphan Lifschitz's documentary, *Claire Denis, la vagabonde* (1995), a scene from *U.S. Go Home* is presented in which Grégoire Colin dances to an American pop song alone in his small room, without a word of dialogue. Claire Denis comments that she used sound (here, a song) to replace dialogue. In effect, she often uses music and dance in connection with powerful images to refuse communication through the exchange of spoken words. Strong emotions often cannot be communicated through language, but sometimes they can find an outlet in music. Many of her characters find such moments, as if they were subtracted from the narrative for the space of a song and allowed to be caught up in private, introspective worlds. If music is experienced in a group, rarely do we have the sense that those present share the same response to, or need for, that music. And we may already have (or may develop) affective relationships to those songs, which become attached to this or that character, just as they were chosen by Claire Denis because of their importance to her. These "narrative parentheses" via music allow her to provide insight into a character without being overly explicit.

More than a *mise en scène* of the image, Claire Denis has created a narrative structure increasingly based on fragmentation—scenes may be interrupted by other scenes, the connections being both metaphorical and metonymical—and that turns on questions of identity. In these films, "complex" sexual identity—by which I mean that which goes beyond biological categories—is inseparable from other kinds of identity that are so often reduced to clichés: homosexuality, immigrants and their relationship to France, ethnicity, age. Her intertwining narratives, with multiple important characters, allow her to manifest different kinds of conflicts and modes of being as questions of desire and power in all their social specificity, without, however, giving the impression that their resolution is possible (other than on a formal, or in other words, a narrative level) because the forces in question resist explanation and resolution for individuals as well as the social collectivity.

## I CAN'T SLEEP / J'AI PAS SOMMEIL

CLAIRE DENIS
Jean-Louis [Murat] followed the entire adventure of the film very closely. I had already chosen his song "Le lien défait" for Camille's performance. The lyrics fit precisely. On the first page of the script I sent to Jean-Louis, I had written down part of a song like the ones they used to write about notorious murderers. I found it in Foucault's book on Pierre Rivière. It ended with: "I know I am a monster, but don't worry, my torture awaits me. . . ." That might have inspired the song that Jean-Louis Murat wrote for the end credits, where he speaks of "the fruit of our entrails."[2]

*I Can't Sleep* was inspired by the infamous case of Thierry Paulin, a serial killer of elderly women who was arrested in Paris in 1987. It is well known that he was black, Caribbean, homosexual, and HIV positive. (By the time this film was made, he had died of AIDS.) Rather than making a detective film with the murderer as protagonist, using suspense as the principal narrative motor, Claire Denis created a narrative structure based on the pathways and accidental crisscrossings (filiations) of multiple characters whose fragmented stories run more or less adjacent to the character who, we find out rather late in the film, turns out to be the murderer. The film begins and ends with a young Lithuanian woman, Daïga, at the wheel of a decrepit Eastern European car—first entering, then leaving Paris. She represents, therefore, a group of immigrants to France, but not those (like the murderer and like the stereotyped image of "the immigrant" in France) from the former colonies. Daïga is looking for her great-aunt and is about to discover, thanks to this admirable elderly lady, an entire network of Slavs who have come to Paris in search of a better life. But she has also come, or maybe it was her primary reason, to meet an ex-lover from the East who promised her a career in Paris as an actress, but brushes her off callously when she appears at his office. (Not defenseless, as it turns out, Daïga will get her revenge later on by smashing her car into his luxury convertible.)

Daïga will maintain a certain reserve from the community of Slavs despite her projection of warmth: an independent, enigmatic young woman, she watches and waits (we don't know why, and probably she doesn't know exactly either). Her story is intercut with the beginning of a parallel narrative, also seen from the outside in a fragmented manner, which unites black Caribbean immigrants, their white French lovers, and a small child that blends these two categories imperceptibly. A second parallel narrative is created inside that one when we begin to find out that the two brothers, born in Martinique, are preoccupied by entirely different conflicts. Théo wants to return home to escape the everyday racism that he experiences working without legal papers ("au noir/in the dark" as they put it in French), but Mona, the French mother of his child, does not want to leave Paris. His brother Camille—the fictional name of the murderer in the film—also has a white French lover, but it is a man and he will turn out to be Camille's accomplice in murdering elderly women. In the first scene with the two brothers, we don't yet know—in fact, we will wait almost an hour to discover—that Camille is a murderer and that the film is built around his crimes. Going back to Martinique doesn't interest Camille ("There's nothing there").

Near the beginning of the film, when these characters are still nameless and undefined, Camille wakes up on the couch in Théo's apartment, where he lives with his child. Mona is not there, although she will keep coming back, a sign of how this couple is living out their love "with difficulty," as Claire Denis described it. But the difficulties of their passions are of another order entirely than those of Camille and his lover, the latter subject to Camille's physical violence that we only glimpse in bits and pieces, but that points to the sadomasochism of their relationship and that the murders contribute to the bond between them.

*I Can't Sleep* insists from the outset on the question of the look, on point of view. But the meaning of the look is never obvious. This scene opens with a camera held very close to the body of a man (Camille) in a suit sleeping on a couch, starting from his feet and ending on the pillow he holds over his head to hide the daylight. As his hands come into view, they display an obvious sign of femininity: red nail polish. He uncovers his face, realizing that someone is watching him. Who?

The reverse shot shows us (only now) the face of a small child. What does this face tell us? It is hard to say: perhaps innocent curiosity. The unexpected visual juxtaposition of the nail polish and the man's body and clothes, obvious to us, doesn't register in the child's look.

A little later on, in a scene intercut with the first meeting between Daïga and her great-aunt, we see Camille in the bathroom, about to remove makeup from his face. When he reaches toward the cosmetics, the child objects firmly: "That's mama's!" In other words, the child doesn't notice Camille's signs of femininity, but he knows what his mother uses. Théo gets his child ready for the day, carrying out naturally the role traditionally reserved for the mother. He seems indifferent to Camille's feminine side (that is, the signs of his transvestism). They speak little, but with familial warmth.

Camille undresses to take a shower, and the camera frames him tightly as he pulls down fishnet tights, revealing naked, muscular buttocks. The angle of the shot, the closeness of the camera, and the flat, bright lighting avoid voyeurism in the usual sense, substituting an opaque view of the body, or of a body filmed in that way. Later, in his transvestite dance performance at a nightclub, Camille will be lit by an intimate chiaroscuro meant to excite a desire that is both diegetic and spectatorial. Here, though, Camille's mixed masculine/feminine appearance is rendered almost banal. These differences in presentation were not accidental. Claire Denis: "Filming the body is really the only thing that interests me. It's rather intimidating, especially when it is men's bodies. I can't say that I was afraid of the subject of *I Can't Sleep* but, from the beginning to the end, I kept asking myself about the kind of look one ought to have for a project like this. Camille's body had obviously been subject to observation, a mystery. And it was necessary to look at it that way."[3]

One of the remarkable things about Claire Denis's films is the way that she, or she and her camerawoman Agnès Godard, who has worked with her since *Chocolat*, presents men's bodies. For although Camille's body was not photographed in an erotic manner in the scene just described, Denis's films provide many other instances when men's bodies are observed and caught by the light in a way that both eroticizes them and makes them enigmatic. What renders these men desirable is their interiority (which is suggested more than it is known), not only the beauty of this or that aspect of their physical presence. It isn't a question of love or sex scenes, but rather the *mise en scène* of the contemplation of these bodies by the spectator or by other characters, usually kept at a distance. That impression comes across strongly even when the editing, the movement of the body in the frame, and the camera movement do not allow the luxury of looking for very long.

The result, in my opinion, is a strange kind of familiarity: even when the camera is close, and the shots are held a long time, one is faced with the impression of "not knowing" these bodies, of being kept separate from them because someone else has had the time to observe them for a long time and knows them so well that a special angle, detail, or expression has been presented that is unique to the person observed. This has nothing to do with the narrative strictly speaking, but it creates a powerful substratum for it. Sooner or later (later for Camille, because he disguises himself so well), one realizes how forcefully these characters suppress their emotions. One has the feeling of catching view of only a small part of the inner conflicts that render them powerful, difficult, unassimilable, and even violent. It is notable that Claire Denis does not photograph women's bodies in the same way.[4]

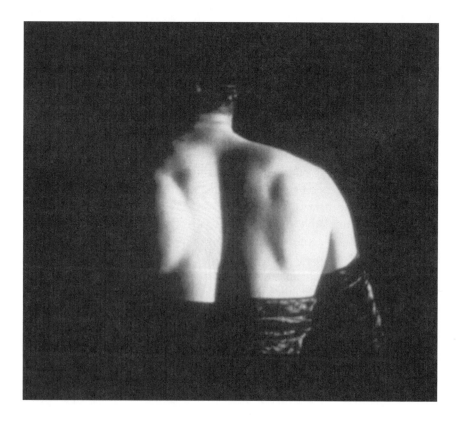

The justly celebrated scene of Camille's transvestite dance in the nightclub is a good example of physical revelation that hides something crucial. The camera reveals Camille's body slowly, as the song progresses and his strapless velour dress begins to slide down his male chest. We see his entire body and costume only once, and then not all at once because the camera is too close. It slowly pans downward to show us Camille in profile bit by bit: head, chest, the long dress tight on strong buttocks, bare feet glimpsed only momentarily but as if they are the most intimate part of his body, fully exposed to view. Camille dances on a platform that runs the length of a small room, very close to men lining its walls who watch silently, never attempting to touch him. At the end of the song, when he turns and extends his arms to balance his weight off the wall at the far end of the room, powerful muscles in his back and shoulders are sculpted by light and shadow, and the song reaches its climax.

This performance, its *mise en scène* so carefully constructed as a wordless, indeed ineffable, story of bodies and looks, displays how Camille mixes exterior signs of masculinity and femininity. The club Denis chose "was like a jail, very much inspired by Jean Genet," entirely different from the kind of early 1980s nightclub where the actual killer, Paulin, "a drag queen," had performed.[5]

> We went looking for something that would be invented for that place, that would be both male and female. Richard [Courcet] and I sort of choreo-graphed the scene together and came up with what we wanted: no falsies, long nails, the band in the hair—those kind of things. So he was also very male, with his wide shoulders, and this worked as something that was in-between, that was more in the spirit of the place. I told Richard that it should be a dance where, in one sense, he's offering his body—dancing very close to the people in the club—but he had to seem tough enough so that they don't dare touch him.[6]

In this scene, Camille reveals another dimension of his seductive side, but gives no hint of his capacity for murder, where he breaks the social bond rad-ically, as Murat's song expresses perfectly: "le lien défait" (the broken link, the tie that has come undone). Near the end of Camille's dance, a low-angle shot shows men crouching to watch him through a grilled metal fence that covers an opening above the stage and makes them look like prisoners in a cage. When interviewers commented on the seductiveness and sensuality of Camille's dance, Claire Denis responded: "Yes, there is desire. It's a scene in which a man offers himself to be looked at, this gesture had to be felt. I thought that there also had to be an element of danger, that offering the body made physical violence a possibility."[7]

   This dance corresponds directly to another, at a birthday party for Théo
and Camille's mother, which seems to function as a counterpoint or even
an antidote, to Camille's performance before the silent, isolated group
watching him. Now the room is crowded, communal, and alive with talking. After singing happy birthday, everyone begins to dance to a joyous
Afro-Caribbean song. Théo and Camille take turns dancing with their
mother and for once, Théo—who is a musician—looks happy. He gives
himself to the moment, to the music, to the pleasures of the dance. His
mother is radiant, moving with him and then with Camille, who takes her
and holds her in his arms, moving with her wonderfully to the music, the
very image of the loving and beloved son, the good son. But underneath
this familial joy, Claire Denis is staging the "lien défait": Camille's profound betrayal of the people who love and trust him, and who think they
know him. No one has the slightest suspicion that Camille could be a murderer, and probably few know of the double life that he leads as a transvestite. The notable exception is Camille's lover, who is seen at the end of
the sequence sitting alone in the corner of the room, the embodiment
of Camille's hidden side. Within the framework of this sequence, the
dance creates a parenthesis, like a little island in which the characters can
give expression to deep and true emotions that seem like an escape from
their behavior elsewhere. The power of this scene extends well beyond its
explicit narrative function.[8]

This choreography of looking as an unspoken duality of revelation and hiding is continued in another way late in the film, when the camera holds on Daïga's face for a long time as she stands outside the door of the hotel staring into the night. What does her expression tell us of this woman who speaks so little? She has crossed paths with Camille several times because they live in the same hotel, but more importantly Daïga has been in his room as part of her housecleaning job and seen the traces of his nocturnal life, notably erotic photos of him. By chance, through another pattern of filiation entirely, she has just examined composite drawings at the police station that correspond to Camille and his lover who have been identified as the serial killers. So at this point she knows who Camille is, and when he leaves the hotel, she follows him. In other words, she takes an active role in pursuing him. When she goes into the café he has just entered and stands next to him at the bar, glancing at him from time to time, it is obvious that he is conscious of her, but he doesn't know why she is there. Perhaps he thinks she is interested in him, which is true, but not because he is attractive. There is even an erotic moment, when she touches his fingers lightly (in a shadowy close-up), reaching for something on the bar, before he tells the waiter quietly that he will pay for her coffee and leaves.

As soon as Camille walks out onto the sidewalk, a patrol car pulls up next to him and he is picked up by the police. When he gives his name, one of the officers comments: "Camille, that's a girl's name," as if underlining the motif of the opacity of his sexual identity, its nonobviousness even though he is perfectly dressed as a man, showing none of the signs of femininity we have seen earlier. At the police station, Camille calmly begins to admit to his murders as he is questioned about the victims, one after another. Daïga follows a different trajectory: contrary to what one might imagine of her, for lack of information it now seems (finally, she is as opaque as Camille; like him in this respect, she masks a side of herself through her charm), she takes advantage of Camille's arrest to search his room until she finds the money he has stolen from his victims. She stuffs fistfuls of it into her clothes. The film ends with Daïga at the wheel of her car, doubtless that very night. She is probably leaving Paris without a word to those she knows there.

Even if Daïga did not turn Camille in to the police, the editing suggests a causal connection on a structural level, for the police stop him immediately after he leaves her in the café, as if they have taken up the pursuit that she began. In the abstract space between the trajectories of these two characters, we have, at the end, the story of a man who is half feminine and who murders elderly women, and the story of a young woman who regains her liberty with the money he has taken from them. The line of nonmotivated causality in the film is constructed in an abstract manner by creating a chain of narratively unrelated actions that link the two characters through the alternation of "their" scenes and cutting to specific shots as if they are somehow linked.

The film began with the same strategy of building a causal narrative chain that was not motivated by the characters but rather by structural juxtaposition, as if it were a kind of abstract, condensed announcement of the story to come for the spectator. (1) From inside Daïga's car as she drives into Paris, we hear a radio announcer (on France-Inter) remind listeners that the killer of elderly women is still on the loose (Daïga doesn't understand French, but we don't know that yet); (2) On the street, in the early morning, Camille beats up his boyfriend, who escapes with a third man in a Mercedes (but we don't know who they are, nor do we have any hint that they are related to the murders); (3) Camille, at his brother's apartment, is still wearing some signs of his transvestite night life (which we have not seen); (4) A new victim of the serial killer is found in the same building in which Daïga's great-aunt lives (but we don't know yet either the aunt or the significance of the building); (5) Daïga meets her great-aunt, who is the same age as the murder victims, and the two of them encounter police agents on the stairs in front of the dead woman's apartment (but they are not told what happened inside) as they go up to the next floor to the apartment of a Slavic friend of the great-aunt who had taken in a number of Slavic immigrants. Little by little, these characters and these narrative events will come closer together, but each character will keep his or her own trajectory. In retrospect, one could say that all the elements of a detective film had been introduced at this point, but not in a way that makes them comprehensible as such: the logical relationship between these events only makes sense later.

## NÉNETTE AND BONI

CLAIRE DENIS
When I went to Marseilles to write Nénette et Boni with Jean-Pol Fargeau, I brought some music with me, including an album by the Tindersticks. I listened to "My Sister" from their second album a lot. This song helped me write. They came to Marseilles during the shoot, they followed the editing process and saw the first rough cut. . . . One day the film's editor, Yann Dedet, and I realized that they were really going to work well with the film. We incorporated some scenes we had cut because the score they had composed worked wonderfully. We were making shots shorter or longer to go with the song, etc. It was the first time I was editing with music. Jean-Pol and I have the impression that narrative doesn't always go through speech. I think Stuart [Staples], with his presence and work, influenced the editing process. He pushed the film towards abstraction. Yann and I also had that tendency, but Stuart, instead of stopping us, liberated us: sometimes we were worried, we wanted more explanatory scenes; Stuart and his music gave us courage to be more elliptical, abstract.[9]

The relationship between the theme of the opacity of sexual difference and dramatic structure functions differently in *Nénette and Boni* than in *I Can't Sleep*. In the earlier film, Claire Denis follows several characters whose paths cross each other intermittently. The story, which also moves forward in a fragmentary manner, is marked by major ellipses that are facilitated by unmotivated changes in the camera point of view, sometimes even within a given scene. But in *Nénette and Boni*, the basic structure doesn't depend on drawing parallels between the stories of the main characters (primarily the two families of immigrants in *I Can't Sleep*). The logic of narrative development in *Nénette and Boni* hovers on the edge of abstraction. The evident dramatic subject—which is presented, moreover, with important gaps in information for the characters in the story as well as for us—is doubled in this film by another level of meaning, more abstract, which is linked to the family and to sexual difference. That is also one of the main lines running throughout *I Can't Sleep*, but in the later film, the logic of the relationship operates differently. The film proceeds according to a metonymic dramaturgical schema that is anchored in rather concrete metaphors that are both comic (that is to say, distanced) and serious.

Near the beginning of the film, a series of brief, fragmented shots shows us the baker's wife walking down the street as she is seen from a moving car by Boni and a friend. We shift to Boni alone in this apartment, reading the first page of his diary out loud, mixing his family history with sexual fantasies about the baker's wife. Boni's images of macho conquest, as he writes and now enunciates them, take place within the history of a broken family ("my dead mother," "the asshole of a father who abandoned us like a coward"). Boni has preserved his mother's room just as it was before she died, as if she were still alive. About his sister, Nénette, not a word.

The encounters Boni imagines with this woman are somewhat pornographic (that's what he calls them), but they are also contained, discreet, and sometimes comical because of the way he recounts them and because their quasi-fetishistic metaphorical support is his adored pet, a little white rabbit. Sometimes he recites his fantasies out loud, at other times we see them in images, whether Boni is sleeping or his eyes are open. In any event, they are masturbatory, for it seems that his affective life is completely trapped by this fictional obsession. Although Boni's introductory scene makes him seem outgoing, talkative, and a sexual braggart, as the film continues, we will see that he can project this confident self-image only on condition of being alone, master of his own house. In the presence of others, he seems reticent and speaks little.

The first scene inside the bakery begins like a fantasy in whipped cream and pink pastries as a slowly moving camera glides past confections, so close as to be almost on top of them, followed by huge close-up shots that make them look like droll sexual symbols. The baker's wife, dressed in pink herself, bends over the counter toward the camera, her bodice revealing her breasts as if an innocent offering for the eyes. But whose eyes? All this is happening in a void. She slowly extends her finger toward the pastries, finds a lottery ticket that had dropped there, and scoops up a bit of whipped cream for herself, which disappears into her mouth. Is this a sexual allegory fantasized by Boni, seen from his point of view? That would not be surprising, for he has already had several "visions." But the sequence continues with several temporal ellipses, which can only be deduced as we go along; they are not obvious but they are possible because of sharp changes in camera position. A fresh angle shows the bakery full of customers. Only now do we see Boni, who is inside the bakery but far from the cash register where the woman of his dreams is standing. Therefore, it is impossible that the camera at the beginning represented his actual point of view. Whose look did it represent? The filmmaker's? Was it a generalized fantasy? Was it supposed to correspond to Boni's, despite the impossibility of the distance?

The fantasy (the imaginary) is shown here to be capable of belonging to a level of abstraction that is no longer associated with any specific character, in contrast to those that Boni has experienced up until this point in the film. As if to underline the scenography of the bakery as an impossible space/time, a shot of the baker appears who looks directly into the camera for a long time and smiles, but his look is not in the direction of his wife, and therefore the axis of his look cannot be motivated by her. He is framed in a rather abstract space that does not overlap with the room we have just seen. This shot appears as a little parenthesis within the scene. It is, however, followed by what would appear to be a reverse shot of Boni, who, according to the rules of classical editing in which the axis of the eye's gaze determines position, is looking at the baker. Up until the moment when Boni arrives at the cash register, following a series of ellipses hidden by close shots of the baker's wife that do not show much of the space around her, the scenography is fragmented and seemingly unreal. After this point, the scene reverts to a classical continuity of space, time, and action rationalized by its characters.

The camera style moves the film deliberately toward the impression of subjective shots regardless of whether or not any given shot is determined to be, sooner or later, the representation of any character's literal point of view. One could also describe this as a scenography in which one is frequently unsure of whether a shot represents someone's (diegetic) point of view. The strategies for accomplishing this effect are beautifully varied and develop further the way in which point-of-view structures were mobilized in *I Can't Sleep* in those instances in which characters were shown to have been looking retroactively, and where the meaning of their look was opaque. Here, the sense of subjective observation is much more pervasive and the opacity-effect (the inability to specify the meaning of these looks) pushed to a much more abstract dimension, one that will be taken to an extreme that one could describe as poetic in *Beau Travail*.

The visual approach that Claire Denis and Agnès Godard developed to portray Nénette and Boni's story ("a film about solitary people rather than a group"[10]) necessitated a change in camera and lens. "We knew that we wanted the opposite of the film I did before. We wanted to work with long lenses and do mostly close ups, to be extremely close."[11] This allowed for

an oscillation of point of view in which a floating, imaginary vision intersects seamlessly with literal point of view shots or with "objective shots,"
thanks also to the tremendous variation in strategies between fixed and
moving shots, using a camera that rested on the shoulder rather than a
Steadycam.

> So all of a sudden, the way that Agnès and I had been working, more or less
> as accomplices, with a 40-millimeter lens so as to give a lot of space to the ac-
> tors, to allow for a choreography to take place between them and the camera,
> was no longer possible because we were working too close up. I had the im-
> pression that this was going to be a big sacrifice for me, but at the same time
> that the film ought to be made that way. What I like about the shoulder-
> camera is that if an actor turns his head a little abruptly, you can always try to
> follow it, whereas with a pan shot it has to be technically perfect. I like the idea
> that it would not be perfect, but aleatory.[12]

When Boni finally reaches the head of the line, his behavior toward the
baker's wife is the opposite of the way he had expressed himself in his diary.
Face to face with the woman herself, he seems dumbstruck and stares
fixedly, yet with no clear meaning in his look. She is the talkative one, smiling and relaxed. After a pause, he asks for a "really long" baguette, an unconscious slip echoing the customers who had been asking for baguettes
that are "really supple." The baker's wife calmly replies that they are all the
same length, and we have just seen who makes them that way, namely, her
husband. The world of Boni's erotic fantasies, in which he, as a man, is all-
powerful, remains an interior world. Boni is at ease in his apartment with
his little white rabbit, to whom he talks and who helps nourish his solitary
daydreams, and not with the woman who inspires them. This woman radi-
ates strength, health, and happiness, a world apart from Boni's situation.
What is more significant for the narrative as a whole is that in Boni's eyes
she represents an idealized image of the family and domestic life, even
though in his erotic scenarios and the "flash" images of his thoughts, her
family is never present. At the beginning of his diary, he wrote derisively
that she was married and saddled with three kids. But the image this film
creates of her, on the contrary, could be taken from an old-fashioned
French song in which a woman dreams about getting married, having children, and running a little bistro or bakery with her husband—a simple future full of life and love. That mood is conveyed by the opening of this
scene, a soft universe blending savory pastries with the warmth of a feminine body.

One of the key scenes in this film continues this motif, but furthers it in the way in which it brings Boni's sister back into his life after he has tried to get rid of her. Its principal elements are: (1) a close-up of the baker's wife's feet, standing in white pompom high-heeled bedroom slippers, with Boni's white rabbit sitting on the floor between them; (2) Boni's erotic dreams that lead to his horrified discovery that his sister is in bed with him; (3) after he makes his sister leave the apartment, Boni sees that she has made a drawing on one of the pages of his diary.

We have seen this rabbit several times: he crosses the film like a metonymic link, one of the film's lines of filiation. The editing contributes strongly to this process, with subtle variations. Three examples: Boni reads one of his fantasies out loud after he has petted and talked to his rabbit, who is now off-screen. On another occasion, we see the baker's wife, dressed in a peignoir with a white fuzzy collar, from outside her apartment as she closes the blinds to her windows. Was she seen by Boni from his pizza truck? It is impossible to tell because the shot that follows, which ought to have established the onlooker in the reverse-field, is taken instead from inside the woman's bedroom. She tosses her peignoir aside, revealing her naked breast fleetingly before her movement takes her out of sight. This can't possibly be an actual point-of-view shot: Boni must be inventing the scene. Next we see the rabbit (its fur resembling the collar of her peignoir) sitting on the dirty tile floor of Boni's apartment. Then he balances it gently in the palm of his hand and begins to recount another of his erotic stories.

The third example: the rabbit appears in a close shot, sitting calmly be-tween the feet of the baker's wife. Her pink high-heeled bedroom slippers have soft pompoms like its fur. This is an impossible image, but it is pho-tographed as if it were real, except that the light is a little too dramatic. The image is offered as a pure fetish. Whereas previously the rabbit had helped direct Boni's fantasies toward the baker's wife, now this linking element ap-pears as a frank metaphor and metonymy of her sexuality. The reverse shot shows us Boni in his bed, his eyes wide open, as if he were staring at this impossible sight.

From the moment that Boni discovers that Nénette has found his diary, the narrative changes. Not only has she read his private fantasies, she has added something of her own, a drawing like a child would make. In it, two stick figures hold hands. In big letters printed underneath, we read: "Nénette and Boni." This is not only a reminder of childhood memories, it is an indirect appeal to her brother to accept her again.

Boni finally lets his sister come back into the apartment, but their con-flict continues and repeats the problems that had divided their parents, the father preferring his daughter and the mother her son. Boni reproached Nénette, who lived with his detested father, for not having come to see their mother when she was dying. Now he finds out that Nénette is pregnant, that she has definitively left her father's home (her father doesn't know that she is pregnant, and we suspect later that he was responsible), and that she has come to him because she needs help. When she is alone in the apart-ment, Nénette examines her mother's room, touching and smelling her clothes. She sits down in a chair and we see, more or less aligned with the axis of her viewpoint in an apparent reverse shot, a silent home movie that fills the entire screen we are watching. The film shows Boni when he was an adolescent, at the seaside. Does this represent a memory-flash of Nénette's, thinking about family vacations in a happier time when brother and sister still lived together? Once again, *Nénette and Boni* passes from a time/space that is "real" to another level of meaning without explanation, either before or ever after.

Another shift in levels of address and *mise en scène* occurs in a curious scene between the baker and his wife (or, the woman who has become his wife). The scene is played without dialogue as we hear one of the Beach Boys' hits ("What Would I Be Without You?"), a song that describes a happiness that is simple, and a love that is direct, pure, and without complications. The space of the filmic scene opens on the image of the woman behind the bar, then a quick shot that shows some American sailors walking outside the open door on a warm summery day, the blue sea behind them, and then a very tight close-up of a hand on the jukebox entering the numbers to play a song. The camera follows this hand up to the face of a sailor— but we have already seen him as the American baker, her husband. From this point on, we have almost shifted registers to abstraction: we observe his face in close-up for a very long time, his eyes looking at the woman off-screen with an intense expression of love, uncertainty, and hope, in keeping with the spirit of the song. Then the field of vision switches to show us the woman cleaning bottles behind the bar. The camera holds on her as she reacts in many small ways to this off-screen look fixed on her. She seems to share the song with the sailor, becoming more and more radiant.

Within the context of the film, this scene, discreet and passionate, turning on these two faces and the music, is the opposite of the sexual stories that Boni makes up. Is this one of his fantasies, a pure idealization? Or is it an imaginary flashback of the couple before they were married? In any event, it seems out of the question that Boni will ever find happiness that is so simple and stable. His life has already been too difficult, and his milieu doesn't offer him much hope.

It is the child soon to be born that advances Nénette and Boni's story, such as we see it in the film. In the eyes of her brother, Nénette remains a child. *Nénette and Boni* has been described by the filmmaker as a love story between a brother and a sister, which is true in a chaste and familial sense. But it is equally true on the level of abstraction and substitution, that is to say, at a structural as well as an affective level: for the child is going to pass from Nénette to Boni. The film advances by fragments of representation of these displacements of desire. The woman Boni finds in his bed is his sister, not the baker's wife. Claire Denis gives us an affectionate and intimate detail of their juxtaposition as man/woman and as brother/sister in a shot in which they are sleeping next to each other, each with one foot protruding from the covers, side by side, one big and one small.

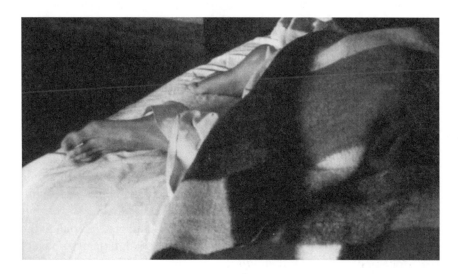

The meetings, real as well as imaginary, between Boni and the baker's wife are less and less present after Boni becomes conscious of the fact that it is too late for Nénette to have an abortion. Instead of projecting erotic fables, the young man begins to take the place of the father "who doesn't exist." This process begins indirectly, but little by little, Boni begins to make conscious decisions and to take on the role of a father who will simultaneously save a lost child and save himself, without ever saying a word to anyone, not even to his sister. When a doctor asks Nénette if the man with her is the baby's father, she replies that he is her husband. Boni does not contradict her. After a second doctor's examination, Boni is the one who takes the photographs from the sonogram that his sister refuses to look at, which show the fetus in its seventh month.

Paradoxically, it is on the very evening that Boni tries to lose himself on the crowded streets because of his confusion about his strong emotions for the baby and his sister's single-minded desire to rid herself of it, which he cannot understand, that the baker's wife encounters him and invites him to get coffee in a café. Alone with her for the first time, but preoccupied by the thoughts that the photographs stirred up in him, Boni listens, mute, his

face unreadable as the woman talks, in all innocence it seems, of her theories about body odor and sexual attraction. We cut to Boni immobile in his
bed, crying silently as if torn apart by his internal conflicts. Nénette takes
care of him, feeding him gently with a spoon, like a child.

In turn, Boni saves his sister's life after she nearly kills herself trying to
carry out a home abortion in a bath of mustard and vinegar. When he pulls
her out of the tub, she must be naked, but the camera doesn't show it. Then
we see Nénette immobile in bed, as Boni had been, dressed in one of her
brother's shirts. Boni gently rubs her stomach with his hand as if he is trying to find the child inside of her. It is Boni who wants to have this baby.
Not that he wants his sister to bear his own child, but he wants to give life
to this child that is already on its way to being born, in place of his sister
who wants to remain a child and deny the entire episode. The displacement
of Boni's desire follows an admirable structural logic.

From this point on, Boni takes his sister's place in several ways, and begins, at the same time, to put an end to his own isolation, to his overly strong
love for his mother and the hatred of his father that preoccupies him. Without a word of explanation to his sister, he begins, shortly before the birth is
due, to rearrange his mother's room. Later, we understand that if he
"wanted more space," it was to have a place for the child. Boni will reinvent
the father-son relationship that he was not able to have by being an affectionate father for this little boy. Moreover, someone kills their father without either brother or sister knowing about it. Who committed this murder,
that was desired more or less consciously by Boni? Earlier in the film, he
shot at his father with a rifle, childlike yet serious, to prevent him from entering the apartment to see Nénette. We see fleetingly that the father is
shot while driving his car. The cause apparently belonged to his past. The
father's story belongs to another system of narrative filiation that the spectator only knows through a few enigmatic glimpses.

After the child is born, Boni kidnaps it from the clinic, showing a rifle he
had hidden in a bouquet of long-stemmed flowers, a beautiful metaphor for
an eminently nonviolent act: the scene seems all the more unreal and abstract in that it is shown like a silent film, the sound masked by a glass par-
tition. Once back home, Boni becomes both mother and father to this child
that he holds in his arms and kisses: an image, finally, of real happiness for
him (for both of them). This composite (and idealized) image, made up of
everything that the child could represent for Boni, has entirely replaced his
erotic reveries.

We see Nénette in bed in the clinic, already in fatigue pants and a
pullover. Smiling peacefully in her sleep, she refuses to be awakened after

having painfully given birth (she arrived too late for an anaesthetic). She did not want to hold or see her son, whom she had designated for anonymous adoption. Presumably, she doesn't know that Boni takes the baby. She had no intention of returning to live with him. She seems relieved, as if she had eliminated that unwanted phase of her life. However, the film does not end on these parallel images of the brother's and sister's happiness, but rather on Nénette's opacity. The last shot shows her in profile, in a tight shot outdoors someplace. She smokes a cigarette, her face has become unreadable again.

## BEAU TRAVAIL

> Claire Denis
> [The New Wave] was a cinema that clearly distinguished between two camps: on the one hand, fiction, and on the other, characters. From the New Wave onward, characters were no longer reduced to their role in the story, pure products of the mechanics of the narrative. They had an independent existence, they were stronger than the necessity to tell a story. That already existed to some extent earlier. In *La Bête humaine*, the instincts driving Jean Gabin are stronger than the script. The films that I love today are those in which the characters have that opacity and that capacity to go beyond the framework of their story.[13]

Claire Denis takes the relationship between character and story, the idea of "characters [who] have that opacity and that capacity to go beyond the framework of their story," to radical extremes in *Beau Travail*. Yet, not unlike Renoir's *Bête humaine*, the dissociative elements of the narrative are anchored in classical formal simplicity, a triangular structure, even when spiraling into violent metaphor in the closing sequence (Galoup's dance).[14] Loosely based on *Billy Budd*, Herman Melville's late, cryptically stylized novel of male bonding, jealousy, and revenge on board a military ship, *Beau Travail* recreates the dynamic of hierarchical power and repressed desire within an isolated regiment of Legionnaires in training on the harsh desert coast of Djibouti. The drama turns on three men: the adjutant Galoup, the commander Bruno Forestier, and the soldier Gilles Sentain. Only after a few minutes do we learn that we are not witnessing this story directly: rather, Galoup is remembering, in flashback, the events that led to his exile from the Legion and to his awkward presence, now, in Marseilles where he no longer has a function. The film blends almost imperceptibly the sense of objective, third-person presentation with Galoup's subjective enunciation, as denoted by his spare voice-over narration or his hand as he writes in a notebook; but as for the images, how often are we led to think that they are his? Our impression of subjectivity or objectivity comes and goes effortlessly, unnoticeably most of the time. That is one of the amazing achievements of the liaison of style and subject in this film. *Beau Travail* is so much carried by "the unspoken," it has so little dialogue, its visual beauty is so stunning, that it has been summed up thus: "the beautiful is therefore the central question of the film."[15] But this view eliminates the nature of the dramatic tensions that motivate this purified story and avoids the history of France in Africa and of the Legion itself that is so tangibly evoked as the visible, meaningful backdrop for the drama: for instance, the ghost-like presence of a rusted WWII tank, a broken, weathered airplane, the remains of a building (was it once a concrete bunker?) now used for military exercises that seem as outdated as those useless relics of war.

Sexual difference remains an essential axis in *Beau Travail*, as in Claire Denis's earlier films, as well as the traces of the colonizing mission of France and its legacy in the French imaginary and in everyday French life. In my opinion, this is why it was important to have Galoup return to Marseilles to tell his story. (The "realistic" reason, according to Claire Denis, was that soldiers who found themselves between tours of duty, while waiting to decide whether to reenter civil society or to reenlist in the Legion, waited in Marseilles.) Moreover, it seems fitting to me that we see almost nothing of that city because Galoup's mind is entirely preoccupied by his past elsewhere, where he has been forbidden to return and that remains too present for him.

It isn't so easy to make the landscape "speak" beyond its narrative purpose without appearing to be superficially decorative. Of course, the great American westerns come to mind, but here I remember the dreamy qualities of certain scenes in *Lawrence of Arabia* or of Terence Malick's *Thin Red Line*. At a certain point, narrative fails; it is meant to fail. Shots appear to us like a series of exquisite "views" of unexpectedly diverse terrain and sea, colors and textures that are unnecessary for the story yet somehow bespeak functionality.

*Beau Travail* conveys such an urgent sense of authorial voice, such power of expression, that I think these fragments must fit into a logical whole that is configured at a higher level of abstraction. Perhaps they are bits of a metaphor, perhaps they help advance a number of themes that are not subservient to an overarching hierarchy (the opposite, in this respect, to the military hierarchy of the Legionnaires): they float, but not without significance. Lines of filiation emerge (the film is still classical in its symmetry), but it is this dimension of the film, I think, that leads critics to compare it to poetry. This way of representing opacity is close to the ineffable, to what Barthes designated as "the third meaning."

In contradistinction to Denis's earlier films, *Beau Travail* is preoccupied with stasis in the guise of forward movement. On the side of progression, Galoup's story moves ahead, and the exercises the soldiers perform seem to become increasingly more difficult as time goes on, in tandem with the mounting pressure Galoup experiences because of his jealousy of Sentain. Stasis is linked both to the blocking of sexual desire (individuals) and to the vision of an antiquated Legion within the context of a much older and more enduring environment and civilization that are completely separate from it. At least three elements keep bringing the narrative back to this idea of the impression of nonprogression:

1. The voice-over narration, spare and dreamlike, which is difficult to place. As in *Apocalypse Now,* the narrator's own mind seems to be affected. Very soon I worry that it may not be trustworthy, Galoup may not be remembering correctly, and besides, we see things he could only have imagined because he was not present.

2. The visual point of view (ours, the camera's) is not necessarily in alignment with the narrator's. Sometimes (as in the director's previous films) we see a late, unexpected onlooker whose look seems to throw the significance of the first one (or two) into doubt. Occasionally this is accomplished through the fragmented shot progression and unexpected, nonmatching angles, which can turn the perception of a subjective shot into an objective (independent) one or vice versa. Is the commandant, the object of our narrator's mythologizing veneration, really there when we cut to those striking shots of Forestier that look like photographs? Or are these images symptoms of a fixation, love-like and neurotic, that led to Galoup's ruin? We see Forestier so little, he speaks so few words during the entire film, that his appearances often seem caught in a twilight between memory and hallucination.

3. Sexual desire is continually blocked and displaced among the men in the regiment, who are learning to form a tight unit despite ethnic, racial, religious, national, and linguistic differences, and the community of Africans who are separate from their world, except for the women who dance with them at night. The new recruit, Sentain, who catches the eye of the commanding officer and Galoup's as a result, seems to be of uncertain ethnic origins. It takes only a few words of dialogue to carry the question of his identity to a more

abstract level: when Forestier asks him about his parents (in a striking shot, they appear to each other in the black of night as they are
about to cross paths, their faces lit from one side), Sentain replies
that he has none. He was found under a stairway. Forestier reacts
with some amazement and then comments "beau trouvaille" [a nice
find], echoing the film's title, *Beau Travail* [a nice job]. It is precisely because Sentain is singled out by the captain—for his bravery
in action after a helicopter accident, but not only for that—that he
is hated so fiercely by Galoup, who becomes obsessed with destroying him ("I became jealous"). Perhaps Galoup needs to destroy Sentain because he wants to avoid the question of desire among men,
sexual or otherwise; before Sentain, it is suggested, Galoup had
channeled his passion for his commandant into a military hero-
worship (imagining his past in Algeria, wanting to be worthy of his
ideal officer) and he had, moreover (unlike Forestier), a relationship of some kind with a woman—but that too is presented in a way
that renders it more and more phantasmic. She is not present when
he leaves to return to France. The beauty of all this comes from the
visual and cinematic fragmentation of unstated, and probably unacknowledged, desire mixed with camaraderie. It is the way these
men are portrayed to us that renders the entire enterprise of training, including the torturous parts, erotic.

Music and dance are crucial to *Beau Travail*. Benjamin Britten's opera, "Billy Budd," provides a foundation of nondiegetic music intermittently throughout the film. Moreover, the entire project was permeated with dance in that Claire Denis worked with the choreographer Bernardo Montet to train her men in their dance-like exercises and the other preparations for the film for some two months in Paris before shooting in Djibouti. Here, however, I would like to draw your attention to one or two instances in which the narrative seems to be diverted through a specific musical parenthesis:

The importance of diegetic music and dance is indicated powerfully in the first shot after the title credit: the soundtrack bursts into loud, rhythmic music—Tarkan's "Samarik"—as beautiful young black women in colorful dresses fill the screen, smiling, dancing with soldiers as others file through the crowded space. These brief dance scenes punctuate the film, bringing with them the theme of sexual difference as the realm away from the men's day-world of hard training. This is where we see Galoup for the first time and witness his desire for a particular woman that keeps returning in the film and in his memories. He touches her bare shoulder, she removes his hand, and his face looks tortured. Then the camera switches positions abruptly, showing him on the opposite side, where she is almost out of sight, but because of that, he seems all the more excluded. In a similar scene later in the film, I thought they were dancing outdoors and we were watching them through a wire fence, as if to underline the idea of containment (nonfreedom) that is so important in

this film. (Another scene, when Forestier watches the men training, shows us the Legionnaires through just such a wire fence.) But when we see Galoup dance alone at the end of the film, we can see that the wall is covered with small square mirrors that gave this visual effect, the reflection of limitations even during these moments of nonmilitary pleasure. Once, to lend an even more unreal and subjective dimension to these musical sequences, we return to the dance as if it surges forth from Galoup's longing—there is no sound at all; the movement is ghost-like, out of reach.

Similarly, Galoup's memories of the woman he desires are deliberately, I think, on the borderline between reality and an aching wish. Once, in daylight, we see a woman in a red evening dress sleeping on a bed, her face turned away from us. It must be the same woman (but we can't really tell). Galoup buys a gift and tries gently to awaken her. He fails, opens her fingers to slip a little box into her hand, and still she sleeps. Did it happen? Did he wish it had happened? All these scenes with the women (prostitutes apparently, although they do not conform to that screen stereotype) must be meant to lend another dimension to Galoup's obsession with Forestier, and then with his self-stated jealousy about Forestier's interest in Sentain. Sexual desire, whether sublimated or diverted or actualized, leads Galoup to frustration and functions as an external sign of his inability to belong anywhere. For this reason, too, he differentiates himself from everyone else several times by dressing completely in black, which is repeated in his final dance. Once we see him in the town, in the same frame as his men. But he is walking in the opposite direction, a vivid image of his separation from them and their esprit de corps.

The film ends with Galoup's explosive dance to "The Rhythm of the Night." In a sense, this scene marks an imaginary return for Galoup to the nightclub scenes in Djibouti, except that it looks like exile rather than memory: he is alone in a room whose walls are covered with small square mirrors that make him appear to be trapped in a fragmenting, reflective cage. As the song goes on, Galoup dances with less restraint, more and more violently, throwing himself to the ground and back up as if transforming his military exercises into a performance that is almost unbearably revealing of his passions, his frustration, and his dead end. Galoup's dance fits the dream-like irreality of the film so perfectly that we can wonder if it is "really happening" or if we are inside his subjectivity. It functions to shift the narrative to a higher level of abstraction and metaphor, as if to supercharge and restate the lines of intense, interiorized force that drove the film to the inevitability of this dark musical expression of Galoup's permanent exclusion from the rhythms of the Legion. Claire Denis had planned to end the film differently, with Galoup lying on his bed holding his pistol across his body. The dance would have preceded that scene in Galoup's spartan room. Of the musical scenes that function as narrative parentheses and further opacity as connected with desire in these films of Claire Denis, this "rhythm of the night" is the most abstract, the most charged metaphorically, the most cut off from the narrative proper. It looks like a self-contained music video, created to sum up the conflictual passions and absence of physical outlet that precede it.

Finally, I would draw your attention to a small musically dominated scene that is not a dance nor is the music diegetic. Among a long series of fragmentary scenes that show us different physical aspects of these men on land or sea where they carry out their exercises, unexpectedly, Neil Young's voice floats onto the soundtrack. We see the men, small in the distance, as they march across rugged terrain to the slow, hypnotic rhythm of "Safeway Cart" (a little-known song). This pace and style of movement were key to Claire Denis's conception of her Legionnaires. As she put it, describing the long training process her actors underwent in Paris to be able to convey the sense that they belonged to a military troupe, even if most of them did not correspond to the physical appearance of the Legionnaire, their transformation had to do with internalizing a specific rhythm.

CLAIRE DENIS

I listened to that Neil Young and Crazy Horse album [*Sleeps With Angels*] for years and I liked that song very much. One day I was trying to explain to the boys that the marching scenes need to be strong but like slow motion. If you see the Legion parading on the Champs-Elysées, you will see all the other army corps walking like any soldier, and then the Legion comes like a slow motion film. To succeed in having every movement for the march in slow motion, I went looking through sounds, music. One day I thought of "Safeway Cart" which gives this hypnotic, gliding feeling, and we used it to work, during [the two months] when we were training. It became so attached to the movie that I wrote a letter to Neil Young and told him that I really needed the song for the movie because it was already part of the movie and there was no way to separate it from the movie. He said yes.[16]

This brief sequence dominated by music doesn't involve a dance, but its rhythm and lyrics create a pause in the narrative, like an opaque emblem in long shot, of the condition of the Legionnaires.

I have proposed a reading of the modes of narration and filiation in three key films of Claire Denis, and in the way she constructs an opacity that pertains to sexual as much as social differences. I close with her description of how her idea of the cinema goes beyond beauty or formal structures as such in order to offer a moral perspective in which her characters are linked to the questions that form the basis of the circumstances in which they find themselves.

To have a moral perspective about your work is fundamental. It is this moral perspective that makes you want to makes films, nothing else. Even the pleasure of framing the image isn't enough. Desire for the cinema ought to go beyond the frame, toward meaning. It should be a desire for a relationship with others. Rivette taught me never to betray my characters.[17]

## NOTES

1. This essay was written before the release of *Trouble Every Day* and *Vendredi Soir.* An earlier version appeared in *La Différence des sexes, est-elle visible? Les Hommes et les femmes au cinéma,* ed. Jacques Aumont (Paris: Cinémathèque française, 2000). All photographs courtesy of the author.

2. *J'ai pas sommeil,* Pressbook, Festival de Cannes 1994, interview by Gaillac-Morgue.

3. Interview with Thierry Jousse and Frédéric Strauss, *Cahiers du Cinéma* 479/80, mai 1994, p. 25.

4. I can only recall two discreet shots of women, when the back of their shoulders are observed in an almost anatomical study of the beauty of the musculature moving beneath their skin: Daïga at the end of her impromptu dance with the Slavic woman who owns the hotel where she lives and works, and Nénette as she is running the water for her bath.

5. "Writing and Directing *I Can't Sleep*: A Talk with Claire Denis," *Scenario* (summer 1997): 186. No author cited. The interview was carried out in English.

6. "Writing and Directing *I Can't Sleep*."

7. Interview with Thierry Jousse and Frédéric Strauss, p. 28.

8. I am passing over two other scenes that show how importantly music guides the progression of the narrative: the affectionate and almost familial dance between women representing two generations of Slavs in Paris, Daïga and the hotel owner who is lodging her, when they hear "A Whiter Shade of Pale" on the radio, and Théo playing the violin with his group in a club, where Camille watches his performance, half-hidden among the people there. Besides sequences in which music plays a direct role, Claire Denis worked carefully throughout with nondiegetic music (DC Basehead, Murat).

9. Strand Presskit (no author cited, no date); original in English, slightly edited.

10. "Claire Denis, les années sauvages de Nénette et Boni," Stéphane Bouquet, *Cahiers du Cinéma* 501 (avril 1996): 55, 56.

11. "Awakenings: Ira Sachs talks with *Nénette et Boni*'s Claire Denis," *Filmmaker* (fall 1977): 38.

12. Bouquet, "Claire Denis, les années sauvages de Nénette et Boni," 55, 56.

13. *Nouvelle Vague: une légende en question*, *Cahiers du Cinéma* special issue (décembre 1998): 70. "Quelques vagues plus tard: table ronde avec Olivier Assayas, Claire Denis, Cédric Kahn et Noémie Lvovsky," interviewed by Charles Tesson and Serge Toubiana, Paris, November 10, 1998.

14. I disagree with Stéphane Bouquet's interpretation that Galoup's dance denotes his liberty from "the group" or in any other sense: "When, at the end of the film, Galoup, excluded from the Legion, now alone, dances his own dance . . . he regains himself as an individual. He is henceforth a singular dance, a body, a consciousness. He knows independence, he is saved, he will not commit suicide. . . . What is important in Denis's films is to regain the self, to escape the dream of fusion, to liberate oneself from the group." I disagree, equally, with Bouquet's view that "the beautiful is therefore the central question in the film" (Stéphane Bouquet, "La hiérarchie des anges," *Cahiers du Cinéma* 545 [avril 2000]: 49).

15. Bouquet, "La hiérarchie des anges."

16. Discussion held at UCLA, April 28, 2000. English in the original.

17. "Noir désir," interview with Serge Kaganski, *Les Inrockuptibles* no. 57 (juillet 1994): 74; reprinted May 12, 2000.

# PART II

# BLACK DIASPORA AND *CREOLIZATION*

The chapters in this section examine the question of blackness and its relationship to French culture and identity. They collectively make the point that, far from representing the opposite of a national identity implicitly defined as white, blackness is an integral part of what it means to be French. Moreover, they demonstrate how a recognition of this fact both arises inexorably from the history of and languages of cultural production, and at the same time gives us a new, more inclusive vision of France.

Édouard Glissant's seminal work in chapter 5 offers an alternate vision of French contributions to world culture. He discusses how, for reasons of both history and language, the French experience in the Caribbean has offered a particularly propitious opportunity for the development of creole cultures. Arguing that one of the key characteristics of globalization today is precisely creolization, the decline of boundaries and essentialist identities, Glissant shows how French culture can best survive and prosper by embracing its creole heritage. The next two chapters consider the relationship between blackness, French identity, and universalism from very different perspectives. In chapter 6, Ethan Kleinberg considers Fanon's interpretation of Hegel's Master-Slave dialectic, in a reading mediated by Alexandre Kojève's presentation of the philosopher's work. He points out that, whereas Fanon's belief that the Master-Slave dialectic differed fundamentally from colonial relations of power was mistaken, Fanon did correctly perceive that the position of the racialized Other was much more radically distinct than was the case of the slave in Hegelian philosophy. Kleinberg asserts that a new post-colonial France must come to terms with its own traditions and practices of racial alienation. In contrast, chapter 7 by Donna Hunter considers the ways in which two non-French black intellectuals made use of French traditions of universalism to argue for better treatment in their own societies. She emphasizes the agency exercised by C. L. R. James and Anna Julia Cooper in selecting those aspects of French Revolutionary history that made the case for racial equality. Hunter thus demonstrates how members of the black diaspora could seize upon the liberatory potential of French universalism, a potential that often went well beyond the intentions of its French creators. The final two chapters in this section take up the theme of creolization and its applicability to the literature of the Francophone Caribbean. In chapter 8, Jean Jonaissaint meticulously analyzes Maryse Condé's *Crossing the Mangrove* in a Caribbean context, showing its clear thematic and stylistic kinship with Jacques Romain's *Masters of the Dew*. Jonaissant criticizes the tendency of many Francophone literary critics to neglect the intertextuality of Francophone literary works, instead preferring to relate them to canonical texts from the metropole and elsewhere. He also emphasizes the importance of Caribbean literary and cultural traditions to Condé's work. Valerie Kaussen's analysis of the Haitian novel *Viejo* by Maurice Casseus in chapter 9 grounds it in the historical context of the American occupation of Haiti and the development of *noirisme*, a fascist ideology that refuted the social and cultural dominance of the Francophone elite in favor of the black Haitian masses. In her study of *Viejo*, Kaussen shows how in this case the interaction of questions of blackness, class, and gender led to the articulation of an alternate form of nationalist consciousness.

The five chapters in this section give a vision of the black diaspora that draws upon, yet is distinct from, traditional models emphasizing Africa and the United States. The authors here show how France has both contributed to the culture of the African diaspora and been deeply shaped by it.

# 5

# THE FRENCH LANGUAGE IN THE FACE OF CREOLIZATION

*Édouard Glissant*

I believe the highest object for literature today is what I call the world-totality [*la totalité monde*]. There is no greater literary object for today's writers. And within this world-totality, we will try to see what French culture is and, consequently, what the French language is—since French culture is among those that are the most fused and identified with its language. The diaspora, if we may call it that, of the French language is peculiar. This language is nowhere concentrated together. It is scattered a bit everywhere. English is concentrated in the United States and Canada; Spanish is concentrated in Latin America, Portuguese in Brazil. These form continental masses, while the French language is scattered here and there in Quebec, in the Caribbean, in Africa, and in Asia. And French butted against the existence and resistance of the languages spoken in the places where it was introduced, such as the Arabic language in the Maghreb, or the Vietnamese language in Vietnam, or the languages emerging from Black Francophone Africa. This has raised a lot of problems, and it is one of the primary conditions determining the way the French language currently exists in the world. And for me, this is paradoxically not a lack, nor a defect, nor a lacuna, it is an advantage. Let me explain why.

By the time colonialism had come to its full fruition and perfection, French had acquired a stature with very particular characteristics. In the eighteenth and nineteenth centuries, it was claimed and proclaimed to be a universal language. Everyone was in agreement. At the court of the czars of Russia and the royal court of England, French was accepted as a universal language, and French was commonly spoken there and elsewhere. This situation is very worrisome for a language: what does it mean to have the stature of being a universal language? It injects a neurotic principle into the language (it can be said that there are neurotic languages), and in this regard, the French language is a neurotic one—perhaps even in the good old literal sense of the word. For, after all, there are good neuroses too.

These linguistic characteristics already sketch out the nature of what will be colonialism in the French style. The genius of France—it's been said before, and I merely repeat it here—tends to assimilate those it administers to those who do the administering. This is clear. French colonialism always tends to assimilate the colonized, to elevate them to the dignity of being French citizens, perhaps even French thinkers. All of which marks out a difference, for instance, with English colonialism. I suspect that English colonialism had a hard time conceiving that a Guyanan could be made into an honorable subject of his British majesty. But, paradoxically, in so doing, English colonialism respected the cultures it disregarded. Which is to say that in the former English colonies the cultural sentiment of the population is much stronger and less ambiguous than it is in the former French colonies. For, in its very disdain, English colonialism respected the cultures involved, while French colonialism, which was humanist and all-embracing, which wanted to turn you into good Frenchmen, contributed to the erosion of cultures, except in the cases where those cultures rose up in opposition and armed rebellion. As, was the case, for example, in Vietnam and Algeria. In any case, there is a fundamental difference between these two forms of colonialism, and between the sorts of societies that resulted from them, as we shall see momentarily.

There is nonetheless one condition, one characteristic that is striking when we examine France's part in the colonization of what was called the New World, that is, the Americas. There is something striking about the fact that wherever the French intervened in an American land, a creole came into being. Francophone creole languages emerged, under the conditions I shall describe, in Haiti, in the lesser Antilles, in Louisiana, and in French Guyana, not to mention the islands of the Indian Ocean. But the other condition for there to be a creole is that there be a peoplement by Africans. For example, in Quebec, there is no creole. So the presence of an African population is a requirement.

And why should the French language have so often authorized the appearance of Francophone creoles? I think there are two reasons. The first is that at the time of colonization, when it was not yet the universal language it subsequently claimed to be, the French language, in the Antilles for instance, and throughout the Caribbean, was primarily represented by the ways of speaking of French sailors from Norman and Breton ports. It seems to me that at the time the West Indies were colonized, the French language had not yet confectioned its organic unity. In other words, at the time Montaigne was writing the famous chapter of his *Essays* on Cannibals, Cervantes had already written *Don Quixote* and Shakespeare was in the process of producing his opus. But Montaigne's language—I'm going to shock you—and Rabelais's language are also creole languages. They are not the language of Malherbe, and even less so the language of Racine. They are languages that are still grappling with the world, that are not yet locked into their own purity and organicness. Rabelais and Montaigne, I maintain, are creole authors. Things happen there: they borrow from all over the place, they pile things up and then mix them together, and then we see something taking place, and it all comes out a certain way, leaving folks astonished— "but what does this word mean there?" and so forth. They are also creole authors because Montaigne has at least ten ways of writing, for instance, the word "donc" [thus]: *donc, adonc, donque, doncque,* etc. It is magnificent, and it is beautiful because it has not yet been purified. It has not yet been sifted through Malherbe's grim sieve. And let's suppose this language was available, that the Breton and Norman sailors who trafficked in the Caribbean and the Indian Ocean were speaking a kind of jargon or awful gibberish, which was awful but open, and which allowed, in my opinion, for this kind of osmosis with what people of African descent in those lands brought to bear in the way of lexical and syntactical elements.

There is also another condition that determined the appearance of creole, and in particular of creoles—for there are *different* creoles, such as the Dutch or Netherlandophone creole known as Papiamento, or the Portuguese-based creoles along the coast of Africa, like the creole of Cape Verde. But Dutch and Portuguese are a bit in the same situation as French. It seems to me that it is because the English and Spanish languages were, during the same epoch, already more sure of their own norm and because they spread out over the continent, that creoles did not spring up from those languages. These are suggestions I'm proposing. Everybody has an idea about the origin of creoles. It has even been said they were invented by children, for what that's worth.

But this other condition that seems important for the appearance of creoles is that they always show up in little islands, or in continental areas that are a bit closed in on themselves, like Guyana. The country must be like a laboratory for creole to appear with that kind of unpredictable outcome generated from, for example, the coming together of a Breton and Norman lexicon with memory traces of African syntax. It is necessary that this takes place in a kind of laboratory, in a closed place. But behold the miracle—that closed place is completely open because it doesn't take place in *one* island, it takes place in an archipelago: the Caribbean. It also takes place in another archipelago, the Indian Ocean, and we shall see that this situation determines what I believe are two current functions of thought: systemic thought, which is continental thought, heavy, dense, sure of itself, magnificent and sumptuous; and archipelagic thought, which is the thought of the archipelago, of the set of islands, which is a fragile, fragmentary, trembling thought, unsure of itself, but which is, perhaps, and in my opinion, the thought that is best suited for addressing today's problems of the world totality.

Consequently, we can see, in this way the French language has had of spreading itself around the world, something like the kernel of the problems confronted today by French culture. This French langage allowed the appearance of creoles, but once a creole appeared, French tried to dominate and stifle it. Now, French developed in its own autonomous way for the Quebecois and the Cajuns, but elsewhere it set itself up in opposition to what we can call the national languages of the Maghreb, of Black Africa, and of Vietnam. In these places, French has tended to regress, whether one regrets it or not, and its final refuge has been to declare itself a kind of lingua franca. I once had a major discussion on French television with the Minister of Francophone Affairs Madame Sudre, who herself hails from the island of Réunion. She said, "Yes, but take an African country where 250 languages are spoken, well the French language is what creates unity, that is, French is what allows everybody a basis for communication." So, I said to her, "I'm very sorry, Madame Minister, but the French language is not what allows everybody to communicate in Africa, or in any given African country." It is the culture of the country, the way people eat, spend time together, dress, make love, value or do not value women, commit crimes or do not commit them. That is what creates unity, not the French language. And people have a command of three, four, or five different languages—which they use to speak! There is no universal language. The belief in a universal language is of a character one could call hospitable, or hospital-like. You go to the hospital when you believe this. Because, truly, it is a sickness to believe there are universal languages. And multilingualism has a contemporary dimension that escapes many of us.

I have a seven-year-old son. He speaks French, English, and creole, all fluently! As for me, I have been in the United States for eight years and I can barely jabber English. He says to me: "No, Dad, not like that," when I utter a word. He says to me, "Dad," and I say, "Stop it! Listen, I read Faulkner and Shakespeare," and he says, "Okay, but you don't pronounce it well. You don't know how to speak." And it's true. Why? Because the part of the brain he uses for language is I'm sure 30 or 40 percent, while I only use about 2 percent. Because I've not been brought up the same way. And, surely, a small child in the streets of Dakar or Rio de Janeiro holds linguistic possibilities that are ten million times greater than mine or yours. And while we may be linguistically competent, these children have something new, very new: they are born into multilingualism, while we were all born within monolingualism. We were born into a monolingual practice even if we know several languages. Our means of functioning is monolingual, even if we know five or six languages. On the other hand, I see children who are born directly into multilingualism—just as they are said to be born in front of a computer screen. And consequently, I told Madame Minister, "No, the French language does not have the vocation of creating unity among Africans. Among Africans, unity or its lack—and I know not every place there is unified—takes place within multilingualism and by common cultural characteristics." And these are the conditions within which I would like to be able to situate the French language at the current moment.

In the Caribbean, what I called the phenomenon of creolization goes far beyond its linguistic phenomenon or stage. When I speak of creolization, I certainly do not mean to bring everything back to the formation of creole languages. That would only be a blind alley. Why, then, do I use the word "creolization"? I use it because in the world-totality today, I think the real harmonies, the real encounters, the real conflicts, the real wars, do not take place between nations, but between cultures. On this everybody seems to be agreed. The problems of the nation will recede with time before the advance of cultural problems. It is thus a question of creolization, just as for creole it was the encounter of heterogeneous lexical and syntactical elements that in a given location interwove to yield an unprecedented outcome. Not a synthesis. Creole is not a synthesis but an unpredictable, novel, and unprecedented outcome of these heterogeneous elements. Similarly, creolization is the contact, conflict, attraction, harmony, repulsion, dissemblance, ressemblance between cultures of the world that come together in the world-totality, that come together, cling together, repel each other, etc., and yield unprecedented outcomes. I call this world a chaos-world not because it is a world in disorder, but because it is an unpredictable world. We can no longer make secure plans, we are done with five-year plans or rationalized planning. That's all over. Our imaginary must become habituated to the unpredictability of the world whole. And so I call "creolization" what happened in the Caribbean, and what has happened in every archipelago, and what happens everywhere today because the world as a whole is becoming creolized. Europe too is becoming like an archipelago, an archipelago where regional realities are like islands, open islands. Little by little, as Europe establishes itself, it also decomposes into islands that are open to each other. Let's not speak of national frontiers. We see the appearance of realities that were dominated by a national entity: Gascon realities, or Basque or Breton or Corsican ones and so forth, which are beginning to meld and which are beginning to forms links with one other. Consequently, creolization does not always take place on the model of what was practiced in the Caribbean, or in other archipelagoes, but it does take place everywhere. And so, what is the principle of this creolization, and in what ways might French culture intervene in it?

This is where I would like to go a little further. I believe that among all these cultures that today oppose each other, come together, move apart, make war to each other, exterminate each other, combine with each other, and so forth, among all these cultures, there are two kinds. There are those I call *atavistic* cultures. Not because they are ancient or traditional, but because they are cultures that have invented, that have had the good fortune or the merit (for being able to touch God is always precious!) of having begotten a genesis, a creation myth of the world, and these cultures are still linked to that creation of the world through an uninterrupted and continuous chain of descent. The most famous example is that of the Old Testament books of Genesis and Numbers. But that's not all. All around the Mediterranean basin there was an appearance of myth, of the creation of the world in this way. And in sub-Saharan African cultures, there are myths of the creation of the world. These are atavistic cultures. That is why, I do not agree with the opposition commonly drawn between Western cultures and Islam. For me, Islam, at this level, is part of the West. That is to say, that the cultures around the Mediterranean basin were the ones that invented the "One." And it is no coincidence that the three great monotheistic religions of the world appeared around that basin, just as they all three claim to be descendents of Abraham. For me, Islam is not in opposition with the West. The opposition between Islam and the West is an avatar internal to Western cultures. That is to say, there is a return of the religious repressed that hangs on and defends itself, but all these cultures nevertheless start from the same atavistic principle. And, for instance, in the Americas, Amerindian cultures *are* atavistic, because they too—and they are the only such cultures in the Western Hemisphere—have produced geneses, stories of the creation of the world to which they are linked through direct descent. We could draw all kinds of differences: genealogical affiliation among Amerindians is not as deadly and dangerous as it is among the cultures of the Mediterranean basin. And the principle of affiliation, the chain of ancestors among sub-Saharan Africans, is not as deadly. It is not closed. You can enter into it. When one was taken prisoner in a traditional African village, through one's own merit and virtue, one could become the chief of the village and so enter into the chain of ancestors of the village. Thus, the chain of ancestors was not exclusivistic, which it is in the West. And the chain of ancestors in the West, its legitimacy, and affiliation are the principles of existence of Western cultures and their literatures. One could go far in this direction, we could study Shakespeare from this standpoint, and so on.

Alongside these atavistic cultures, I believe another kind of culture has come to assert itelf, what I call *composite* cultures, which are cultures that have not engendered or begotten a myth about the creation of the world. Why? Because these are cultures that are *born from history*. My own genesis, what is it if not the belly of the slave ship? This is the place where the peoples of the Caribbean are truly born, and all those transplanted peoples of African descent. We can adopt geneses. For example, we can become Islamic, Christian, Protestant, etc., and we adopt genetic traditions that have already been produced, but we do not produce them as such. That is to say, no people of the Americas, except for the Amerindians, have produced a genesis, a myth of world creation. And this opposition between atavistic cultures and composite cultures is what shakes the world today. Why? Because, under the pressure of the world-totality, the atavistic cultures tend to decompose. That is to say, they tend to renounce their geneses. And composite cultures, on the contrary, have a kind of nostalgia from knowing they could have begotten a genesis. This is not so much a nostalgia of religiosity, or of spirituality, but a nostalgia for something that is not comprehended and that is sacred. This is why the proliferation of sects with a religious character is frightening because each sect tries to take a little bit of genesis from here, a little bit of genesis from there, and then remakes its own genesis, its own creation of the world in the most preposterous way possible. But all the same, this opposition between atavistic and composite cultures is what raises concerns in the world. In atavistic societies, wherever a "composite" locale, that is, a creolizing one, is found, it becomes a priority target for the return of repressed identity, as for example, Beirut in Lebanon, or Sarajevo in Yugoslavia. These were locales where everybody lived together, where one could have relations or get married without being of the same

religion, etc., and that is why those places are truly martyr places for the
current world situation. And as a consequence, this world situation is one
about which no one knows what to do. Wherever one turns, there is the return of repressed identity. And I maintain we cannot change that, no military, sociological, economic solution will obtain as long as we have not
changed the imaginary of human peoples today. And what does it mean to
change the imaginary of human peoples? It is to accustom ourselves to the
idea that we can no longer live as we once did in the mode of our unique
root identity, which kills everything around it. We have to get habituated to
the idea that if I can change my own identity by exchanging it with some
Other, that does not mean that I will disappear as an identifiable person. It
does not mean that I will disappear into some gaping hole. It does not mean
that I will be suspended in midair. It does not mean that I will vanish into
some incomprehensible fantasm.

We should get used to the idea that the identities of human peoples today *are* relational identities—what I call rhizomatic identities, that is, the
root that digs down but that also extends its branches laterally toward other
roots. And as long as we have not changed the mentalities, the imaginaries
of peoples and human communities today, nothing will happen—and that is
why I say that poetry and literature have an immense role to play in all this
and that the world-totality is the real object of literature today. There will
be solutions for ten or fifteen years, but there will always be the return of
repressed identity, there will always be the old atavisms that will want to
display themselves in an imperative manner and there will always be new
composite formations that will proceed in an impulsive or tender manner
toward atavisms, that is, toward forms of legitimacy.

And so, it seems to me that in this panorama the function of French
culture is precisely *not* to be universal, nor to take a leadership role, nor
anything of the sort. And it seems to me that the advantage of the French
language is that it is scattered a bit everywhere. That there are French languages today: I have *my* French language, I may despise it, I may say dumb
things, I may say good things, but it is *my* French language. It is not the language of Madame de Sévigné, and it is the not the language of Monsieur
d'Ormesson.[1] It is my own language. There is the language of the Québécois, and that is their own language. But we can also reach across to each
other through these languages, and as a consequence, the role of France
and French culture—once the French have understood that they no longer
rule the world but are a *part* of the world, and that this responsibility must
be shared—is to allow this meandering of a language that goes everywhere,
so to speak, that has neither continental weight nor the weight of a system,

and that becomes like an archipelago. French becomes archipelagic, it becomes multiple, and it must come to understand in contradistinction to
every lingua franca [*sabir*],[2] that one does not preserve a language by
letting others perish. For with every language that disappears, there disappears forever a part of the human imaginary. This we cannot allow. Everything possible must be done so that the languages of the world are
preserved. And when I am warned about the threat of the growing
Anglo-American lingua franca, I reply that the first language that is threatened by the Anglo-American lingua franca is the English language itself,
because it is threatened with no longer living the electrifying advances, prudent retreats, obscurities, and weaknesses that every language must know.
From the moment a language becomes the mechanism of a lingua franca,
when *everybody* can speak it *indifferently*, that language dies. And so, in the
Francophone world, I have been told, we must fight against the Anglo-
American language. I say no, we must fight for the survival of every language in the world against every codification and we must also fight for the
English language, which is also threatened by this lingua franca. Let me
conclude, then, by stating that in this multiplicity of our chaos-world, and
in the context of ongoing creolization, the French language has no universal calling, but French is situated within a set of diversities that grants it a
privileged status at the moment and that will bring it to the forefront of the
world's lived reality on the condition that it ceases to believe it is the only
language in the world.

## NOTES

*This chapter was translated by Georges Van Den Abbeele.*

    1. Known for her elegant letters to friends and relatives, Madame de Sévigné
(1626–1696) is often deemed to exemplify the classical French prose style. The
contemporary journalist and novelist Jean d'Ormesson (1925– ) is a current member of the Académie française, and is likewise considered by many to be the con-
summate modern prose stylist of French. TRANS.

    2. Glissant uses the French word *sabir* where I have put lingua franca. Sabir, ac-
cording to the *Larousse du XXe siècle*, is "a language of mixed Arab, French, Italian and Spanish elements" spoken in the Levant and Mediterranean basin. Sabir
thus functioned as a very specific kind of lingua franca in that area. The word's use
as a common noun implies the sense of a composite speech rather than the dominance of any one language over the others. TRANS.

# 6

# KOJÈVE AND FANON: THE DESIRE FOR RECOGNITION AND THE FACT OF BLACKNESS

*Ethan Kleinberg*

This chapter began as a reading of one work, Frantz Fanon's *Black Skin, White Masks*, which became an investigation into the tension between two separate themes: one from an early chapter entitled "The Fact of Blackness" and the second from a section of the last chapter on "The Negro and Recognition" entitled "the Negro and Hegel." But as I began exploring this tension in earnest I realized that I was dealing not with one figure but two: Fanon's focus in his chapter on Hegel is on the "Desire for Recognition" and his reading of this theme requires a serious consideration of Hegel, but of Hegel as read by Alexandre Kojève. Here I must admit that the more obvious choice would have been to read Fanon in relation to Sartre, but as pertains these two themes the influence of Kojève is far more direct and the juxtaposition of Kojève and Fanon is far more elucidating—especially in understanding a phenomenon of hybridization in French philosophy involving the teleological Hegelian dialectic and German phenomenology. In moving from the two themes to the two figures I realized that what is at stake in understanding the internal tension in Fanon's work is a larger understanding of the relationship between these two philosophical projects, and the ramifications of this conflation on Fanon's project and our understanding of the colonial system.

In *Black Skin, White Masks*, Fanon attempts to differentiate between the Master-Slave dialectic in Hegel (and here it is Kojève's reading of Hegel to which I am referring) and the master and slave in the colonial system.[1] In doing so Fanon is attempting to find a third place from which the colonial situation, distinct from the Hegelian situation, can be addressed. But in his attempt to distance the colonial slave from the Hegelian Slave, Fanon actually parallels Hegel's movements. Fanon is correct in his diagnosis of an incompatibility between the Hegelian system and the colonial system but this becomes explicit not in his critique of the dialectic, but in his phenomenological investigation into "the Fact of Blackness." It is only through the conflation of the teleological Hegelian dialectic with phenomenology that the fundamental incompatibility of the Hegelian system and the colonial system becomes visible.

It is this incompatibility that I wish to explore by first looking at Fanon's attempt to distance himself from Hegel and the subsequent subsumption into the dialectic, and then attempting to understand the bearing that the phenomenological component of Fanon (and Kojève) has on this movement.

Toward the end of *Black Skin, White Masks* in the section entitled "the Negro and Hegel," Fanon attempts to distinguish his reading of the colonial condition (the black condition) from the Master-Slave dialectic as proposed by Hegel, Fanon presents a footnote on page 220 where he "sums up" the distinctions between the two.

> I hope I have shown that here the [colonial] master differs basically from the master described by Hegel. For Hegel there is a reciprocity; here the master laughs at the consciousness of the slave. What he wants is not recognition but work.
>
> In the same way, the slave here is in no way identifiable with the [Hegelian] slave who loses himself in the object and finds in his work the source of his liberation.
>
> The Negro wants to be like the master.
>
> Therefore he is less independent than the Hegelian slave.
>
> In Hegel the slave turns away from the master and turns toward the object.
>
> Here the slave turns toward the master and abandons the object.[2]

But by looking at this footnote in relation to Alexandre Kojève's reading of Hegel we will see that the two readings are actually parallel, equivocal.

In Kojève's interpretation of Hegel, as presented in his seminars at the *École Pratique des Hautes Études* from 1933 to 1939, the relation of the Master to the Slave is the result of the "Struggle for Recognition."[3] Kojève constructs a dualistic ontology (following Heidegger not Hegel) in differentiating between an animal/object world and a human world: "For a man to be truly human, for him to be essentially and really different from an animal, his human Desire must actually win out over his animal Desire."[4] This human Desire is essentially differentiated from animal Desire. Animal Desire is immediate gratification, it is pure negation (being hungry and eating) but as such "the I created by the active satisfaction of such a desire will have the same nature as the things toward which that desire is directed: it will be a 'thingish' I, a merely living I, an animal I."[5]

For the human to transcend the animal/object realm and ultimately attain Self-Consciousness, the human must transcend given natural reality. Human Desire must be directed toward a non-natural object. But the only thing that goes beyond the animal realm is to desire another's desire. This is to say to desire the desire of another. To be human is thus to wish to be recognized as a human being and not as an object or animal.

Fanon follows this logic and is in accord with Kojève when Fanon states: "As soon as I *desire* I am asking to be considered. I am not merely here and now, sealed into thingness."[6] For both Kojève and Fanon the fruition of human Desire is to have the value that I represent be the value desired by an Other. But for my value to be recognized by the Other, the Other must first see me as a human and not as an animal or thing.

Here Kojève introduces what he claims to be the fundamental difference between the animal and the human realm:

> Now all Desire is desire for a value. The supreme value for an animal is its animal life. All the Desires of an animal are in the final analysis a function of its desire to preserve its life. Human Desire, therefore, must win out over this desire for preservation. In other words, man's humanity "comes to light" only if he risks his (animal) life for the sake of his human Desire. . . . And that is why to speak of the "origin" of Self-Consciousness is necessarily to speak of the risk of life (for an essentially non-vital end).[7]

To be human, and thus worthy of an Other's recognition, is to put one's human Desire, the desire for recognition, above one's animal Desire, the desire to live.

Here too, Fanon echoes Kojève in his explanation of *desire*: "I demand that notice be taken of my negating activity insofar as I pursue something other than life; insofar as I do battle for the creation of a human world— that is a world of reciprocal recognitions."[8] In Fanon's explanation it is a "demand that notice be taken," that recognition be given, to his "negating activity" insofar as it is in pursuit of something other than life. He is prepared to accept the risk of his life for the sake of his human Desire, a desire for recognition that will be satisfied by the "creation of a human world—that is a world of reciprocal recognitions."

But in this statement there is a discord between Fanon and Kojève, a flaw in Fanon's understanding of Hegel that is the basis of his differentiation between the colonial situation and the Hegelian Master and Slave. Fanon assumes that there is a reciprocal relationship of recognition in Hegel, which is not present in the colonial relationship between the white master and the black slave. This assumption is made when Fanon asserts that "The other, however, can recognize me without struggle" and he attempts to support this assertion with a quote from Hegel: "The individual, who has not staked his life, may, no doubt, be recognized as a *person*, but he has not attained the truth of this recognition as an independent self-consciousness." In Hegel according to Fanon, it is only the "I" that must struggle for recognition. Therefore any "I" who does not engage in the struggle for recognition, who has not staked his life, will simply be recognized *by* the Other, who is somehow exempt from the equation except as recognizer.

But the struggle for recognition is a binary equation with the necessary condition that both parties see each other as equals, as worthy of each other's recognition. As stated above, the desire for recognition can only be fulfilled by obtaining the Desire of another human. For an individual to achieve the recognition of an Other, he must first prove that he has overcome his animal Desires, that he has overcome his fear of death and is worthy of my Desire. The only possible means of proving this assertion is by risking one's life for the sake of one's Desire, by proving that one's desire for recognition is more important than one's desire to live in a purely biological sense. "Therefore to speak of the origin of Self-Consciousness is necessarily to speak of a fight to the death for recognition."[9] According to Kojève, the initial encounter between human beings is necessarily violent and potentially lethal.

But in Kojève's reading, this struggle for recognition serves not only to distinguish the animal from the human world but also to distinguish two classes of humans: those who have overcome their animal Desires (Masters) and those who have not (Slaves). According to Kojève, the human world is distinguished from the animal world by the decision to fight for recognition, to fight for pure prestige. Then the question is whether one sticks to the fight and overcomes his animal Desire or doesn't. It is precisely to this point that the passage in Hegel, taken from chapter 4 of the *Phenomenology of Spirit* and quoted by Fanon, is addressed. The Slave may be seen as a "person," in the biological sense, but also because in some way he has distinguished himself from the animal world (the world of objects). I want to earmark this moment in Kojève because it will later become crucial for our understanding of Fanon. But the Slave has not attained the "truth of this recognition as an independent Self-Consciousness," he has not overcome his fear of death and thus is not recognized by the Other as worthy of recognition. Here we see that the battle for recognition is a paradox.

If both combatants turn out to have overcome their animal Desires, then one of them must die. If one does die, then he is returned to the inanimate form of a mere thing and as such his recognition is of no value to the victor who must journey off to search for recognition elsewhere. If, as is and must be the case, one decides that one would rather live than die and gives in to one's animal Desire, then the two have distinguished themselves as unequals. The victor enslaves the loser, who now recognizes the victor as Master without being recognized himself. But the Master is not satisfied with the recognition of a Slave who has not proven to be fully human and thus continues in search of validation. Thus contrary to Fanon's assertion, there is no recognition possible with or without struggle. At this stage of the dialectic, for Hegel, like for Fanon, there is no reciprocity of recognition.

To return to Fanon's footnote we now see that the "master" does not laugh at the consciousness of the slave but, perhaps worse, ignores it as beneath him. For Kojève's Hegel and for Fanon the relationship of the Master to the Slave is the same: "What he wants from the slave is not recognition but work."[10]

But then the question arises at what stage is there reciprocity? The answer is at the end of history. Kojève tracks this teleology that begins with the distinction between Master and Slave but is propelled by the Slave's relationship to work. The Slave is forced to work by the Master, and in turning to the object the Slave develops a mastery over nature that transforms the world. This transformation is seen in the evolution of civilization from the Pagan State, through the Christian World, to the modern Bourgeois World.

With the emergence of Christianity the entire "world" becomes a world of pseudo-masters and pseudo-slaves or rather "masterless Slaves." The Master is no longer a concrete manifestation on earth but instead God above. Once again the Slave's confrontation with death is avoided through the creation of an after-life. The masterless Slaves do not overcome their slavery until they replace theism with atheism overcoming their fear of death and attaining Self-Consciousness. It is only after this final stage that there can be reciprocity of recognition.

Thus when Fanon points to the abolition of slavery without battle to expose the differences between the colonial situation and the Hegelian dialectic, he does not contradict Kojève's Hegelian schema but steps into it.

Historically, the Negro steeped in the inessentiality of servitude was set free by his master. He did not fight for his freedom. Out of slavery the Negro burst into the room where his masters stood. Like those servants who are allowed once every year to dance in the drawing room, the Negro is looking for a prop. The Negro has not become a Master.[11]

The satisfaction of overcoming the fear of death, of being recognized as a human being, of attaining Self-Consciousness is denied the Negro in emancipation but this denial is precisely the deferral, the lack, that Kojève anticipates. It creates the dis-satisfaction that is the motor of history that forces the Slave to work, to master nature, which leads to the Enlightenment where he comes to terms with Universal Reason, and eventually to the Revolution that will replace theism with atheism where every man overcomes his fear of death and whose fruition will be the end of history and the creation of a world of mutual recognition, a world of reciprocity.

When Fanon claims in his footnote that "the [colonial] slave here is in no way compatible with the [Hegelian] slave who loses himself in the object and finds in his work the source of his liberation," one must ask "Why?"

When Fanon continues that "the Negro wants to be like the Master," we can respond that for Kojève, too, the Slave wants to be like the Master in overcoming his fear of death and moving toward Self-Consciousness.

And when Fanon points out that "in Hegel the slave turns away from the Master and turns toward the object," we can point out that this is by force and not by choice. The Master forces the Slave to work. In work, the Slave turns toward the object and eventually masters the object. Ironically, it is this mastery over the world of objects (forced upon the Slave by the Master) that allows the Slave to eventually overthrow the Master himself. So what is the essential difference between the colonial system and the Hegelian system that Fanon is trying to enunciate?

The answer is unclear so long as Fanon attempts to determine the differences from within the framework of the dialectic he is trying to critique. His desire to find a place alongside the Hegelian dialectic that will eventually allow him into the dialectic through violent and Marxist action betrays his debt to Hegel.

Fanon's critique is blunted when he is in the dialectic but it is most powerful in the phenomenological investigation into the conditions prior to the "Struggle for Recognition." The difference between the Hegelian and colonial systems is implicit in his understanding of "the Fact of Blackness," not explicit in his critique of the dialectic itself. There is an incompatibility between the system that Kojève is describing and the system that Fanon is trying to understand, which is not addressed when Fanon steps into the dialectic precisely because the determining moment is prior to the dialectic.

What becomes clear in "The Fact of Blackness," and here we shift our position and use Fanon to read Kojève, is that the economy of Hegel's system is such that it does not allow space for a radically Other. Fanon sees that there is no room for the colonized in the historical progression of Hegel as read by Kojève but the Other, the black, is not denied a place because he is "recognized without struggle" or because "he did not fight for his freedom," which is Fanon's claim. Instead, it is because prior to the moment of confrontation the fact of blackness disqualifies the Negro from participation in the Hegelian teleological progression.

If we return to Kojève's lectures we remember that the struggle for recognition differentiates two tiers of humans (Masters and Slaves), but there is a prior duality in Kojève that is between human being and things. It is this distinction between human and thing that ultimately puts the Hegelian dialectic in question.

In Hegel's teleology, the battle for recognition is fought between two individuals who both seek recognition and this battle constitutes the appearance of a stage in the history of Self-Consciousness as an expression of a developing entity. In Kojève's reading we find an Husserlian twist in his attempt to understand how it is that "things" appear to us. Seen in this light as "contemplative and descriptive" the Kojèvian project takes on an epistemological nature in its attempt to understand the way an object is given through its appearance first and foremost.[12] The conflation of Hegel's teleological dialectic with phenomenology forces Kojève to confront not only the relation between humans (as in Hegel) but also the relationship between the human world and the animal world (as in Heidegger) and the way that these worlds make sense to us through appearance (as in Husserl).

In the struggle for recognition there is an epistemological moment prior to the confrontation where the "I" must determine the ontological nature of the Other as potentially human or as animal/object (a moment peculiar to Kojève's reading of Hegel's *Phenomenology of Spirit*). The one who fights must initially visually recognize the Other as a potential human and not as a mere thing or object. Thus some sort of previous referent is required so that confirmation of human potential can be made and the initial struggle can begin. Seen in this light the entire Hegelian project is a system placed within an already existing, and working, epistemological structure that is unquestioned. At the basis of this structure is the necessity for the "I" to confirm itself as self and not as object; to do so the "I" looks not to the radically Other but to one like himself, an homologous Other, in order that he may affirm his position as a self from outside. The "I" looks to itself in order to dictate the criteria to confirm the human potential of the Other. For the Other to be human, the Other must be like me and if the Other is like me then I am not an object. From its ontological inception in Hegel's system, the "I" that first speaks, that has animal Desires and overcomes those Desires, that struggles for recognition and progresses toward Self-Consciousness is a European "I," a white "I," and by all indications a male "I." The Negro in his blackness is not the same, he is radically Other and if allowed into this economy places the white self in question. To avoid this dilemma the radically Other is labeled as object and excluded.

Within Kojève's phenomenological reading of Hegel the possible thingness of the Other, and the subsequent possibility of the thingness of the self, is pointed to. Within the work of Fanon it becomes explicit: "I arrived in the world anxious to make sense of things, my soul filled with the desire to get to the origin of the world, but then I discovered myself an object . . . an object in a world of other objects."[13]

Fanon presents the phenomenological problem at hand but also a subsequent existential dilemma. Fanon sets out upon the phenomenological task of attempting to understand how it is that things make sense to us in the world we live in only to discover that within the epistemological framework that he is investigating he is an object

We have determined that the attainment of Self-Consciousness is contingent upon the Desire of the Other. To be human is to wish to be recognized as such. To return to a quote from Fanon, "As soon as I desire I am asking to be considered. I am not merely here and now, sealed into thingness."[14] But what if the Other does not respond to your request? What if the Other does not recognize you as human potentiality but fixes you in the animal realm, as a "thingish I, a merely living I, an animal I."[15] Here again it is crucial to remember that for Kojève there is no difference between the animal realm and the object. In Kojève's construction, the struggle for recognition is contingent upon the initial visual confirmation that the opponent is potentially a human being and not a mere object. As a potential human, the satisfaction of one's desire for recognition is a possibility. The "Fact of Blackness" denies this possibility.

The black is always already fixed in the realm of thing. It is encoded in his skin and in the colonized world in which he lives. He is denied access into the historical progression by the gaze of the white Other who arrests any possibility of teleological development by denying the possibility of black Self-Consciousness. The black is "sealed into thingness." Furthermore, once relegated to the position of an object, a "thing" in the schema of an Other and more specifically the white Other, the possibility of ontological investigation is denied.

For not only must the black man be black; he must be black in relation to the white man. Some critics will take it on themselves to remind us that this proposition has a converse. I say this is false. The black man has no ontological resistance in the eyes of the white man.[16]

Here we see the potentially schizophrenic nature of this unbalanced equation. The black must not only understand his self as a black self, but also as a black self in relation to a white self. By contrast the white self is its own totality. Thus there is no dialectic but a white self that is whole and a black self that is split and fragmented.

The colonized people are denied an originary self, or rather the status of their self is placed in permanent question by the process of colonization: "His [the black's] metaphysics, or, less pretentiously, his customs and the sources on which they are based, were wiped out because they were in conflict with a civilization that he did not know and that imposed itself on him."[17] The colonized people are defined from without by the colonizer, they are denied access to the economy of human Desire with the result that their desire for recognition is left permanently unrequited.

In Kojève the constitution of the self is within one's control, one makes the choice between Master and Slave. In Fanon's understanding of the colonial system, it is determined by the colonizer:

Sealed into that crushing objecthood, I turned beseechingly to others. Their liberating gaze, sliding over my body making it free from encumbrance, endowing me once more with an agility that I had thought lost, and by taking me out of the world, restoring me to it. But just as I reached the other side, I stumbled, and the movements, the attitudes, the glances of the other fixed me there, in the sense in which a chemical solution is fixed by a dye. I was enraged, I demanded an explanation. But nothing came. I burst apart. Now the fragments have been put together again by another self.[18]

In his attempt to escape the object-like state in which he has found himself, the black desires the recognition of the Other to free him from his state of object-like encumbrance. He knows that the recognition of the Other will free him from the world of things, or rather that he will return to it as a Human. But in the Hegelian economy into which he has been thrown, the Other whose recognition he desires, the Other whose recognition is of value to him is the Master Other, the white Other. And the white Other does not see the black's human value. For the black, Self-Consciousness is denied. He is fixed by the gaze of the Other. He is classified and he is marked. He has no ontological resistance so he bursts apart. For the colonized, the being that is recognized by the colonizer is not constructed in the Kojèvian sense, but given in the way that a botanist gives a name to a plant. In his attempt to construct a self in the Western metaphysical tradition Fanon discovers that "the elements that I used had been provided for me not by 'residual sensations and perceptions primarily of a tactile, vestibular, kinesthetic, and visual character,' but by the other, the white man, who had woven me out of a thousand details, anecdotes, stories."[19]

The black, the colonized, is denied history and is placed in a state of explicit *Geworfenheit*. He is thrown into a world of symbols and meanings that are not his own. Therefore at the moment of initial confirmation prior to the possibility of a struggle for recognition there is an epistemological assertion. A moment when the Western epistemology usurps the position of the indigenous system of knowledge, incorporates it, and subordinates it to its hierarchy. From the very moment that the white colonizer sets foot onto "his" colonial territory, he has determined the inhabitants as less than he, unequal and unworthy of his human Desire. This "fact" is reenforced by the color of the inhabitants' skin and the European understanding of what this means. The black is redefined in European terms and as such is excluded from human potentiality. This moment of visual and taxonomical confirmation is at the basis of the Hegelian dialectic but might also shed light onto the recent French obsession with the question of the veil. The veil does not allow for the immediate visual confirmation and reenforcement of the Western epistemological structure that dictates how one is to respond to the Other. Is the Other like me and thus worthy of my recognition, is the Other less than me?, a black?, a woman?, an unknown? The veil denies the visual confirmation of the Other as radically different or homogenous, as threatening or tame, and thus disturbs the basis of this Western model by pointing to this originary moment of classification that is so crucial to Fanon. As a human, he is a black human, he is herded, he is civilized, and he is fixed by the color of his skin: by the Fact of his skin: "My body was given back to me sprawled out, distorted, refashioned, plunged into mourning on that white winter day. The Negro is a beast, the Negro is bad, the Negro is vicious, the Negro is ugly."[20]

Labeled and classified, denied the possibility of Self-Consciousness, filled with the desire for recognition that has no outlet, the black self is radically destabilized:

> On that day, completely dislocated, unable to be in the world with the Other, the white man who unmercifully imprisoned me, I took my self away from my own presence [*être-là*], far away, and made myself an object. What else could

it be for me but a detachment, a tearing out, a hemorrhaging that curdles the black blood through all my body. But I did not want this revision, this thematisation. All I wanted was to be a man among other men.[21]

Unable to be human by the fact of his skin, the black in reaction, in defense, in desperation must occupy the only space given him: he must make himself an object.

The questioning of the relationship of the self to the object, self as object is the logical extension of Kojève's phenomenological investigation into the economy of being in the Hegelian dialectic (this is especially true in the work of Lacan). But in Fanon there is also an important political dimension. One common critique of the problematic nature of applying Marxist models to the colonial world, and thus a critique of Fanon's politics, is that Marxism as the heir to the Hegelian dialectic is in fact a continuation of the same epistemological structure that has dominated the world for the last two hundred years. This criticism exposes the hypocritical nature of assuming the teleological fruition of historical development in non-Western countries through the imposition of Western European political and metaphysical values. By this logic, Marxism is not the solution to colonialism but the logical conclusion of it.

Despite Fanon's Marxist tendencies, through his phenomenological work we see that the initial problem occurs prior to any economic or historical determinant. By denying the black (the colonized) a human space in the Hegelian system, the economic solution that Marxism can provide does not address the fundamental conflict prior to the dialectic: the moment of exclusion, the denying of a place, the refusal to recognize the radically Other.

In a Marxist utopia the black will still be black and will still live under the imposition of an identity given him by the white, one that he has himself internalized. Even in the "modern" world where slavery is abolished, and science "after much reluctance . . . has conceded that the Negro is a human being; *in vivo* and *in vitro* analogous to the white man," the residue remains and is inherent in the first encounter.[22] Even in this modern world, Fanon laments: "I am given no chance. I am over-determined from without. I am the slave not of the "idea" that others have of me but of my own appearance."[23] In a world of given meanings, the initial moment of confirmation is dictated by the epistemological world into which you are thrown.

Thus the fact of blackness is a constant state of breakdown in the Heideggerian sense of the word where things no longer show up as making sense or having reason, the groundlessness of the black's position is explicit and this causes anxiety. This anxiety is compounded by a reenforcement from without and a realization from within that to ease the anxiety the black man must become what he is not, white. This is an impossible task that heightens the anxiety that tears at the core of his existence and leads to a rage of unfulfilled violence. Forced into the Hegelian schema and denied the possibility of Self-Consciousness, the struggle for recognition is sublimated and internalized. Seen in this light, Fanon's concern with the high suicide rate among blacks becomes more clear. Frustrated, denied, unfulfilled, and forced to attain an impossible goal, the movement to overcome death that would lead to Self-Consciousness is turned inward in a futile gesture.

But the gesture is not necessarily suicidal. Fanon evokes Bigger Thomas and Robert Jones in Chester Himes's *If He Hollers Let Him Go*, who both eventually explode in acts of violence that they cannot control. "The Negro is a toy in the white man's hands; so in order to break the infernal circle he explodes."[24] But like the suicide this attempt at action is futile, it is "expected, anticipated" and simply confirms the white man's convictions.

Returning to Fanon's footnote with the realization that the "Fact of Blackness" is disqualification from the struggle for recognition, the incompatibility between the Hegelian and the colonial systems becomes clear: "For Hegel there is reciprocity; here the [colonial] master laughs at the consciousness of the slave." The colonial master laughs at the slave in the way that one laughs at a circus animal wearing clothes. For the colonial master, the consciousness of the slave is that of an animal. "In the same way, the slave here is in no way identifiable with the slave who loses himself in the object and finds in his work the source of his liberation." The black does not lose himself in the object through work but loses himself as object, as indistinguishable from the object, and from this imposed thingness there can be no "liberation." "The Negro wants to be like the Master." He wants to be liberated from thingness, he desires to be recognized by the Other as equal to the Other and thus necessarily he wants to be white. The colonized slave does not master the world of objects so that he might one day overturn the Master, instead he *is* the world of objects and what's more he has made himself an object. The colonized slave *is* what is mastered and from this "mere thinglike" position he does not wish to "overturn the Master" but merely to enter the economy of human being: "Therefore he is less independent than the Hegelian slave." The colonized slave does not want to rule but merely to be recognized as human potential, to be allowed the *possibility* that his Desire for Recognition be satisfied. "In Hegel the slave turns away from the master and turns toward the object. Here the slave turns toward the master and abandons the object." From his position within the dialectic, the Hegelian Slave is the motor of history and turns to the object so that he may one day become Master. In the colonial system, the slave is excluded a human place and relegated to a thing-like existence. The slave is an object and the only way that he can enter into the dialectic, that he can satisfy his desire for recognition, is somehow to abandon that which makes him an object, the "Fact of Blackness." The colonized slave thus turns toward the Master to absolve him of his blackness.

The tension one senses in Fanon's text lies in his contradictory analyses of the "Fact of Blackness" and the "Desire for Recognition." His answer to the colonial problem is dictated by his desire to enter into the dialectic and to achieve recognition through violent contest. He points to the American black who is engaged in a war that will eventually end with a "white man and a black man hand in hand."[25] This appears to be a happy synthesis if ever there was one, but Fanon's analysis of the Fact of Blackness makes this optimism untenable.

For Fanon, the most important moment in his analysis is the moment of the fight, the decision to engage in the struggle for recognition. It is this moment that he feels will give the colonized a place that had been denied by the colonizer. But by engaging in the fight, he engages in a battle that he has already lost, or rather that he has been excluded from since the beginning. For us it is this moment of exclusion that is essential. Fanon's phenomenological investigation exposes what Kojève incidentally uncovered in his conflation of methodologies: an epistemological structure prior to the Hegelian dialectic that first and foremost privileges the same and negates the Other. In isolating this moment, Fanon anticipates a new way of trying to understand the Other by making a space for the Other prior to the restrictive classifications of the Western epistemological structure.

In "postcolonial" France, a France of growing diversity, the colonized have come "home." But by moving onto French soil (and here I mean France) the issue of place has become more acute. The Debré Law, intended as a legal codification of the initial moment of visual confirmation and classification that Fanon isolated in his work, shows the extent to which the postcolonized Other must still live in a position of marginality in relation to the Western epistemological structure. To come to terms with a postcolonial world, and not merely a world of postcolonization, will be to come to terms with this moment of subjugation. To be able to make a place for the Other prior to our current understanding so that the economy of Desire will not be the desire for recognition of my value by an Other who is recognizable as the Same, but to desire the respect and knowledge of the Other as Other.

# NOTES

1. Kojève translated Hegel's terms *"Herr"* and *"Knecht"* into the French terms *"Maître"* and *"Esclave"* ("Master" and "Slave"). In English, Hegel's terms are usually translated as "Lord" and "Bondsman" or "Servant," which is closer to Hegel's intended meaning. The first complete translation into French of Hegel's *Phenomenology of Spirit*, by Jean Hyppolite in 1939, retained the translation as *"Maître"* and *"Esclave."*

2. Frantz Fanon, *Black Skin, White Masks*, trans. Charles Lam Markmann (New York: Grove Press, 1967), 220–21.

3. An overview of the lecture series was written by Kojève and published in the January 14, 1939, issue of *Mesures*. This is probably the best-read version of Kojève's interpretation of Hegel's *Phenomenology of Spirit*. The lectures themselves as recorded by Raymond Queneau were published by Gallimard as *Introduction à la lecture de Hegel* in 1947.

4. Alexandre Kojève, *Introduction to the Reading of Hegel*, trans. James H. Nichols Jr. (Ithaca, N.Y.: Cornell University Press, 1993), 5.

5. Kojève, *Introduction to the Reading of Hegel*, 4.

6. Fanon, *Black Skin, White Masks*, 218.

7. Kojève, *Introduction to the Reading of Hegel*, 6–7.

8. Fanon, *Black Skin, White Masks*, 218.

9. Kojève, *Introduction to the Reading of Hegel*, 7.

10. Fanon, *Black Skin, White Masks*, n.8, 220–21.

11. Fanon, *Black Skin, White Masks*, 219.

12. Kojève, *Introduction à la lecture de Hegel*, 449.

13. Frantz Fanon, *Peau Noire Masques Blancs* (Paris: Éditions du Seuil, 1952), 108, my translation.

14. Fanon, *Black Skin, White Masks*, 218.

15. Kojève, *Introduction to the Reading of Hegel*, 4.

16. Fanon, *Black Skin, White Masks*, 110.

17. Fanon, *Black Skin, White Masks*, 110.

18. Fanon, *Peau Noire Masques Blancs*, 108, my translation.

19. Fanon, *Black Skin, White Masks*, 111.

20. Fanon, *Peau Noire Masques Blancs*, 111–12, my translation.

21. Fanon, *Peau Noire Masques Blancs*, 111, my translation.

22. Fanon, *Black Skin, White Masks*, 119.

23. Fanon, *Black Skin, White Masks*, 116.

24. Fanon, *Peau Noire Masques Blancs*, 133, my translation.

25. Fanon, *Black Skin, White Masks*, 222.

**7**

# "HISTORICALLY PARTICULAR USES OF A UNIVERSAL SUBJECT"

*Donna Hunter*

Within a volume devoted to new directions in historiography, this chapter examines an old direction in the historiography of the French Revolution, but from a vantage point afforded by new perspectives. It does so not to further distance new from old or to champion one over the other, but rather to situate beliefs that now seem passé or reactionary in the context of the 1920s and 1930s, when they were a strategic and progressive if not radical response to particular intellectual and political needs. The old direction in question is the one that universalized the achievement of the French Revolution, making it the heritage of all freedom-loving individuals regardless of class, race, or gender. C. L. R. James (1901–1989) and Anna Julia Cooper (1858–1964), Anglophone descendants of Africans brought across the Atlantic as slaves, recognized and celebrated their own liberation in the ideology that had freed the slaves at least briefly during the French Revolution. James, the internationally famous polemicist for world revolution, and Cooper, the less well-known American educator, both wrote about what the French Revolution and the thinking that prepared it had done for the cause of abolition: James, in *Black Jacobins: Toussaint L'Ouverture and the San Domingo Revolution* (1938);[1] and Cooper, in a 1925 dissertation for the Sorbonne on French attitudes toward slavery during the French Revolution, a study that deals extensively with the slave revolt in Saint-Domingue.[2]

In recent years, a number of works have appeared that address the problems and problematic of universality in a culturally diverse world, in response to a general tendency to make difference the focus of theoretical and political debate. *Contingency, Hegemony, Universality: Contemporary Dialogues on the Left* by Judith Butler, Ernesto Laclau, and Slavoj Zizek is an especially intelligent contribution. Its authors talk of reformulating or even constructing universality. "Contingent," "alternative," and "competing" are adjectives applied to "universality," a word that can very logically be made plural. To quote Butler: ". . . the articulation of universality does change over time and changes, in part, precisely by the kinds of claims that are made under its rubric which have not been understood as part of its purview."[3]

Opinion on universality varies. Two examples that follow represent the range I have encountered in texts either on James or on the Haitian revolution. Grant Farred critically assesses James's "proclivity toward universality": "One of the key features of the West Indian's [James's] writing is his recurrent, but undertheorized, proclivity toward universality. This capacity for the universal reveals a minor irony in James's work. While his writing supposedly keeps its sights firmly on a single site, there is in James a tendency to implicitly pronounce on conditions with which the original location has little in common. Therefore, even as James's writing manifests a strong sense of historical locale, his work is regularly underwritten by an appeal to a transhistorical constituency."[4]

Aimé Césaire sees universalism differently in the closing pages of *Toussaint Louverture: La Révolution française et le problème colonial*: "Certainly the law had been decreed, but it still had to be applied. But to which peoples? To the peoples of Europe? To all peoples? To colonial peoples? False universalism has accustomed us to so many deviations, the rights of man have so often been defined as the rights of European man, that the question is hardly superfluous." But false universalism gives way to principles brought to life. "When Toussaint Louverture came, it was to interpret literally the Declaration of the Rights of Man, to show that there was no pariah race, no marginal land, no people that did not count. It was to incarnate and emphasize a principle, indeed to bring it to life. . . . The struggle of Toussaint Louverture was this struggle for the *recognition* of man, and that is why he, and the revolt of the black slaves of Saint-Domingue, occupies such a place in the history of universal civilization."[5]

This chapter examines how, accurately or inaccurately, two rather different persons in two rather different pieces of writing made use of the universal subject fostered by the French Revolution to suit particular objectives. It shows how certain aspects of a mythic supra-French identity could for non-French people be a source of pride, hope, and legitimation. If women were excluded by the Declaration of the Rights of Man, the ideas it introduced also produced enough contradiction to open the door that at first was closed to them. If people of color in French colonies were included by the law of February 4, 1794, and then excluded by Napoleon's *Code noir*, the former could never be entirely revoked once promulgated since it too was the consequence of taking the Declaration of the Rights of Man at its word. James and Cooper are black intellectuals of the early twentieth century who were freed by books and the words they contained, both the books they read and the books they wrote, a sort of liberation that itself exemplifies an old direction upon which the new historiography casts a poignant and instructive light. As Henry Louis Gates Jr. has put it, "What seems clear upon reading the earliest texts by black writers in English . . . is that the production of literature was taken to be the central arena in which persons of African descent could establish and define their status within the human community."[6]

In a volume concentrating on French identity and its discontents, this contribution introduces a note of content, internationalism in place of nationalism, and at moments a shift away from colonialism, race, and gender toward a universal personhood. But those were the moves that persons of color made in certain eras when citing, apostrophizing, or embracing certain facets of French political, cultural, or intellectual identity. This is a measure of how far contemporary debate and struggle have moved from earlier positions and how historically particular and contingent the strategies of past and present are. James and Cooper could make use of French universalism precisely because they were *not* French and therefore did not have to worry about the realities of French racism. They also wrote before the major decolonization struggles and before the rise of large nonwhite populations in France made French racism a more obvious contradiction to French universalism.

The Trinidadian C. L. R. James and the African American Anna Julia Cooper furthered their own analyses of subjugation and emancipation by choosing to believe some part of the French view that the French Revolution was for all peoples and all times. Cooper maintained that "legal slavery and the trade in slaves became an issue—indeed a major issue, an issue that epitomized other issues—in the struggle over the rights of man during the French Revolution" and that the French Revolution would have been more of a revolution if the question of slavery had been addressed more forthrightly. James subscribed to a view that latter-day proponents of the Revolution have held that the violence of that revolution, and for James of all revolution, was the crucible in which a finer world was produced. *Black Jacobins* appeared on the heels of his *World Revolution, 1917–1936: The*

*Rise and Fall of the Communist International,* published in 1937, and in the same year as *A History of Negro Revolt,* a book that opens with a chapter on Saint-Domingue.[7]

An emblem of this intellectual reinterpretation might be found in the way the *Place de la Révolution* became the *Place de la Concorde,* less a renaming than a fantasized convergence of revolution, revolution concluded, and a peaceable and everlasting republic. The change of name is also a rejection if not an erasure of revolution. It first occurred during the Directory, the government that followed the Thermidorian reaction, and was reiterated in 1830 at the start of the July Monarchy to undo the naming of the same space during the Restoration after the last two monarchs of the Old Regime.[8] The abiding or overarching message, as historically wishful or amnesiac as it might be, is the grand one of transforming the discord of the radical phase of the French Revolution into its opposite. Not for nothing was the jet that crossed a great ocean in a single leap, the ocean separating an Anglophone from a Francophone world, called the Concorde. The abstraction, of the *place* and the plane, is a powerful symbol and sign of a deep Frenchness, a *France profonde* not in the usual sense of a corner of France where the culture is venerable and uninterrupted but a France whose achievements are international if not transnational or even universal as well as national or regional.

The question simply put is: What does it mean to "think French"? As opposed to be or look French. And to delimit the question further: what could it mean to think French in the Anglophone world of persons of the African diaspora in the Caribbean or the United States in the 1920s and 1930s?

This chapter had an earlier title, "Translating Slavery: The Reading and Writing of C. L. R. James and Anna Julia Cooper on the Subject of the Saint-Domingue Revolution." It began with an interest in situating *The Black Jacobins* within the Francophone world. How was it received? When was it translated? What use have French historians of the French Revolution or of the revolution in Saint-Domingue made of its argument? There was also the desire to learn what drew the Anglophone James, born in Trinidad and a resident of England, to write a study on a French colony. The answer might seem obvious enough: an intellectual of African descent formed by the colonial culture of the Anglophone Caribbean, a man whose own ancestors, I believe, were brought from Africa as slaves, would, like many a person of African descent, be interested in the story of the only successful slave revolt, the first colony to be decolonized, and the establishment of the first and most long-lived black republic, the Haitian Republic.

But it seemed that the crossovers of language, political program, and intellectual tradition between the Anglophone and Francophone Caribbean and between England, the United States, and France were worth examining, especially in light of the work that has appeared on James as a major if maverick Marxist thinker since his death in May 1989 and in light of recent studies on colonialism.[9]

In fact, the earlier title of this chapter was drawn directly from one such study, *Translating Slavery: Gender and Race in French Women's Writing, 1783–1823*, a volume edited by Doris Y. Kadish and Françoise Massardier-Kenney.[10] This book literally translates a group of writings by French women in France on the question of slavery, writings by Olympe de Gouges, Mme de Staël, and the novelist Claire Duras. But it also figuratively translates the selections because it reads them across the divide between the situation of women residing in France and the situation of slaves in the French colonies. It also reads them across the divide between their time and their language and our moment and not only the English language but also the concerns about gender and race that have been articulated in an Anglophone intellectual and political community. Kadish has also published an article that looks at perceptions of the "black terror" unleashed by the revolution in Saint-Domingue from a female point of view.[11] It is an article that openly works with a Jamesian (C. L. R. Jamesian) model, by shifting the Jacobins and the Terror from Paris to Saint-Domingue, a move that she does not question or contextualize, so accepted has the idea of "black Jacobins" become.

Such shifts in gender, race, language, and place opened my eyes to a possible alignment between James's book and a doctoral dissertation written in French by an African American woman, Anna Julia Cooper, *L'Attitude de la France à l'égard de l'esclavage pendant la Révolution*. Cooper defended her dissertation at the Sorbonne in 1925 when she was sixty-six years old, one of many remarkable achievements in her long life. Born in slavery in 1858, Cooper earned both her B.A. and M.A. from Oberlin College and spent many decades as a teacher and administrator at Dunbar High School in Washington, D.C., a public school famous for educating the children of that city's black middle class, children who went on to distinguished careers in many different fields. In 1988, Cooper's dissertation was translated into English, so great was the interest in making available to those who read English and not French what this African American woman had had to say.[12]

But why would Cooper have chosen to study what the French had thought about slavery in the first place, or to write her dissertation in France for a

degree from what was then the premier French university? She was interested in what had been written during the Enlightenment that argued the
abolition of slavery, in particular the writings of the Abbé Raynal, author of
the once famous and once again famous *L'Histoire des deux Indes*. She was
interested as well in the work of the Société des Amis des Noirs and in the
legislation implemented, when the Jacobins were in power, that abolished
slavery for the first time in all French colonies in February 1794. Were her
reasons for gravitating toward what the French had said and written about
slavery or revolution close in some way to those of James? What did French
thinking and the fate of the French colony of Saint-Domingue mean to the
two of them? It is true that Cooper's work as an intellectual and educator fits
into the moralizing if not moralistic black middle-class ideology of racial
uplift, hardly James's point of view.[13] But I would argue that for these two
Anglophone persons of African descent, persons whose personal or longer
family history included the experience of slavery, "thinking French" was to
join forces with a venerable radical tradition.

   If James restored agency and responsibility for the Saint-Domingue revolution to the slaves, men and women who freed themselves through their
own thinking and actions, he nonetheless gave a great deal of credit to the
Abbé Raynal for having planted the idea in the head of the young Toussaint
Louverture, one of the rare slaves who was literate, that he might be the
black liberator the abbé had prophesied. And, more significant when one
asks about the French connection, James titled his book *Black Jacobins*
even though the Jacobin Club in Paris had little or nothing to do with revolutionary thinking or action in Saint-Domingue. For Stuart Hall, James
"shows the connections *between* the ideas of the French revolution in Paris
and the forms those ideas took in Haiti for black French citizens, and in so
doing, establishes the Haitian revolution as an integral part of the French
revolution. . . . Haiti becomes another theatre of the revolution—an astonishing idea! The revolutionary forces in Haiti are, precisely, *black* Jacobins."[14]

   The Jacobin in "black Jacobins" was thus used transhistorically if not
somewhat ahistorically.[15] The "white Jacobin" was seen as a legendary political radical who although not a person of the people supported their cause
and advancement. By extension (and it is a surprising extension as Hall's exclamation point indicates), the black Jacobin is the man of the people who
secures his own freedom from slavery as well as monarchy. For James,
Michelet is the greatest historian of the French Revolution—greater than
Jaurès, the socialist, or Mathiez, the admirer of Lenin—not because he devotes attention to the cause of the slaves in the French colonies (he does

not), but, I would speculate, because he is an eloquent and passionate sup-
porter of the people, the revolutionary proletariat in James's terms.[16]

In 1949, *Black Jacobins* appeared in French as *Les Jacobins noirs*.[17] It
was translated by Pierre Naville, a Marxist sociologist born in 1904 and thus
an almost exact contemporary of James's, who published studies on work
and professionalism in the twentieth century and on eighteenth-century
materialism and Marxism. In his preface Naville explains how both timely
and prophetic he finds James's book to be. It describes how a French colony
fell, something that was happening and needed to happen as Naville saw it
in all those countries, Indochina in particular, where France was then still
overlord. (France's later loss of Indochina was, of course, due to the same
cause that brought about its loss of Saint-Domingue: a war for independence fought by those who had been colonized if not enslaved.) When one
looks for traces or acknowledgment of James's thinking in two of the most
famous Marxist studies of the French Revolution, Soboul's work on the
*sans-culottes* and Guérin's on the *bras-nus*, there are none.[18] Guérin's 1956
work on decolonization in the West Indies makes extensive use of several
works by Eric Williams, a protégé of James's, but makes only three brief references to two publications by James (neither *Black Jacobins* ).[19]

James's views on "permanent revolution" at the time he wrote *Black
Jacobins*—not to mention his involvement with Trotsky and Trotskyism—
probably put his study at odds with the Stalinist interpretation of revolution,
and of the French Revolution, favored by the French Communist Party
(PCF). In *Black Marxism,* Cedric Robinson simply states, "It was as a Trot-
skyist that James would author *The Black Jacobins*." And adds, "it is not difficult to unearth a critique of Stalinism" within his study of the Haitian and
French revolutions.[20] The Stalinism of the PCF could explain why James's
book was consequently overlooked or actively ignored even after it was
available in French translation. Naville engaged with the text in 1949 because the end of the French colonial empire was a high priority for him, politically and ethically. He also engaged with it because he remained loyal to
Trotsky's views. In 1928 he had been excluded from the PCF because of
these loyalties; in 1945 he was forced to abandon an academic career in psychology, a discipline dominated by members of the PCF, for one in sociology.[21] Even if James broke with Trotsky well before 1949, Naville did not; it
was as a Trotskyite that he translated the work that James had written as a
Trotskyite eleven years earlier.

To return to the pairing of James and Cooper, certain aspects of the
French Revolution had a significance for them that transcended (the word
is used advisedly) many (but not all) of the historical details about the

French Revolution, French abolitionist thinking, or the Jacobins in particular. They are not France's discontents, but an earlier generation of
non-French people who found inspiration and legitimation for their own
identity as free persons of color in the heritage of the French Revolution.
There were other Anglophone blacks thinking about Saint-Domingue if
not "thinking French" in 1938. Jacob Lawrence, twenty-one in 1938, did a
series of forty-one paintings on Toussaint Louverture and the Saint-
Domingue Revolution. He attributed his interest in the theme to the intellectual and cultural atmosphere of the Harlem Renaissance. In an interview
in the 1980s he specifically mentions men on street corners talking to each
other and addressing passersby about the relevance of Toussaint.[22] In addition to what he heard in the streets of Harlem, Lawrence might have been
stirred by the play *Haiti* by W. E. B. Du Bois that was produced
in 1938 at "the Negro branch," as it was called, of the Federal Theatre in
Harlem.[23]

Claims of universality are not the topic of this volume, far from it, but a
now fairly discredited position exercised a powerful sway over intellectuals
and political activists all over the world for close to one hundred and fifty
years (if not longer). If the Rights of Man as first promulgated did not include women, men without property, or persons of particular religions or
professions who had traditionally been discriminated against in France, it
left the door open for those groups to make a case that the Reason (capital
"r") that underlay the Rights could not rationally be denied them. A case in
point is a poster designed in 1989 by Tibor Kalman to commemorate the bicentennial of the Declaration of the Rights of Man. Over the face of a black
woman seen in extreme close-up, the full text of "Article 35" is printed:
"When the government violates the rights of the people, insurrection is,
for the people and for every part of the people, the most sacred of rights
and the most indispensable of duties." There is no reference to the abolition of slavery, the end of colonialism, feminist struggle, or opposition to
racism, but the image makes all those interpretations possible.[24]

In conclusion, I would like us to see James and Cooper as people of the
book, a book written in French as well as English. James's tombstone bears
this interpretation out: it is an open book.[25] One page bears his full name,
his dates, and the inscription, epithet as well as epitaph, "A Man of Letters."
The facing page has an excerpt from his book on cricket, *Beyond a Boundary* (1963), a penetrating study of the colonial mind and also something of
an autobiography: "Times would pass, old empires would fall and new ones
take their place, the relations of countries and the relations of classes had
to change, before I discovered that it is not quality of goods and utility

which matter, but movement; not where you are or what you have, but where you have come from, where you are going and the rate at which you are getting there."

James's grave is just outside the small town in Trinidad where, as a boy, he lived in a house overlooking a cricket green. A photograph of James from the 1940s shows him in what, I think, would have been the attire he wore to cover cricket matches, his work when he first arrived in England.[26] The blazer and flannels (as well as the cigarette and body English) are those of one "England made," who, to paraphrase further the title of Graham Greene's early novel, *England Made Me* (1935), was also unmade and re-made by the colonial experience and his own examination of it.

Before his death, James set the terms of his funeral very strictly: the Trinidadian government was in no way to be involved; instead a trade union with which he had early been associated, the Oilfield Workers, was put in charge. In the mid-1930s, a strike by these workers set off repercussions throughout the Caribbean. That strike has been said to have been one of the catalysts for *Black Jacobins*, an account of other black workers improving their lot through concerted revolt. Did James or the union design the gravestone? In either case, it is both revealing and touching, and at first glance, surprising. C. L. R. James a "man of letters" like the writers buried in Poets' Corner? But surprising only until one remembers the power of the book, the power of reading and writing books, the power of booklearning in the lives of the disenfranchised and the dispossessed. The power of books and bookish ideas has had its effect not only in personal lives (an enlarged self-identity not to mention upward social mobility) but also in the polities people so empowered have striven to establish.

To return to the start of this chapter, we might listen to the comments of Henry Louis Gates Jr. on the "shared text of blackness": "If writing, then, was a crucial terrain of black struggles in the Age of Enlightenment, the concern to make themselves heard—that is, to inscribe their voices in the written word—was a primary motivation for those former slaves who chose to narrate the stories of their enslavement and redemption." Put in other words, those ex-slaves "met the challenge of the Enlightenment by writing themselves into being."

> Precisely because successive Western cultures have privileged written art over oral and musical forms, the writing of black people in Western languages has remained political, implicitly or explicitly, regardless of its intent or its subject. The very proliferation of black written voices, and the concomitant political import of them, led fairly rapidly in our literary history to demands both

for the coming of a "black Shakespeare or Dante," as one critic put it in 1925, and for an authentic black printed voice of deliverance, whose presence would, by definition, put an end to all claims of the black person's subhumanity. In the black tradition, writing became the visible sign, the commodity of exchange, the text and technology of reason.[27]

If for forty years, from 1949 until his death in 1989, James planned a full-length critical study of Shakespeare and if Anthony Bogues, the author of a study of James's early political thought, could liken him to Caliban, leading the reader to think of James (or the black intellectual in general) outwitting Prospero (the white magus who controls reality and irreality on a Caribbean island),[28] what can we make of Anna Julia Cooper's more modest projects and her biographers' less radical claims for her as a thinker? Are James and Cooper in the end too different to be paired?

Here too Gates is an aid in understanding the importance of Cooper's autobiography, *A Voice from the South* (1892). In a foreword he characterizes it as "one of the original texts of the black feminist movement": "It was Cooper who first analyzed the fallacy of referring to 'the Black man' when speaking of black people and who argued that just as white men cannot speak through the consciousness of black men, neither can black *men* 'fully and adequately . . . reproduce the exact Voice of the Black Woman.'"

Further testament to the very large reach of books such as Cooper's comes in the final sentences of the same foreword when Gates states that the series in which Cooper's autobiography is reprinted, The Schomburg Library of Nineteenth-Century Black Women Writers, is dedicated to the memory of his mother, Pauline Augusta Coleman Gates, who died in 1987, a year before the series began to appear.: "It was she who inspired in me the love of learning and the love of literature. I have encountered in the books of this set no will more determined, no courage more noble, no mind more sublime, no self more celebratory of the achievements of all Afro-American women, and indeed of life itself, than her own.[29] A mother whose will, courage, mind, and self are the equal of those pioneering figures in Afro-American literature inspired a love of learning and literature in her son. She is the reader who makes the connection with writers that then leads another reader to writing, not to mention the re-publication of many overlooked writers.

James's tombstone—it appears to be made of aggregate slabs (cement with pebbles mixed in) and has a simple base, one could not say pedestal, of larger stones cemented together—puts one in mind of the monumental stacks of the Bibliothèque Nationale of France (*"four open books placed*

*face to face,*" in the words of the architect, emphasis his). This is the evocation of the mind, at the same time lofty and silly, that makes the French a
people of the book, and France the storehouse for books as well as the place
where more will be written.[30] As outlandish as the conceit is, there is a way
in which a germ of its meaning contains aspects of what the French put into
words and into books in the eighteenth century, a germ that has taken root
in other soils in other seasons. If this chapter argues for a measure of liberation through literacy and grand ideas, it does so out of respect for James
and Cooper.

## NOTES

I would like to thank Tyler Stovall for encouraging me from the start to explore my interest in James and *Black Jacobins* and for carefully reading what in the end I wrote.
His review essay, "Histories of Race in France," *French Politics, Culture & Society* 18,
no. 3 (fall 2000), was particularly helpful in distinguishing the various roles and guises
that universality has assumed regarding race and identity. Equally valuable were many
passages in *Paris Noir: African Americans in the City of Light* (Boston: Houghton Mifflin, 1996), especially those pertaining to Anna Julia Cooper. I would also like to thank
Jorge Canizares Esguerra for his supportive response to my work, the staff at the
Smyrna Press for their prompt response to a query, and Vévé Clark for instructively as
well as graciously giving me a copy of *Black Jacobins* in the bicentennial summer of
1989. My warm thanks as well to Georges Van Den Abbeele for his patience.

    1. First published in England by Secker and Warburg; published later the same
year in the United States by Dial Press. A second revised edition appeared twenty-
five years later, as a "Vintage Book" (New York: Random House, 1963). The author
added an appendix, "From Toussaint L'Ouverture to Fidel Castro," that in itself is
justly famous.
    2. *L'Attitude de la France à l'égard de l'esclavage pendant la Révolution* trans-
lated into English as *Slavery and the French Revolutionists (1788–1815)* by Frances
Richardson Keller (Lewiston, N.Y.: Edwin Mellen Press, n.d.). Cooper was only the
fourth African American woman to earn a doctorate.
    3. Judith Butler, Ernesto Laclau, and Slavoj Žižek, *Contingency, Hegemony,
Universality: Contemporary Dialogues on the Left* (London: Verso, 2000), 163. Two
other titles that point to this contemporary concern for separating spurious or
empty universality from more valuable forms are Alessandro Ferrara's *Reflective
Authenticity: Rethinking the Project of Modernity* (London: Routledge, 1998); and
Lynda S. Bell, Andrew J. Nathan, and Ilan Peleg, eds., *Negotiating Culture and Hu-
man Rights* (New York: Columbia University Press, 2001). Sue Peabody's *"There
Are No Slaves in France": The Political Culture of Race and Slavery in the Ancien*

*Régime* (New York: Oxford University Press, 1966) trenchantly brings out the an-
tinomy that can exist between thinking in metropole and colony over questions of
identity and rights. Not to be overlooked are *Against Race: Imagining Political Culture Beyond the Color Line* (Cambridge, Mass.: Harvard University Press, 2000),
Paul Gilroy's brave and challenging book, and Naomi Schor's incisive article, "The
Crisis of French Universalism," *Yale French Studies* 100 (2001): 43–64. Unfortunately, I discovered the issue of *Differences* devoted to universalism (vol. 7, no. 1,
spring 1995) too late to shape my thinking in this article.

4. Grant Farred, *Rethinking C. L. R. James* (Cambridge, Mass.: Blackwell,
1996), 5.

5. Aimé Césaire, *Toussaint Louverture: La Révolution française et le problème
colonial* (Paris: Présence Africaine, 1981), 342–43. Hegel, and with him Marx and
many a Marxist, is inclined to give history past and history future such a sweep.

6. "The Talking Book," Introduction to *Pioneers of the Black Atlantic: Five Slave
Narratives from the Enlightenment, 1772–1815,* ed. Henry Louis Gates Jr. and
William L. Andrews (Washington, D.C.: Counterpoint, 1998), 2.

7. Reissued as *A History of Pan-African Revolt* (Chicago: Charles H. Kerr, 1995).

8. See Todd Porterfield, "The Obelisk at the Place de la Concorde," in *The Allure of Empire: Art in the Service of French Imperialism, 1798–1836* (Princeton,
N.J.: Princeton University Press, 1998), 13–41.

9. Since his death in 1989 a great number of James's writings have been printed
for the first time, reprinted or gathered together in anthologies. Among the reprints
are many items that previously had a very limited circulation. Three works are especially noteworthy: *American Civilization,* ed. Anna Grimshaw and Keith Hart
(Oxford: Blackwell, 1993); *The C. L. R. James Reader,* ed. Anna Grimshaw (Oxford:
Blackwell, 1992); and *C. L. R. James on the "Negro Question,"* ed. Scott McLemee
(Jackson: University of Mississippi Press, 1996).

Among the interpretive and biographical studies, the following stand out: *Rethink-
ing C. L. R. James,* ed. Farred, 1996; *C. L. R. James's Caribbean,* ed. Paget Henry and
Paul Buhle (Durham, N.C.: Duke University Press, 1992); *C. L. R. James: His Intel-
lectual Legacies,* ed. Selwyn R. Cudjoe and William E. Cain (Amherst: University of
Massachusetts Press, 1995), especially "*The Black Jacobins*: An Assessment," 81–160;
Kent Worcester, *C. L. R. James: A Political Biography* (Albany: State University of
New York Press, 1995); and Paul Buhle, *C. L. R. James: His Life and Work* (Chicago:
Sojourner Truth, 1981).

The recent literature on colonialism and postcolonialism is vast. Srinivas Arava-
mudan's *Tropicopolitans: Colonialism and Agency, 1688–1804* (Durham, N.C.:
Duke University Press, 1999) is especially thought-provoking given my topic, in
particular the last chapter, "Tropicalizing the Enlightenment" (289–325). Neferti
Tadiar's "The Dream-Work of Modernity: The Sentimental Education of Imperial
France," [*boundary 2* 22:1 (spring 1995)] was equally stimulating.

Studies on suffrage, rights, and citizenship have also been a help in sorting out the
extension of the Rights of Man to women and people of color: Joan Wallach Scott,

*Only Paradoxes to Offer: French Feminists and the Rights of Man* (Cambridge, Mass.: Harvard University Press, 1996); Pierre Rosanvallon, *Le Sacre du citoyen: Histoire du suffrage universel en France* (Paris: Gallimard, 1992) and *Le Peuple introuvable: histoire de la Représentation démocratique en France* (Paris: Gallimard, 1998); and Sophie Wahnich, *L'impossible citoyen: L' étranger dans le discours de la Révolution française* (Paris: Albin Michel, 1997), especially "Nationaliser la raison universelle, universaliser la loi nationale," 170–85, and "Conclusion: Relancer les dés de l'universel," 347–62. Also very useful was "Une citoyenneté paradoxale, affranchis, colonisés et citoyens des vieilles colonies" by Françoise Vergès, in *L'Abolition de l'esclavage: Un combat pour les droits de l'homme*, ed. Chantal Georgel, Françoise Vergès, and Alain Vivien (Paris: Editions Complexe, 1998), 17–44.

There was not time to consider the numerous, and usually conservative, studies on the supposed universality of French language and culture, from Rivarol's *Discours sur l'universalité de la langue française* (1784) to Manuel de Diéguez's *Essai sur l'universalité de la France* (1991).

10. Doris Y. Kadish and Françoise Massardier-Kenney, eds., *Translating Slavery: Gender and Race in French Women's Writing, 1783–1823* (Kent, Ohio: Kent State University Press, 1994).

11. "The Black Terror: Women's Responses to Slave Revolts in Haiti," *The French Review* 68, no. 4 (March 1995): 668–80.

12. See note 3 for publication details of the translation. On Cooper, see Leona C. Gabel, *From Slavery to the Sorbonne and Beyond: The Life and Writings of Anna J. Cooper* (Northampton, Mass.: Department of History of Smith College, 1982), Smith College Studies in History, vol. XLIX; and Karen Baker-Fletcher, *A Singing Something: Womanist Reflections on Anna Julia Cooper* (New York: Crossroad, 1994). Cooper herself wrote an autobiography that was published when she was thirty-four, *A Voice from the South by a Black Woman of the South* (1892); this volume has been reissued in The Schomburg Library of Nineteenth-Century Black Women Writers (New York: Oxford University Press, 1988) with an introduction by Mary Helen Washington and a foreword by Henry Louis Gates Jr.

13. On the ideology of racial uplift, with which Cooper is closely associated, see chapter 5 in Kevin K. Gaines, *Uplifting the Race: Black Leadership, Politics, and Culture in the Twentieth Century* (Chapel Hill: University of North Carolina Press, 1996).

14. "Breaking Bread with History: C. L. R. James and the Black Jacobins," Stuart Hall interviewed by Bill Schwarz, *History Workshop Journal*, no. 46 (autumn 1998): 25. The featured theme for this issue was "Haiti Remembered." Hall goes on to say that James enlarges the historical role of the revolutionary forces by calling them black Jacobins. I would like to thank Jonathan Beecher for this valuable reference.

15. For a pointed examination of the issues involved in calling the Haitian revolutionaries "black Jacobins," see John D. Garrigus, "White Jacobins/Black Jacobins: Bringing the Haitian and French Revolutions Together in the Classroom, " *French*

*Historical Studies* 23, no. 2 (spring 2000): 259–75. The "back formation," "white Jacobins," points to what had previously been an unspoken element in the name "Jacobins." It is "black Jacobins" who draw attention to "white Jacobins," something James was aware of when he first baptized blacks "Jacobins." Whether the blacks who made the Haitian Revolution were in fact Jacobins (i.e., members of a Jacobin Club or proponents of the views of such clubs) is basically immaterial. Through the thinking revealed by their actions, the black Jacobins were what James understood Jacobins to be at their revolutionary best. In addition to clarifying what was meant or could be meant by "Jacobin" during the French Revolution (and in 1938), "the Revolution in Saint-Domingue/Haiti poses the question 'Who is French?'," as Garrigus puts it (p. 259), a question central to this volume on French identity.

Cedric Robinson astutely points out that James, a black Victorian, needed to become what he understood by "black Jacobin" before he could write his famous book. See "C. L. R. James and the Black Radical Tradition," in Robinson's *Black Marxism: The Making of the Black Radical Tradition* (London: Zed Press, 1983; Chapel Hill: University of North Carolina Press, 2000), 241–86.

16. Bibliography to *The Black Jacobins*, rev. ed. (New York: Vintage Books, 1963), 383–84. I base my speculation on Michelet's frequent and highly charged evocations of "le peuple" as a major force in French history, a tendency Barthes, for one, draws attention to in his study on *Michelet* [Michelet (Paris: Seuil, 1975), 160–61]. Michelet's *Le peuple* (1846) is the prime example of this historiographical and rhetorical tendency.

For recent and excellent analyses of the Haitian Revolution, see chapters 5 and 6 in Robin Blackburn, *The Overthrow of Colonial Slavery, 1776–1848* (London: Verso, 1988), and Carolyn E. Fick, *The Making of Haiti: The Saint Domingue Revolution from Below* (Knoxville: University of Tennessee Press, 1990). Both Blackburn and Fick express their debt to James and share the position he stated in the foreword to the 1980 edition of *Black Jacobins* (London: Allison & Busby, 1980): "I made up my mind that I would write a book in which Africans or people of African descent instead of constantly being the object of other peoples' exploitation and ferocity would themselves be taking action on a grand scale and shaping other people to their own needs" (v). Or, more succinctly, all three are convinced that "it was the slaves who had made the revolution" (vi).

17. *Les Jacobins noirs. Toussaint Louverture et la révolution de Saint-Domingue* (Paris: Gallimard, 1949). The book was reviewed favorably in *Les Temps modernes* 5, no. 52 (février 1950): 1527–29, by Louis Ménard, for whom nonetheless: "There is a problem: to what extent was the framework of bourgeois principles that served Toussaint not a new form of exploitation of the black proletariat, more subtle but thus also more removed from a true liberation?" James may insist on the role of the *enragés*, but Ménard sees bourgeois principles at work, not the spontaneous movement of the masses.

Cedric Robinson points to this same contradiction: "the ambivalent pride of place presumed for this Westernized ideologue [Toussaint]" who had former slaves hunted down and executed when they did not accept his compromises (*Black Marxism*, p. 278). For James, "Toussaint's failure was the failure of enlightenment, not of darkness" (*Black Jacobins*, p. 288; cited p. 278, *Black Marxism*). For Robinson, this is a sad case of rationalization. Perhaps James and Robinson are both right in their different ways: the Enlightenment had its failures; bourgeois revolution was bourgeois; and James did pride himself on being Westernized, a "Black European" in his own words. The claims of the universal subject and his rights can be extended to transmute bourgeois values into effective emancipatory discourse and action, but then again those same claims can contract.

I would like to thank Margaret Gordon and Elisabeth Remak-Honnef, both librarians at the University of California–Santa Cruz, for their assistance in locating reviews of various editions of both *Jacobins noirs* and *Black Jacobins*. No easy task.

18. Albert Soboul, *Les sans-culottes parisiens en l'an II*, 1958; 2nd ed. 1964; Daniel Guérin, *La Lutte des classes sous la Première République*, 1946; reissued, 2 vols., 1968; abridged under the title *Bourgeois et bras-nus*, 1973. In the year *La Lutte des classes* first appeared, James completed a translation, with the intention, one would suppose, of seeing the book published in English.

19. Daniel Guérin, *Les Antilles décolonisées* with an introduction by Aimé Césaire (Paris: Présence Africaine, 1956); translated as *The West Indies and Their Future* (London: Dennis Dobson, 1961). James, unlike Eric Williams, is identified only in the notes, not the text; *Black Jacobins* is not cited. Kent Worcester maintains that Guérin's book owes a great deal to exchanges between the author and James. Cf. his *C. L. R. James: A Political Biography* (Albany: State University of New York Press, 1996), 222. Guérin and James did maintain a decades-long correspondence. Williams and James, on the other hand, were sharply at odds about independence in the West Indies, but not before 1960–1961, several years after Guérin's book first appeared. The less suspicious explanation might be that Williams was a better source for a book on the future of the West Indies since he, not James, wrote at length about that part of the world in the twentieth century.

20. Robinson, *Black Marxism*, 265.

21. Michel Eliard, "Présentation," *Naville, la passion de la connaissance*, ed. Eliard (Toulouse: Presses Universitaires du Mirail, 1996), 12. For more on the political ramifications of Naville's intellectual choices, see Patricia Vannier, "Pierre Naville: de l'écriture automatique à l'écriture de l'automation" in the same volume.

22. Ellen Harkins Wheat, *Jacob Lawrence, American Painter* (Seattle: University of Washington Press, 1986).

23. William Dubois [sic], *Haiti* (New York: Random House, 1938); one of three plays in a volume of Federal Theatre Plays. To develop the theme of the "people of the book" a little further, mention deserves to be made of a bronze statue of Du Bois at Fisk University that shows him standing next to a stack of books. The mature Du Bois faces the building that was the library at the time the statue was erected; he was also exceedingly eminent when he was a sixteen-year-old undergraduate

at this historically black college. Books read and books written cross paths along the sightlines from the statue to the former library.

James also wrote a play about the Saint Domingue Revolution, *Toussaint L'Ouverture*, that was performed in London in 1936, two years before *Black Jacobins* was published or even in large part written. None other than Paul Robeson played the title role. There was talk of Eisenstein making a filmed version with Robeson in the lead. A revised version of the play, adapted by Dexter Lyndersay and James, is reprinted under the title *The Black Jacobins* in Anna Grimshaw, ed., *The C. L. R. James Reader* (Oxford: Blackwell, 1992), 67–111. More recently Peter Blake has turned the revised play into an opera of the same name.

24. For a reproduction of the poster, see Liz Farrelly, *Tibor Kalman: Design and Undesign* (London: Thames and Hudson, 1998), 16. Article 35 occurs in the Declaration of the Rights of Man and the Citizen of An I (June 23, 1793). Kalman's poster was one in a series commissioned for the *bicentenaire* by a French advertising agency known for its political interventions in the public sphere. For the full set, see *ARTIS 89, Pour les droits de l'homme: histoire(s) image(s) parole(s)* (Paris: ARTIS 89, 1989).

25. For a photograph of the gravesite in Tunapuna, see K. Worcester, *C. L. R. James: A Political Biography*, p. 212. Worcester also reproduces separately the face of the tombstone that bears the passage from *Beyond a Boundary*. Tellingly, this reproduction of James's "last page" is opposite the first page of his introduction (p. x).

26. Photograph of James from 1940s on cover of *Rethinking C. L. R. James*, ed. Farred, 1996. Between 1938 and 1953 James was in the United States, where he did not cover cricket matches. If my speculation about what he wore when he did is correct and if the photograph is, as it is said to be, from the 1940s, then James's Anglicisms were even more striking in an American context.

27. "Introduction," *Pioneers of the Black Atlantic*, 3–4.

28. *Caliban's Freedom. The Early Political Thought of C. L. R. James* (London: Pluto Press, 1997). The first chapter of this book begins with the following quotation from *Beyond a Boundary*: "To establish his own identity Caliban, after three centuries, must himself pioneer into regions Caesar never knew." The "regions Caesar never knew" are outside western Europe and the Mediterranean basin, regions Caesar obviously knew. A paraphrase of the same quotation, minus the reference to Caliban, forms the dedication to *C. L. R. James: His Intellectual Legacies*, ed. Cudjoe and Cain, 1995: "To the people of the Caribbean who, in pioneering regions that Caesar never knew, made C. L. R. James who and what he became."

29. "In Her Own Voice," *A Voice from the South* (New York: Oxford University Press, 1988), xiii and xxii.

30. For differing views on the symbolism of the L-shaped towers that house the books, see Dominique Jamet and Hélène Waysbord, "History, Philosophy, and Ambitions of the Bibliothèque de France" and Anthony Vidler, "Books in Space: Tradition and Transparency in the Bibliothèque de France," in *Future Libraries*, ed. R. Howard Bloch and Carla Hesse (Berkeley: University of California Press, 1995),

74–79 and 137–56, respectively. The architect's own words are on p. 147. The essays were originally published as a special issue of *Representations* 42 (spring 1993). That issue was preceded by a conference at the University of California–Berkeley, on the "Très Grande Bibliothèque and the Future of the Library." For symbolism of another sort, consider that François Mitterand announced the idea of the TGB on Bastille Day, 1988.

One passage from Vidler's essay (pp. 151–52) warrants quotation since it neatly ties the "Très Grande Bibliothèque" to universalism, a false universalism that makes James's gravestone a true and effecting monument to productive and particular uses of universalism.

> For Perrault [the architect, Dominique Perrault], . . . the question was precisely the production of a *universal* [emphasis Vidler's] object, one that might serve as the open signifier of a host of universalisms: the universalism of the classical tradition; the universalism of knowledge, and, more importantly for the scheme's immediate resonance in the Mitterand circle, social if not Socialist universalism. Supporters of this latter form of universalism, identified with the French republican tradition and more generally with the values of the French Enlightenment, have found in the Perrault library a rallying point against a host of contemporary particularisms based in identity politics and given special urgency by the pressures of the post-colonial condition. Its reassuringly abstract forms, tied to no specific agenda, provide an implicit solution—or at least an impartial and undifferentiated coverall—to the multiple and violently competing visions of "France" and "Europe" currently breaking up the traditional Socialist coalition.

# FOR A CARIBBEAN INTERTEXT: ON SOME READINGS OF MARYSE CONDÉ'S *CROSSING THE MANGROVE*

*Jean Jonassaint*

Among North American literary critics, there is a tendency to read Maryse Condé's *Traversée de la Mangrove* [*Crossing the Mangrove*] (1989) in relation to William Faulkner's works, especially *As I Lay Dying* (1930). In so doing, these critics situate this Francophone novel within a North American rather than a Caribbean literary tradition. Moreover, the most important and definitive "transtextual" relationships (as Gérard Genette defines the term[1]) with Condé's text seem to be the following: (a) the Caribbean oral tradition (more accurately the *oraliture* as the Haitian critics say or the *orature* to use the African Anglophone critical term[2]), especially that associated with wakes and funerals, as Condé notes in an interview with Françoise Pfaff;[3] and (b) the Haitian novel, *Gouverneurs de la Rosée* [*Masters of the Dew*] by Jacques Roumain, a passage from which is cited in Condé's novel for its formative role on one of her characters, Carmélien.[4]

How can such a critical oversight be explained? Especially since Roumain was the first Francophone Caribbean novelist to have his work compared with Faulkner, by none other than Michel Serres in his article "Christ noir" for the journal *Critique*.[5] What do such *partial* readings of Francophone literature have to tell us? These are the questions that concern me while I try at the same time to reveal the complexity of these allogeneous Francophone texts.[6] In order to answer these questions, I will dwell more specifically on one such transtextual relationship, that of Condé's novel to Roumain's work, for it is among the most obvious cases as evidenced by the intertextuality and metatextuality of the extended citation in *Crossing the Mangrove* of a fragment taken from *Masters of the Dew* along with the commentary that surrounds the citation. Thus, by following out these unbeaten paths, I will try to read *Crossing the Mangrove* as a rewriting of *Masters of the Dew*.

Of course, I am not in the least attempting to reduce Condé's text to a version or (even a loose) adaptation of Roumain's novel. And, still less, am I interested in challenging any connections between this story and other novels, contemporary or otherwise, including Faulkner's *As I Lay Dying* as Michael Lucey has done, or Brontë's *Wuthering Heights* as shown by R. H. Mitsch, even though these comparative studies merit some reservations.[7] What I do maintain, however, is that the transtextual relations (intertextuality, metatextuality, hypertextuality, and even architextuality) between *Crossing the Mangrove* and *Masters of the Dew* are fundamental and decisive. And the critical silence or quasi-silence about this transtextual relation is symptomatic of a problem that goes well beyond the analysis of Condé's work to implicate Francophone studies in general.

In fact, in the body of criticism I have read on *Crossing the Mangrove*, (comprising more than twenty articles or book chapters), I have found only six brief references to Roumain. Françoise Lionnet (without ever using the term) underscores an architextual relationship between *Traversée* and *Gouverneurs*. Both, according to Lionnet, place themselves in "the tradition of peasant novels."[8] Leah D. Hewitt and Lydie Moudileno note a certain "intertextuality" between the two works.[9] But none of them, it seems to me, perceive, much less reveal, the fundamental web of transtextual relations between the two novels. Besides, this is in no way the purpose of these articles.

To the best of my knowledge, with Yvette Bozon-Scalzitti's "La Mort de Francis Sancher" (1998), where it is stated that *Crossing* is "a rewriting of *Masters of the Dew*" in a short but interesting demonstration,[10] the only notable exception is Christiane Ndiaye's 1996 article, "De Césaire à Condé: quelques retours au pays natal," which completely slipped by me in 1998 while I was writing a first version of the results of this research,[11] just as it has escaped the attention of many of Condé's exegetes ever since. Indeed, both De Souza—in a brief and interesting comparison of the issue of the return to the native land in *Masters of the Dew* and *Crossing the Mangrove*— and Larrier—in drawing parallels between Manuel and Sancher, and the metaphor of the *man-tree* and the "return to the native land" motif—fail to consider Ndiaye's work or even Bozon-Scalzitti's article.[12] The same omissions are found in Fulton, Hayes, and Malena—who appear to be unaware of Roumain's text.[13] Despite the fact that Ndiaye does not specifically address the parallels between *Masters of the Dew* and *Crossing the Mangrove*, she does however claim that Condé's novel reconsiders the "story of the return to the native land," as does Roumain's novel. This argument comes close to Condé's in "Order, Disorder, Freedom, and the West Indian Writer." In this article, which Ndiaye does not mention, Condé states that "Like *Return to My Native Land*, *Masters of the Dew* became a sacred text, a fundamental text. According to a Guadeloupean critic, every West Indian novel is nothing but the rewriting of *Masters of the Dew* and *Return to My Native Land*."[14] Moreover, it is striking that Ndiaye ignores the relation between Condé and Roumain in both her title and analysis. Ndiaye begins her analysis of Condé's novel by claiming: "The year following the publication of *Solibo Magnifique* [*Solibo Magnificent*], Maryse Condé published her novel *Crossing the Mangrove*. Its parallels with previous similar texts is quite evident: the novel also tells the story of a 'foreigner' whose 'return' radically transforms the lives of those around him, generally for the better, but in his own case, for worse."[15] However, no other text in her entire corpus (Aimé Césaire's *Cahier d'un retour au pays natal* [*Return to My Native Land*], Joseph Zobel's *La Rue Cases-Nègres* [*Black Shack Alley*], Jacques Stephen Alexis's *Compère Général Soleil* [*General Sun, My Brother*], Emile Ollivier's *La Discorde aux cent voix*, and Patrick Chamoiseau's *Solibo Magnifique* [*Solibo Magnificent.*]) comes closer to her description of *Crossing the Mangrove* than the story of Roumain's Manuel, whose life is sacrificed for the revival of Fonds-Rouge.

Moreover, the title of the article, which primarily insists on a Césairean and of course Caribbean filiation, with its reference to Césaire's famous *Return to My Native Land*, and the pairing of Césaire and Condé, completely fails to mention Roumain, and Haitian novels, which make up 50 percent of the study corpus. The title of Ndiaye's article is a *tour de force*, enabling her to suggest implicitly that the myth or motif of the "return to the native land" goes back to Césaire's text. However, this myth lies at the very heart of Caribbean popular imagination. It is present in Haitian voodoo when the *sèvitè* (the servant, the follower) returns to Guinea after his or her death. This myth runs parallel to that of Ti-Jean in the Guadeloupean context, which Simone Schwarz-Bart writes of in her 1979 novel *Ti-Jean L'Horizon*. This myth is also present in the Haitian storytelling popular tradition, when the storyteller ritually returns to his native land, where his audience is, to bring back and tell the story that he has witnessed elsewhere.[16] However, beyond these popular forms, the tale of the return to the native land is a recurrent motif in the very first novels of the Haitian tradition in the twentieth

century—*Thémistocle-Épaminondas Labasterre* by Frédéric Marcelin
(1901), *Séna* by Fernand Hibbert (1905), *Mimola* by Antoine Innocent
(1906), *La Famille des Pitite-Caille* by Justin Lhérisson (1905), etc. Indeed,
this motif of the return to the native land has enabled me to differentiate between novels of the Haitian diaspora and novels of the Haitian tradition in
my book *Le Pouvoir des mots, les maux du pouvoir: Des romanciers haïtiens
de l'exil* (1986). As I stated in this work, ". . . if novels such as *Les Thazar* by
Fernand Hibbert (1907) or *Masters of the Dew* by Roumain (1944) begin
with the return to the native land after an enriching experience abroad, novels of the diaspora more generally, on the other hand, end (or sometimes
even begin) with the departure from the native land, as in *L'Onction du
St-Fac* by Wèche (1980)."[17]

Although the return to the native land is by no means an exclusively Haitian or Caribbean motif, appearing initially in Homer's *Odyssey* and the biblical parable of the return of the prodigal son, it does have particular roots
in both popular and intellectual circles in the Caribbean. However, neither
Césaire's *Return* nor Roumain's *Masters* can be said to have founded this literary myth of the Francophone Caribbean as Ndiaye implies; and it is further misleading for Ndiaye to insinuate that Roumain was inspired by
*Return*, when she writes: "Was Roumain directly inspired by Césaire or,
rather, have these two writers integrated the privileged fetishized images
of the literary world of the period?"[18] Furthering her analysis by comparing
the beginnings of both novels, Ndiaye also insists on the texts' similar oppositions between actual drought and misery (in the narrative present) and
ancient abundance and happiness. Nonetheless, this opposition that Ndiaye
considers a novelty in Caribbean literature is the central motif in Roumain's
first novel, *La Montagne ensorcelée* (1931), prefaced by Jean Price Mars.
Here again, the character in the midst of the village conflict is a foreigner,
a woman named Placinette, who, like Manuel, will be assassinated to ap-
pease the vengeful gods.

Ndiaye's neglect of Roumain is therefore manifest. In her commentary
on Condé, she fails to mention this Haitian writer's name and work directly.
Even in the conclusion, when she refers to the similarities between *Masters*
and a novel by Sembène Ousmane, she simply directs the reader to a footnote, with no comments, consisting merely of the title of an article by Victor Aire, "Affinités électives ou imitation? *Gouverneurs de la Rosée* et *Ô
Pays, mon beau peuple!*"[19] Such silence is probably a sign of the times but
also of a more structural problem concerning Francophone literary criticism. Indeed, how can Ndiaye claim that Condé's text, like Roumain's, tells
the story of a "return to the native land," and yet not have seen, nor men-

tioned, the privileged links between the two texts, particularly the way in which Condé reconsiders the central motif of the regenerating and liberating springhead in Roumain's *Masters*?[20]

Indeed, this almost universal silence among critics of *Crossing the Mangrove* concerning Roumain's influences should be questioned. But, before getting to this reading of the readings of *Crossing the Mangrove*, it is important first to illustrate, if not document, how and why *Crossing the Mangrove* is a rewriting of *Masters of the Dew*. To do so, I will analyze certain elements of Condé's text: (1) the title; (2) the *incipit* (opening passage); (3) the main character (and his name); (4) some motifs of its tragic plot; (5) and finally, (the status of) the quotation taken from Roumain.

## THE TITLE(S)

We need to underscore a certain, if not exact, similarity between Condé and Roumain's titles: both are syntagms of the type, NP [human] of (Det) NP [nature], which forms an almost perfect chiasmus.[21] Both syntagms express an impossible desire to master nature. For, just as one would not know *how* to "cross the mangrove," one would not know *how* to "master the dew." It is remarkable, moreover, that Condé, like Roumain, capitalizes the names of the natural object. "Mangrove," like "dew," is a common noun, and the use of capital letters here is rather unusual, and inappropriate; even though in the case of Roumain, one could say that this merely reflects a dated practice. It is not a question, then, of a particular mangrove or of a specific dew, but of *the* Mangrove and *the* Dew, as if to render the act even more enormous or impossible. It seems to me that such syntagmatic, orthographic, and semantic coincidences are not the result of chance, even though Condé seems to suggest that they are,[22] and even though readers like Patrick Chamoiseau, dwelling on the title, have not noticed any references to *Masters of the Dew*.[23]

Moreover, I would like to note the singularity or oddity of this title in relation to the system of titles in Condé's novels.

1. All of Condé's titles are thematic, none are rhematic (to make use of Genette's distinction in *Paratexts*[24]). With only two exceptions, *La Vie scélérate* [*Tree of Life*, literally: *A Wretched Life*] and *La Migration des coeurs* [*Windward Heights*, literally: *The Migration of Hearts*], Condé's titles all refer to proper names of places and/or characters. *Crossing the Mangrove* is the only title that refers to a natural domain,

unhistoricized, untamed, nature in all its grandeur and wildness, which undoubtedly accounts for the capitalization of "Mangrove."

2. With the exception of those titles that are proper nouns [PN] (*Heremakhonon*, *Ségu*, and *Désirada*) and of *I, Tituba, Black Witch of Salem* (which is a *hapax* among Condé's titles), all the titles—except *Crossing the Mangrove*—start with a definite or indefinite article (*La migration des coeurs*, *Une saison à Rihata* [*A Season in Rihata*]), and fall under one or the other of the following syntactic forms: Det NP (*La Vie scélérate*, for example), or Det NP preposition [Det] NP (*Une saison à Rihata*). So, *Crossing the Mangrove* is a clear exception to the series, and of course, it is the only title by Condé to include a capitalized common noun. Even in *La colonie du nouveau monde* [*The Colony in the New World*] and *Les Derniers rois mages* [*The Last of the African Kings*], which should (or at least could) have capitalized "nouveau monde" and "rois"—since these fixed syntagms are generally considered to be proper nouns (of place or person)—they are left in lower case.[25]

## THE *INCIPIT*

Beyond the similarity between the titles of the two novels there are the similitudes of their *incipit*, not just in the narrow sense of the opening sentence but the first few lines, even the first paragraph. In "Pour une sociocritique, ou variations sur un incipit," Claude Duchet has shown everything that can be extracted from a reading of opening passages and how these come to characterize different types of novels. In his "Qu'est-ce que le roman historique?" Jean Molino shows that the topos of the date, which is one of the distinctive characteristics of the historical novel, is also a key element of the *incipit*.[26] Without claiming to pursue my analysis beyond that of these eminent predecessors, I would nonetheless like to analyze the *incipit* of Condé's novels, on the one hand, to emphasize some of their recurring characteristics, and on the other hand, to show how *Crossing the Mangrove* sets itself apart by similarities with the opening passage in *Masters of the Dew*. In fact, even a quick reading of the *incipit* of Condé's novels brings some common and systematic characteristics into view.

1. Except for *I, Tituba, Black Witch of Salem* (but is the opening evocation of "one day in 16°°" really an exception, is a truncated date really a date?), the *incipit* of Condé's works never actualizes the topos of the

date. Moreover, this component of the nineteenth-century historical or even realist novel may be completely foreign to the universe of Condé's characters, as seen in the *incipit* to *Tree of Life*, which is appropriate to cite here:

> My forebear Albert Louis was not yet the forebear of anyone that day but a handsome Negro of around thirty-two years of age. I say *around*, for, as everyone knows, they paid scant attention to birth certificates in those times. The people of the plantation simply remembered his being born in the year of the terrible hurricane that downed trees and cabins from one end to the other of both Basse- and Grande-Terre and swelled to overflowing the tranquil Sanguine, which usually provided the islanders with just enough water to fill their water jars and wash their clothes nicely white. . . .[27]

The temporal reference used here ("the year of the terrible hurricane . . ."), instead of a more traditional form of chronological dating (month/day/year), refers to a natural catastrophe (which is in no way an isolated or historical event), one event among others of the same sort, a hurricane, thus hard to pinpoint with precision, as the narrator admits. This manner of dating the story, of inscribing a given chronology into the narrative, is not unique to Condé. It is a feature common to the *orature* that is put to use in a number of Caribbean novels. I am thinking, among others, of Simone Schwarz-Bart's famous *Pluie et vent sur Télumée Miracle* [*The Bridge of Beyond*] (1972), which begins the tale of the Lougandor lineage with "the abolition of slavery" rather than with the year 1848.

2. All of Condé's novels begin in the assumed voice of the narrator, whether impersonal or not, with the exception of the second book of *Ségou*, *La Terre en miettes* [*The Children of Segu*]: the celebrated exception that confirms the rule, but even so, we need to consider to what extent this really is an exception or not. On the one hand, can one really separate a reply, in the case of a second volume of *Segu* a question, from the commentary that frames it, either following or preceding it? "Mother, why do you love him more than me? Why does his arrival make you so happy that you pay no attention to me anymore?"[28] Should we not construe the assumed voice of the narrator that follows the question as an integral part of the narrative's opening? In which case, it is less an opening that begins with the voice of a character, than a double-voiced opening: character and narrator. On the other hand, the *incipit* of the *second* volume of a novel is not really

the opening of a novel, only the beginning of its second half. Such an affirmation is tautological and debatable, of course, but it is completely defensible, both vigorously and rigorously, in the case concerning us. Because the same title was given to both volumes, and a long author's note summarizing the first volume is included in the second, these two volumes are shown to be dependent on a single corpus and sequence, one preceding the other, the one being necessary in order to understand the other. It is self-evident that the novel *Segu* is constituted by a set of two volumes and that the beginning of the first volume *is* the real *incipit* of the novel. There cannot be more than one beginning. Such is moreover, as far as I can tell, the point of view taken by Condé's editors who list or market *Segu* as a single novel in two volumes.[29]

3. Every *incipit* is a narration or description, except for *Heremakhonon* and *Ségou: Les murailles de terre* [*Segu*]. Here again, we need to analyze these exceptions more closely to see precisely to what extent they are or are not, in point of fact, exceptions.

The incipient remarks of the main character/narrator that open *Heremakhonon*, like all argumentative or reflective discourse, are not devoid of narration or description. This is illustrated by the two mininarratives inserted into those opening comments: (a) "Blondes are dyeing their lips with henna and running to the open market on the rue Mouffetard for their peppers and okras"; (b) "Seven hours in a DC-10. On my left, an African, desperately trying to make small talk. Behind me, a French couple, as average as they come."[30] Furthermore, this *incipit* may not be typical of the openings of Condé's novels. As she emphasizes in the preface to the new (edited and amended) edition of *Heremakhonon*, under the title of *En attendant le bonheur*, her "conception of writing and of novelistic structures has considerably evolved since this first novel."[31]

As for the first paragraph of *Ségou: Les murailles de terre*, it is more an epigraph than the beginning of a story, as its italicized and sententious imperative form implies: "*Segu is a garden where cunning grows. Segu is built on treachery. Speak of Segu outside Segu, but do not speak of Segu in Segu.*"[32] And so, the opening of the story, properly speaking, would be the ensuing narration/description that reports the questions Dousika asks at dawn as he awakes.

4. All of the *incipit* of Condé's novels open onto family or ancestral portraits, providing a more or less detailed genealogy of the main character. The opening to *I, Tituba, Black Witch of Salem* is a com-

pelling example: "Abena, my mother, was raped by an English sailor on the deck of *Christ the King* one day in the year 16°° while the ship was sailing for Barbados. I was born from this act of aggression. From this act of hatred and contempt."[33]

It would be fastidious here to analyze every *incipit* of Condé. This example alone, it seems to me, is sufficiently explicit and typical of the ways in which the opening passages to Condé's novels are real family albums, as further confirmed by the initial sentence to *Desirada*: "Ranélise had described her birth to her so many times that she believed she had actually played a part—not that of a terrorized and submissive baby, whom Madame Fleurette, the midwife, wrenched out from between her mother's bloodied thighs—but that of a clear-sighted witness, a major role, her very mother. . . ."[34] In fact, Condé's *incipit* are words of life, not of death as in *Crossing*. Indeed, if certain novelists like Balzac leave a mark on the reader's consciousness, on mine at least, through memorable openings that create the scene and establish the setting, Condé instead attempts right from the start to trace back lineages, to sketch out family portraits, to set up a genesis. She tries this in *Crossing the Mangrove*, but fails because Léocadie Timothée, the spinster with a worn-out body on the edge of death, is not a proper subject, she is not the main character, nor is she the stuff of a main character, and her lineage is rather sterile.

In fact, the kind of genealogical certitude found in *The Last African Kings* or *Tree of Life*, for example, is impossible with *Crossing the Mangrove*; every genealogy, including that of the main character, Sanchez/Sancher, being problematic. On the one hand, this character is enigmatic, and the object of the novel is precisely an attempt to reconstitute his story, to ascertain his identity in the same way police speak of "identifying the victim." This is not an identity that could lead to lost or mythical origins or to a stable image of the subject, and this is precisely what L. D. Hewitt points to as the detective-story element in this novel.[35]

On the other hand, right from the beginning of the story, Francis Sancher is dead, and this information, like everything we learn about him, is mediated (transformed) by the consciousnesses of the characters present at his wake and who knew him during his brief sojourn at Rivière au Sel, where he came, after a considerable amount of wandering, for his final voyage, death. Even the parts that are told from the point of view of the impersonal narrator are not entirely free of the intervening consciousnesses of the characters. Condé gives preference to an internal focalization, i.e., the narrator, even though impersonal (extradiegetic) tells the story from the point of view of the character on whom the narrative is centered. Thus, the narrator is no better informed than the character.

Having demonstrated the singularity of this *incipit* in Condé's work, we now need to show its similarities with the opening passage in Roumain. The initial sentences of both novels are short and simple exclamations. The ellipses points in Roumain's text do not allow us to forget that the "nous mourrons tous . . . [we're all going to die[36]]" spoken by Délira Délivrance is an exclamation that she repeats elsewhere, just like Léocadie Timothée's "Mon coeur n'a pas sauté! [My heart did not skip (translation modified)]," which opens *Crossing the Mangrove*. Both sentences are denials, counter-truths, because we know that Léocadie's heart not only *skipped* at seeing Sancher's cadaver, but that it *leapt*, since she subsequently vomited. As for the people of Fonds-Rouge, they are not all going to die. Manuel alone pays with his life for regenerating the village by his quest for the spring of water and consequent unity of its inhabitants. And the words of Délira are less a prophesy than a hopeless cry of hope (if one can allow me this oxymoron), a call to life, a cry to reject death. And so, it is a matter of noting that both of these initial sentences must be read and interpreted beyond their apparent meaning.

On the one hand, "Mon coeur n'a pas sauté!" is a fixed form cast from a very common creole expression in Guadeloupe that signifies astonishment, surprise, panic, fear ("kè an mwen soté"); more so in its negation ("kè an mwen pa soté") which expresses courage or bravado. It does not mean a heart attack as a flatfooted French gloss might suggest, even though such a malaise is often associated with the shock of a "kè soté" (to cite the Haitian version of this expression). On the other hand, for a Francophone reader unfamiliar with the Guadeloupean language, or any other so-called French-based Caribbean creole, "Mon coeur n'a pas sauté!" signifies, "My heart did not fail me, I escaped death." So, as with the opening passage in Roumain, Condé refers, first and foremost, if not to death then at least to the semantic field of death. Besides, Léocadie's exclamation only expresses her initial reaction upon discovering the cadaver of Sancher, just as Délira's exclamation expresses her feelings at the blighted devastation her land has become. Moreover, in both cases, we have a bit of monologue from the old woman, whom the narrator presents using both first and last names: "the old woman . . . Délira Délivrance" (MD 23); "Mademoiselle Léocadie Timothée, a former elementary school teacher now retired for over twenty years" (CM 1, translation modified). On the contrary, Délira's husband, Bienaimé, and Léocadie's neighbor, Léo, are indicated only by their first names.

Undoubtedly, there is much more we could say about these two *incipit*. For example, both draw on a particular Christian discourse that is prevalent in the Francophone Caribbean (the "Jesus-Mary-Holy-Virgin" that Délira invokes; the "Eternal Life" alluded to by Léocadie). In both cases, the use of free indirect style and internal focalization leads one to believe that the narration is assumed by the character whose name also gives the title to the chapter (or section). It seems to me, though, that my remarks have sufficiently illustrated the compelling similarities between the two *incipit* and how, up to a point, one rewrites the other. Moreover, can we not say that this modeling of a creole form ("Mon coeur n'a pas sauté!"), this creolization of French (the groundbreaking contribution of *Masters*), is, consciously or not, an homage to Roumain and his unique Caribbean work, a work that is read in schools and a work that interested Carmélien, the only work with *The Brothers Karamazov* (CM 186), as far as I can tell, from among those written by the many well-known authors previously evoked, to be explicitly quoted in Condé's novel?[37]


## THE MAIN CHARACTER(S)

Both characters have names in three parts—to parody the title of Roger Dorsinville's novel, *Un homme en trois morceaux* [*A Man in Three Parts*]—spelled out the same way, with a hyphen between the two components of the surname in addition to a Hispanic first name: Manuel Jean-Joseph/ Francisco Alvarez-Sanchez. Both spent time in Cuba, and according to some of the characters, they retain speech patterns influenced by the Spanish language. And for both, their stay in Cuba defined a place of transformation and maturation: disillusionment for Francisco in his dealings with the Cuba of Castro's revolution; politicization for Manuel in his tussles with the syndicalism of Cuba during the time of Batista's corrupt dictatorship. And, of course, this Cuban sojourn crowns them with a certain aura, at least in the eyes of the inhabitants of Rivière au Sel and Fonds-Rouge.

Both characters return to their country with the fixed intention, or at least conviction, that they will die there, even though the meaning of this expression (or gesture) is not the same. For Manuel, this determination never again to leave his native land is a pact of hope. He says to his mother: "No more crying, mama. From today on, I'm here for the rest of my life." (MD 44) While for Francisco, the sense of his return home is entirely different; it is a radical rejection of life, a profound gesture of despair that emerges when he confides in Dinah: "That child must never open its eyes to the light of day. . . . An ill omen is upon him as it is upon me. He'll live a life of calamities and he'll end up dying like a dog as I shall soon do. I have come here to end it all. To come full circle. To put the finishing touches, you understand. Return to square one and stop" (CM 83).

Of course, both die prematurely: Sancher's death is an enigma for the inhabitants of Rivière au Sel, but completely explained (and explainable) by the Guadeloupean authorities (CM 5–10); Manuel's death is an enigma for the Fonds-Rouge authorities, but a momentous event for the inhabitants (MD 159–61). In both novels, this death "foretold," to parody the title of García Márquez's *Chronicle of a Death Foretold* (it was known that Sancher had come to Rivière au Sel to die, to that mythical place of genesis from which his family originated; just as Papa Legba had foretold in barely veiled terms the impending death of Manuel), is redemptive for the villagers of Rivière au Sel as well as for those of Fonds-Rouge. Francis's wake becomes a cathartic space, a place for monumental decisions: thus Mira, for example, affirms, "My real life begins with his death" (CM 193), while Délira's meeting with the members of the rival clan on the night of Manuel's burial allows for a resolution of old conflicts and the reconciliation demanded by the sacrifice of her son's life (MD 179–83).

Other motifs in Roumain's novel are likewise transposed unaltered or transmuted in *Crossing the Mangrove*. Let's recall two that seem to me pretty self-evident: the child to be born after his father's death; and the first love by the water: the spring for Manuel and Annaïse (MD 117–18), the gully for Sancher and Mira (CM 32, 34, 36–38). Furthermore, it is important to note that this waterhole is not only the place where love blossoms between Mira and Sancher, but is also the place where Carmélien discovers his own feelings of love and sexuality, precisely by the sight of Mira's naked body. That waterhole is further understood by Carmélien's consciousness to be a kind of spring and one closely linked to *Masters of the Dew* (CM 143–45, 146). How then can it be explained that Ellen Munley did not make the connection between the water themes in *Crossing* and *Masters*, in her article "Du silence de la mort à la parole de la vie: à l'écoute de l'eau et du vent dans *Traversée de la Mangrove*" (1995)?[38]

Is this a blindness or a misunderstanding of the corpus, or both? To answer such a question runs the risk of idle speculations, or at least taking us away from the purpose of this study: *Crossing the Mangrove* as a rewriting of *Masters of the Dew*. And I think of *Masters* not only as a text by itself, but also as exemplary of a certain narrative model that I call the traditional Haitian novel (that set of works published primarily between 1901 and 1961), as opposed to those novels concerning Haitian modernity (that other set of works, written from within or without Haiti, especially since 1968). Now, one of the pertinent characteristics of the traditional Haitian narrative is precisely, as with Condé's narrative, that it is a tragic one.[39]

## OF TRAGIC(S)

Indeed, traditional Haitian novels all peddle narratives of a fatal loss linked to a (forbidden) quest for pleasure and/or power articulated by two compulsory sequences: an initial one in the form of an anticipatory discourse (a *warning* or a *caution*); a final one in the form of a retrospective discourse (a *clarification* or an *explanation*).[40] But, contrary to Greek tragedy, Haitian tragedy is not inscribed within a logic of prediction or predestination, but rather within one of prescription/ prohibition (closer to the biblical tradition of the Fall of Man).

Also, in opposition to the Greek tragic hero, the Haitian protagonist has a certain freedom of choice, and can on occasion avoid the worst of his or her circumstances. Thus, for example, in *Mimola* by Antoine Innocent (1906), Lala avoids a precocious and imminent death by accepting the call of the loas, whereas Léon, who stands in open opposition to their will, slips into insanity. In fact, in traditional Haitian novels, the tragic syntax is actualized in this specific way:

(DO NOT) DO [*PROHIBITION/ PRESCRIPTION*], OR ELSE [*WARNING OR CAUTION*] (NOT) HAVE DONE [*TRANSGRESSION*], THAT IS [*EXPLANATION OR CLARIFICATION*].

This syntax is especially good at soliciting concern or anxiety in the reader through his/her apprehension of a fatal denouement (implied by any warning, whatever it may be) and of its (moralizing) reassessment by duplication or diegetic redoubling—a *mise en abyme* that almost every clarification imposes at every turn, since it involves a *reprise*, a revisiting of the facts. This is the syntax, the grammar of traditional Haitian novels, which makes these counterexemplary narratives into (effective) exemplary "lessons of life."

In *Masters of the Dew*, the death of Manuel is presented precisely as the outcome of his violating a series of both political and sexual prohibitions that are linked to his quest for a source of water that would also reunite the villagers, and then also, to his quest after Annaïse, hence quests that are tragic because forbidden. But the erotic quest (just as is the case in *Crossing the Mangrove*) seems to be the crucial one in bringing about Manuel's downfall because Gervilen Gervilus, the love-struck cousin of Annaïse, is the one who murders him. Similarly, the hatred that spins around Sancher, and the desire to kill him that lurks within offended fathers or brothers, spurned wooers or lovers, is a direct consequence of his amorous (or presumed sexual) relationships with the inaccessible (idolized) girls of the Cité. On this point, Carmélien's comments are totally explicit: "I can't hide the fact that I hated him more for what he did to Mira than for what he did to my own sister Vilma" (CM 141). In other respects, even though it more manifestly takes from the fable form of classical Greek tragedy—the death of Sancher, for example, is not only foretold and inevitable, but it is also *told* in accordance with the classic tragic rules for unity of time and place, as L. D. Hewitt so well points out[41]—Condé's novel is tempered by this grammar specific to Haitian tragic narrative, and consequently it plays on two codes at once (allogenous and indigenous).

Indeed, the anticipatory (or prospective) discourse of Sancher speaking to Dinah about his past and future lineage (CM 83), is at once both PREDICTION and PROHIBITION. *Prediction* in Sancher's tragic story, which is the main narrative (story 1), but *prohibition* in the (future, potential) tragic narrative of his illegitimate and orphaned children (story 2). Also, one could read the story of Sancher's life as emblematic of the tragic story (to come) of his progeny. And, as in the tale of the woodcutter Viandélou, in *Le Crayon de Dieu* [*The Pencil of God*] (1952) by Philippe Thoby-Marcelin and Pierre Marcelin, which is also an emblem of Diogène Cyprien, the hero in this novel, it is merely a pretext for a moral lesson. And, it is not a coincidence that Condé chose the structure of the Caribbean wake, which is *par excellence* a time/space of catharsis (explanation)—which is also what opens *Masters of the Dew* in order to tell this tale, this passage from life to death, deployed between the two distinctive sequences of the tragic narrative: the prospective discourse of the warning or caution and the retrospective discourse of the explanation or clarification.

## ON THE QUOTATION FROM ROUMAIN: PROVISIONAL CONCLUSIONS

If the transtextual relationship between Condé's text and that of Roumain has been revealed on so many levels (intertextual, metatextual, hypertextual, architextual), how can one explain the lack of critical commentary on these similarities? It seems to me that three kinds of response tied to the three aspects of the symbolic object (author, criticism, text) can explain this literary oversight.

1. Author's Way: Condé herself remains silent on this link with Roumain. He is neither named in the text, nor in the accompanying textual materials (authorial paratext), nor even in her interviews with Pfaff where she does in fact make note of, or recognizes, several other literary influences or intertextual links.[42] Thus, Condé's attitude toward Roumain is similar to that of Haitian novelists in exile, and thus in alignment with a certain strategy or attitude taken by writers from peripheral (or Southern) spaces who tend to deny or ignore indigenous literary influences.[43] It is necessary perhaps to qualify such an assertion, for according to Lucienne Serrano, Condé is said to have "spoken of particular works like *Gouverneurs de la Rosée* and *Cahier d'un retour au pays natal* as literary models" at a "conference on Caribbean literature."[44] On the other hand, in her article "Order, Disorder, Freedom, and the West Indian Writer," Condé clearly recognizes *Masters* as a "fundamental text" of Francophone Caribbean literature.[45] Furthermore, one must admit that Condé is one of the most generous Francophone Caribbean writers, and without a doubt, the one who has written the most extensively on contemporary Caribbean writers, mainly in her numerous contributions to *Présence africaine* and in her books: *La Parole des femmes: essai sur des romancières des Antilles de langue française* and *Penser la créolité*.[46]

2. Critic's Way: A Francophone criticism that is overly sociological or thematic cares little for text-based effects, and in particular, any transtextual relations by or within the Francophone corpus.[47] Thus, during a study project on Mehdi Charef's *Le Thé au harem d'Archi Ahmed* [*Tea in the Harem*], it occurred to me that what had not been noticed, much less analyzed, was the transtextual relationship between this novel and Proust's *À la recherche du temps perdu* [*Remembrance of Things Past*]—something that is already apparent in their similar nine-syllable titles. There are many signs, however, that point to this relationship to Proust (whether conscious or not): from the special friendship between Pat and Madjid (which seems to suggest a certain latent homosexuality) to the name of the housing complex where the main characters live, "la cité des fleurs [the city of flowers]" which includes its very own Madeleine who gives so many pleasures to all

those young boys. And then there is the following comment by the narrator: "she'd love him like crazy to make up for *lost time* [*le temps perdu*]. And though we might not notice it, women have their ways of making up for *lost time* [*temps perdu*]."[48] Moreover, we should not discount the structure of Charef's novel, presented as a series of microtales, more or less autonomous, but tightly linked together via the central figure of Madjid—a structure akin to the *1001 Nights*, which Proust, if not his narrator, dreamed of "redoing" in *Remembrance of Things Past*, as Georges Cattaui has suggested, repeating the very words of the narrator at the close of *Le Temps retrouvé* [*Time Recaptured*].[49] Also, there is that rather troubling set of parallels: Mehdi (author)/Madjid/Mehdi (the main character's brother, who is always immersed in reading or writing)/Mame Marcel, with of course, Marcel (Proust) and Marcel (the presumed narrator).

Moreover, Francophone criticism remains only spottily aware of its own corpus written over a range of three centuries (as opposed to the commonly held assumption that Francophone literature was born in the twentieth century) and three continents (Europe, America, Africa). So, for example, in the introduction to her dissertation on "the writer as character in Francophone West Indian novels" between 1980 and 1990, written under the direction of Ann Smock, Vèvè A. Clark, and Maryse Condé at the University of California, Berkeley, Lydie Moudileno (who, in other respects, is a fairly attentive reader of Caribbean texts) asserts:

If it were a question of the Caribbean novel of French expression, it would have been necessary . . . to include Haiti. Here again, it turns out that the corpus is limited to authors from the departments of Outre-Mer [i.e., Martinique and Guadeloupe] because I know of no Haitian novel published in the last few years which displays what I consider an "obsession with the writer." Only Dany Laférière's [*sic*] novel, *Cette grenade dans la main du jeune Nègre, est-ce une arme ou un fruit?* [*Why Must a Black Writer Write About Sex?*] (1993) might have found a place in this dissertation. If it had only been published a few years earlier, that is, before my choice of materials had been completed, the whole direction, and certainly the theses and hypotheses of this study would have been altered."[50]

Now, it so happens that Laferrière's first book, *Comment faire l'amour avec un nègre sans se fatiguer* [*How to Make Love to a Negro*] (1985), which is about the "writer as character" to use Moudileno's term, is undoubtedly one of the most typical novels within the context of Francophone Caribbean literary production between 1980 and

1990. Moreover, this novel is a good example of what Genette calls a "hypertext," another factor that should compel critics to study this novel, which has been a major success, including a paperback version in the popular French "J'ai lu" series and a film adaptation in 1989 (directed by Jacques W. Benoit) that was released for international distribution. Furthermore, this novel is extensively evoked in *Cette grenade dans la main du jeune nègre, est-ce une arme ou un fruit?*[51]

Such mistakes are also a consequence of, among other things, the limited circulation (or poor dissemination) of these works and the lack of reliable reference tools that characterize (and obviously handicap) Francophone studies. And, on this last point, it is useful to recall Alain Baudot's 1977 comments (which are unfortunately still accurate today) about Lilyan Kesteloot's 1963 work, *Les Écrivains noirs de langue française: naissance d'une littérature* [*Black Writers in French: A Literary History of Negritude*].

Became a classic—and a kind of best-seller—in Black African literary studies . . . this straightforward survey of the literature needs a serious overhaul. While it is an essential reference indeed for the documentation it provides on the Negritude movement among the West Indians (Césaire, Damas) and Africans (Senghor) living in Paris, and especially concerning the content of the reviews, *Légitime Défense*, *L'Etudiant noir* and *Tropiques*, quite rightly generous in its evaluation of Césaire's thematics, [and] useful for the concluding analysis it makes of a questionnaire distributed to some 20 contemporary Black writers . . . , this work nonetheless exhibits two major flaws for a study of such scope: a comprehensive timidity in its methodological outlook and a worrisome misapprehension of Haitian literature (and even the literature of the lesser Antilles prior to the 1930s).[52]

3.  Text's Way: The indigenous intertext, hypotext, and architext are often hybrid, belonging to at least two traditions. Now, the best-known and most studied tradition is precisely the European one. Also, it should come as no surprise that Francophone criticism—educated in the canons of Europe or the North—has a tendency to ignore the other part (the flip side) of its object of study, which is never a simple object nor simply an object, since it exists as an allogeneous text. Indeed, one of the characteristics of allogeneous texts is that they are tempered by an at least twofold semiotics, drawing their models from two semiotic orders: an allogeneous one, which is visibly manifest, especially on the level of the written language; the other, an indigenous one, lodged or recessed within its deep structure like the model of the Haitian tragic

tale, which works as a kind of blotter for *Crossing the Mangrove*. Deciding which semiotic order oversees or inspires a given writing strategy, a given narrative motif, a given figure of speech, is often difficult, if not risky, because the allogeneous and indigenous semiotics often share common characteristics or may even mutually influence each other.

For example, the structure of Condé's text takes as much from Caribbean orature and the mortuary wake of Caribbean plantation culture as it is a reappropriation, whether consciously or not, of the form of Faulkner's *As I Lay Dying*. But Faulkner's novel is itself unquestionably a transferral or rewriting into American high culture of a form taken from the popular culture of Southern plantations. And we must not forget that this actualization of a Faulknerian structure is no stale imitation. Condé innovates, or at least transforms, this structure to generate a response uttered in the speech of the Caribbean night: from dusk to foredawn (the deceased being evoked only at night?) in opposition to Faulkner's story "On the Road" (entirely typical of the American imaginary), the "story of a long funerary voyage" to pick up Carson McCullers's expression cited by Michel Gresset in his preface to the bilingual Folio edition of *As I Lay Dying*.[53]

Commentators like L. D. Hewitt have noted the similarities between Condé's novel and classical tragedy (in terms of unity of time and place). Yet they did not draw the link between the tragic and Roumain's text. Here again, we need to raise questions about this silence or blindness, but space does not allow me to give an adequate answer and perhaps there are not even any good answers to give. Nonetheless, these silences concerning Roumain's tragic narrative remain symptomatic of a general malaise in Francophone studies, of an incapacity to grasp the set of works in this vast arena as an organic whole, or as a network of changes and exchanges between texts, writers, scholars, readers, etc.

How do these passages or exchanges take place from one semiotic system to another, from one text to another, from one author to another, or even from one (national) literature to another? I hesitate to answer this question, at least at this point in time. And given the present state of research on this matter, even venturing a hypothesis seems premature. Nor do I claim that my project to read *Crossing the Mangrove* as a rewriting of *Masters of the Dew* is any more valid than other readings. I do suggest, and moreover insist on what seems to me to be the critical point, namely, that one cannot afford to ignore this black side of the mirror, this dark side of the text: the manifest or latent inscription (in terms of surface or deep structures, to borrow terms consecrated by modern linguistics) of indigenous semiotic systems in the text: citation, translation, the reappropriation of motifs, forms, and fixed expressions taken from indigenous speech, etc.

The textual, though partial, reinscription (*mise en abyme*) of the narration/description of the sexual act between Manuel and Annaïse is only partial since Condé saw fit to truncate the quotation from Roumain. Now, this is a classic erotic scene of Francophone literature, to the point of being a selection for anthologies.[54] The partialness of the quotation should not let us forget that what is not (textually) cited has been paraphrased, or rewritten on two, perhaps three, occasions: (1) immediately following the quotation, by the remainder of Carmélien's nascent sentiments of love triggered by the sight of Mira naked (CM 143–44); (2) in Mira's account of her first meeting with Sancher at the water's edge where, as with Annaïse and Manuel, their bodies were united for the first time (CM 36–38); (3) with Léocadie's memory of a scene from her youth when she saw under the shade of an "amandier-pays [almond tree]"[55]—a word not without its hyphenated parallel in Roumain's novel: "figuier-maudit [mysterious fig tree]" (MD 117)—a couple making love on the beach, hence at the edge of the sea (CM 113), that great expanse of water that is, for her too, the definitive inception of her amorous quest.

Indeed, is it not the sea, a "nasty sea," that gives Léocadie the strength to go to her fellow teacher, Déodat Timodent, and declare her love to him (CM 117–18)? Of course, when she shows up at Déodat's door and becomes paralyzed by his fearful attitude, Léocadie does not follow through with her plan, despite her intentions. Even though she had the courage to go as far as the doorstep of the man of her dreams and could have declared her love to him (I am clearly extrapolating), there was only this fear, even dread, that she read in his eyes and words (CM 118).

Perhaps the quotation from Roumain is a trap, a "banana skin" for critics to slip on, like the famous reference to the complete works of Rabelais that the character of Gabriel takes with him to Paris in *One Hundred Years of Solitude* and that, as García Márquez says in *The Fragrance of Guava*, has caused many critics to go astray.[56] Or the Roumain quotation could be an important point of critical departure, even a necessary point of entry into Condé's texts. I do not wish to decide between these alternatives, but the quotation carries at least the trace of a transtextuality (intertextuality, metatextuality, hypertextuality, and even architextuality) that has to be (and must be) questioned, at the risk of completely missing the (indigenous) other side of this allogenous text.

## NOTES

This chapter is an updated and expanded version of my article, "Sur des lectures de Traversée de la Mangrove de Condé," *Cahiers Francophones d'Europe Centre-Orientale*, vol. 10 (2000): 419–41. I would like to thank Georges Van Den Abbeele, Tyler Stovall, and Sharon O'Toole Dubois who have provided this English translation.

1. For Genette, *transtextuality* ("all that sets the text in a relationship . . . with other texts") is the very subject of poetics and implies "five types of transtextual relationships." (1) *Intertextuality* is "the actual presence of one text within another" (quotation, allusion); (2) *Paratextuality* is the "relationship . . . that binds the text properly speaking . . . to what can be called its *paratext*: a title, a subtitle, intertitles; prefaces, postfaces, notices, forewords, etc.; marginal, infrapaginal, terminal notes; epigraphs; illustrations; blurbs, book covers, dust jackets, and many other kinds of secondary signals." (3) *Metatextuality* is "the relationship [which] unites a given text to another, of which it speaks without necessarily citing it (without summoning it)." (4) *Hypertextuality* is "any relationship uniting a text B (which I shall call the *hypertext*) to an earlier text A (I shall, of course, call it the *hypotext*), upon which it is grafted in a manner that is not that of commentary" (relationship of transformation or of imitation). (5) *Architextuality* is the generic relationship that the text entertains with others said to be of the same genre or modality. Gérard Genette, *Palimpsests: Literature in the Second Degree*, trans. Channa Newman and Claude Doubinsky (Lincoln: University of Nebraska Press, 1997), 1–7.

2. On the emergence of both terms, see Anne Malena, *The Negotiated Self: The Dynamics of Identity in Francophone Caribbean Narrative* (New York: Peter Lang, 1999), 116, note 2.

3. Françoise Pfaff, *Conversations with Maryse Condé* (Lincoln: University of Nebraska Press, 1996), 72–73.

4. I cite Richard Philcox's translation of *Crossing the Mangrove* (New York: Doubleday, 1995), 142–43. All further references to this text will be by page number only, preceded by the initials CM. The original text of *Traversée de la Mangrove* was published in Paris by Mercure de France in 1989. For *Masters of the Dew*, I will cite the translation by Langston Hughes and Mercer Cook reissued in the "Caribbean Writers Series" by Heinemann (London and Kingston, 1978). *Gouverneurs de la Rosée* by Jacques Roumain was originally published by Roumain's widow in French in 1944 in Port-au-Prince, then subsequently reissued by EFR editions in Paris in 1946. All further references to this text will be by page number only, preceded by the initials MD.

5. Michel Serres, "Christ noir," *Critique* 308 (1973): 3–25.

6. By allogenous, I mean works produced in a language that is not the language (or at least not the first language) of the referential space (that is being represented) and/or of the writer, a language that is thus both other and host, making it even doubly allogenous.

7. Michael Lucey, "Voices Accounting for the Past: Maryse Condé's *Traversée de la Mangrove*," in *L'Héritage de Caliban*, ed. M. Condé (Pointe-à-Pitre: Éditions Jasor, 1992), 123–32; Ruthmarie-H. Mitsch, "Maryse Condé's Mangroves," *Research in African Literatures* 28, no. 4 (1997): 54–70.

8. Françoise Lionnet, "*Traversée de la Mangrove* de Maryse Condé: Vers un nouvel humanisme antillais?" *French Review* 66, no. 3 (1993): 478.

9. Leah D. Hewitt, "Inventing Antillean Narrative: Maryse Condé and Literary Tradition," *Studies in Twentieth Century Literature* 17, no. 1 (1993): 89; Lydie Moudileno, "Portrait of the Artist as Dreamer: Maryse Condé's *Traversée de la Mangrove* and *Les Derniers rois mages*," *Callaloo* 18, no. 3 (1995): 636.

10. Yvette Bozon-Scalzitti, "La Mort de Francis Sancher, ou l'adieu aux armes de Maryse Condé dans *Traversée de la Mangrove*," *Women in French Studies* 6 (1998): 68–69. This article, whose arguments on *Crossing* as a rewriting of *Masters* are similar to some that I present here, without doubt, has been published after my first presentation of this research on January 20, 1998, at Northwestern University, under the title "Condé lectrice de Roumain." So, it seems to me irrelevant to discuss it at this point.

11. Christiane Ndiaye, "De Césaire à Condé: quelques retours au pays natal," *De paroles en figures. Essais sur les littératures africaines et antillaises*, eds. C. Ndiaye and J. Semujanga (Montreal: L'Harmattan, 1996), 137–77; and see my "Sur des lectures de *Traversée de la Mangrove* de Condé," *Cahiers Francophones d'Europe Centre-Orientale* 10 (2000): 419–41. This article, which should have been published in 1999, was a synthesis of the communications delivered between January and March 1998 at Northwestern University and the French Institute in Leipzig, respectively. I return to this publication and Ndiaye's article—as well as Yvette Bozon-Scalzitti's of Roosevelt University, "La Mort de Francis Sancher"—in the concluding chapter of my book in progress, *Lecture de la lecture: littératures francophones et transtextualité*, in which I reread some of my readings of Francophone texts, considering that a critical epistemological approach without autocriticism would make no sense—or would simply be vain pretence.

12. Pascale De Souza, "*Traversée de la Mangrove*: Éloge de la créolité, écriture de l'opacité," *French Review* 73, no. 5 (2000): 824–25; Renée Larrier, "A Roving 'I': 'Errance' and Identity in Maryse Condé's *Traversée de la Mangrove*," *Esprit Créateur* 38, no. 3 (1998): 89–90.

13. Dawn Fulton, "Reading Death: Allegory in Maryse Condé's *Crossing the Mangrove*," *Callaloo* 24, no. 1 (2001): 301–9; Jarrod Hayes, "Looking for Roots among the Mangroves: Errances Enracinées and Migratory Identities," *Centennial Review* 42, no. 3 (1998): 459–74; Anne Malena, *The Negotiated Self*.

14. Maryse Condé, "Order, Disorder, Freedom, and the West Indian Writer," *Yale French Studies* 83, no. 2 (1993): 126.

15. Ndiaye, "De Césaire à Condé," 171.

16. Cf. Jean Jonassaint, *Des romans de tradition haitienne. Sur un récit tragique* (Paris: L'Harmattan and Cidihca, 2002), 149–50.

17. Jean Jonassaint, *Le Pouvoir des mots, les maux du pouvoir: Des romanciers haïtiens de l'exil* (Paris: Arcantère, 1986), 246–47.

18. Ndiaye, "De Césaire à Condé," 143.

19. Victor Aire, "Affinités électives ou imitation? *Gouverneurs de la Rosée* et *Ô Pays, mon beau peuple!*," *Présence francophone* 15 (1977): 3–10.

20. Ndiaye, "De Césaire à Condé," 175.

21. Jonassaint's comments here refer, of course, to the standard generative grammar with its key terms Determiner or Determinator, Noun Phrase, Verb Phrase, and the syntactic and semantic ordering of the titles as they appear in French: *Traversée de la Mangrove* and *Gouverneurs de la Rosée*. His ensuing comments also presuppose an understanding of French rules for capitalization in titles, i.e., *only* the first word or proper nouns are to be capitalized with all others to be in lower case. TRANS.

22. Pfaff, *Conversations with Maryse Condé*, 71.

23. Patrick Chamoiseau, "Reflections on Maryse Condé's *Traversée de la Mangrove*," trans. K. M. Balutansky, *Callaloo* 14, no. 2 (1991): 389–95.

24. Gérard Genette, *Paratexts: Thresholds of Interpretation*, trans. Jane E. Lewin (Cambridge: Cambridge University Press, 1997), 81–89.

25. Condé herself writes "Nouveau Monde" (New World) with capital letters for both "Nouveau" and "Monde" in *Heremakhonon* (Paris: Union Générale d'édition, 10/18, no. 1033, 1976), 12.

26. Claude Duchet, "Pour une socio-critique, ou variation sur un incipit," *Littérature* 1 (1971): 5–14; Jean Molino, "Qu'est-ce que le roman historique?," *RHLF* 2–3 (1975): 195–234.

27. Condé, *Tree of Life*, trans. Victoria Reiter (New York: Ballantine Books, 1992), 3.

28. Condé, *The Children of Segu*, trans. Linda Coverdale (New York: Viking, 1989), 5.

29. See the bibliography of Condé in the Folio edition of *Traversée* (Paris: 1995) where *Ségou* is listed as one title with two subtitles. See also the note from Laffont on the dust jacket to *La Colonie du nouveau monde* (Paris: Robert Laffont, 1993), which follows the same protocol.

30. Condé, *Heremakhonon*, trans. Richard Philcox (Washington, D.C.: Three Continents Press, 1982), 3.

31. Condé, *En attendant le bonheur* (Paris: Seghers, 1988), 11.

32. Condé, *Segu*, trans. Barbara Bray (New York: Viking, 1987), 3.

33. Condé, *I, Tituba, Black Witch of Salem*, trans. Richard Philcox (Charlottesville: University Press of Virginia, 1992), 3.

34. Condé, *Desirada*, trans. Richard Philcox (New York: Soho Press, 2000), 3.

35. Hewitt, "Inventing Antillean Narrative," 84.

36. These ellipses points do not appear in the English translation.

37. The poem by Dominique Guesde, supposedly taken from *La Guadeloupe Pittoresque* (CM 119), is most likely apocryphal, or at least coming from a fictional author or an illustrious unknown, for this author cannot be found in the

*Catalogue du fonds local* in the Schoelcher library, neither for the years 1883–1985, nor for 1986–1993 (cf. Bibliothèque Schoelcher, *Catalogue du fonds local 1883–1985* [Fort-de-France: Conseil Général de la Martinique, 1987]; and *Catalogue du fonds local 1986–1993* [Fort-de-France: Conseil Général de la Martinique, 1994]). As for the other literary references, whether real or fictional, they are limited to the names of authors and/or of titles: Émile Étienne, *Parler de Petit-Bourg* (fictional); Carpentier, Césaire, Chamoiseau, Cheikh Anta Diop (real); *Wonders of the Invisible World* is a real title modified by Condé into the story of the Alvarez-Sanchez family (CM 197). On the other hand, one must underscore the first phrase of the third part of *Amitié du Prince* [*Friendship of the Prince*] by Saint-John Perse, "Each season I shall return, with a garrulous green bird on my wrist" (cf. Saint-John Perse, *Collected Poems*, bilingual edition English and French, trans. W. H. Auden et al. [Princeton, N.J.: Princeton University Press 1983], 85, which is reproduced at least three times in the novel (CM 137, 234, 251). But this quotation is more or less explicit, the different narrators presenting it in various manners: a «recitation» (Sylvestre Ramsaran), a «declamation» (Émile Étienne), or an obsessional sentence of Francis Sancher (the impersonal narrator). Furthermore, it is obvious that the Saint-John Perse intertext in *Crossing the Mangrove* ought to require more attention than it has received here, than the paragraphs written by Bozon-Scalzitti ("La Mort de Francis Sancher," 69–71) and Malena (*The Negotiated Self*, 80) on this issue, or the short and problematic comment by Raylene Ramsay ("The Nature of Hybridity in Maryse Conde's *Traversée de la Mangrove*," *Nottingham French Studies* 39, no. 2 [2000]: 216–17), especially since the property bought by Franciso Alvarez-Sanchez at Rivière au Sel is that of a certain Alexis (which is the real first name of the poet Saint-John Perse, Alexis Saint-Léger Léger, and the last name of the Haitian physician and novelist, Jacques Stephen Alexis whose famous title Condé recalls, *Compère Général Soleil* [*General Sun, My Brother*] (CM 129). Those two examples show well how the Caribbean intertexts (from literary or popular culture) are present in *Crossing*, and not taking them into account could lead to some obvious misreadings. On the contrary, I am not sure that the Dostoyevsky quotation should deserve the same attention.

38. Ellen Munley, "Du silence de la mort à la parole de la vie: à l'écoute de l'eau et du vent dans *Traversée de la Mangrove*," *L'Eau: Source d'une écriture dans les littératures féminines francophones*, ed. Y. Helm (New York: Peter Lang, 1995), 113–27.

39. See Jonassaint, *Des romans de tradition haïtienne*, 207–30, 264–73, from which the following commentary on tragedy is taken.

40. The terms "caution " or "warning" and "clarification" or "explanation" are used here not in their literal or current sense, but in a very specific way that expresses more adequately perhaps the original French concepts, *mise en garde* and *mise au point*. They translate a certain pragmatic relationship between text and reader or text and spectator. Therefore every narrative or discursive segment

that allows the reader or spectator to apprehend the denouement to come is a *warning* just as every narrative or discursive segment that in one way or another informs the reader or spectator about the outcome of the crisis is an *explanation* that allows an evaluation, interpretation, or understanding of the denouement.

41. Hewitt, "Inventing Antillean Narrative," 84–85.

42. See Pfaff, *Conversations with Maryse Condé*, 60–62, 65, 74.

43. See Jonassaint, *Le Pouvoir des mots*.

44. René Depestre, *Le Métier à métisser* (Paris: Stock, 1998), 174.

45. Condé, "Order, Disorder, Freedom, and the West Indian Writer," 125–26.

46. Condé, *La Parole des femmes: essai sur des romancières des Antilles de langue française* (Paris: L'Harmattan, 1979); Maryse Condé and Madeleine Cottenet-Hage, eds., *Penser la créolité* (Paris: Karthala, 1995).

47. There are, of course, exceptions, like Alec Hargreaves, who devoted a number of excellent pages to intertextuality in his book, *Immigration and Identity in Beur Fiction* (New York: Berg, 1991); Kathleen Gyssels, who broached the question of transtextuality in the Schwartz-Barts for her dissertation, *Filles de solitude: essais sur l'identité antillaise dans les (auto-)biographies de Simone et André Schwarz-Bart* (Paris: L'Harmattan, 1996); or Keith Walker who wrote an enlightening chapter in *Countermodernism and Francophone Literary Culture: The Game of Slipknot* (Durham, N.C.: Duke University Press, 1999) about intertextuality in Tahar Ben Jelloun's *L'Enfant de sable* (Paris: Seuil, 1985); English translation: *The Sand Child*, trans. Alan Sheridan (San Diego: Harcourt Brace Jovanovich, 1987).

48. Mehdi Charef, *Le Thé au harem d'Archi Ahmed* (Paris: Mercure de France/ Folio, 1983/1996), 28, emphasis added; English translation: *Tea in the Harem*, trans. Ed Emery (London: Serpent's Tail, 1989), 23; emphasis added.

49. See Georges Cattaui, *Marcel Proust* (Paris: Editions universitaires/ Classiques du XXe siècle, 1958), 70. Moreover, this hypothesis, which proffers *1001 Nights* as a model for *la Recherche*, and which is taken up again by Dominique Jullien in *Proust et ses modèles: les "Mille et une nuits" et les "Mémoires" de Saint Simon* (Paris: Corti, 1989)—an argument that follows that of Jean Rousset in *Forme et signification* (Paris: Corti, 1962)—has been reproduced by Anthony Albert Everman in his book *Lilies and Sesame: The Orient, Inversion and Artistic Creation in "À la recherche du temps perdu"* (New York: Peter Lang, 1998). Without forgetting the excellent article by Alain Buisine, "Marcel Proust: le côté de l'Orient" (*Revue des sciences humaines* 214 [1989]: 123–44), which indirectly addresses this question, is it surprising to note the lack of research on the links between Proust's text and *1001 Nights*? Is this another side of an ideological bent that refuses to admit that every "clash between cultures" implies a twofold network of mutual influences, irrespective of the inequity of their exchange. In the same vein of thought, one should consider the silence of Beckett criticism on the incongruous reference to Toussaint Louverture, the Haitian hero, in *The Unnamable*. This question is the object of a chapter in my book-in-progress, *Lecture de la lecture: littératures francophones et transtextualité*.

50. Lydie Moudileno, *L'Écrivain comme personnage dans les romans antillais francophones*, Ph.D. dissertation in French, University of California–Berkeley (1994).

51. Dany Laferrière, *Cette grenade dans la main du jeune nègre, est-ce une arme ou un fruit* (Montreal: VLB, 1993); English translation: *Why Must a Black Writer Write About Sex?*, trans. David Homel (Toronto: Coach House Press, 1994), 17–23.

52. Alain Baudot, "Antilles et Guyane," *Guide culturel: Civilisations et littératures d'expression française*, eds. Reboulet and Tétu (Paris: Hachette, 1977), 196–97.

53. William Faulkner, *Tandis que j'agonise/ As I Lay Dying*, bilingual French/English edition (Paris: Gallimard, Folio, 1990), 15.

54. Gérard Clavreuil, ed., *Erotisme et littératures* (Paris: Acropole, 1987), 79–81.

55. Note that in *Les Derniers rois mages* [*The Last African Kings*], trans. Richard Philcox (Lincoln: University of Nebraska Press, 1997), Condé writes "amandier pays" [almond trees] without a hyphen (p. 23). The use of these hyphens (or their absence) is once again a stylistic feature *not* reproduced in the English translations of Condé as well as Roumain. TRANS.

56. Gabriel García Márquez, *The Fragrance of Guava: Conversations with Gabriel García Márquez*, trans. Ann Wright (London: Verso, 1983; and Faber and Faber, 1988), 72–73.

# 9

# "HEREDITARY ANTAGONISM": RACE AND NATION IN MAURICE CASSEUS'S *VIEJO*

*Valerie Kaussen*

In the opening chapter of *Viejo* (1935), the main character, Mario, a migrant cane-cutter (termed a *viejo*) arrives in Port-au-Prince where his joyful homecoming is interrupted by the sight of an American soldier marching before the Haitian Palais National. As Mario gazes in dismay at this spectacle of imperialism, an elderly passerby comments,

> yes, yes, another colonizer, and to whom we didn't even sell the land at its worth. The first taker and it was done! The first colonizer, the one from before 1804, was also against you. They're all brothers, united together with all the instincts of their race, with all the prejudices of the white caste, civilization and cult, and the entire closed circle of the white world.[1]

The elderly man describes the U.S. occupation (1915–1934) as a historical repetition, a return to the colonial period, prior to the Haitian independence of 1804, when Haiti was not yet Haiti, but the French sugar colony Saint Domingue. Both "colonial" moments are depicted as expressions of a racially determined conflict between white and black, with the French and the Americans united by their membership in the white caste, their worship of the white cult, and their instinctive rejection of all imagined Others.

To many Haitians the U.S. occupation indeed seemed like history repeating itself.[2] As Jacques Roumain, founder of the Haitian Communist Party (and Haiti's best-known writer internationally) argued: "the parallel between the class structure of St. Domingue and the present Republic of Haiti is quite striking: French colonists and American Imperialists; 'affranchis' and the present day bourgeoisie; slaves and the Haitian proletariat."[3] Roumain surely refers here, in part, to the occupation's controversial reestablishment of the *corvée*, a form of forced labor that originated in French feudalism and had not been seen in Haiti since the early nineteenth century. Paradoxically, the *corvée* was justified as a necessary evil that would hasten the country's much-needed modernization. The *corvée* was not the only example of the way the U.S. occupation's labor practices paralleled those of the French colonial past: as *Viejo* narrates, during the occupation a migrant labor system became the norm in which poor Haitians, mostly peasants, were shipped by the thousands to U.S.-owned sugar plantations in Cuba, in a system of indentured servitude that was widely termed "slave trafficking."[4] Thus, for the majority of Haiti's population, the white marines represented a kind of resurrection of that historical enemy of freedom, the French overlord, and the American presence, despite its rhetoric of progress and modernization, signified a paradoxical return to an archaic past of hard labor, plantations, and chain gangs.

However, alongside representing the parallels between French colonialism and U.S. imperialism, especially through the example of the migrant laborer, or *viejo*, Casseus's novel also demonstrates the differences between these two institutions, attempting to map the ways that Haiti of the twentieth century was no longer Haiti of the eighteenth, and U.S. economic imperialism was not the same as the French colonial slave regime. In *Viejo*, what distinguishes the colonial past from "modern" imperialism is the way in which the latter's direct exploitation of bodies and material resources is accompanied by a more subtle campaign, one waged on the level of the mentality or the subject. Along with *corvées* and a new traffic in slaves, the United States imported into Haiti ideologies of uplift, progress, and pragmatism. As one historian puts it, the U.S. military saw itself as ambassadors of a modern industrialized nation that would assist Haiti "to pull [itself] up by its bootstraps if only Haitians would follow the formula of the American success story."[5] *Viejo* wages a relentless critique of the U.S. mission by representing a Haiti flooded by American consumer goods and the "Yankee dollar," thus insisting upon the ways that this liberal agenda was clearly a mask for U.S. economic expansion into the region both as a market for U.S. goods and as a site of investment. *Viejo* could be interpreted as a complex response to the words of the occupation's financial adviser, Arthur Millspaugh, who stated that the "shiftless" and "indolent" Haitian peasants "if they are to be citizens of an independent self-governing nation, . . . must acquire . . . a new set of wants" (Schmidt 158). Liberal market ideologies favoring competition, efficiency, and the individual are thus linked, in *Viejo*, to the expanding U.S. market, which is gradually creating a "nouvelle race" of Haitians who worship, instead of traditional values of nation and race, a dangerous foreign money economy with its "new set of wants." *Viejo* thus seeks to represent the ways that the often paradoxical effort to "modernize" Haiti, to make it more penetrable to U.S. investment, was pursued both materially and ideologically, often depicting the latter as the more insidious form of colonization.

However, although *Viejo* identifies and seeks to define the modern ideological forms of subjection that accompanied the occupation's mission, it does so by marshaling its own archaisms. As the quote with which I open this article suggests, colonial Saint Domingue and Occupied Haiti become versions or typologies of a primordial universal story: the instinctive battle between the races, outside of history and always already prior to colonialism, the occupation, and modernity itself. For Casseus, racial strife, or "the hereditary antagonism of two races, two colors" ("l'antagonisme héréditaire, raciale, de deux couleurs") (52), is an archaic story and a kind of originary state. As such, it is the essential truth behind black enslavement under both the French colonial system and U.S. imperialism. Haiti's two historical moments of foreign domination become typologies, varying versions of a universal same, thus assuaging anxieties aroused by the "newness" of the modern imperialist method of the United States.

Maurice Casseus was a fellow-traveler of *noirisme*,[6] François Duvalier and Lorimer Denis's proto-fascist cultural and political movement. *Noirisme*, also termed the Griot movement, was an extreme variant of the *indigénist* movement, whose cultural nationalism developed in response to the U.S. occupation.[7] *Noirisme* acknowledged its debts to European fascism and scientific racism and sought to understand Haiti's history exclusively in terms of racial conflict, specifically conflict between the ruling mulatto elite and the black majority. A famous Haitian proverb—a poor mulatto is a black man, and a rich black, a mulatto—suggests that *noirisme* interpreted what was clearly a class/race phenomenon as one of race exclusively. Haitian sociologist Laënnec Hurbon argues that *noirisme* was the discourse of a growing black bourgeoisie who desired full participation in the social and economic institutions that traditionally excluded them.[8] Thus, according to *noiriste* ideology, the solution to the problem of social upheaval in Haiti lay in the rise to power of a black elite who would represent the needs, desires—and vengeance—of the impoverished black majority.

For the *noiristes*, the legacy of colonialism with its strict class and color hierarchies was identified as the root of the "Haitian problem"—economic dependence, class division, misery, and abject poverty for the majority. As evidenced by Roumain's Marxist analysis quoted above, the *noiristes* were not alone in emphasizing the importance of Haiti's colonial past in understanding its current predicament. But where the Marxists viewed the colonial legacy in terms of class structures, the *noiristes* described the continued presence of Haiti's colonial past in terms of biological residues. According to Duvalier and Denis, history traced the degree to which individual races pursued successfully their "mission," i.e., the flowering of their unique gift to the world community of races, or "le concert des peuples."[9] Throughout their ethnological and political writings, Duvalier and Denis argue that social and racial divisions inherited from the colonial period were detrimental because they had suppressed the development of a genetically determined "psychisme profond," or true Haitian "génie" or spirit. In an essay entitled "Question d'anthropo-sociologie: le détérminisme racial," published in a 1939 issue of *Les Griots*,[10] Duvalier and Denis suggest that it was not so much the socioeconomic effects of racial inequality that had stunted the growth of the Haitian racial ideal, but rather the influence of the white race's most base biological elements: "pirates, buccaneers, scavengers, and freebooters, *habitués* of the Salpêtrière"[11] (*Eléments* 120). Duvalier and Denis go on to ask: "how could all of this magma brought into contact with the African Negro give rise to a Community valued for its elevated collective consciousness and the grandeur of its spiritual ideal?" (120). According to Denis and Duvalier, colonialism brought to the island of Hispaniola a crude and debased genetic influence, a criminal race of pirates, mad men, delinquents, and derelicts. The "feverish period of colonization" (*Eléments* 120) is the product of this gene pool, and dominant in Denis and Duvalier's list of debased white genetic traits is the theme of greed and materialism. Criminality, greed, and the impulse toward economic expansion are here biologized as white and, in a reversal of the European narrative of progress, it is *this* biological material that is held responsible for Haiti's underdevelopment.

Similarly, *Viejo* defines the U.S. occupation in terms of genetic pollution, as ushering in a racial influence that debases and degenerates. Imperialism as the invasion by greedy white barbarians is represented in the character "Cap," short for "captain" but also resonating with "capitalism," a figure who would fit comfortably into Denis and Duvalier's gallery of colonial rogues. Cap, a former marine captain, is a reject of the U.S. military (he has been court-martialed for striking a superior) but nonetheless finds protection in occupied Haiti. Cap is never depicted as uttering a full sentence, and he seems almost cretin-like as he communicates through monosyllabic American expressions: "hey baby!" Cap is also red-faced and obese from eating and drinking excessively, and he is usually shown in the novel lewdly propositioning prostitutes. Closely associated with money and commodities in the novel, Cap has grown rich in Haiti by speculating on the Port-au-Prince market, which he has flooded with an artificially sweetened lemonade, the quality and salubrity of which the newly established American-run "Service d'Hygiène" chooses to overlook. He invades Haiti's borders with new tastes and desires: for low-quality lemonade, as well as for American luxury products, the latter with which he lures away Mario's girlfriend: "[Mario] knew all too well that the rich fabrics, the lotions bearing a new American brand-name, the manicure set, and the hair ornament had all come from the local Marine commissary" (149).

The process of capital penetration into Haiti is thus represented by Cap who, like capital and its attendant ideologies, has the power to cross national boundaries and to freely move about unencumbered by limitations—legal, economic, or institutional. Through Cap, the novel imagines capitalism as transgression, criminality, and piracy, as not subject to certain "natural" laws, particularly of national sovereignty: "what need did he have of superficial ornamentation: his white skin sufficed. Would this passport assure his welcome in the next world as well?" (40). With the "passport" of his white skin, Cap may enter any world at will, and the authority of his whiteness permits free reign to his appetite, allowing him to appropriate what he has no "right" to: black Haitian women. Predictably, black women are associated in *Viejo* with the national ground; the nationalist aim of the imagined connection between black women and the *terre-patrie* is particularly emphasized when Mario muses that after sleeping with his girlfriend Olive, "he felt himself to be a master, a sort of colonizer" (55). But like the nation, Olive's body will be claimed by the "real" colonizer Cap, whose desire will "infect" not only her body but her own desire, her subjectivity: "Olive recalled the miraculous gift of her own body enveloped in the white embrace of Cap, who blindly desired her, and whom she, in turn, desired with equal blindness" (91). In desiring Cap, Olive joins the "nouvelle race" of Haitians, "who pray to the idol of the 'Dollar'" (56), or who participate in the project of uplift, the desire for social mobility. The creation of this new, i.e., modern race, enslaved to the twin desire for material gain and its ideological expression, whiteness, is represented in *Viejo* as the spread of an infectious disease: "the reign of the dollar introduced onto the black island the supremacy of a skin that spread like leprosy" (15).

In *Viejo*, Cap is a figure for the ambivalent transforming processes of capitalist modernization, an embodiment of invisible market forces and ideologies that disintegrate the traditional values—race, nation, family—with which they come into contact. At his touch, the touch of the world market, "all that is solid melts into air," i.e., traditional constraints dissolve. In response to these deterritorializing potentials of modernization, *Viejo* regrounds unseen market forces in raced bodies, the better to combat them. Paradoxical to his ability to dissolve and transgress boundaries, then, Cap, like the French pirates and scavengers ("magma") of Duvalier and Denis's colonial era, is a figure of grotesque physicality, seen in his obesity and his drunken, clumsy movements. Cap's whiteness is defined as a base materiality, a crude and weighty matter that overwhelms whatever comes into contact with it. In *Viejo*, whiteness as "magma" is inextricable from the base materialism of colonialism and the occupation; whiteness is the physical embodiment of the capitalist market and the market finds its most pure expression in whiteness.

By contrast, *Viejo* defines blackness as in its essence opposed to the materialism, alienation, and debased systems of value associated with modernity. In *Viejo*, blackness is represented as ideal and spiritual in contrast to the weighty "magma" of whiteness. In this respect, *Viejo* follows the international trend of primitivist art of the nineteen twenties that derived in part from Oswald Spengler's massively influential work, *The Decline of the West*. The latter argued that, whereas Western civilization was in a state of decline and decadence, African cultures were still close to nature, and were thus youthful and vigorous, the repositories of spiritual and authentic human values. *Viejo's* construction of mythic African ideal is most directly described in a scene where Mario, dancing to the drums of a *vaudou* ceremony, feels the call of his African ancestry: "his soul had mounted upon something that he couldn't quite define but that carried him far away into the unknown land of his ancestors . . . this was the mother country, the hot sands that burnt the souls of his feet and the palms of his hands, the thick jungles stalked by nude bodies" (52). The Haitian national soul is located in this African "mother country" of hot sands, thick jungles, and nude bodies. Blackness is here defined as sensual, natural, pastoral, but also ideal and spiritual.

In *Viejo*, Mario signifies this African-based black essence. His role in the novel is to present an absolute opposition to the white race and all its imagined corollaries—market ideologies, money, modernity—each threatening to contaminate the spirit of "oldest Africa" that defines Haiti's national identity. In this respect, *Viejo* fits squarely into the cultural politics of Haitian *indigénisme* and its more right-wing variant *noirisme,* which called for an embrace of the negative, a celebration of the terms that European culture deemed barbarous, ugly, and unclean. In general, *indigénisme* and *noirisme* pursued this goal by locating the Haitian nation's African soul in the countryside, and in the *vaudou*-practicing peasantry who was supposedly isolated and unsullied by contact with the U.S. presence and with modernity in general. What is especially interesting, then, about *Viejo,* is that Casseus chose to depart from the indigenist norm by setting his novel of resistance in the urban space of Port-au-Prince, heart of the U.S. imperialist campaign, and by choosing to portray a social type, the *viejo,* specifically created out of the conditions of contact, movement, and capital penetration initiated by the U.S. occupation. The *viejos,* disenfranchised peasants forced to migrate to U.S.-owned cane plantations in Cuba to work, were a population of deracinated figures. Ironically resembling Duvalier and Denis's impure colonial rogues, they were on the fringes of society, returning to Haiti as working-class heroes with some cash, gold teeth, and Spanish surnames. Figures of hybridity and cultural contact on the peripheries of the capitalist world market, the *viejos* were representatives of the degradations and possibilities created out of the conditions of U.S. empire.

Viejo of course identifies the modern forces that produced the *viejos* as deep threats to Haiti's African-derived authenticity. In response, the novel insists, on the one hand, that the surface realities of racial contact cannot touch the pure biological inheritance from Africa, the soul of the Haitian nation. But on the other hand, the racial contact of colonialism and imperialism is paradoxically necessary to the novel's articulation of the absolute truth of race, which, in *Viejo,* is racial strife, or the "hereditary antagonism of two colors."

Mario, then, along with the African pastoral motherland, contains within his "racial unconscious" histories of contact between Africa and the West, i.e., enslavement. Casseus depicts his main character as nearly overwhelmed by this biologically inscribed history of trauma: "his heart grew heavy under the weight of the black continent with all of its deserts, its grains of sand, its Pyramids, with all of the waves of the mysterious Nile, and the dirty foams of the Mississippi strummed upon a banjo" (15). Mario carries within his unconscious a mythic racial history, imagined here as a storehouse of sorrowful images of slavery, emblematized by the Pyramids and the Mississippi. Despite its occasional realism, then, the description of the *viejo's* experience in Cuba ultimately serves the articulation of this grander allegorical narrative. As a canecutter on a U.S.-owned sugar plantation in Cuba in the nineteen twenties,

Mario performs "the beastly labor that built the Pyramids" (17). The reference to the biblical narrative of captivity and enslavement here of course emphasizes this description's typological aims, as do the descriptions of hard labor on the cane plantation that are aestheticized and almost romanticized: "the stooped backs of beautiful polished ebony, molded muscles that mirrored the sky, the heaving of chests with each stretching forth of the arms" (17). The lyricism of these passages suggests an attempt to represent hard plantation labor, not so much realistically, but in terms of a set of timeless aesthetic images, the latter recalling at once Egypt, the Deep South, Saint Domingue, and twentieth-century Cuba.

Implied in this vision of slavery as the timeless condition of the black masses is also the moment of violent black revolt, expressed most purely and gloriously, according to *Viejo*, in the Haitian Revolution. The Haitian Revolution is evoked in *Viejo* as the great transformative moment when Africa triumphed over France, when whiteness was negated. *Viejo* identifies the spirit of the revolution then as African, associating it, rather than with the French-speaking and Catholic Toussaint Louverture, with the African slaves Bouckman and Mackandal, leaders of early slave revolts, and described by Casseus as "those savage and primitive wretches, flea-ridden vagabonds and the true sons of Africa" ("ces gueux sauvages et primitifs, ces vagabonds pouilleux, fils légitimes d'Afrique") (87)—Rimbaud-esque, embracing their otherness and bent on destroying the white world.

In *Viejo*, then, enslavement is in part invoked as a means of "resurrecting" the Haitian Revolution, the typological event that must be repeated in order to rout the second colonizer and liberate the "enslaved" nation. Through the novel's representation of a racially determined and thus ever-repeating history, neoenslavement on the Cuban cane plantation and a labor strike among Haitian canecutters become repetitions of Saint Domingue enslavement and the Haitian Revolution, prefigurings of the inevitable revolt that will chase the United States from Haiti's shores. Mario calls the strike, which he terms a "revolution," for the second of January, Haitian independence day, suggesting the novel's use of Haitian labor struggle in terms of nationalist display. The symbolic nature of the strike—and the Haitian Revolution itself—is further emphasized by the way Casseus narrates it, with the strike finally acting only as a backdrop for a scene of much greater affect in which Mario engages in a fight to the death with a white manager: "he lunged at me and hit me in the face with his stick. Damn! My friend, I don't know what went through my head, but Lord, I became enraged when that pig struck me. With one blow I had him down on the ground and I crushed his head against the old machine cogs and rail debris that were lying there" (28). A response to the real conditions of his oppression, Mario's violence is nonetheless depicted as the eruption of primitive rage, of his racial unconscious.

In *Viejo*, revolutionary violence, by being racialized, is also aestheticized. The representation of the labor struggle in Cuba as a theater of symbolic racial redemption undermines the scene's potential as a political allegory of revolution, one with concrete material aims. *Viejo's* depiction of black revolutionary violence thus conforms to Walter Benjamin's argument about the Fascist aestheticization of politics. In the familiar epilogue to "The Work of Art in the Age of Mechanical Reproduction," Benjamin writes that "the logical result of Fascism is the introduction of aesthetics into political life,"[12] i.e., an aesthetics of the aura that requires passivity and inaction from its spectators. Benjamin goes on to argue that the Fascist aestheticization of politics offers the masses the gift of expression as a compensation for taking away their "right to change property relations" (241). Fascism thus provides the opportunity for collective expression, but doesn't seek to alter the property structures that are the objects of mass political participation. Similarly, the *noiriste* response to Haiti's recurrent economic crises and the cyclical revolts of the peasantry was effectively to deny the notion of class in favor of race exclusively, the latter becoming the rallying cry of an elite group whose leadership would "redeem" the black masses while leaving the structure of power and the distribution of capital unchanged (Hurbon 101).

The act of killing the white "master" in Cuba is not revolutionary, then, as it has no transformative outcome. In the nationalist fantasy depicted in *Viejo*, the scene functions to render Mario a symbol of the violent *potential* of his race, and of Haiti's historical role as the site where whiteness is negated. Mario then operates as a symbolic reminder of this nationalist essence to those who have capitulated to the Occupier and his materialistic mission. In one brief episode, a kind of tableau, Mario contemplates a black Haitian soldier, who is a member of the American-trained civilian military police, *La Garde d'Haïti*. The scene represents clearly the symbolic function of *Viejo's* protagonist:

> For a long time [Mario] took pleasure in cataloguing the stigmas of the new race that was on its knees before the dollar and was being kicked in the ribs. In the sight of the man giving the military salute to the American corporals he contemplated the distorted image of the glorious battle that had liberated him by overthrowing enslavement. He heard the inferno of the sugar refineries grow and rise toward the stars. But by the time it reached him, the vision had shriveled up and was nothing more than a meager reddening of the sky before

it finally faded away. Mario then understood that he still preferred the miserable life of the sugarcane harvest to the role of human beast bent down under the foreign boot. (14)

This fixed image or tableau contrasts the "slave" Mario and the American-trained soldier, in order to compare two forms of "enslavement," the physical and the ideological, paradoxically defining the former as potentially more human. Mario may have led a "miserable life" in Cuba but the soldier is a "human beast," animalized by his ideological subjection, and thus the one who is "truly" enslaved. In *Viejo*, direct physical repression is the site of resistance, because it putatively does not compromise those under its domination. Their racial unconscious remains untouched. But, in contrast, the racial unconscious of the American-trained soldier, site of the black will to revolt, has been colonized, here. As a slave to ideology, the soldier is not truly black, but rather a member of a "new race," a miscegenated race that worships the dollar instead of the African drum. This new race is a modern one: fallen, fractured, and, having internalized the master's law, in collusion with its own enslavement. The American-trained soldier thus represents a "deformed" image that Mario's presence in the tableau is designed to heal in two ways: by regrounding ideological subjection with figures of physical subjection (the soldier is "kicked in the ribs," on his knees, a "beast bent down under the foreign boot"), and by resurrecting, from his own unconscious, that image's "essence," the black racial essence, of slave revolt and the apocalyptic flames of the burning sugar-cane factories, i.e, the absolute negation of white colonization.

The above scene encapsulates the role assigned to the main character of *Viejo* in the student-led nationalist struggle that occupies one of the novel's loose narrative threads. For the group of students (a coalition of mulattos and members of the black bourgeoisie) who are in the process of fighting for Haiti's liberation, Mario is a national exemplar, an object of inspiration, and the living embodiment of black authenticity, defined in terms of the twin experiences of enslavement and overthrow. He is at once the eternally sorrowful slave, complacent and child-like: "you were hardly intellectual and cultivated, Mario. But there was so much sensitivity in your beautiful, sad and sweet expression, like an animal resigned to its fate" (37); but also a vector of racially inscribed violence, one of the "savage and primitive . . . vagabonds," one of the "true sons of Africa" (87). A key scene represents the students discussing the strike and assigning to Mario his role in their struggle:

Mario had listened to them pensively. But finally when the intensity of the speeches had subsided, he nodded his fine woolly head:

"Oh, friends," he said, "if only I could do something too by your sides. I'm older than the rest of you—I'm thirty years old—and I don't know all the things that you know. But at thirty, I'm still in the prime of my youth, yes I am!"

When Mario had finished, André David contemplated his sad face, took that humble woolly head into his hands and gazed deeply into those soft and tranquil eyes:

"I've only known you for a few days, Mario," he said, "but listen up: the words that you just uttered must ignite a revolution that will usher in the second Independence. Damn it! . . . Bouckman, Biassou, Mackandal knew nothing about diplomacy and treaties. In hand-to-hand combat, they had only broken swords in their black fists, and when they were armed with nothing but their teeth and nails, they eviscerated the enemy, smashed in their skulls, crippled them, and then hung the long bluish strands of white entrails under the mighty Negro sun. Good lord! Have we got their blood in our veins, yes or no? . . . what is it that we're doing here?" (87)

In Mario's timid and innocent offer of assistance, the students identify the soul of the revolution, the energy and drive that will incite a "second Independence." But clearly, rather than Mario's *words* it is the sight of Mario's body, of his "fine woolly head" that inspires the students here. True to *noiriste* ideology, the educated elites speak for the black man of the mass, translating his racially determined silence into the poetry of national revolt. For as one of the "true sons of Africa" (87), Mario is not expected to speak the language of the civilized. He must symbolize, rather, the eternal potential for its destruction, and an embodiment of the master's phantasmic fears of the barbaric, blood-thirsty, and irrational black African.

As *Viejo* suggests, in the *noiriste* nationalist project, historical violence, Haiti's history of slave revolt, is racialized as the genetic inheritance of the black masses. As such, mass violence operates as a weapon for those who claim alone to have the power to contain it, the Haitian black elite. As a scene following the student strikes depicts, those who control the masses, also control this engine of barbaric rage. In the scene, Haiti's political old guard tries to prevent one of the students from speaking at an important political meeting, and in response the student threatens the assembled with the violent wrath of the silenced for whom he speaks: "no, Mr. President, you may not restrict me from speaking, for look at the people in the doorway listening to me. They won't allow it. They'll tear you to pieces" (113). The young member of the nationalist movement speaks for the people and lays claim to their violent tendencies, using the latter as a weapon in a project that, far from including them, will ensure that they remain silent witnesses peering over but never crossing the threshold into the "civilized" domain of political process.

Imagining black violence as a racially encoded trait of course eliminates the need for transforming the conditions that produce it. In *Viejo*, the representation of the revolutionary violence of the enslaved, whether in Saint Domingue or Cuba, is drained of its radical challenge to the existing socioeconomic order, be it dominated by French colonialism, contemporary U.S. imperialism, or the Haitian *bourgeoisie*. *Viejo* thus demonstrates, perhaps inadvertently, the ways that *noirisme*, far from challenging Haiti's inherited colonial—and capitalist—model, sought to uphold it. As Hurbon has written, according to *noiriste* ideology, Haiti's problems would be solved, i.e., social upheaval "neutralized," by finding "intellectuals able to speak for the masses, and thus keep them in a docile position" (92). Hurbon then adds cryptically, "a soothing discourse for the local bourgeoisie as it was for the imperial metropoles." Haunted by the former Master's values of civilization vs. barbarism, *noirisme* would justify its bid for power by maintaining an "enslaved" and thus restless and violent populace; "controlling" the latter would be their *raison d'être* for joining the "master" and participating equally in "his" civilization.

Like *indigénisme, négritude,* and other black cultural movements of the nineteen twenties and thirties, *noirisme* inverted the race hierarchy of Western thought without challenging Western ideologies of absolute racial difference nor the economic motives that underlay them. Thus, the literary exploration of *noiriste* nationalism in *Viejo* demonstrates the stakes of a familiar nativist black poetic aesthetic pushed to the extreme: if oppression and a concomitant will to violence are the inescapable inheritance of an impoverished black populace and the basis for a black cultural (and, in Haiti, national) aesthetic, how will the black masses ever escape this condemnation to silence and barbarism? The perpetuation of colonial socioeconomic structures are now written into the discourses that claim to resist them, perhaps most vividly expressed in the *noiriste* celebration of enslavement as the most "authentic" state, and symbol, for the black masses. In the attempt to carve for themselves a place in a capitalist world order that, as history has shown, indeed precluded Haiti's participation under any other terms, *noiriste* nationalists depended on the perpetuation of a benighted, dependent, and impoverished black majority. As *Viejo* shows, in this imagining of enslavement as the location for the heroic negation of white oppression is emblematized the final and utter triumph of the white "master" and his insidious forms of control.

# NOTES

1. Maurice Casseus, *Viejo* (Port-au-Prince: Editions "La Presse," 1935), 7; all translations are my own.

2. Despite the 1804 anticolonial revolution that established Haiti as an independent nation, the class/race system created by French colonialism had never been fully dismantled. Haiti's elite French-educated mulatto class, mostly descendants of the colony's free persons of color *(les affranchis)* had stepped into the shoes and the mansions of the departing French *colons* and maintained the abject poverty, if not enslavement, of the mass of the population—the black, *kreyol*-speaking peasantry. When the United States invaded and began its military occupation of Haiti in 1915, Haiti's elite was in a sense demoted. As one historian puts it, "to the Marines, a mulatto was just as much a 'nigger' as a coal-black peasant from the countryside" (Schmidt, xii). Occupation officials established Jim Crow–style segregation and the Haitian elite found itself combating the kind of racism that the class of *affranchis* had encountered one hundred years earlier.

3. Jacques Roumain, *Analyse schématique* (1934), (new ed., Port-au-Prince: Editions Idées Nouvelles, Idées Prolétariennes, 1999), 33.

4. See Brenda Gayle Plummer, *Haiti and the United States: The Psychological Moment* (Athens: University of Georgia Press, 1992), 111.

5. Hans Schmidt, *The United States Occupation of Haiti, 1915–1934* (New Brunswick, N.J.: Rutgers University Press, 1971), 155.

6. Casseus was born in 1909 in Port-au-Prince. He is a minor writer in the canon of Haitian letters, having written, in addition to *Viejo*, only one novel, entitled *Mambo* (1949), which, like *Viejo*, has been out of print since its initial publication. Casseus's name never appears on the list of writers closely associated with *noirisme*, which includes Carl Brouard and Magloire St. Aude. Nonetheless, his poetry appeared in the pages of the *noiriste* journal *Les Griots*, and *noiriste* ideology, in its most extreme forms, clearly informs many passages of *Viejo*. To such an extent does Casseus's work feel *"noiriste"* that in *Literature and Ideology in Haiti, 1915–1961* (Totowa, N.J.: Barnes & Noble, 1981), Michael Dash opens his chapter on *noiriste* literature with an analysis of one of Casseus's poems, "Le Tambour racial."

7. Members of the *indigénist* group, including Jacques Roumain, Emile Roumer, and Carl Brouard, came from a variety of political orientations, but their political differences tended to be unacknowledged throughout the occupation period in the interest of the common cause of national liberation. Once the United States began to dismantle the occupation in 1930, however, rifts in the indigenist group emerged, with indigenist intellectuals eventually splitting into two camps, the Marxists and the ultranationalists, or *noiristes*. The *noiriste* movement eventually resulted in the election of Duvalier as president of Haiti in 1957, thus ushering in one of the nation's bloodiest dictatorships.

8. See Laënnec Hurbon. *Culture et Dictature en Haïti: L'imaginaire sous contrôle.* (Paris: L'Harmattan, 1979), 87.

9. Lorimer Denis and François Duvalier, *Le problème des classes à travers l'histoire d'Haïti* (Port-au-Prince: Collection Les Griots, 1959), 143.

10. Reprinted in *Oeuvres Essentielles,* Docteur François Duvalier (Port-au-Prince: Collection Oeuvres Essentielles, 1968), 115–21.

11. A mental institution in Paris.

12. Walter Benjamin. "The Work of Art in the Age of Mechanical Reproduction," in *Illuminations,* trans. Harry Zohn (New York: Schocken Books, 1969), 241.

# PART III

# ORIENTALISM AND THE MAGHREBIAN PRESENCE IN POSTCOLONIAL FRANCE

Just as no part of the French empire was more central to the colonial endeavor than North Africa, no group of migrants has loomed larger in the French imagination since World War II than those from the Maghreb. Contemporary France is a nation where discussions of race, a taboo concept in universalist discourse, are subsumed under the rubric of "immigration"— and "immigrants" usually implies Algerians. The marked intolerance toward North Africans in a nation proud of its history of tolerance arises from several sources, including the bitter, unresolved legacy of the Algerian war, questions over the place of Islam in the lay republic, and above all the enduring contradiction between universalism and humanism key to the history of modern France. The four chapters in this section explore the presence of North Africa in contemporary France from a variety of perspectives. All call into question facile demarcations between colonialism and postcolonialism, as well as insisting on the central role of Maghrebian France in elaborating a new French identity.

The chapters by Hafid Gafaiti and Driss Maghraoui use Maghrebian immigration as a mirror to analyze contemporary French society. In chapter 10, Hafid Gafaiti demonstrates how conflicts over North African immigrants illustrate deep tensions over citizenship and universalism in modern France. He argues that these conflicts arise not just from the colonial past, but also from the continued colonial character of the relationship between France and the Maghreb. Gafaiti also explores the important role of race in the development of modern societies, noting that race and universalism are not opposites, but two sides of the same coin. Chapter 11 by Driss Maghraoui also emphasizes the importance of the colonial heritage in understanding contemporary tensions over immigration, focusing in particular on discourses of citizenship and race. He considers the ways in which new social movements have arisen out of the conflicts over French politics and identity, and analyzes one such group, the *organisation politique* and its conceptualization of a new sense of what it means to be French. In contrast to these first two chapters, the chapters by Ali Yedes and Nancy Wood, concentrate on non-Muslim Algerians, considering the experiences of French settlers and Jews. Both groups left Algeria *en masse* for France after 1962, and yet both remain profoundly linked to Algerian culture. Chapter 12 by Ali Yedes looks at the many ways in which the *Pieds-Noirs* of Algeria were shaped culturally by their interactions with Algerian Muslims during French colonial rule, showing how these cultural affinities went together with racist views of the Arabs. He shows how the exodus to France intensified this contradiction, and at the same time sharpened feelings of difference from the French of the metropole. In chapter 13, Nancy Wood uses the techniques of history of memory to analyze the Jewish population of Algeria both during and after French rule. Wood begins by asking why so many in France today (for example Jacques Derrida and Hélène Cixous, both Jews of Algerian descent) are so interested in Algerian Jewish identities, then explores how the historiography of Algerian Jewry has changed over the years. She underscores a new tendency to critique assimilation and emphasize instances of Jewish/Muslim cooperation rather than hostility.

These four chapters not only outline the Maghrebian contribution to modern French culture, but also demonstrate how contradictions in the very notion of what it means to be French surface in the treatment of those incorrectly considered to be outsiders.

# 10

# NATIONALISM, COLONIALISM, AND ETHNIC DISCOURSE IN THE CONSTRUCTION OF FRENCH IDENTITY

*Hafid Gafaiti*

In recent years, the issue of immigration has appeared to be not only an essential feature of the formation of French identity, but also a central element in the cultural and political debate in modern France. However, contrary to the racist ideology of a growing portion of the French population and media and to the increasingly consensual allegations of leaders from both the Right and the Left against immigrants, it has been established that the immigrant population in France has remained basically stable over the last sixty years. Indeed, the figures on immigrants in the 1930s and the 1990s in France are practically equivalent and amount to 7.5 percent of the total population.[1]

What has changed is not the proportion of immigrants, but, on the one hand, the composition of the immigrant population in France and, on the other hand, the ways in which it is viewed and considered. A symptomatic indication of this phenomenon is that the political debate has become predominantly centered on policies of immigration, and that events of the 1990s have led to an important body of work on the subject not only in France but also in Europe and the United States.

It is evident that the interest in this issue corresponds to the evolution of the postwar economic situation and the change of policies directly related to decolonization. In this perspective, as a consequence, the status of the "immigrant" changed and new categories were produced to describe and relate to this new component of French society.

In this chapter, I will argue that this situation and the sociological as well as the ideological and intellectual categories produced to deal with what has become the "question of immigration" probably reflect more on the French and the way they view themselves than on this half-real and half-imaginary being that they created and call the *immigré*. In order to do so, I will concentrate on the genesis of conceptual constructions produced to represent North African immigrants and on the evolution of their status within French society. Indeed, the structural relationship between universalism, colonialism, nationalism, and racism is best illustrated, in the case of Modern France, by the evolution of the concept of the North African immigrant. Besides, an important element in the discussion of the relationship between what, in France, is considered the "French" and the "Other" is provided by the singularization of the North African immigrant community. My analysis will combine a necessary historical perspective and a reflection on the image of the immigrant in contemporary French society.

## FRANCE AND IMMIGRATION: THE TERMS OF THE DEBATE

For decades, the parameters that defined French identity went unquestioned, and actually masked the fact that, like in all countries, immigration is at the heart of the constitution of France as a nation. In this sense, the history of France is the history of the denial of fundamental elements of its own identity. It is precisely the model of the nation upon which republican France is founded that has led to the historical amnesia concerning the role of immigration in the development of French society. The ideas of assimilation, uniformity, and universality of the French model of the nation—"la République une et indivisible"—have been crucial in masking ethnic, regional, and other differences.

For a long time, the debate on immigration suffered from a lack of historical contextualization. In fact, the conceptual opposition between the French and the immigrants is a relatively recent phenomenon resulting from the emergence of the nineteenth-century idea of the nation-state. It is, indeed, in the course of the process of reevaluation of French sociocultural and ideological values that took place during the French Revolution and its aftermath that the categories of "national" and "foreigner" were produced. In this respect, the study of immigration in France requires that we take into account its genesis and that we consider it as an inherent element of French history and not as an external object to be explored separately from France itself. Indeed, a basic consideration of French history, even by nonhistorians, indicates without ambiguity that, like any other country's, the fate of France was largely determined by various fluctuations of populations and numerous fluxes of immigration from different parts of the world. In spite of the different readings and interpretations that historians may produce about it, this phenomenon has been ongoing since prehistoric times and is very accurately traceable from, at least, the Germanic and Roman invasions to the present.[2] Recently, Fernand Braudel and other historians have challenged the previously unquestioned dogma of the homogeneity of France's population and cultural identity. In other words, as Gérard Noiriel puts it,

Individuals are free to represent their past in any way they wish, to display or to hide their "ethnic," national, or socioeconomic origins. Collectively, however, to take seriously the diversity of the current French population involves a change in outlook on the recent past. Immigration can no longer be considered an issue that affects us from without; it must be understood as a problem that is internal to the history of contemporary French society. Indeed, to illustrate its problematic, this book could very well have been entitled *Immigrants into Frenchmen*. . . . As Fernand Braudel wrote in his last book: "To define the French past is to locate the French within their own existence" (Braudel 1988–1990). Beyond simply stating the "truth," to explain contemporary France's indebtedness to immigration is, therefore, to provide millions of inhabitants of this country with the possibility of legitimately locating their personal history, or that of their family, within the "master narrative" of French national history. What makes immigration such an important dimension of recent history, however, is that it raises epistemological questions of greater relevance to contemporary France. It is not the immigrants themselves who are particularly interesting but, rather, the explanatory principles that must be mobilized if we are to address the unanswered questions of French republican history: what is the relationship of real individuals to institutions (state, party, nation)? What is the role of uprootedness in the formation and the consolidation of a society? How can the issue of "origins" and "feelings of belonging" be incorporated into the so-called history of mentalities? How are criteria of class, nationality, and gender combined in the definition of individuals and of the groups to which they belong?[3]

Until very recently, sociologists and politicians, critics and theorists have had the tendency to describe the relationship between the French and immigrants in terms of oppositions, putting forward binary terms such as assimilation and difference, national and foreigner, universal and particular. One should explore to what extent this series of dichotomies is an accurate reflection of reality considering that the notion of "nation" is an ideal construction based on the idea of unity and homogeneity that the social, ethnic, and cultural facts of every country structurally and permanently contradict.

Most of the time, modern France is characterized as an entity molded in the crucible of a Jacobinism that erased all distinctions; it is described as a monolithic structure that destroyed the particularities of regions, populations, cultures, and political organizations in order to replace them, in fact to remodel them, in a unique and homogeneous republican universalism. I would like to suggest that an assessment of the philosophical foundations of French universalism leads us to rethink, from a different and productive perspective, this concept, which is at the basis of the representation of the French national myth, and the central notions such as French identity, citizenship, assimilation, integration, constituting the current debate about French society and immigration.

## THE ENLIGHTENMENT'S ETHNIC DISCOURSE

Most postcolonial discourses have emphasized the fact that French universalism is in fact another form of particularism, and on that basis opposed it with categories such as difference and diversity. However, even though they are oppositional categories, universalism and particularism are constitutive parts of a metadiscourse that encompasses them. Indeed, they are constituents of the Enlightenment concept of "Man" as the central anthropological project of modern European discourse on both the individual and society, on the West and the rest.[4]

In "Writing 'Race' and the Difference It Makes," reflecting on the concept of race on the basis of a study of the conditions of publication and subsequent reception of the work of Phillis Wheatley, Henry Louis Gates Jr. explains that throughout the eighteenth century, one of the questions that seemed fundamental to Europeans was whether Africans could ever produce literary works or be able to deal with the sciences and the arts. For them, the answer to this question would determine if Africans were part of humanity—as they conceived it and of which they considered themselves the models—or not. If, according to the Eurocentrist classification of species, Africans were not capable of producing formal thought and aesthetic works, it followed that they were naturally destined to slavery.

Why was the creative writing of the African of such importance to the eighteenth century's debate over slavery? I can briefly outline one thesis: after

René Descartes, reason was privileged, or valorized, above all other human characteristics. Writing, especially after the printing press became so widespread, was taken to be the visible sign of reason. Blacks were "reasonable," and hence "men," if—and only if—they demonstrated mastery of "the arts and sciences," the eighteenth century's formula for writing. So, while the Enlightenment is characterized by its foundation on man's ability to reason, it simultaneously used the absence and presence of reason to delimit and circumscribe the very humanity of the cultures and people of color which Europeans had been "discovering" since the Renaissance. The urge toward the systematization of all human knowledge (by which we characterize the Enlightenment) led directly to the relegation of black people to a lower place in the great chain of being, an ancient construct that arranged all of creation on a vertical scale from plants, insects, and animals through man to the angels and God himself.

By 1750, the chain had become minutely calibrated; the human scale rose from "the lowliest Hottentot" (black South Africans) to "glorious Milton and Newton."[5]

What Gates's demonstration illustrates is that this problematic—which constituted the basis of modern Western thought and ideology and paved the way for the nineteenth-century European ethnic discourse and colonial ideology—indicates clearly that the idea of universalism is not opposed to the idea of race, but that they constitute a dyad, the two sides of the coin, the two faces of Janus. Indeed, it is necessary to stress that there is a structural link between the eighteenth-century universalistic ideal and the Enlightenment's racist classifications that later justified the European colonial enterprise. It is also important to add that, on the one hand, our world was largely shaped by this philosophical perspective and, on the other hand, that the issue of immigration in France is still significantly associated with this country's colonial past. Along with Etienne Balibar, I would like to suggest that "it is a question of the 'internal liaison' which was established between the notions of Mankind, the Human species, of the cultural progress of Mankind, and of the anthropological 'prejudices' concerning races or the natural bases of slavery. It is a question of the very notion of race, whose modern meaning dates from the Enlightenment—that great blossoming of universalism—and affects its development in return: not in a tangential way, external to its 'essence,' but intrinsically."[6] From this perspective, it appears that racism is not an external dimension of modern societies, following the development of the age of discovery, the Industrial Revolution, capitalism, and the second wave of French colonialism. Again, it important to insist with Balibar that "there is no clear line of 'demarcation' between unversalism and racism. It is not possible to define two separate entities, one of which includes all ideas which are (potentially) universalist, whilst the other includes all ideas which are (potentially) racist. I would express this in a Hegelian terminology: universalism and racism are determined opposites, which means precisely that each one affects the other 'from within.'"[7]

Racism is not a deus ex machina creation or a virus that contaminates the city from time to time. It is at the core of modern ideological constructions of notions of nation and state on the basis of which, along with the economic factor, most of the political debate on immigration is carried out. In this respect, Benedict Anderson's affirmation regarding the structural separation between the two processes is not defensible. In *Imagined Communities*, distinguishing between nationalism and racism, Anderson argues:

> The fact of the matter is that nationalism thinks in terms of historical destinies, while racism dreams of eternal contaminations, transmitted from the origins of time through an endless sequence of loathsome copulations: outside history. Niggers are, thanks to the invisible tar-brush, forever niggers, Jews, the seed of Abraham, forever Jews, no matter what passports they carry or what languages they speak and read. (Thus for the Nazi, the *Jewish* German was always an impostor.)
>
> The dreams of racism actually have their origins in ideologies of *class*, rather than in those of nation: above all in claims to divinity among rulers and to "blue" or "white" blood and "breeding" among aristocracies. No surprise then that the putative sire of modern racism should be, not some petty-bourgeois nationalist, but Joseph Arthur, Comte de Gobineau. Nor that, on the whole, racism and anti-semitism manifest themselves, not across national boundaries, but within them. In other words, they justify not so much foreign wars as domestic repression and domination.[8]

This vision is strikingly essentialist, but such a formalist systematisation has become rather common in postcolonial theory with a perspective that increasingly ignores the historicity and epistemological contexts of concepts and ideological productions. Furthermore, it is surprising that Anderson states that racism and anti-Semitism do not function across national boundaries in view of human history and, in the modern era, World War II, the anti-Semitic ideology of Nazism and fascism, and the continuous oppositions and conflicts between people or cultures of different origins or civilizations.

Contrary to what Benedict Anderson affirms, racism and nationalism do not have separate historical developments or structures. Indeed, they are not two distinctive essences because modern states are built on the basis of nationalism of which racism is constitutive. This is certainly true in the case of French nationalism that developed at the same time France was defeated in 1871 and began to expand its colonial Empire.

## THE FRENCH NATION

In France, the construction of the idea of nation is attached to the Revolution. Indeed, 1789 constitutes a landmark of the identity of Modern France built on fundamental principles. These principles include the Enlightenment concepts of Man, reason, and the association of free men as conceived in Jean-Jacques Rousseau's *Contrat Social*. In this respect, Ernest Renan's "Qu'est-ce qu'une nation?" constitutes the quintessence of this ideological discourse and the fundamental reference of the French national myth and conception of the nation. In this lecture delivered at the Sorbonne on March 11, 1882, Renan develops his notion of the French nation in the following way.

A nation is a soul, a spiritual principle. Two things, which in truth are but one, constitute this soul or spiritual principle. One lies in the past, one in the present. One is the possession in common of a rich legacy of memories; the other is present-day consent, the desire to live together, the will to perpetuate the value of the heritage that one has received in an undivided form. Man, Gentlemen, does not improvise. The nation, like the individual, is the culmination of a long past of endeavours, sacrifice, and devotion. Of all cults, that of the ancestors is the most legitimate, for the ancestors have made us what we are. A heroic past, great men, glory (by which I understand genuine glory), this is the social capital upon which one bases a national idea. To have common glories in the past and to have a common will in the present; to have performed great deeds together, to wish to perform still more—these are the essential conditions for being a people. One loves in proportion to the sacrifices to which one has consented, and in proportion to the ills that one has suffered. One loves the house that one has built and that one has handed down. The Spartan song—"We are what you were; we will be what you are."—is, in its simplicity, the abridged hymn of every *patrie*.

More valuable by far than common customs posts and frontiers conforming to strategic ideas is the fact of sharing, in the past, a glorious heritage and regrets, and of having, in the future, a shared programme to put into effect, or the fact of having suffered, enjoyed, and hoped together. These are the kinds of things that can be understood in spite of differences of race and language. I spoke just now of "having suffered together" and, indeed, suffering in common unifies more than joy does. Where national memories are concerned, griefs are of more value than triumphs, for they impose duties, and require a common effort.[9]

Renan's conception of the nation has prevailed over previous conceptions and is posited as the specific French model in contrast with notions of communities based on tribal relations, heredity, or blood. As a consequence, traditionally, the opposition between the French model born out of the Enlightenment and embodied by the Revolution and the other models based on ethnicity as in the case of Germany and its idea of the *Deutsche Volk* is generally construed as the antagonism between French universalism and German particularism. Comparing the two conceptions, Renan makes the following statement:

> A community of interest is assuredly a powerful bond between men. Do interests, however, suffice to make a nation? I do not think so. Community of interest brings about trade agreements, but nationality has a sentimental side to it; it is both soul and body at once; a *Zollverein* is not a *patrie*. (18)

If the Germans developed a kind of biological racism, the French actually produced a form of cultural racism. As discussed earlier and as can be seen in Renan's formulation, along with the philosophy of universalism, the French systematically developed an ethnic discourse that is not fundamentally different from the German model. However, this ideological distinction continues to inform the Republican discourse of not only most French politicians from both the Right and the Left, but also the thought of most French intellectuals and political activists who systematically endorse this concept of the nation. It is also from the perspective of this model that the French ongoing resistance to multiculturalism is explained and justified. What is remarkable is that this conception, the synthetic formulation of which is constituted by Ernest Renan's seminal text, still significantly informs French laws and ideology across the board and continues to justify the most anachronistic and racist discourses and immigration policies of Descartes's country.[10] Indeed, Renan's classification has had a central influence in the conceptualization of the distinction between French nationals and foreigners who live in France and who became French through naturalization or other processes, as in the case of the "Beurs." As Maxim Silverman relevantly points out,

> The profound institutionalisation of social relations transformed the hazy distinction between nationals and non-nationals into a clear division between them. The state and the nation, whose origins and history were *not* the same, then became inextricably intertwined. As Lochack points out, the state became the "juridical personification of the nation." . . . It is through the power of the national state (or rather the state-hegemonised nation) that foreigners

were no longer "those who are born outside the frontiers of the state but, in a much more profound way, those who do not belong to the *body* of the nation." . . . The construction of the "national" and the "foreigner" was part of the same historical process.[11]

In this respect, the hierarchy and distinction between social or ethnic groups as the basis for inclusion in or exclusion from the French community—structurally linked to the debate on nationality and citizenship at the center of which the "Beurs" currently are—has its roots in the history of France and, in recent times, more decisively in the relationship between France and its colonies. Indeed, throughout the nineteenth century, France developed its nationalism inside (Metropolitan France) and outside (French colonies) on the basis of a deeply rooted racist ideology. Under various forms, even after the decolonization following the end of World War II, this process continued. This ideology and the policies associated with it took various designations such as *universalism* in the eighteenth century, *mission civilisatrice* in the nineteenth century, and *coopération technique et culturelle* in the second half of the twentieth century. Today, it is continuing, somehow subtly, under a different disguise, in the shape of the French government's official policy of "Francophonie."[12]

## COLONIALISM, ETHNICITY, AND "RACE"

Once it began the colonization of North Africa, France established a distinction between the French and the non-French. Following the 1830 conquest of Algeria, it immediately created a system of apartheid by establishing different types of subjects: the colons, the Jews, and the Algerians designated as *"indigènes"* or *"musulmans."* It also quickly proceeded to establish ethnic distinctions among the colonized as well. The ethnic classifications and the racist categorization it operated between the Arabs and the Berbers, the two most important ethnic groups in North Africa, on the one hand, reproduced the classification of Eurocentric discourse on peoples and races, and, on the other hand, contributed to its colonial project. We will see how this classification will be reversed and used in the modern context in order to marginalize the contemporary North African immigrant population.

Among the "indigènes," who constituted the majority of the population, colonial ideologists quickly proceeded to distinguish between the Arabs and the Berbers in order to justify and develop their racist ideology, an operation that led to what is commonly known as the "Kabyle Myth."

Their view was that there is a permanent conflict between the two dominant ethnic groups of North Africa. As Rachid Tlemçani puts it in *State
and Revolution in Algeria*,

> Typically, traditional colonial discourse and Orientalism regarded the "ignoble
> Arab" as living in a state of despotism in opposition to the "noble savage" living
> in a state of tribal democracy. According to E. Gauthier, one of the most dis-
> tinguished orientalists in the 19th century, an inherent conflict exists between
> the Berbers and the Arabs. Maghribi history, according to him, is dominated by
> a permanent confrontation between "two biological parts fundamentally op-
> posed in their eternal behavior. . . . The Maghrib has always been cut into two
> irreconcilable halves. . . ."[13]

In order to colonize and establish the superiority of the French over the
North African people and assert the continuity between Algeria and France
as two parts of the same entity, a decisive step in French universalist discourse—but in fact assimilationist ideology—the French had to further explain and reinforce their classification of races. As Tlemçani further
explains, more of this racist ideology can be found in Viscount Caix de St.
Aymour. In *Questions Algériennes: Arabes et Kabyles*, he wrote:

> Arabs cannot be transformed whereas the Kabyles can be assimilated. . . . Arabs
> are lazy, soft, slow . . . almost sad and fanatical. The Berber is hardworking, en-
> terprising, practical . . . and finally not very religious. Accordingly, "If we have
> one duty in Algeria, it is to combat Islam, our eternal enemy, in all its manifes-
> tations," so as to Europeanize culturally the "moderate Moslem"; i.e., the
> Berbers of Greater Kabylia. Therefore, as Captain Carette concluded in 1848:
> "Kabylia . . . must in a few years become the most intelligent auxiliary of our
> enterprise and the most useful associate in our tasks."[14]

This process consisted in the development of a racist/colonial discourse
on the Algerian community based on the concept of the "Kabyle Myth."[15]
It was completed by the principle of the so-called Latin heritage of North
Africa. Indeed, in *Le Sang des races*, Louis Bertrand, the prominent colonial ideologist, argued that the French conquest of Africa was in fact a reestablishment of the Latin heritage of this continent.[16] The central targets
of this discourse were the so-called North African Arabs and Islam. According to him, the Islamization of North Africa broke the link of this region with Europe of which it is part. He claimed that Islam was a dark
parenthesis that France had to destroy in order to renew and develop the
process of civilization initiated by Rome when it occupied this region. It is
remarkable that throughout the colonial period and even today, most North

Africans call the French, and Europeans in general, "romi" (singular) or "raoama" (plural), a designation indicative of the continuity that they, on their part, see between the Roman conquest and the French colonization.

## THE STATE, THE CHURCH, AND THE COLONIES

The important role of ethnic representations cannot be underestimated. Another essential aspect of the French discourse consisted in the assimilation of the concepts of "race" and religion. In this respect, the attention must be brought to the fact that the so-called civilizing mission was anything but a secular operation. If one of the aspects of the French Revolution was an expression of the separation between the State and the Church and if French republicanism was supposed to be built in part on the appropriation of the power of the Church and the repression of religion in the public sphere, the "Mission Civilisatrice," as the result of republican nationalism and Napoleonic imperialism was, at the same time, a colonial enterprise and a religious crusade. Indeed, the progressive separation between the Church and the State *in France*—which, from the point of view of the religious authorities, was formally completed only in 1962 by the Vatican Council—corresponded to the collaboration between these two bodies *in the colonies*. Indeed, as Charles R. Ageron[17] explains, the French government let the Church organize its activities—schooling, medical help, and conversion of the colonized populations—as part of the process of colonization. In this respect, there was a total collaboration between the politicians, the military, and the missionaries.

This redistribution of power and territory had the advantage, on the one hand, of being a compromise with the still powerful Church institutions and the still important sensitivity of the French public over religious matters and, on the other hand, of constituting a significant alliance in the process of domination of the conquered people. In fact, there was a division of labor between the State and the Church in the sense that the aim was to dominate the Algerians, on the one hand, culturally, through the destructuration of their system of education and its replacement by the French school system as a fundamental instrument of promotion of the colonial ideology and, on the other hand, religiously through the action of the Church that, along with the State and colonial ideologists, saw in Islam a vital element of Algerian identity that needed to be fought and possibly eradicated.

In Algeria, the representative of the Church, Cardinal Lavigerie, initiated an active campaign of conversion of the natives to Christianity. This operation was a total failure except for in the Kabylie region where a limited number of people embraced the religion of the colons. In Kabylie, the ideological discourse on the "Kabyle Myth" reinforced the proselytism of the French Church. As Tlemçani observes,

> Furthermore, Islam and the Arabic language were the other side of the target of French Orientalism, which reached its highest point at the time when France was penetrating the hinterland of Algeria. The colonial authorities strove to discourage the pilgrimage to Mecca and to disrupt the old ties between the rural areas and urban Islam. Orientalism found its expression in the "Kabyle Myth" even under the pen of prominent specialists in Arab affairs. Analyzing the pseudo-differences in the intensity of religious beliefs between the Arabs and Berbers and in particular, the Kabyles, Colonel Daumas et al., wrote in 1847: "They (the Kabyle people) have accepted the Koran, but they have not embraced it. . . . They have escaped the universal consequences of the Islamic faith by still obeying the sacred law of work, more or less rehabilitating their women and practicing a number of customs that bespeak equality, and Christian commiseration."[18]

However, although they had a relative influence on some Kabyle communities, ultimately both enterprises failed. The resistance to colonialism was strong as was Islam in the struggle against the French attempts to impose their religious and cultural domination on the Algerians.

The influence of historical representations has always been important in the relationship between all people and, in this case, especially between the Algerians and the French. But, in spite of the Enlightenment and the universalistic discourse that led to the supposedly distinctive secular vision of the French, the religious factor was as important in the nineteenth century as it is today. One cannot fail to observe the continuity of the structural hostility toward North Africans who are viewed not only as undesirable immigrants but also as Arabs and Muslims. This continuity and the ongoing importance of this factor can be seen in the systematic marginalization of Islamic communities. An illustration of this fact has been given more explicitly since the 1970s in the debates about the structural impossibility of integration of the Muslim immigrants in France and in the mid-1980s drastic changes of nationality laws aimed at denying immigrants or their descendants of Muslim confession or cultural background French citizenship. As Patrick Ireland explains in his *The Policy Challenge of Ethnic Diversity: Immigrant Politics in France and Switzerland*:

> A turning point was reached with the student demonstrations in late 1986 and early 1987, which forced the government to withdraw planned educational re-

forms (the Devaquet Plan). Many in the movement of high school and college students had cut their activist teeth in the marches and rallies of SOS-Racisme. Their reluctance to forge an alliance with striking railroad workers bespoke the absence of working-class consciousness that typified much of the second generation. The death of an innocent Beur bystander, Malik Oussekine, at the hands of the security forces underscored the stake that young people of foreign extraction had in the social struggles of their genera-tion in contemporary France. . . .

A few months later the government proposed a reform of the Nationality Code (the Chalandon Reform). Many leaders and intellectuals of the French right had decided that Islam, seen as blending the private and public spheres of authority irretrievably, made the assimilation of Muslims into secular, re-publican France far more unlikely than that of the earlier Catholic and Jewish immigrants. . . . The commission that Chirac appointed to devise a plan pro-posed eliminating the automatic nature of second-generation immigrants' ac-cession to French citizenship, in order to stem the "mass" naturalization of second-generation immigrants and to revalorize the acquisition of French cit-izenship. The list of offenses that precluded it was to grow significantly longer. The government eventually backed off on requiring evidence of assimilation and an oath of allegiance. Yet a conscious, expressed desire to be French would become the sine qua non of citizenship acquisition.[19]

Thus, it appears that, structurally, there is no difference between the nineteenth-century colonial discourse and the current views of either Jean-Marie Le Pen or the majority of both the French political leaders across the board and the French electors. In 1989, the controversy over the issue of the Islamic scarf in schools was an even more dramatic symptom of the re-jection by the French of multiculturalism in general and Arab–Muslim identities in particular.

## GENESIS OF THE CONCEPT OF "IMMIGRÉ"

In order to grasp the dimension of the evolution of French policy on immi-gration in general and the North African community in particular, one has to consider how the concept of the "immigré" was produced. Following the conquest of Algeria in 1830 and throughout the nineteenth and twentieth centuries, the French colonial authorities produced an ethnic discourse that would serve as the basis of and justification for their policies.[20] Along with economic and political factors that determine the development of im-migration in France, this discourse shaped the representation of North

African immigrants within France. On the other hand, the colonial situation and French imperial policies led to a space of migration between Metropolitan France and the colonies of the Empire. This space of migration explains the contradictions but also the structural relations between colonialism, racism, and immigration in France.

> However, another major aspect of the process of nationalisation of French society, and one less frequently discussed in this context, is the development of colonialism under the Third Republic. . . . Colonialism established a "space of migration" between the "metropole" and the colonised countries (and vice versa) which was a classic channel for the mobilization of foreign labor. . . . At the same time as "internationalising the economic system" . . . colonialism established, as we know, political, juridical and cultural structures which institutionalised the distinction between nationals and "natives" ("indigènes"), or citizens and subjects.[21]

Indeed, as subjects of the Empire, members of the colonies could travel to France and work, technically without restriction. In fact, restrictions were systematically determined by the economic needs of France and the political conditions of the Empire. Similarly, although they were considered French subjects, the law would not apply to them in the way it applied to French citizens and they would, therefore, not benefit from equal rights.

Initially, in the framework of the imperial space of migration, Algerian immigration in France increased in the 1930s when, following the commitment of Algerians on the French side in the struggle against Germany during World War I and, following the end of the conflict, the European economic context led to a strong demand for labor. As noted by Neil MacMaster in his article, "Patterns of Immigration, 1905–1954: 'Kabyles' and 'Arabs,'"

> Because of her unusually low birth-rate, subsequently compounded by heavy losses in the First World War, France encouraged foreign labour immigration. The strict controls on the emigration of Algerians to France were partially removed by a circular of 28 January 1905 and scrapped entirely by the law of 15 July 1914. The opening of the door coincided with the growth of a large pool of underemployed and impoverished peasants, themselves the product of the enormously destructive impact of colonialism on the traditional Algerian economy and society (appropriation of lands, uprooting and dislocation of tribes, growing demographic imbalance between population and resources, etc.).[22]

As far as Algeria, the most important colony of the Empire, was concerned, immigration was actually at first mostly limited to the Kabyles, that is to say Algerians of Berber origin from the northern regions. This fact is linked to the colonial ideological discourse based on the "Kabyle Myth" referred to earlier. It is not surprising that, for a short period, between the two world wars, in spite of the ongoing hostility toward them, Algerians were regarded not only as "subjects" of the Empire but also as allies. This evolution of their status can be tracked in literary works, and namely in Jean Genet's play *Les Paravents*. After World War I, World War II saw them on the side of France, on the front line against Nazi Germany, along with the people of many African nations and other colonies. The situation was to change dramatically when, following the slaughter of 50,000 of their people by the French army on May 8, 1945, the Algerians decided to start their War of Independence against France.

The process of decolonization of other countries is parallel to the theme of treason when the French refer to the Algerians.[23] Indeed, while most French colonies were decolonized without the necessity of shooting a single bullet, in the case of Algeria, because Algerians were forced to conduct an armed struggle for independence, between 1954 and 1962 France used all its might, ranging from napalm, phosphorus bombs, systematic rape of women, and torture, to kill nearly 15 percent of the Algerian population. The fact that France was defeated in spite of the savage war it waged as a whole but ironically carried out and led to its summit of atrocity by a government of the Left of which Mr. Mitterand was the virtuoso, recast the short-lived image of the good Algerian. Algerians came to be seen as the absolute Others in the sense that, according to the French imperial representation, they betrayed the mother-country (*la mère patrie*). In this context, the distinction between the Kabyles and the Arabs quickly disappeared and Berbers were from then on referred to as Arabs in the same way their so-called Arab ethnic enemies were designated.

The confrontation between France and Algeria took place inside and outside France. The defeat of France and of the French Imperial model— Algeria was supposed to be the first "*colonie de peuplement*" and, therefore, the laboratory and model for the development of the colonies of the Empire—that the independence of Algeria incarnates after 1962 and the evolution of the international context from the 1960s on have contributed significantly to the representation of North African immigrants and their descendants. Paradoxically, these descendants were called immigrants of the "second generation" although they were born in France and were, therefore, legally French nationals.[24]

As far as the international context is concerned, the Cold War during which the confrontation between the communist bloc and the Western world was paralleled and intertwined with the conflict between Israel and the Arab countries, the strengthening of the Arab League, the constitution of a panarabism, and the developing power of Egypt as a model and leader for the Arab world contributed to the production of the image of the "Arab." At the same time, the economic boom in Europe in the 1960s resulted in an increase of North African immigration that, along with the exacerbated tensions linked to the ongoing Algerian War of Independance and the progressive evidence of the future defeat of France, led to the miserabilist image of the "phony, vicious, and treacherous Arab." From there on, the term "Nor'af" (North African) was produced to characterize a particular segment of the global immigrant population. Following that, in the 1970s the term *"Maghrébin"* (Maghrebin) was coined to further singularize it. Progressively, in France, the word immigrant (*immigré*) came to identify essentially the members of the North African community. Indeed, the other main groups, such as the immigrants of Spanish and Portuguese origin, were progressively assimilated, that is to say they became "invisible" in French terms. In recent years, the Gulf War and the rise of Muslim fundamentalism in general and in Algeria in particular complicated the contradictions and exacerbated the tensions between the French and their important minority of Arab–Muslim origin or cultural background.

The singularization of North Africans in general and of Algerians in particular also meant their automatic exclusion from the French community. As Jean-Marie Le Pen, whose extreme right-wing party, Le Front National, until recently represented more than 10 percent of the French electorate, put it: "Ethnically, culturally, and religiously, the North African cannot be integrated in French society." Patrick Ireland comments on the rise of the party of Le Pen and explains the conditions of the mid-1980s cohabitation between the Socialist presidency of François Mitterand and the right-wing government of Jacques Chirac in the following terms:

> Jean-Marie Le Pen adapted his message to the changing times, linking the immigrant—specifically, the North African—presence not only with crime but even with the rising incidence of AIDS in the country. The FN was gaining working-class support and seemed to be replacing the PCF as the mouthpiece for the disaffected. . . . Certainly, it had become fully installed in French political life. . . . Such developments overshadowed more positive ones for the immigrants as the list of municipal and departmental consultative bodies lengthened steadily.
>
> The period of cohabitation that followed the mainstream right's narrow victory brought more-repressive immigration policies. For years, its top leaders

had shamelessly bent to the political winds of the moment on these issues. . . . The new prime minister, Jacques Chirac, made an explicit connection between delinquency, terrorism, and immigration. Identification checks and expulsions of illegal immigrants and refugees multiplied, with non-Europeans incurring much of the wrath of the new hard-line interior minister, Charles Pasqua. His policies, codified later that year, made it clear that the new government rejected the notion of a multicultural France. . . . The left remained silent, apparently terrified by the amount of public support for such measures.[25]

While this expression of radical racism is not surprising on the part of the leader of the extreme Right, it is often shared by members of various mainstream parties such as the more traditionally conservative or democratic movements—UDF, Chirac's RPR—, some left-wing parties, including the Socialist Party and the French Communist Party at times, and numerous otherwise "progressive" intellectuals. In a recent poll carried out by Sofres, the French polls central agency and published on May 30, 2000, by *Le Monde*, the most important French daily, it appears that a metamorphosis has taken place in French society in the last fifteen years. Indeed, the recent implosion of the Front National and its subsequent division into two parties, the Front National of Le Pen and the Mouvement National Républicain (MNR) of Bruno Mégret, does not actually reflect a weakening of the extreme Right. Rather, it indicates that the views of the extreme Right have been progressively appropriated by the more traditional and mainstream political organizations. The extremist positions of the FN and MNR are considered acceptable when expressed by the leaders of UDF, RPR, PS, or other parties. Comparatively, while in May 1999, 73 percent of the French considered that the FN constituted a danger for democracy, a year later only 62 percent made that judgment. However, as revealed by *Le Monde*'s journalist Gérard Courtois, the French feel increasingly comfortable with the ideas that have been making the success of Le Pen's party in the last fifteen years.

Thus, while, traditionally, the French recused the ideas of the president of the FN on immigration, when these are expressed without link to the name of the extreme right's leader, nearly six out of ten (59%) consider that "there are too many immigrants in France." Similarly, 64% are favorable to a reinforcement of the power of the police authorities. And 73% consider that "we do not defend the French traditional values enough." The taboo about an important part of the ideological foundation which made the success of the extreme right—defense of traditional values, fear of immigration and feeling of insecurity—seems to be in the process of disappearing. Similarly, the weakening of the extreme right and the failure of its management in cities conquered in 1995 transforms its electors into an increasingly attractive additional force for a portion of the right, especially among the followers of Démocratie Libérale and RPR.[26]

The author of this article, entitled "Extrême Droite: ce n'est pas fini" (Extreme Right: It Is Not Over), concludes that the French think that the extreme right is less dangerous but that more of them approve of its views.


## FROM THE "IMMIGRÉ" TO THE "BEUR"

To a large extent, considering the continuity of the colonial and postcolonial relationship between France and Algeria, the attitude of the French toward the North African immigrants is an extension of the colonial ideological edifice. The coinage of the word "Beur" corresponds to the evolution of French society, the political context of the 1970s and 1980s in both France and Algeria, and the change in the very notions of immigration and immigrant in France. Until the late 1970s, there was an understanding and explicit agreement that North African immigration in France was temporary. Having been promoted on the basis of bilateral agreements between France and the governments of Algeria, Morocco, and Tunisia, immigration meant a collaboration between France and the other countries leading to the provision of a North African labor force for specific projects that were part of the reconstruction or modernization of the European country. It was taken for granted that the immigrants would go back to their original countries after having fulfilled their contract. This understanding was very clearly supported by official policies such as the Algerian programs of reinsertion of former immigrants in the economy and by what one could call the strong myth of return. Indeed, every immigrant planned—and many did complete—their return, which culminated in the realization of a dream: go back to one's village, build a house, see one's children grow up, and die decently in one's own country.

The limits of the French economy, the increasing problem of unemployment throughout Europe, and important political conflicts between France and mostly Algeria changed this situation and had a fundamental impact on the issue of immigration and the representation of immigrants in the French political and public sphere. In 1974, following the nationalization of the oil industry and the subsequent disagreement between Socialist Algeria and France on the price of Algerian oil and gas, the government of Valéry Giscard-d'Estaing called back the 28,000 French engineers and technicians who were still largely exploiting the energetic resources of the Algerian Sahara. France's move was the result of the failure of its neocolonial policies such as the attempts to perpetuate its control on the oil industry, to have commercial privileges, and to impose the continuous use of the French language in Algeria. Indeed, in spite of continuous economic and political pressures, unlike many former colonies of the French Empire, Algeria was actively developing its economy, industry, education, and army in order to assert its independence. In this context, along with increasing racism and violence against North Africans in the country of Descartes and Rousseau, immigration became a political weapon in the hands of the Algerian regime, which called off the bilateral agreements and unilaterally canceled immigration to France.

Having itself evolved on the issue of immigration and retaliating against the Algerian government's radical positions, the French right-wing government took revenge by deporting immigrants or, later, by offering some of them a package to leave the country. While many Portuguese accepted this deal, most Algerians did not. The reason for this attitude is explained in part by the Algerian situation itself and in part by the choices made by the immigrants' children. Indeed, on the one hand, in spite of important progress linked to the socialist policies of the regime, the Algerian economy was still weak and did not offer comparable conditions to returning immigrants who had grown accustomed to their, albeit meager, standard of living in France. On the other hand, Algerian immigrants being mostly of peasant origin refused the socialist policy and the collectivization of the land in their own country. Finally, and most importantly, their children, born in France, speaking most of the time only French and having extremely tenuous relations with the country of their parents, did not want to go live in Algeria, Morocco, or Tunisia. Two other factors discouraged those who will later be called the "Beurs" to fulfill their parents' dream of return to the motherland: for the males, two years of harsh military service in Algeria complicated by an undeclared war with Morocco over the Western Sahara and, for the females, Islamic and traditional rules that women born and living in a Western environment could not accept in the heavily patriarchal societies of North Africa.

In brief, contemporary immigration in France developed in part against both France and Algeria. The immigrants chose to stay and live in France and thus challenged the policies and pressures of both countries' regimes. The consequences of this situation and these choices were going to change the very nature of French society. Indeed, as observed by Silverman,

The change from an economic to a social/cultural perspective on immigration parallels the change in focus from immigrants as a simple labor force ("les travailleurs immigrés" or "la main-d'œuvre étrangère") to immigrants as social actors or victims, from the "first" to the "second generation," from immigrants as single men on temporary work and residence permits ("une immigration temporaire") to families settled in France ("une immigration sédentarisée"). In the 1980s "les jeunes" became the major symbol of the new focus on the "problems" of installation and integration. Both official reports and research at large reflected (or constructed?) this new perspective on immigration. Therefore, the production of the figure of the "immigrant" and of Beur literature and culture in general corresponds to this historical change and to the shift of the perspective on immigration.[27]

In the 1970s and 1980s, the status of immigrants changed drastically. Indeed, North African immigration is linked, first, to the French colonization and, second, to the consequences it had on both the French and Algerian economies. In light of what I said earlier, historically, the first element concerns the evolution of the function of immigrants in modern France, and the second the change of status of the immigrants' descendants. This new situation and the new status of immigrants, and of their children in particular, designated as the second generation, led to the currently exacerbated tensions within the French social fabric and to an increasing racism and discourse of exclusion. It also put the issue of immigration at the center of the political debate. The consequences were enormous in the sense that the predicament of the immigrants in general, and of the important North African and Muslim community in France in particular, compel the French to rethink the very foundations of their national and cultural identity. It is in this context that the French have been confronted again with the issues they thought clarified by their Revolution: nationality, citizenship, republicanism, secularity, etc.

## POSTCOLONIALISM AND IMMIGRATION

The "Beurs" are the French descendants of North Africans who are not given access to full citizenship in France. It is obvious that this situation is contradictory only if one does not take into account the distinction between nationality and citizenship that is at the center of France's ideological and institutional edifice. The "Beurs" are French nationals but they are not considered French citizens. Their continuing exclusion from the "breast of the Mother-Land" is a logical continuation of the relationship between nationalism, colonialism, postcolonialism, and racism that the North African has come to incarnate in the definition of French identity, an identity that functions on the basis of a simultaneous process of obligatory ideological inclusion *and* actual economic and social exclusion. As Silverman puts it on the basis of his development of Balibar's analysis,

[The] term "the post-colonial era" can suggest a clean break with the colonial era and obscure the relevance of the colonial legacy today. Etienne Balibar maintains that the suggestion that decolonisation closed a chapter in French history and allowed France to open new avenues of development and communication (notably in the context of Europe) perpetuates a myth and is the source of a common misunderstanding of the structures of contemporary France. "In fact it is the opposite which is largely true: contemporary France has been formed through and by colonization." . . .

It is not simply a question of colonial mentality which has persisted in the post-colonial era—especially with the immigration of former colonised peoples and the repatriation of over a million "pieds noirs" (the European settlers in Algeria) at the end of the Franco-Algerian war in 1962. It is more fundamentally a question of the juridical structures of the French state which were largely formed in the context of management of the colonies abroad and immigrants at home, and which are still the source of forms of exclusion today. Balibar sees colonialism as a fundamental determinant of contemporary racism: "Racism in France is essentially colonial, not in terms of a 'leftover' from the past but in terms of the continuing production of contemporary relations."[28]

When considering the "Beurs," two tendencies opposed each other, at least until the mid-1980s, the discourse and political positions of the Left and that of the Right. This ideological and political confrontation on the issue of immigration led to the production of the oppositions I mentioned, and which can be synthesized in the apparently opposed terms of integration and exclusion. However, in fact, this opposition is mostly apparent and in actuality essentially semantic. As confirmed by most polls of the last decade and most recently by the *Le Monde* June 2000 polls mentioned, currently, there is an anti-immigrant global consensus in France that has considerably reduced the previous distinctions between the discourses and policies of the Right and Left. An illustration of this fact is that the previous socialist government of Mr. Lionel Jospin endorsed and carried out practically unchanged the immigration policy of the preceding right-wing governments of Jacques Chirac and Edouard Balladur: the 1994 drastic anti-immigration laws of Charles Pasqua are still implemented in their near totality. Similarly, access to equal rights for immigrants or French citizenship is as difficult under the current government as it was under the previous one.

The tension over the issue of immigration and the French focalization on the North African community and the "Beurs" come from the fact that immigration from various countries and from the former colonies of France in particular challenge French society and its model at all levels: economic, political, philosophical, cultural, social, and religious. In fact, it shakes the very epistemological and ideological foundations of universalism on which modern France constructed its identity. The racialization of the French discourse on immigrants in general and North African immigrants in particular functions on the basis of the colonial history of France, the economic context, and the ethnico-religious representation of the Arab–Muslim as the absolute Other. In this respect, the rhetoric of universalism and republicanism is what it is: an ideological cover-up.

## NOTES

1. See Fernand Braudel, *L'Identité de la France: les hommes et les choses* (Paris: Flammarion, 1990), 207–8.

2. See Jean Carpentier and François Lebrun, eds., *Histoire de France* (Paris: Editions du Seuil, coll. Points, 1987; reedited 1992), 17–96, and Alfred Fierro-Domenech, *Le Pré carré: Géographie historique de la France* (Paris: Robert Laffont, 1990), 15–49.

3. Gérard Noiriel, *The French Melting Pot: Immigration, Citizenship, and National Identity*, trans. Geoffroy de Laforcade (Minneapolis: University of Minesota Press, 1996), xxvii–xxviii.

4. In his discussion of the Euro-American conception of literary theory exemplified by Paul de Man, Kwame A. Appiah appropriately objects to the claim of its universality and challenges the idea of its application when confronted with different textual models and narratives originating in other, and in this case, African, traditions.

> It is hardly outrageous, I think, to suggest that literary theory in Kambouchner's stricter sense, taking for its subject the "text in general," is not, after all, something we need to be especially concerned with if our interest is in the peculiar characteristics of the African written text. It does not follow that we must think the project of literary theory, again in Kambouchner's strong sense, is uninteresting; far from it. To the extent that African writing fails to conform to a literary theory in this strong sense, that is a problem for the theory, revealing it as yet another local principle masquerading as universal, and this is a problem we can begin to address only and precisely by a serious analysis of African texts. . . .
>
> The deductive-nomological model, you will recall, seeks to see explanation in terms of a reduction of some particular events to be explained to a general pattern: a derivation of this specific pattern of events from the wider pattern of laws of nature. And

though there is, no doubt, truth in the claim that one way to understand a historical event is to see it as fitting into a general pattern—perhaps the aftermath of the French Revolution just *is* better understood as part of a pattern that is found also in the Russian Revolution—it is also true that the historian's concern remains often with the particular event. Historians do not need to confirm or discover the patterns that nomothetic sociology seeks to discover, for they may use known patterns to explore the minute particularity of some local configuration of fact. If the nomothetic impulse is to seek general patterns, call them laws or what you will, we might gloss the idiographic impulse—the chronicler's impulse—as the desire to put our general knowledge to the service of a particular narrative.

Kwame A. Appiah, *In My Father's House: Africa in the Philosophy of Culture* (New York: Oxford University Press, 1992), 64.

    5. Henry Louis Gates Jr., "Writing 'Race' and the Difference It Makes," in *"Race," Writing, and Difference* (Chicago: University of Chicago Press, 1986), 8–9.

    6. Etienne Balibar and Immanuel Wallerstein, *Race, Nation, Class: Ambiguous Identities*, trans. by Chris Turner (London: Verso, 1991), 11.

    7. Balibar and Wallerstein, *Race, Nation, Class*, 13–14.

    8. Benedict Anderson, *Imagined Communities: Reflections on the Origin and Spread of Nationalism* (London: Verso, 1983), 136.

    9. Ernest Renan, "What Is A Nation?," in *Nation and Narration*, ed., Homi K. Bhabha, trans. Martin Thom (London: Routledge, 1990), 19.

    10. For example, it is, indeed, this paramount conception that accounts for the normally paradoxical association of the conservative Charles de Gaulle and Régis Debray, the former companion of Ché Guevara. As noted by Keith Reader,

The most obvious divergence between Cohn-Bendit's political thought and that of Debray is the latter's stress, central to his work from its earliest days, on the importance and inescapability of the nation-state. It is essential to grasp that, for Debray, the two halves of that compound noun are of equal, and symmetrical, importance; that is one reason for his polemical admiration for de Gaulle, whose "certain idea of France" led him to oversee the nationalization of the principal banks along with Renault and Air France immediately after the Liberation. His attachment to the republican model of the nation-state is most vividly demonstrated in the essay "Republic or Democracy," with its exaltation of the French republican values of citizenship, lay politics, and reason over and against "Democracy"'s supposed stress on communitarianism and civil society.

"Three Post-1968 Itineraries: Régis Debray, Daniel Cohn-Bendit, Marin Karmitz," in *Rethinking 1968: The United States and Western Europe*, A Special Issue of *South Central Review* 16.4; 17.1 (1999–2000): 94.

    11. Maxim Silverman, *Deconstructing the Nation: Immigration, Racism and Citizenship in Modern France* (London: Routledge, 1992), 29–30.

    12. It goes without saying that there is a fundamental difference between Francophonie as we understand it in the current sense of the word in Francophone

Studies and the ideology of Francophonie as conceived and used by the French official institutions in their ongoing enterprise to fight Anglo-Saxon culture and language and to dominate the former colonies of France economically, politically, and
culturally as can be seen in such forums as the annual "Sommet de la Francophonie" involving fifty-three Francophone countries—most of which were colonies of
the French Empire—and presided over by the French president.

13. Rachid Tlemçani, *State and Revolution in Algeria* (London: Zed; Boulder,
Colo.: Westview Press, 1986), 198.

14. Tlemçani, *State and Revolution in Algeria,* 198.

15. See Patricia M. E. Lorcin, *Imperial Identities: Stereotyping, Prejudice and
Race in Colonial Algeria* (London: I. B. Tauris, 1995), 252–53.

16. Louis Bertrand, *Le Sang des races* (Paris: Albin Michel, 1926 [first published, 1899]).

17. See Charles Robert Ageron, *France coloniale ou parti colonial?* (Paris: PUF,
1978), 189–234.

18. Tlemçani, *State and Revolution in Algeria,* 199.

19. Patrick R. Ireland, *The Policy Challenge of Ethnic Diversity: Immigrant Politics in France and Switzerland* (Cambridge, Mass.: Harvard University Press,
1994), 85.

20. It is interesting to note in this process the total collaboration between ideology
and literature throughout the whole enterprise of orientalism. As Edward W. Said
argued in *Orientalism,* literature and the arts contributed significantly to the production of European ideological discourse on the Orient. For the French the Orient
started in North Africa. In this respect, the most important voices of ethnic discourse
in the nineteenth- and early twentieth-century colonial France were not only military
officers but also writers such as Louis Bertrand and Robert Randau.

21. Silverman, *Deconstructing the Nation,* 30.

22. Neil MacMaster, "Patterns of Immigration, 1905–1954: 'Kabyles' and 'Arabs,'"
in *French and Algerian Identities: From Colonial Times to the Present,* ed. Alec G.
Hargreaves and Michael J. Heffernan (Lewiston, N.Y.: Edwin Mellen Press, 1993), 21.

23. In Tassadit Imache's novel, *Une Fille sans histoire* (Paris: Calmann-Lévy,
1989), the Algerian father is seen simultaneously as the enemy and the traitor, even
more so since being Kabyle and fair, he is considered to be even more guilty due to
the fact that his appearance could mislead the French into thinking that he is a
member of their community. See chapter 2, especially pp. 17–25.

24. See Patrick Weil, *La France et ses étrangers* (Paris: Gallimard Folio, 1991),
474–75.

25. Ireland, *The Policy Challenge of Ethnic Diversity,* 84.

26. Gérard Courtois, "Extrême Droite: ce n'est pas fini," *Le Monde,* mardi 30
mai 2000; my translation. The RPR (Rassemblement pour la République) is the
leading party of the current French president, Jacques Chirac.

27. Silverman, *Deconstructing the Nation,* 11.

28. Silverman, *Deconstructing the Nation,* 34.

# ⓫

# FRENCH IDENTITY, ISLAM, AND NORTH AFRICANS: COLONIAL LEGACIES, POSTCOLONIAL REALITIES

*Driss Maghraoui*

## INTRODUCTION

Rai music is synonymous with the name of Cheb Khaled in France today. Everybody knows who he is, and they are many musicians who use the same style. Khaled's music is a hybrid of Algerian tone and French language, of French intonation and Algerian dialect. When we listen to his songs, we are in both Wahran and Paris at the same time. His music is played at different clubs in France. Gradually, music in France is no longer just about Edith Piaf, Jacques Brel, Jacques Dutront, or Serges Gainsbourg; it is more and more made of different tunes, and open to different cultural tones. In the meantime while we still enjoy the *Bouillabaisse, Choucroute, Hachis parmentier*, and the *Bananes flambées* at different restaurants in Paris, we can no longer escape the delicacies of *couscous, Mechoui, Mergès, Chawarma*, and a variety of other ethnic foods in the streets of St. Michel, Montparnasse, and Barbès. This kind of diet is part of an everyday reality of life in Paris and in most major cities in France.

Whether in the field of music or in the culinary world, or in the arts and literature, French society is culturally diverse. This "real" cultural diversity is very much representative of the real people who live within French society. It is there and it has been there for quite a while. Cultural diversity and the existence of non-European communities in France are by no means the product of a postcolonial reality. Different ethnic groups have a long history in France

and their histories are very much part of France, as much as "nos ancêtres les
Gaulois." The current issues of immigration and race relationships in France
should therefore be negotiated in the present as much as in the past in order
to recover the histories of those who have been excluded from French "historical memory." That's an important issue that I'm not going to deal with here.

Instead I would like to deal with the debate about immigration and identity and situate it in its cultural, historical, and economic contexts. I argue that
in order to better understand the problems of race relations, Islam, and the
North African presence in France, we need to locate them historically within
a persistent colonial mentality and vision. To take a closer look at how the notion of identity is being reshaped in France today, I propose at the end of this
chapter to look at the discourse of an association known as "l'Organisation
Politique: un Comité des Gens de partout." I want to stress that its discourse
is very much outside of what the *Organisation Politique* has termed as the
"parliamentary field of politics" and official thinking about immigration. This
organization can better be situated as part of a group of associations that are
defined from within the civil society, and outside of political parties and labor
unions. I would like to argue that the gradual emergence of the associative
movement for the past two decades is itself symptomatic of the changing political landscape and of the very notion of "French" identity.

The issue of immigration and cultural difference has been very much the catalyst of this change. Contrary to the generally held belief that the problem of
race relations and a multicultural society is the product of postwar immigration,
I insist here that the colonial period was at the heart of deep-rooted stereotypes
and racism within French society. The problems of present-day ethnic marginalization and discrimination should therefore be viewed from a historical perspective. Europeans and the French in particular have often defined their own
identity in relation to the "other" as a figure of barbarism, fanaticism, and backwardness.[1] France was the champion of the universalizing ideals of the *mission
civilisatrice* for the colonized people. Based on a similar colonial rational,
France wanted its different ethnic communities to be integrated and transformed into French citizens. The emergence of "ethnic dilemmas" is not as recent as it might appear.[2] For the purpose of this chapter I will concentrate
mostly on issues regarding the North African community. West Africans,
Asians, Turkish, and other ethnic groups share some similar problems.

The Maghrebian community, however, represents a few characteristics
that are specific to it. First, according to the 1990 census there were
473,000 Algerians, 396,000 Moroccans, and 135,000 Tunisians. Their children, who are labeled as "foreigners born in France," amount to 140,000
Algerians, 176,000 Moroccans, and 70,000 Tunisians. (I will say more about

how these labels are indicative of the problems of how immigration is debated in France.) The Maghrebian community is therefore the largest non-European ethnic community in France. The second characteristic about the Maghrebian community is its symbolic association with Islam. A third aspect, which is not necessarily unique to North Africans, is their shared experiences as being originally "immigrants" from countries that were under French colonial rule. Finally the debate about North African immigration in France is more specifically revealing of the inherent contradictions of the liberal democracy and its unifying values. The combination of these factors makes their problem more acute.

## THE CULTURAL CONTEXT

The symbolic association with Islam made the Maghrebian community subject to cultural stereotypes and racism at different levels of French society. There is first the phenomenon of *surmédiatisation* as it occurred during the *affaire du foulard*.[3] Second, some prominent intellectuals have contributed to the creation of a collective fear of Islam by the publication of a very alarmist literature about the growing presence of the religion.[4] Finally any acts of violence by radical Islamic groups become immediately associated with the presence of the Muslim community in France. International politics and events are automatically related to domestic debates about immigration. For a while the Algerian war of liberation, the Islamic revolution in Iran, the emergence of the *Front Islamique du Salut* in Algeria, the Gulf War, and more recently the events of September 11, 2001, have become a clear test of interethnic relations in France. Often the media coverage contributes to a phenomenon of homogenization about the Muslim community in France with the subsequent results of an irrational collective fear of Muslims. The "Maghrebin" becomes equated with the "religious Muslim," who is violent, repressive, and undemocratic. Hence, the idea is constructed that the "Maghrebian" is incompatible with the supposedly "secular" and "Democratic" attributes associated with French identity. During the Gulf War, for example, the North African community came under intense coverage from the media and its sensationalist reporting. As Alec G. Hargreaves and Timothy G. Stenhouse put it, "in France, the Maghrebian community came under intense media scrutiny, with much speculation that it might function as a fifth column against the allied war effort."[5]

The problems of representation of the "Muslim" require no elaboration here. The dominant French and "Western" imagination of Islam in general has been quite generous with its representation of Islamic fanaticism, fundamentalism, and violence to say the least.[6] The ideology of colonialism played and still plays a significant role in the debates about Islam and immigration. In many ways the postcolonial discourse about the Maghrebian community in France is reminiscent of a colonial discourse that is still entrenched in the "mental framework" of France's political leaders and in a substantial segment of French society in general. I believe that there is a "colonial syndrome" attached to the debate about immigration. Today, French political leaders, from both the Left and the Right, reproduce the same discourse on immigration as those of the colonial administrators.

## HISTORICAL CONTEXT

It was in the eighteenth century that the notion of *politique musulmane* first came into the jargon of French politics.[7] It was a conscious attempt to take into consideration the realities of the Muslim world as part of an overall strategy of colonial rule. Concerns about Islam emerged therefore in the colonial context. As early as the Napoleonic expedition of Egypt in 1798, the question of how best to govern and control the Muslim subject was raised by Napoleon himself. During the nineteenth century, the idea of the presence of a geopolitical entity known as the "Muslim world" became more apparent for the West with the rise of Pan-Islamism under the leadership of Jamal al-Din al-Afghani and Mohammed Abduh. Pan-Islamism was considered a major threat to the colonial interest of France, which had millions of Muslim subjects under its control. It became gradually clear that a better understanding of the Muslim world was fundamental to the colonial interest of France. New institutions and chairs in different universities were created to study Islam. One of the first ministries to be interested in *la question islamique* was, quite revealingly, the *ministère des colonies*, which created in 1899 a special section of information about the Muslim populations under its control. Known later as *Section des Affaires Musulmanes et des Information Islamiques*, it played an important role for information and coordination between different ministries.[8] The French military also established its own *Section d'Outre-Mer et de l'État-major de l'Armée au ministère de la Défense*. Its main role was to engage in a propaganda campaign for the recruitment of Muslim soldiers in World War I. At the university level between 1895 and 1902, a series of chairs were opened for the study of different aspects of Islam. In 1895 a chair of Islamic law was opened at the *Université de Paris* and in 1902 another chair of Muslim sociology was presented to Alfred Le Châtelier, a colonial sociologist and one of the most dedicated proponents of the *politique musulmane*. Before Samuel Huntington, Le Châtelier in his own way warned about the "clashes of civilizations." What I want to insist upon here is that interest in the study of Islam came as a result of a colonial context that considered the religion to be a threat. We should keep in mind that Algeria was always at the background of any debate about Islam and French identity. In 1848 Algeria was declared a French territory. The French settlers were strong supporters of the politics of assimilation, but paradoxically opposed its logical outcome, which would normally grant full citizenship to Algerians. Because of the senatus law of 1865, Algerians did not have any political representation and were not permitted to hold public office. To have equal status with the French, it was strongly believed that Algerians had to acquire French culture, which was an impossibility according to the colonial ideology. After 1914 the colonial lobby made every effort to present North Africans as "primitive" and "medieval" and open to the temptations of metropolitan France.[9]

One aspect about the debate of immigration that observers tend to ignore is that the first wave of North African labor migration to France came as a result of the colonial situation. Originally the Arab and Muslim presence in France drew a kind of curiosity similar to the Orientalist fascination with the exotic. But gradually the exhibition became a social and cultural reality, and fascination turned into fear. In the interwar period France was faced with the presence of a Muslim community within its metropole. Most of them were brought in as a result of the war effort that was imposed upon North Africans among other ethnic groups from Asia, West Africa, and the Middle East.[10] The idea of the *politique musulmane* was no longer debated as part of a colonial space, but as an issue within the hexagon itself.[11] It is in this newly created context that the notion of an *Islam à la Française* emerged.

In the 1920s the *Mosquée de Paris*, the *Hôpital Musulman*, and the *Institut Musulman* were all established under the guidance of Si Kaddour Ben Ghabrit, who started his career as an interpreter and became the prototype of what the *colons* referred to as *évolués*. The idea of an *Islam à la Française* was supposed to reinterpret the religion according to the ideals of the French republic in a paternalistic way. The most fundamental question was whether or not Islam was compatible with the principles of *laïcité*? In a more pragmatic way the question was asked: could immigrants from a non-European racial stock (mainly Muslims) be assimilated into French society, absorb French identity, and become respected citizens? There were those who responded that Muslim subjects are worthy of citizenship only if they are "sufficiently civilized (*évolués*) to deserve the granting of political rights of the French citizen."[12] There were also those like Robert Montagne who held more "liberal" views but were weary of ethnic diversity and threatened by the challenge of other cultures to French identity. Montagne believed that "it is liberalism which imposes itself, but a prudent liberalism which is aware of the distance that separates an assemblage of different people and tribes from a modern nation."[13] The evocation of the assemblage and tribes can be translated in today's political rhetoric into a fear from the cantonisation of neighborhoods, the fracture of French society along ethnic lines, and the emergence of identity politics.

In the 1920s the response of the French extreme Left to the Paris mosque as a symbolic presence of Islam in France was unambiguous. As invoked in the Arabic communist journal *Al-alam al-ahmar* (red flag), Islam was associated with the "*marabouts* and corrupt clergy," both signs of ignorance and imperialist control.[14] Like the position of present-day political parties in France, there has always been a certain consensus about Islam and immigrants from North Africa. At the same time the language about immigration and assimilation has often been evoked in racialized terms. Ideological considerations and references to universalism were always part of how French identity was constructed as part of a political community, but that did not preclude the presence of the most intolerable forms of racism.[15]

During the colonial penetration of North Africa in the nineteenth and twentieth centuries, France was faced with the Islamic social and cultural realities of the majority of the populations they sought to colonize and control. Because of the monolithic and essentialist view that colonial ideology often constructed about Islam and Muslim society in general, it formulated two opposing alternatives regarding its colonial policy in the Maghreb. The first one consisted of a systematic destruction of Islamic institutions in order to engage in a process of "*assimilation*." This was especially the case of Algeria, which was administered as a set of French *départements*. The attempt to repress the Islamic identity and Islamic symbols in different spheres of Algerian society contributed further to the strengthening of Islam as a symbolic field of reference. Resistance to colonialism in Algeria came originally from local centers such as the religious brotherhoods. By the end of the nineteenth century, the *Salafya* movement, which was a kind of Pan-Islamism, became one of the major religious and intellectual sources for resistance against colonialism.[16] The nationalist movements in North Africa would later on recast the discourse of the *Salafya* movement in their own language of resistance.

The second alternative for control typical of French colonial ideology was the so-called *"politique d'association"* or *"politique des égards,"* which was practiced first in Tunisia and established more systematically in Morocco, both countries being protectorates of France. The *politique d'association* consisted of controlling the population through the use of the local religious elite and ostensibly showing respect for local Islamic traditions and institutions.[17] In 1900, Robert de Caix, an "indigénophile" and one of the defenders of the politics of association, wrote in the revue *L'Afrique Française* that "with a little bit of thought we will start to conceive of our colony not as three detached départements, but as a slice of this Orient where the race is so tenacious, where traditions are so powerfully resistant that people live indefinitely attached to them. . . . It means that in our treatment of the diverse ethnic elements of the colony, the *jus sanguinis* has to prevail over *jus soli.*"[18] Robert de Caix goes on to explain that the Roman Empire declined because it granted citizenship to different ethnic groups and he concludes that democracy is not for export. It is very hard to dissociate this colonial mentality from either the racialist arguments that led to the Pasqua laws or the racist discourse of today's *Front National.*

## THE ECONOMIC CONTEXT

The economic context of the 1980s and 1990s is an important aspect of the debate about immigration in France. It is a period that witnessed the gradual decline of the nation-state as the guarantor of social solidarity through the funding of welfare programs. The economic changes that Europe in general and France in specific have been experiencing have disrupted the traditional role of the centralized French state and subsequently contributed to the emergence of racist and nationalist movements, which targeted "immigrants" of different ethnic origins. The processes of economic globalization have weakened the national market that constituted one of the bases of power of the French nation-state. This economic process has led to the emergence of the so-called "régimes globalitaires."[19] This globalization has led to a series of economic deregulations, which have had serious effects on the social fabric of French society. The phenomenon of globalization has further weakened social cohesion and aggravated economic inequalities. Immigrants from different ethnic groups became the scapegoats for the economic and social degradation that the country was faced with. This degradation is gradually being perceived not in terms of socioeconomic groups, but in terms of cultural and ethnic categories. As Tahar Ben Jelloun once stated, "it is almost traditional that whenever there is a serious economic crisis voices will be raised to say it's the fault of the foreigner—of that looming shadow, unseen because unrecognized, yet found guilty in advance."[20] Because of the ethnic origin that characterizes them, the Maghrebian popular classes are not identified as a working class, but as an ethnic class. This social grouping contributed further to the mystification of the North Africans as a homogeneous group.

## THE IMMIGRATION DEBATE AND ITS LANGUAGE

Since World War II and with the gradual increase in the number of North Africans, first as "colonial workers," or soldiers, and later as an important social component of the economy in France, the debates about immigration revolved around some key terms that were and still are reformulations of a persistent colonial ideology as I outlined above. They include such terms as "assimilation," "insertion," and "intégration."[21]

### "L'Assimilation"

From an etymological point of view, the term "assimiler"[22] means "rendre semblable" or "établir une comparaison." To assimilate is to "cause to resemble" or "to make alike." "Assimiler" means the process by which a social or ethnic minority adopts the dominant values and the traditional behavior of the society into which it is inserted and within which it is ultimately fused. The term assimilation is by itself revealing of the relationship of power between those who assimilate and the ones who are being assimilated. In the political sphere of French society the term assimilation has been more commonly used by the Right. Assimilation is hence a kind of cultural passport that right-wing political parties require in order to obtain citizenship rights. It involves a denial of one's own cultural background and the acceptance of a supposedly "French identity." This was exactly the position that was taken in the case of Algeria when Algerians had to give up the so-called *statut de l'indigénat* in order to get French citizenship. But even for the proponents of this notion of "assimilation," the "Maghrébin" is inherently incapable of "assimilation" because of his/her religious and cultural background.

### "L'Insertion"

This term is more commonly used by the Left. The "insertion" refers to a kind of attachment of one group to the other. It is a process by which a specific ethnic group is collectively implanted into French society. The idea of insertion was mainly socioeconomic. It targeted immigrants with social and economic problems that are specific to them as an ethnic group. It did not take into consideration the broader issues, but dealt with the problem in a pragmatic and technocratic way. Immigrants were thought of as guest-workers. Overall the notion is itself ambiguous when it comes to the methods or modalities by which this *insertion* is supposed to take place. The question of how the affirmation of identity and respect for difference is possible in a dominant culture is not addressed. Regardless of the neutrality that the term insertion may suggest, French leaders from different political spectrums viewed it as a long-term process that would ultimately lead to the *"assimilation"* of the Maghrebian community. Those who oppose the idea of "insertion" argued that the existence of different communities would lead to a concentration of various ethnic groups into a kind of ghetto that would lead to more social conflicts and cultural confrontations. After the 1970s, the inadequacy and racist connotations of the concept of *insertion* became more apparent with the popularization of the idea of *seuil de tolérance,* which was closely associated with it.

## "L'Intégration"

"Intégrer" means "assembler en un tout." In a way this concept is a different version of the same principles associated with "assimilation." "Integration" is often not clearly defined and may have different meanings. It has been used by both the Center and Left within French political parties. As opposed to the notion of "assimilation," "intégration" requires the active involvement of different public institutions to intervene and make individuals part of the "imagined community." In political discourse, this notion is presented as a kind of "choice" between either "integrating" into the "French" nation or keeping a kind of cultural umbilical cord with the country of origin with the prospect of an eventual return. The term integration often implies such notions as cultural "fusion" or "absorption," which again presupposes an existing dominant culture. Since the 1980s it is the idea of integration that has been adopted as part of the political consensus concerning immigration. As Adrian Favell explains, "France's public philosophy of integration combines high universalist ideals with a 'mythical' retelling of a long historical tradition that grounds these ideals, and their working out in practice, in the institutional particularity of the French nation. . . . Such a normative theory exerts a price on those it is applied to: a price perhaps not worth paying."[23]

The classical reference to French republicanism as the basis of political citizenship is usually Ernest Renan. In his writings, Renan epitomized the ideals of the Third Republic and its ability to forge the French nation through the inclusion of diverse regional cultures. France, in comparison to Germany's ethnical conceptualization of the nation, has been viewed as a more open society. Among French intellectuals today Renan is still celebrated as the promoter of the abstract idea of French identity in which inclusion is not determined by race or culture, but by a rational and conscious choice individuals make to be part of the nation. This reference to Renan is astonishingly surprising to anyone who has a modicum of knowledge of modern Middle Eastern history. First Renan had always associated the success of secularism and science with Christianity. It was Renan who once wrote that "the progress of the Indo-European peoples will consist in departing from the Semitic spirit. Our religion will become less and less Jewish. Our religion will be that of the heart . . . and we will be more and more Christian."[24] More relevant to my point here are his views of Islam and its incompatibility with modernity. "The Arab, and in a general sense the Muslim, are further apart from us more than any other time. The Muslim and the European are to one another like two different species, having nothing in common in the manner of thinking and feeling."[25] In a more violent tone Renan finally states: "the essential condition for the expansion of European civilization is the destruction of the Semitic thing *par excellence*, the destruction of the theocratic power of Islamism. . . . When we reduce Islamism to its religious and individual state, it will disappear. . . . Islam is the most complete negation of Europe. . . . Islam is fanaticism. . . . Islam is the disdain of science and the suppression of the civil society, restricting the human mind and closing it to rational thinking."[26] In a synergetic and contradictory way, Renan is hence the symbol of French republican ideals of inclusion for some contemporary French intellectuals, but at the same time he is the paradigm of denigration of Islam and the exclusion of Muslims.

Since the 1980s the philosophy of republicanism about Islam and cultural diversity has been much more open. But it is according to the traditional principles of integration that this openness manifested itself. There is a contradiction inherent in this philosophy. While it calls for the freedom of individual cultural, religious, and linguistic expressions, it nevertheless insists on the idea of the French model of political unity that rejects "the logic of there being distinct ethnic minorities, and instead looking for a logic based on the equality of individual persons."[27] The French government envisioned that the associations under its control would be an important means of integration. The phenomenon of associations, if controlled, was therefore perceived as the ideal mechanism of adapting religious identity to republican ideals. These associations pose however another problem: "it is a suspicious echo of the model of the moral socialization of children, proposed by French Swiss psychologist Jean Piaget, in which the child follows a step-by-step socialization through the discipline of authority, rules, and then principled public association. . . . The most fundamental problem related to Islam in France relates to the fact that it is still not officially recognized as a public religion on a par with Catholicism, other Christian denominations and Judaism."[28]

What has so far framed the debate about immigration in France is the notion of a specifically French political and cultural heritage. As part of the nation-building process since the Third Republic, republicanism and the citizen-based formulation of individual rights have always been key concepts for French identity. But if regional peasants in the nineteenth century were turned into Frenchmen through the educational system and military service,[29] the case was not the same for Muslim immigrants who were excluded from their rights based on the notion of *jus sanguinis*. The Pasqua laws in fact used the same principle of ethno-cultural belonging as the basis for nationality when it did not automatically grant citizenship to "second generation" children of immigrants. Whether in the past or in the present, republican ideals have been a mythical reality as far as Muslim immigrants are concerned.

## THE LE PEN EFFECT

In April 24, 1988, the head of the *Front National* in France received 4,375,000 votes, which represented 14.39 percent of the suffrages. Since then, the Right has been able to put the issue of immigration and French identity at the center of political debate in France. More importantly, Jean-Marie Le Pen gave a certain legitimacy to the themes of his party. By associating "illegal immigration" with juvenile delinquency and crimes, he has been able to draw too much attention to a mythical reality about "l'invasion des immigrés" and the necessity to stop this "invasion." The discourse of the Right in France used also the notion of decline of the French nation as a way of demonizing the presence of different ethnic groups. As a result, the current debate over the issue of immigration and identity has shown an increasing popularity for the ideas of the traditional right-wing doctrine associated today mostly with Le Pen and his *Front National*, but also with Bruno Mégret and the *Mouvement National Républicain*. Since 1988 the political space in France has remained open to the rhetoric of the *Front National*, which was able to win a series of local elections in places like Marignane, Orange, Toulon, and Vitrolles. The Pasqua laws and the Debré laws were clear indications of how political parties in France were responding to the right-wing ideology. A kind of Lepénisation of the discourse on immigration has taken place. Whether it was initiated by Pierre Joxe in 1990, Charles Pasqua in 1995, or Jean-Pierre Chevènement in 1999, the debate on immigration and the "Question Musulmane" has been closely connected with security measures to "control" the Muslim community.[30] In the hope of winning the elections, French political parties have contributed to the perpetuation of a racist ideology that represents non-European communities as a threat to the French nation and Europe in general. The growing influence of the Italian National Alliance under the leadership of Gianfranco Fini, and the success of Jorg Haider's party and his access to power in Austria, confirmed the persistent potential and popularity of right-wing political discourse throughout Europe. Le Pen preyed on those events to declare that "it will serve the cause of right wing parties in Europe to defend the citizens against immigration, against insecurity, unemployment, corruption. . . ."[31] The end result of the Lepénisation of the immigration debate in France came in April of 2002 when 5.5 million French people voted for the extreme Right.

The tacit condemnation of the Austrian government by most European countries should not, however, obscure the fact that the European Union has been itself indirectly implicated in the problem. In their research on the European Commission in Brussels, the anthropologists Cris Shore and Annabel Black discovered that the commission had set up a number of committees to explore "ways of making Europeans more aware of their common cultural heritage and developing European identity." Shore and Black argue that the notion of "European identity is now accepted as a given and unproblematic entity in official EC discourse. What this has led to is a conscientious attempt to build a more coherent sense of European culture by constructing a series of symbols that emulate, and in many ways are intended to replace, those which traditionally define the nation-state."[32] The European flag, passports, driving license, and anthem are examples of such constructed symbols. Yet the promotion of the notion of "European identity" is in a sharp contrast with how members of the public think of themselves. The attempt to inculcate the idea of a homogeneous European culture within the community at large is more likely to be challenged by the consistent and highly integrated sense of nationalist consciousness in each individual country in Europe. But whether the EC officials succeed or not in the creation of a European "imagined community," the fact remains that the promotion of any form of collective consciousness—at either the national or supranational levels—is very likely to exacerbate the situation for non-European ethnic groups. As Shore and Black put it, "promoting the idea that Europeans are heirs to a common cultural heritage may simply add to the tide of xenophobia and racism currently sweeping through Europe."[33]

## THE CRISIS OF REPRESENTATION AND THE EMERGENCE OF THE ASSOCIATIVE MOVEMENT

The idea that the "emergence" of associations is recent is probably inaccurate. Religious institutions have been an important component of civil society in France for centuries. Neither purely religious nor secular, alternative forms of social action have also been popular in cities like Lyons and Paris. For example, in the 1550s the journeymen printers of Lyons organized themselves according to what Natalie Davis called a "secularistic" principle, which meant "the use of nonreligious sanctions and techniques to influence social action, and the assumption by laymen of increasing responsibility in directing social activities formerly directed by the clerical estate."[34] It is this kind of assumption that led the journeymen to form the *Companie des Griffarins* around 1524. To better their standard of living and collectively confront potential economic adversity, many skilled artisans and workers resorted to the phenomenon of *Compagnonnage*.

In its more secular form, the *association* was, however, the creation of postrevolutionary republicanism. In 1866, one of the first examples of such institutions was established by Senator Jean Mace. Known as *La Ligue de l'Enseignement*, its goal was to defend republican ideals of secular education in the creation of the "French citizen." After its creation, the *Ligue* was counterbalanced by a number of associations with a clearly more religious overtone: *Union Chrétienne de Jeunes Gens* in 1867, *Association Catholique de la Jeunesse Française* in 1886, and *Union Chrétienne de Jeunes Filles* in 1894.[35] Religious associations emerged in response to what they perceived as a threatening phenomenon to their identity: secularization and Enlightenment thought. The growth of the associative movement in France continued during the first two quarters of the twentieth century. One of the major characteristics of the associations during this period was their inclination toward either religious discourses (Catholicism, Judaism, or Protestantism) or traditional political ideologies ranging from the extreme Right to the extreme Left. Here the phenomenon of Boy Scouts,

youth clubs, and educational centers became more popular. After World
War II, larger associations were created. Among these, the *Fédération Nationale des Maisons de Jeunes et de la Culture* and *Peuple et Culture* were
quite active. Gradually the associative movement became more institution-
ally organized under the so-called *Comité pour les Relations Nationales et
Internationales des Associations de Jeunesse et d'Éducation Populaire*
(CNAJEP). The key concept to their philosophy is the idea of *éducation
populaire*, which they view as the basis of social relationships, cohesion, and
integration in France. Up to 1968 the associative movement entertained a
rather cordial and diplomatic relationship with the French government, political parties, and trade unions.

The movement of May 1968 constituted a turning point in the history of
social movements in France. Alain Badiou explains that the events of May
1968 occurred "not only outside of the PCF and labor organizations, but in
a more explicit and violent way against the PCF and labor organizations."[36]
It was a moment when "young workers and students said 'non,' which
meant that they brought about an abrupt rupture in the consensus" of both
the Gaullist government and the syndicalist movement. In a way, May 68
was an ephemeral but influential experimentation with the spontaneous
practice of "démocratie de masse," "aller aux usines," and "servir le peuple."[37] The weakness of the movement was ultimately related to its lack of
program and organization, but its legacy remained an important factor in
the emergence of the associative movement in the following decades.

Since the 1970s social movements in France have no longer been mo-
nopolized by trade unions (*syndicats*), but have issued in new forms of social action that Alain Touraine called "les nouveaux movements sociaux."
Essentially a critique of the traditional Marxist analysis of class, the new
conception of social movements stresses the notions of agency, the individual, and the social actor in political action. Touraine was able to break away
from class analysis in order to promote a theory of social movements that
presents social subjects as the main force of relations. According to
Touraine, social subjects fight for control over their historical realities and
it is this historicity that provides collective groups with self-consciousness.
Therefore, the notion of collective identity is explained by Touraine in
terms of an active choice on the part of social groups that have the capacity
to act and make a change.[38] The most important event that made the concept of "nouveaux mouvements sociaux" popular was the 1973 strike of the
workers of the Industrie Horlogère du Doubs, which fabricated watches
known as Lip.[39] Faced with the imminent closure of their factory, the workers took over its management and administration out of their own initiative.

The case of the *mouvement du Lip*, as it was called, became a symbol of the New Left in France. For many, the events of the Lip represented the most concrete actualization of the ideals of May 68.

The 1980s and 1990s witnessed a sort of "crisis of representation" of workers, "immigrants," and the unemployed. The last two decades required therefore a rejuvenation of the notion of *citoyenneté* and democracy. In the recent political and economic contexts, a new form of militantism and mobilization around different associations has emerged. These include neighborhood associations, religious associations, associations within ethnic and cultural references, women's associations, and others. Today there are about 750,000 associations in France. They are a very important instrument of "participatory democracy" and "active citizenship" among a number of social actors who join together around specific themes and projects. They include associations like *Droit au Logement* (DAL), *Agir Contre le Chomage* (AC), and *Comité des Sans-Logis* (CDSL), all of which were created in the 1990s. The political discourse of most of these associations is often critical of the government, political parties, and trade unions. They constitute a form of militancy from the very basis of civil society and are situated in a contestatory field of politics that may be the most accurate representative of the problems of civil society. To echo Natalie Davis's formulation above, associations are now directly the result of the assumption by laymen of increasing responsibility in directing social activities formerly directed not by the clerical estate but by the secular state.

As far as the immigration issue is concerned, the phenomenon of *associations* is very much symptomatic of the weakness and inability of the French government and political parties to represent democratically the Maghrebian community and other ethnic groups in France. Their mobilization has manifested itself more and more in terms of being part of a "cultural identity" in French national space. While these associations are not homogeneous, they confront a common problem, which is related to the rise of racism and the *Front National*. The particular and local aspect of this social mobilization is revealing of the general weakness of the French state with its monopoly over cultural reproduction. According to Jocelyne Cesari, the phenomenon of associations has made various "collective identities" more visible. It has also contributed to the breakup of the "exclusive relationship of allegiance between the individual/citizen and the state." Cesari believes that " there is a reactivation of a civil relationship to the detriment of a civic relationship."[40] There is therefore more of a tendency for mediation between groups as defined in civil society, and less relations with universal institutions such as political parties and labor

unions. The universal notion of the nation-state and its capacity to generate the symbols of cultural integration and social cohesion is no longer
compatible with the growing diversity of the French population and its cultural landscape. It is in the context of this newly emerging phenomenon of
associations that the *Organisation Politique* can be situated.


## THE *ORGANISATION POLITIQUE*

My interest in the *Organisation Politique* is related to two important aspects of its discourse. First, it is strongly anchored in a new wave of philosophical thinking about the nature of the state, democracy, identity, and
politics in France. Although not directly stated in any of the tracts that I will
use here, there is an intellectual and theoretical basis for the *Organisation*
that is easily traced to the work of a new generation of philosophers.[41] Their
work represents a major challenge to the traditional perception of French
politics from either the Left or the Right. The May 1968 movement played
an important role in the formulation of new concepts about democracy as
related to the notion of agency and active citizenship. The second important aspect about the *Organisation* is related to its distance from any political ideology. This break with ideological orientation is, however, not devoid
of intellectualism as it is traditionally associated with French politics. With
the *association* we see the application of the most abstract ideas into the
most concrete form of political activism. While the activities of the
association manifest themselves at the most local level, their philosophical
basis challenges the most fundamental notions of abstract ideas of republicanism and liberal democracy.

One of the most important aspects of the *Organisation* is its conception of
the meaning of politics. *La politique*, according to the association, is not the
consequence of specific historical circumstance, economic considerations,
or state perspective. Its members stress, on the contrary, their distance from
all of these factors.[42] It is rather politics that creates its own parameters and
not vice versa. It is a search for the possible, or what is referred to as *le
champ du possible*. As opposed to the possible *en extériorité* (the socialist
version of the state), it is the idea of the possible *en intériorité* that frames
their action: "it means, for us and for individuals, that the state does not mediate between given social situations and politics. Instead there is an active
individual thought about politics which organizes its own singular relation
with the state."[43] This position is reminiscent of the May 1968 movement
that I mentioned above. It challenges the role of the state, political parties,

and trade unions as the representative of individuals and proposes a more active role for the citizen. Reading Sylvain Lazarus, we see similar *énoncés*: "the people are intellectually neither incapable nor powerless."[44]

The philosophical basis of the discourse of the *Organisation* may also be closely connected with the work of Alain Badiou, whose project can be described, at least from one perspective, as the rejuvenation of Plato. In his book *Conditions*, Badiou states that "Plato affirms that justice is by no means an inner norm, a qualification of what is there. Justice is affirmed by an inner action. . . . The submission of political will to the theme of the community as a figure of good will in politics predisposes this will to the field of sophistry. It is therefore not surprising that this will . . . is extenuated today by the sophistic argument: if the community is impossible, the politics of emancipation do not represent any good will."[45] Badiou in a way is arguing for the ideal city, which is by no means utopian, but real. "This reality (*réel*) is the subjective prescription of what it is that's possible to do."[46] The idea of the *possible* is closely related to what Badiou calls *énoncés prescriptifs*. The *énoncés* of the politics of emancipation are themselves connected with the principle of political subjectivity. So, contrary to Althusser, Badiou believes that the politics of emancipation is an integral part of the *lieu de penser*. It is therefore not necessary to separate the practical aspect from the theoretical aspect of politics.[47] How do some of these abstract notions of political philosophy translate into the language and action of the *Organisation Politique* as a disruptive element of the status quo in French politics and policies about immigration?

To start with, the main slogans of the *Organisation* represent a clear break with the language of all political parties: (1) to say and practice the idea that France is the country of all those who live in it; (2) to say and practice the idea that the people who are here are from here, that they are not foreigners to this country; (3) to search for another alternative for this country.

The individuals associated with the *Organization Politique* present themselves as "Militant politiques des gens de partout." There is no social or religious characteristics that unify them together. Instead they all share a critical political position toward the country and the state that they put in simple terms. They state that "for us the country is made up of people who live within it, today they are from everywhere, that is why in our view, a government can not be democratic unless it is a government for the people from everywhere."[48] For almost ten years three major aspects summarize their position. First, they have kept a distance from the state and the political parties or what they refer to as "L'espace parlementaire." Their public declarations are meant to produce a counter-discourse to the government, the political parties, and the media. Second, for them the very debate about the "immigration problem" is the product of a political corruption in which the *Front National* is a determining factor. Third, their discourse is devoid of ideological abstractions and references to universalistic political principles. Instead, they are pragmatic in their enunciation and concentrate on specific cases and local problems.

According to the *Organization Politique*, the debate about immigration in France is part of what they call "La Politique du mode parlementaire de la Politique, C'est le consensus." Few key terms reflect this consensus: "immigration," "illegal immigration," "insecurity," "second generation" . . . etc. All of these terms reflect a continuum with the discourse of Lepenism. For example the term "illegal immigration" is presented as a coded term that implies a state of insecurity, terrorism, and Islamism. For them the people who are being stigmatized as "illegal immigrants" are in fact people who have lived and worked in France for many years and who have been denied the possibility of regularizing their situations. The *Organisation* also objects to the notion of "jeunes issus de l'immigration," or "jeunes immigrés," who in reality were born in France and who hold French citizenship. The persistence in the use of such terms as "second generation" only confirms the character of exteriority that is attached to the young generations who were born in France. In some cases, the term "second generation" is applied to people who are third or fourth generation.

For the *Organisation*, the present context of parliamentary politics does not provide any progressive and independent alternative to the discourse of Le Pen. In fact, they view the crisis of parlementarism as one of the causes for the emergence of the *Front National*. "C'est la politique de l'état qu'il faut changer si on veut arrêter la montée en puissance du front national." The political parties are perceived as state organizations and not as representatives of the interests of social classes. This for them explains the similarities that exist between French political candidates.

In the overall political discourse of the "Organisation Politique," reference is never made to any French specificity. "Tous les gens qui vivent ici, aujourd'hui des gens de partout, font partie du pays." The term "immigré" is not used. Instead individuals are identified in terms of their socioeconomic conditions. As stated in one of their tracts: " to designate some people as 'immigré' is to lie: these people are from this country . . . the category of 'immigrants' can exist only in an oppositional relation to another category, 'the French,' which would exclude all those who do not conform to it, because of their religion, color or names. The category of 'immigrants' is in reality a dangerous political category, which makes

Lepenism more effective in the government, among the parties, and among people."

An articulation of the ideas of the *Organisation* was more clearly expressed in its response to the Pasqua laws. "We are responsible for the idea that there are policies which are prescribed by the people for the state to be democratic." In the terminology of Alain Badiou, this is an *énoncé prescriptif* because "the democratic prescription of the state is today very weak. . . . The Pasqua 'laws' radically contradict the democratic prescription of the state . . . and we hold that a space of thought and political consciousness is possible beyond consensus." Here again, the idea of the *champ du possible* is applied to refute the Pasqua laws as discriminatory in accordance with the "necessity of the community." "Our idea is that we have to invent . . . and forge pertinent new political *énoncés.*" The *énoncés* are "prescribed in the possible realities, *énoncés pratiquables*, capable of annihilating state practices." For the *Organisation*, a militant political action consists of "confronting the state by the evocation of local political situations." It means that the Pasqua laws contribute to "the construction of a state-informed opinion about an internal enemy who, designated as *immigré, clandestin, irrégulier*, is separated from the rest of the population." This is why "we challenge the racial republicanism of the Pasqua Laws."


## CONCLUSION

This chapter is an attempt to relate the issue of immigration and race relations in France to a persistent colonial mentality, especially in regard to Islam and North African Muslims. I have tried to show that the inadequacies of republican ideals are closely connected to a colonialist vision of the universal ideals of what it means to be French. In the nineteenth century, colonial ideology revealed the intrinsic contradictions of its "civilizing mission" as it related to its Muslim subjects within a colonial space. With the gradual presence of Muslims in France beginning in the 1920s, colonial ideology was still a strong factor in the way North African and Muslim immigrants in general were perceived. Based on the same colonial ideals, France has wanted its ethnic communities to be "inserted," "assimilated" or "integrated" into the abstract notion of the nation-state. It has reformulated a new discourse in the guise of a broad respect for the ideals of republicanism in response to Lepenism, but it has not transcended its racialist mode of expression. Islam is still considered a threat to the secular notion of the nation-state and it has never been considered an official religion on a par with Christianity and Judaism.

My analysis of the discourse of the *Organisation Politique* was intended to show the disruptive aspect of associations that speak in the name of an emergent civil society that is in contradiction with the official discourse of the state and political parties. It represents the "real" cultural diversity I mentioned in my introduction. The *Organisation* is at the same time the voice of a civil society that is realizing its identity not in terms of being "French," but in terms of being *"des gens de partout."*

## NOTES

1. See Edward Said, *Orientalism* (New York: Vintage, 1979) and Bernard Cohen, *The French Encounter with Africans: White Response to Blacks, 1530–1880* (Bloomington: Indiana University Press, 1989).

2. Nathan Glazer, *Ethnic Dilemmas, 1964–1982* (Cambridge, Mass.: Harvard University Press, 1983).

3. A. Peroti and P. Toulat, "Immigration et Media: le Foulard Surmédiatisé," *Migrations Société* 2, no. 12 (novembre–lécembre 1990): 9–45.

4. Gilles Kepel, *Les Banlieues de l'Islam* (Paris: Seuil, 1987).

5. Alec G. Hargreaves and Timothy G. Stenhouse, "The Gulf War and the Maghrebian Community in France," *The Maghreb Review*, vol. 17 (1992): 42.

6. See Edward Said, *Covering Islam* (New York: Pantheon Books, 1981) and *Orientalism* (New York: Vintage, 1979).

7. See Henry Laurens, "La Politique Musulmane de La France," *Monde Arabe: Maghreb Machrek*, no. 152 (avril–juin 1996): 3–12.

8. Jalila Sbai, "Organismes et institutions de la politique Musulmane," *Monde Arabe: Maghreb Machrek*, no. 152 (avril–juin 1996).

9. See Neil MacMaster, *Colonial Migrants and Racism: Algerians in France, 1900–1962* (New York: St. Martin's Press, 1997), 134–52.

10. For a general history and synthesis of this aspect of history see Marc Michel, *L'Appel à L'Afrique* (Paris: Sorbonne, 1982) and Jacques Fremeaux, *L'Afrique à l'Ombre Des Epées* (Paris: SHAT, 1991).

11. This statement should not preclude the fact that the colonial relationships of power were imported through the institutionalization of different forms of control. In 1928 for example, the *Services de Surveillances, Protection et Assistances des Indigènes Nord Africains* was active throughout France.

12. Louis Milliot, "Notre Politique Musulmane," *L'Année Politique Française et Etrangère, 1926–1927*, 113–35. Quoted in Henry Laurens, "La Politique Musulmane de La France," *Monde Arabe: Maghreb Machrek*, no. 152 (avril–juin 1996): 3–12.

13. Quoted in Henry Laurens, "La Politique Musulmane de La France," *Monde Arabe: Maghreb Machrek*, no. 152 (avril–juin 1996): 11.

14. See Neil MacMaster, *Colonial Migrants and Racism: Algerians in France*, 106.

15. Christophe Charle, "Sentiment National et Nationalisme en France au XIX Siecle," *Bulletin de la Société d'Histoire Moderne et Contemporaine*, nos. 1–2 (1996): 22–27.

16. This fear of Pan-Islamism as a force of nationalistic sentiment can be clearly noticed from the interest, in both the *Revue des Deux Mondes* and the *Revue du Monde Musulman*, paid to Islam and Pan-Islamism during the first part of the twentieth century.

17. Henry Laurens, "La Politique Musulmane de La France," *Monde Arabe: Maghreb Machrek*, no. 152 (avril–juin 1996): 8.

18. Quoted in Laurens, "La Politique Musulmane de La France," 9.

19. Ignacio Ramonet, "Régimes Globalitaires," *Monde Diplomatique* (janvier 1997): 1.

20. Tahar Ben Jelloun, *French Hospitality: Racism and North African Immigrants* (New York: Columbia University Press, 1999).

21. For a good discussion of the meaning and history of these terms see Mohand Khellil, *L'Intégration des Maghrébins en France* (Paris: Presses Universitaires de France, 1991).

22. "Le processus par lequel une minorité sociale ou ethnique (souvent caractériseé par un niveau économique inférieur) adopte les valeurs dominantes et les comportements traditionnels de la société dans laquelle elle s'insère et avec laquelle elle finit par fusionner (*Dictionnaire Encyclopédique Alpha*)."

23. Adrian Favell, *Philosophies of Integration: Immigration and the Idea of Citizenship in France and Britain* (New York: St. Martin's Press, 1998), 151.

24. Ernest Renan, *Oeuvres Complètes*, tome 2 (Paris: Calmann-Lévy, 1948), 333.

25. Renan, *Oeuvres Complètes*, 323.

26. Renan, *Oeuvres Complètes*, 333.

27. Favell, *Philosophies of Integration*, 70.

28. Favell, *Philosophies of Integration*, 77.

29. As shown by Eugen Weber in *Peasants into Frenchmen: The Modernization of France* (Cambridge, Mass.: Harvard University, 1977).

30. Nathalie Dollé, "Qui Représentera les Musulmans de France?," *Le Monde Diplomatique* (janvier 2002): 6.

31. Christiane Chombeau, "Le FN et le MNR Esperent Etre Banalisés grace à 'l'Effet Haider,'" *Le Monde*, 13 février 2000.

32. Cris Shore and Annabel Black, "The European Communities and the Construction of Europe," *Anthropology Today* 8, no. 3 (June 1992): 10.

33. Shore and Black, "The European Communities and the Construction of Europe," 11.

34. Natalie Zemon Davis, *Society and Culture in Early Modern France* (Stanford, Calif.: Stanford University Press, 1987).

35. Martine Barthelemy, "Les Associations dans la Société française: un État de Lieu," *Les Cahiers du Cevipof* 10, no. 2 CNRS (juin 1994).

36. Alain Badiou, from the text of the film "L'École de Mai: 1968–1978" by Denis Levy (1979), p. 3.

37. Alain Badiou, from the text of the film "L'École de Mai: 1968–1978."

38. Alain Touraine, *The Return of the Actor: Social Theory in Post-Industrial Society* (Minneapolis: University of Minnesota, 1988).

39. Serge Depaquit, "Les Interrogations du Syndicalisme francais," *Monde Diplomatique* (janvier 1997): 4.

40. See Jocelyne Cesari, *Etre Musulman en France: Associations, Militants et Mosquees* (Paris: Khartala, 1994).

41. Two important thinkers come to mind: Alain Badiou and Sylvain Lazarus. Badiou's works include *L'Être et l'événement* (1988), *Manifeste pour la Philosophie* (1989), and *Conditions* (1992). Sylvain Lazarus's most important work is *Anthropologie du Nom* (1996).

42. The name of their journal, *La Distance,* is revealing of their position.

43. See *La Distance Politique*, no. 16 (avril 1996): 1–2.

44. Sylvain Lazarus, *Anthropologie du Nom* (Paris: Seuil, 1996), 191.

45. Alain Badiou, *Conditions* (Paris: Seuil, 1992), 219.

46. Badiou, *Conditions,* 221.

47. Badiou, *Conditions,* 233.

48. Most of the quotes that follow are taken directly from tracts that I collected between 1993 and 1998.

## ⑫

# SOCIAL DYNAMICS IN COLONIAL ALGERIA: THE QUESTION OF PIEDS-NOIRS IDENTITY

## Ali Yedes

Over the course of decades of French colonial settlement in Algeria from 1830 to 1962, the European-Algerian community, commonly called the "Pieds-Noirs," gradually grew farther and further apart—culturally and socially—from the French of France. Born and raised in a North African space, the Pieds-Noirs were fully exposed to the various groups that populated it. The new space included the undeniably strong pull of the Arab/Berber population, which accentuated even more the difference between the Metropolitan French and the European-Algerians. Having settled in North Africa for generations, how many French traits did the European-Algerians still keep with them? And, for that matter, how many North African traits did they come to carry in all aspects of life? The purpose of this study is to examine the conflicted character of Pieds-Noirs identity as revealed in their colonial relationship to the indigenous Arab/Berber population, in their *native* relation to the Algerian land, and ambiguous ties to Metropolitan France and its inhabitants.

The Pieds-Noirs shared the Algerian space with the indigenous population, and eventually shared the culture that came with both the space and its occupants. Not only were they influenced by the culture that was around them, but they also became part of it, even if they refused to admit it, and did not want to be associated with the people that were identified with that culture. It would have been very difficult, for example, for a European-Algerian to avoid the impact of Ramadan, the fasting month for

Muslims. During this spiritual and festive month, Moorish cafés were closed and the streets were almost deserted of Arabs and Berbers, particularly during the diurnal fasting times. At night, however, festivities would last till dawn and European-Algerians were definitely part of these. In *Jeunesse de la Méditerranée*, Gabriel Audisio relates his pleasant Ramadan nights as a matter of fact and not as a single, accidental experience: "Oriental celebrations, music, dancing, and the dramatization of a story from *A Thousand and One Nights. . . ."*[1]

Close contact between the settlers and the indigenous population was inevitable and unavoidable. This fact is quite understandable when we realize that Algerian cities had long included both European and Arab/Berber as well as mixed neighborhoods. Communities were often mingled together in the same space, even sharing, as Pierre Nora reports, "the same apartment buildings": "Arab neighborhoods are next to the European cities; [Arabs] work on European properties. . . . Out in the country, the Arab community was inoculated with a French presence. On a map, the indentations of the Arab population infiltrate right into the heart of the European settlement in a network that defies all partitions."[2]

Living in the same neighborhoods and sharing the same apartment buildings in North Africa meant a lot more, in terms of human contact and interaction, than doing so in France, or in Europe, for that matter. As Audisio recounts in 1957, the warmth of emotion, the boiling passion, the relaxed Mediterranean lifestyle ultimately led both communities to interact:

> Insofar as they inhabit the same places, where they move about, see and meet each other, all these populations have lived side-by-side or face-to-face for more than a hundred years. They are condemned to live together, as their fellow compatriot Camus told them. And, inevitably, some of their customs were influenced by each other: for example, the eating of couscous among Europeans and the wearing of Western trousers among Arabs, and among all of them, a certain accented speech, certain expressions, certain typical gestures.[3]

It is important, here, to remember that a good part of the early European settlers, such as the Spanish, the Maltese, and the Sicilians, already had had a significant exposure to Arab culture, throughout their history. Some of the places where these settlers originated still carried a pronounced Arabic influence in their language and customs. Nora tells of "a Spaniard [who] would listen in rapture to [what he believed to be] Andalusian music on the radio, until he learned from the announcer that it was Arab."[4] On this matter, too, Audisio, offers an eloquent elaboration: "Think of Dante, steeped in Muslim eschatology. Think of medieval Sicily where Norman kings ruled

over a civilization whose care and creation they left to the Arabs. Think of
Malta . . . where Christians worship Jesus Christ in a language akin to that
of the Koran. . . . And think of the Andalusia of old."[5]

Regardless of national origin, though, European-Algerians were well
aware of their now mixed ethnicity. The North African space, with its specific climate and the fact of its indigenous culture and traditions, was the
reality to which they belonged and by which their specific identity as "Algerian" was shaped and defined. As Audisio puts it:

> The Algerian is already conscious of his ethnic and mental particularity. He
> believes in the climate and in the influence of the milieu, and sometimes
> he does not hesitate to find in himself something Berber (we could also say
> something Arab, and some Algerians are not afraid to admit it, but Berber
> sounds better, since it is the beneficiary of a favorable prejudice). He knows
> that he is a specific mixture.
>
> One should always go back to Cagayous' famous answer to the question:
> "Are you French?—Algerians, we are."[6]

Isolated farmers, small village communities, and the poor working class in
urban areas were the most exposed to and influenced by the Arab/Berber milieu and culture. They, more than others, shared the same type of life as the
indigenous population and ended up adopting Arab/Berber manners and customs; but middle-class and wealthy settlers also received their share of influence from the indigenous Arab/Berber majority. Though seemingly more
distant from the native inhabitants, these classes still interacted in specific
ways with the Arab/Berber Muslims. Even when this rapport was a patronizing one, the proximity was often close enough to establish a certain bond, *on
the individual level*, between certain members of different groups. The
overtly intolerant and hard-line attitudes of the colonizers against the indigenous Arabs/Berbers in general did not always hold up on the individual level.
As colonizer/colonized, they both carried a certain hatred and *mépris* for one
another as members of those opposing *groups*, but as individuals, each had a
friend or acquaintance that he/she would get along with; a person to whom
he/she wished no harm. Even at the very height of the battle of Algiers, according to General Jacques Massu, who infamously oversaw the brutal suppression of the Casbah at the behest of the European-Algerians who
demanded the most extreme harshness on his part, every arrest of an Arab
triggered the intervention from a European on his/her behalf: "They all had
their Muslim!," he later testified.[7]

In the practice of daily life, each group needed the other. The colonizer
needed the colonized, mostly to perform labor, and the colonized needed

work in order to survive. So much so that the tense, political undercurrent of grudge bearing and mutual disdain was usually put aside when the immediate needs of both communities were at stake. The warmth of inter- action between the European-Algerians among themselves was "sponta- neously extended," *on the individual level*, to indigenous Arab/Berber acquaintances: "Brotherly and easygoing familiarity was also spontaneously extended to Arabs (more officious between themselves than the French were to them), which gave Europeans reasons to be surprised when they were accused of being racist" (Nora, 164). In a place where the gen- eral condition of social and political life was under constant tension, and where anguish, insecurity, and fear of the other were common sensations working *both* ways between oppressor and oppressed, the individual rela- tionship offered a locus of exception to socially determined human relations. Members of the colonizing group had an opportunity to prove to themselves that they were not, after all, deprived of human feeling and that they were capable of relating to others on a sympathetic, personal level.

Moreover, these European-Algerians were well aware of their own con- flicted condition; they wanted to maintain their superiority over the indige- nous people but they did not know any other lifestyle except the one that was urging them, reluctantly or not, closer to the Arab/Berber population. Ironically, the more they felt distant from and inferior to the Metropolitan French, the more they felt the Arab/Berber people should be inferior to them. They tried hard to establish a distance between the indigenous peo- ple and themselves yet they could only be the North Africans they in fact were by narrowing that distance with the rest of the Algerian population, an effort whose ever-intensifying paradox could only lead to their doom at the end of the Algerian war.

The European-Algerians were caught therefore in an insuperable dilemma: on one hand wishing to be distanced sociopolitically from the in- digenous Arabs/Berbers in order to mark their superiority; on the other hand, affectively grounded in the reality of an adopted culture that was sig- nificantly assimilated to the Arab/Berber lifestyle. The effort in distancing oneself from the Arab was particularly pronounced among the educated elite of European-Algerians, who carried themselves with a borrowed atti- tude of French snobbism. One such group was even behind an organized snob movement, the goal of which was to recuperate the "lost" European essence (as if it had ever existed) of the European-Algerians. This move- ment gained momentum through its magazine interestingly titled *Afrique*, whose editor was no less than Robert Randau, the author of *Les colons*, ar- guably the best-known Algerian colonial novel.[8] Randau and his group took it upon themselves to point out to their fellow European-Algerians the dangers of totally divorcing themselves from the metropole and of losing their European character. If they continued along in the same lifestyle, Randau warned, at the rate they were going, they would become as African as the rest of the indigenous people, without the French character that made them "superior." Randau wrote, alarmingly, that "européanisme" and the sense of differentiation between one race and the other, which he considered a valuable inherited tradition from the first colonizing settlers, was already slowly disappearing among the younger generation: "The descendants of the early colonists have gradually lost the essence of their Europeanism and the sense of the old differentiations between the races," he sadly declared.[9] Randau's movement sought above all to increase cultural relations with France, in an effort to reawaken the greater French soul in the wayward European-Algerian. In order to reach this goal, "oriental" or North African influences had also to be avoided. North African cultural manifestations that they considered threats to their goal of ethnic purification ranged from bazaar displays to Arab feasts, belly-dancing, Numidian horsemanship, and muezzins calling for prayer on minarets.

It goes without saying that these efforts to establish a distance from the indigenous culture came into the fore only precisely *because* the people behind these efforts realized the incontestable fact of their deep immersion in North African culture, whether they liked it or not. At the same time, the European-Algerians needed a corrective for the inferiority complex created by the Metropolitan French attitude toward them. As the Metropolitan French associated them with the dominated indigenous community, the European-Algerians were at pains to show them—and themselves—how distant and different they were from the despised Arab.

In order to mitigate the already soiled, inferior image encapsulated in the derogatory term "Pied-Noir," many European-Algerians, like those associated with Randau's group, attempted the illusory task of proving to themselves and to others that they were as French as any to be found in the hexagon: "In the street, at the slightest incident, the argument comes up: "I am French [je suis français]" pronounced, by the way, with an accent: *froncé*. "I am *froncé*, monsieur, I am as *froncé* as you are!" (Nora, 52).

Endless frustration marked the European-Algerian relation with the "Françaoui," their nickname for the Metropolitan French, who could not possibly understand their Algerian side. It is interesting to note that the word *Françaoui* was a North African Arabic word meaning a French person. As a matter of fact, indigenous Algerians used this word indifferently for the Metropolitan French as well as the European-Algerians. For the

Arab/Berber Algerian, they were both *Françaouin* (plural of *Françaoui*). The European-Algerians, in turn, bounced back onto the Metropolitan French the very name the indigenous Arab/Berbers employed in order to identify the colonizer as belonging to a separate community. The use of such an Arabic word to refer to the Metropolitan French reveals the European-Algerian psychological attitude toward the French, that they somehow considered the Metropolitan French foreigners to their community, since they consciously "baptized" them with such a distancing name.

European-Algerians who left Algeria, even for a while, missed the space, the culture, and the indigenous people that they would keep their distance from back home in Algeria: "What French Algerian does not feel exiled in the metropole? It is not only the sun he misses, or his family, but the familiar Arab with whom he feels more confident and has more in common with than the French of France; the one with whom very often he spent his 'salouetche' childhood" (Nora, 177). European-Algerians in Paris for education or other reasons were invariably thrilled to find fellow North Africans, whether European or Arab, with whom to share complaints about France, its weather, and its people. They would seek out North African circles where they could savor North African dishes they were brought up with and would always miss. One of the characters in Randau's *Les colons*, "exiled" in Paris to study Law, runs every evening to a fellow Algerian compatriot's home in order to treat himself to various dishes of couscous, zelabia dipped in honey, and other typically North African pastries and dishes.

European-Algerians felt rejected by the Metropolitan French. Remarks such as the following abound: "In the metropole, people do not like us . . . the atmosphere is unbreathable: they puncture our tires. In Lyon, they even refused us a room in a hotel" (Nora, 46). Their accent, their idioms, and their definitely non–French-like *allure* brought laughter and contempt from the French. As Daniel Leconte explains:

> What refined Parisian society reproaches in the French Algerians is, above all, the "bougnoulisé" that he is. It **is** his exuberance that they take for vulgarity, his references that they attribute to bad taste, his way of speaking that they consider coarse, or his attitudes that they consider out of place. Thinking that they are denouncing his lack of culture, what they refuse to recognize is in fact his "difference."[10]

For the French, the "Pieds-Noirs" were viewed as inferior, belonging to an inferior continent, Africa, their feet steeped in its "blackness," so to speak. The Pied-Noir aspiration to equality with the French of the hexagon provoked even more scorn and disdain.

Most of the European settlers in Algeria were originally escaping the harshness that struck Europe during the Industrial Revolution. As victims of the unmerciful working and living conditions in the industrial factories, they saw in exile an opportunity to set themselves free from the lingering life of misery. Factory workers in the industrial cities were often adapted provincials who had a certain nostalgia for agricultural lands. Algeria seemed the perfect solution for these people who would not hesitate to seek refuge in land even if it was through colonization. These workers were also looked down upon as they belonged to the lower social class. When these workers left France and other European countries, they were desperately hoping to improve their standard of living (Nora, 82–84; Baroli, 41–45, 109–18). In the eyes of the conventional French, however, they were always those who belonged to a low-class group who abandoned their country out of desperation. They were still looked down upon. After generations of settlement, they were still haunted by the image of being inferior to the Metropolitans even if they were now economically successful.

The Metropolitan French managed to find more reasons to look down upon the European-Algerians. The fact of sharing the North African space with their indigenous occupants, the *bougnouls,* made them, if not *bougnouls* like them, at least *bougnoulisés* ("bougnoulized"). This word, *bougnoul,* was first used in Senegal by the white colonizers as a denigrating name for indigenous people there. The word had been used, ever since, to designate all colonized Africans, those north as well as south of the Sahara (Le Robert). Living among the indigenous Arabs/Berbers, and, in the case of the *petits colons* of the remote villages, speaking their language and involving them in family events, was a concession dictated by the necessity of coexistence. Already looked down upon because of their class origin that led them to leave their country and live in exile, the European-Algerians found themselves even more *déclassés* and *bougnoulisés* because of their coexistence with the Arab/Berber "inferior" race.

In his study of *Les Pieds-Noirs,* Daniel Leconte notes that among the defining elements that linked the European-Algerian settlers together was the "mentality of a *lost homeland.*"[11] This involved the painful sense of being excluded from the mother country, the metropole that was ungrateful to its sons and daughters. Convinced that he/she has been cheated and used by a society that, in a way practically created and shaped his/her destiny in order to satisfy its economical and political thirst, the European-Algerian held a "tenacious" grudge against the metropole. The idea of the existence of two types of French, those of Europe, the masters, and those of Algeria, the servants, was unbearable.

The European-Algerians also wanted to be French for the status that being French carried in colonial life. In other respects, however, they tended
to be not only satisfied but also proud of being Algerian. The vacillation between the desire to be French and the conviction of being also Algerian was
a constant emotional dilemma in the European-Algerian soul. Among
themselves, they were Algerians but also a special category of French; in
the presence of the Metropolitan French, they insisted on being Algerians
but also wanted to be considered as French as them. With the indigenous
Arabs/Berbers, they justified their superiority and privileges by being
French and they saw their patronizing association with them as a compromise to their "Frenchness" that was now soiled, in the eyes of the metropole. This compromise was something they had to live with, a sacrifice that
had to be made, imposed by the necessity of North African life together.
They thus saw themselves as a superior type of Algerian, since they belonged to the politically privileged group, the colonizer.

Musette, Robert Randau, and Albert Camus among other Algerian writers expressed the unique, complex character of the European-Algerian in
their literary works. The following passage from Randau's *Les colons* is typical:

> – Above all, we have to be Africans.
> – You're right, let's liberate ourselves, damn it! In Paris, they think there are
> two kinds of French in the world, those of Europe, the masters, and those of
> Algeria, the servile. Men of Algeria, we will only obey the laws that are good
> for Algeria and that we have already discussed in advance. I feel that France
> is less and less my fatherland, but I confess France remains my ideal.[12]

Even renowned writers like Camus were not protected from the Metropolitan scorn for the Pieds-Noirs. Daniel Leconte, among others, mentions the
clashes that Camus himself had with the Parisian intelligentsia who saw in
him a *déclassé* mingling with the refined crowd of the capital (Leconte,
146).

Small wonder, in the face of such adverse relations with France, that the
claim on Algeria became such a passion for the European settlers. A powerful psychological sense of belonging to its land came to prevail over the
questionable legitimacy of their presence there. Indeed, this emotional
bond of "belonging" was willingly separated from the intricacies of political
life.[13] The justification of their existence was more dedicated to asserting
the necessary sense of this belonging to themselves than persuading some
"other": the legitimate, threatening indigenous Arabs/Berbers, on
one hand, and the scornful, disowning Metropolitans, on the other. The

European-Algerians, as it were, needed a justifying narrative for their colonial presence in Algeria. For them, it was the Algeria that bore *their* impact that mattered. The most important part of Algerian history began with the landing of their ancestors on the Algerian land and chronicled their endeavors to reshape it. They also provided themselves with "legitimate" reasons for their settlement: the "reconquest" of Christian Africa was an easy "justification." The land of Saint Augustine and where remnants of sites related to other Christian saints could be found was also part of their Christian heritage. Religion provided a convenient excuse for belonging and appropriation. For them, history started with North Africa as part of the Roman Empire, froze with the arrival of the Arabs, and started all over again with the French occupation. It was the grand fantasy of "reappropriating" what should by all rights have been a Christian land, while turning a deaf ear to the actual historical process of colonization. As far as the ethics of occupation were concerned, in their eyes, it was the Arabs who had started the process by usurping what should have been an extension of the Christian world. The European-Algerian perception became rather hazy, though, when it came to accepting the reality of the recorded historical events of the occupation of Algeria, leading up to its virtually inexplicable war of liberation, and what for them could only be the scandal of decolonization, the metropole's final act of betrayal. The prospect of abandoning the Algerian land was unbearable. Where else could the settlers go? France, for them, was a place of exile, and postwar Algeria had become a place of turmoil. The turmoil of physical violence, however, was but the final act in that other turmoil of the settler's fatal love and attachment for a native land no other could replace. Well before the former became overt, the tumultuousness of the latter had already long bred tension, anguish, and despair into the seemingly apparent ease of colonial life.

Ultimately, whether in France or in Algeria, the European-Algerians were bound to have neither a definite direction in terms of identity nor a sense of balance. They were not sure they were French, nor were they sure of being Algerians. In his early sociological study of Algerian society, Pierre Bourdieu argues that the colonial environment created by the European-Algerians was a powerful work of negation by which they no longer felt themselves to be foreigners at all: "Little by little, the European creates an environment that reflects his own image and which is the negation of the old universe, a universe in which the European[-Algerian] no longer feels himself to be a foreigner, and by a natural reversal, the [indigenous] Algerian ends up being perceived as a foreigner."[14] The European-Algerians wished and tried to be both Algerians and French; but would they be accepted as such by either party? In the end, rejected by both sides, they belonged to a group of their own, living in an imaginary world, with an identity of their own, separate and distant from either side. Bourdieu concludes, "as the Europeans distance themselves from the Arabs, so too do they distance themselves from France, not only from the ideal of France . . . but from the 'French of France'" (Bourdieu, 115–16).

The European-Algerians thrived on opposites and contradictions: they wanted to be Algerian but did not want to be associated with the indigenous Algerian character, nor did they accept the Metropolitan French conception of themselves as "Pied-Noir;" on the other hand they wished to be French, while insisting on their being different from the French of France. It is Pierre Bourdieu again who provides us with a valuable analysis related to this matter: "The 'Pied-Noir' defines himself/herself by defining the *Françaoui* in opposite terms: on one side, there is generosity, virility, the cult of the body, that is to say pleasure, strength and physical beauty, a cult whose temple is the beach: on the other side, meanness, impotence, intellectualism, asceticism, etc. But the self-definition is also drawn in opposition to the Arab who, in his or her eyes, embodies, on the contrary, instinctual life, a lack of culture, ignorance, routine existence, etc. All this leads to a definition of oneself that is quite contradictory" (Bourdieu, 113). The European-Algerian's complex psychological state led to an inner world of ebb and flow between contradictory desires, wanting to be either French or Algerian, or both at a certain time, and neither French nor Algerian. Alienated in Algeria, alienated in France, the European-Algerians were in the end perfect foreigners, both to themselves and to the spaces they inhabited, remaining in constant search for an ever-elusive identity. Here, again, Bourdieu points out the sense of despair that resulted from the frightening reality of belonging nowhere: "the disarray that results from losing the ties of belonging that founded the psychological and social stability of the individual in traditional communities" (Bourdieu, 123).

The ease of European-Algerian colonial life was thus always marred by a bittersweet taste. As Pierre Nora pertinently notes, "a profound despair dominates all the social relations" of the European-Algerians (157). Even in the heyday of the colonial regime, the European-Algerians were constantly worried about the future of Algeria. There was always the deep concern about whether the colonial life was going to last and about what would become of them if the French occupation came to an end. What made things worse was the pervasive belief that the mother country (France) did nothing for the colony. Indeed, the future of Algeria constituted such a dominating theme that all communities were affected by it and took part in it. In *La vie quotidienne des Français en Algérie*, Marc Baroli notes:

In public squares, in cafés, and in the street, conversations take their normal course, and, if we believe Feydeau, all of them tackle a single subject, the future of Algeria. Everybody has an opinion, including the Jews, the Moors, and even women; newcomers themselves do not stay long before voicing their own. Only these, at least during their first days, do not share the general opinion that quickly comes out from all the talk: "France does nothing for the colony."[15]

The European-Algerians felt insecure in their own space. They found themselves between two forces: the first was the Muslim population behind the scene, silent but whose presence alone was a lurking threat. The second was the metropolitan authority against which the European-Algerians could not do much if this authority refused to intervene in the case of a dispute: the center of decision making being in France, it was too far for the pressure of the European-Algerian population to be efficient. Baroli notes: "Thus, caught between the indigenous masses and the metropole, the French Algerians experienced a sense of isolation, and this feeling came to heighten their own particularities" (Baroli, 252).

At the same time, every European-Algerian had some kind of authority over every indigenous Muslim. The army, whose organization reflected the stratified reality of Algerian colonial life, itself constituted a model in a place where the physical display of virility was an acknowledged cultural value and virtue. Moreover, the military group assigned to Algeria had the authority to execute any suspect without a trial. In the very few cases where a trial was held, the *colons* or settlers directed it the way they wanted, according to their benefit. During the Sidi Mokrani rebellion in Kabylia, accused Arabs/Berbers, whose lands were confiscated, were tried by juries composed solely of European-Algerian community members (Nora, 89).

And while the Pieds-Noirs had no effective sway over the distant metropolitan authority, the French government, for its part, could not bring itself to impose any controlling law on the French community in Algeria. Not only were European settlers politically out of control, but there seemed to be no limit to their claims and demands. Demanding one favor after the other, all their requests were clothed with a coat of legitimacy, yet without any sign of satisfaction or satiation upon their petitions being granted. Their claims were that of desperate colonials who wanted to have their hands full of impossible guaranties. Their insecurity was such that they wanted to make sure that nothing related to their native land of settlement would one day slip from their hands. What they demanded in Algeria was to appropriate the land and lord over the indigenous Arabs/Berbers who populated it, and who were the image of a historical reality that stated the potential threat of a reappropriation: "With the ardor of people in despair, these 'French' demanded guaranties from the metropole. What they sought in Algeria was Algeria with its two aspects: the land and the Arab. Thus, from the outset and spontaneously, they set themselves in opposition to any evolution, they blocked history" (Nora, 87).

Beyond the promulgation of such "guaranties," the government authority, political or judicial, was almost absent as far as the European-Algerian was concerned. The authority that did exist was the one applied to the indigenous people. The settlers yelled, shouted, and complained furiously about the lack of rigorous measures toward the indigenous Arabs/Berbers. Once they got the government to adopt the necessary tough measures to support and maintain their privileges—such as the Warnier Law of 1873, which aimed at "frenchifying" the Arab, Muslim land; or the 1874 *Code de l'Indigénat*, which introduced extreme repressive measures against the indigenous people, reinforcing their total subordination to the mercy of French administrators and community members—all they had to do was to block any evolution toward more lenient attitudes. As for the assertive claim to run their own affairs without metropolitan interference, it is again a character in Randau's novel who makes an exemplary deathbed statement to one of his Arab farmers: "Ahmed Cheik, I am no scribbler or whiner for justice; justice, I create it for myself. I am not a lazy Arab like you, I am a colonist."[16]

More generally, the European-Algerians became experts in political manipulation, what they themselves called "politichiennerie" (Nora, 98). In the course of a century and a half of colonial rule, dealing with politics had become a long habit that allowed them to get familiar with the ins and outs of *both* the Right and the Left and use each to their benefit. The popular character of Cagayous created by Musette expresses very well the rather insecure but defiant attitude of the cornered European-Algerian: "Politics, we stuff it inside a basket and sit on it till it becomes just like the date bread the Arabs eat."[17] At social gatherings, they would take pleasure in making fun of the government in the rudest way. They would laugh at government decisions and consolidate their opposition to them by such mocking slogans as the following: "'De Gaulle, he says: *auto-determination*, we tell him: why not *bicycle-determination*?' They give the finger! And in unison they strike up: 'We are the Africans'" (Nora, 27). Such gestures let them revitalize their frail sense of unity against both the metropole and the indigenous Arabs/Berbers; a unity they also knew, deep inside, would not mean much without the support of the metropole. Neither would it be of any significance when tested by the frightening indigenous majority.

Eventually, of course, the unbearable dread of leaving the native country turned to reality, and what the European-Algerians were afraid of, the independence of Algeria, happened. The desperate, resigned attitude of the European-Algerians, during their forced exile, after the liberation, led them to a state of emotional destitution. The strength of their attachment to the land was measured by the enormously deplorable state of deception, grief, and desolation they fell into when they had to leave Algeria. Leaving the Algerian land, for them, meant being uprooted from the homeland. With this "uprootedness," the inner world of the European-Algerians was struck twice: on one hand, the colonial figure in them was obviously killed; on the other hand, and perhaps more importantly, their childhood was also killed. Now they could connect with childhood only *in memory* with no more physical space to relate to. In *Les Pieds-Noirs*, Daniel Leconte quotes Alain Ferry talking about his mother:

> Rosette died for having had to leave Algeria. Not the whole of Algeria, with its history of colonization, its war of liberation, or its Secret Army Organization [OAS]. Just a tiny, native corner of Algeria, which did not belong to us in the juridical capitalist order of things, but it was our piece of land; that's where we acquired our beings, our memories, . . . that's where she was our queen without even trying, without having to show it as in the talismanic evidence of some power that is accountable to nobody because nobody would ever think of asking about it. (285–86)

Leconte goes on to remark that there were thousands of people like Rosette for whom, after 1962, life held no meaning, and they ended up withering, slowly, to their death. Leconte also mentions that during the winter of 1962–1963, obituary columns of the southern French newspapers were full of European-Algerian names. What these newspapers did not specify, Leconte adds, were how many were suicides, individual epilogues of a collective tragedy (244). The European-Algerian community, now scattered in an austere and indifferent French milieu, could not find the right place for its sense of communal joy to be reborn. The height of despair was perhaps best expressed by a European-Algerian woman, relocated in France after Algerian independence: "They stole our past. Here, when people see each other, they talk about their roots, their soil, they can do that, not us. As for us, we can do no more than listen to them, we cannot live in this country because we do not have a place that is ours, we no longer have a country" (Leconte, 248).

In an effort to mitigate their "uprootedness," many of the European-Algerians who were forced to relocate to France after independence chose to settle in the South, not to be deprived of the Mediterranean climate that was so much a part of their physical and cultural environment. Despite the material advantages that the French government agreed to offer to those who would settle in the North, many rejected this choice, preferring the "gratuity" of the sun that they hoped would heal their open wound. As for those unfortunates who had no alternative, settling in the North was a good reason to gain the sympathy of their Algerian expatriots: "The biggest problem was the dispersion. Some found themselves in Marseille, in Albi or Toulouse, the others in the North, poor things . . . , " declared a European-Algerian "refugee" (Leconte, 246). While the foggy climate of the North was associated with the cold indifference and the gloomy moods of its inhabitants, it happened that, *wherever* they ended up residing in France, they could not easily adapt to the new metropolitan culture. Solidarity, generosity, and exchange of services, which were fundamental values in a North African context, were perceived as "quaint" in "modern" French society. Many European-Algerians came to the conclusion that there was no such a thing as "social life" in France. In Algeria, *le quartier* (the neighborhood) was the place "par excellence" for socializing. Animated by a mixture of cultural, social, political, and religious differences, *le quartier* was the heart of public activities and daily entertainment. In France, by way of contrast, they passed their neighbors daily, but they hardly talked to each other, let alone socialized (Leconte, 245–48).

Algeria, as a place of birth for these exiles, remains a matter of record. Though this "native" status was well disputed by the legitimate indigenous Algerians, the two irreconcilable worlds of colonial Algeria have yet to be painfully faced. What cannot be denied are the truths and the realities of two peoples who shared the same space for over a century and a half: one was legitimate, and the other born and raised there with nowhere else to go. Which truth and which reality would prevail is also a matter of record: the cultural and ideological truth of "belonging" to a specific space of settlement, or the political and historical one that recalled the legitimacy of the indigenous Algerians. The image of Rosette as her family's natural "queen " reigning over their little piece of the native Algerian land still suggests a prevailing notion of innocence, ease, and belonging, one that was irreconcilable—to the point of becoming inconceivable—with the expropriation of that land from its indigenous owners. The "romanticization" of the past, particularly as colored through nostalgic childhood memories, is a normal tendency for exiles, but it should not be forgotten that this same past is seen by the indigenous Arabs/Berbers of Algeria with a different eye indeed, and all the more so in recent years as so many of those indigenous

Algerians have in turn made the trek north, themselves settling in the land the Pieds-Noirs hailed from but never considered home.

## NOTES

1. Gabriel Audisio, *Jeunesse de la Méditerranée* (Paris: Gallimard, 1935), 110.
2. Pierre Nora, *Les Français d'Algérie* (Paris: René Juillard, 1961), 185.
3. Gabriel Audisio, *Algérie méditerranée. Feux vivants* (Limoges: Rougerie, 1957), 28.
4. Nora, *Les Français d'Algérie*, 135–36.
5. Audisio, *Algérie méditerranée*, 35–36.
6. Audisio, *Jeunesse de la Méditerranée*, 113.
7. Cited in Nora, *Les Français d'Algérie*, 182.
8. Robert Randau, *Les colons* (Paris: E. Sansot et Cie, 1907).
9. Cited in Nora, *Les Français d'Algérie*, 52.
10. Daniel Leconte, *Les Pieds-Noirs: histoire et portrait d'une communauté* (Paris: Seuil, 1980), 157.
11. Leconte, *Les Pieds-Noirs*, 101.
12. Leconte, *Les Pieds-Noirs*, 145–46.
13. On this strong emotional sense of belonging as a basis of political identity, see Michael Ignatieff, *Blood and Belonging: Journeys into the New Nationalism* (New York: Farrar, Strauss & Giroux, 1994).
14. Pierre Bourdieu, *Sociologie de l'Algérie* (Paris: Presses Universitaires de France, 1961), 114.
15. Marc Baroli, *La vie quotidienne des Français en Algérie, 1830–1914* (Paris: Hachette, 1967), 87.
16. Cited in Nora, *Les Français d'Algérie*, 173.
17. Musette [Auguste Robinet], *Cagayous. Ses meilleurs histories*, ed. Gabriel Audisio (Paris: Gallimard, 1931), 129.

# ⓭

# REMEMBERING THE JEWS OF ALGERIA

## Nancy Wood

J'ai quitté mon pays
J'ai quitté ma maison
Ma vie, ma triste vie se traîne sans raison
J'ai quitté mon soleil
J'ai quitté ma mer bleu
Leurs souvenirs se réveillaient
bien après mon adieu.

Soleil, soleil de mon pays perdu!
Des villes blanches que j'aimais
Des filles que j'ai jadis connu.

These lyrics are sung by Enrico Macias, the enormously popular *chanteur,* described by *Le Monde* as the Charles Aznavour of France's *pied-noir* and Maghrebian community alike.[1] In his song "Adieu mon pays," Macias recalls memories of the sun and of the blue sea of "mon pays perdu," of last glimpses of his homeland as the ship puts distance between him and the quayside, and of the "waves" of regret that overcome him. Macias, a Jew from Constantine, left Algeria in 1962, shortly after Raymond Leyris, spokesperson of the Constantine Jewish community and master singer of *malouf,* a version of Arabo-Andalusian music, was assassinated by two FLN militants during the final stages of the Algerian War. Leyris's death was the symbolic trigger for a rapid exodus of Jews from Algeria, including that of

Macias, who, on the ship *Le Ville-d'Alger*, composed "Adieu mon pays."[2]
However, if it is tempting to interpret the lyrics of Macias's song, and indeed his enormous popularity among France's *pied-noir* community, as
symptomatic of the *"nostalgérie"* that is said to exercise such an enduring
affective hold over former Français d'Algérie, in the case of Macias this interpretation would be both too simplistic and unjust. It would not account
for the 8,000 Egyptian fans who turned up to his concert in 1979, the hundreds of Maghrebians who mingled with *pieds-noirs* at his Paris concert in
1995, the women waving their headscarves as they danced to his music, nor
for the insults—"Sale juif," "Ami des Arabes"—directed at him by the Front
National.[3] Macias's Jewish-Algerianness is a more tangled identity to un-
ravel, just as the memories evoked in his songs articulate an equally complex relationship to his "pays perdu."

Far from the venues of French popular culture, philosopher Jacques
Derrida also confirms a "disorder of identity" (*trouble d'identité*) that lies at
the heart of his self-designation as a "Jewish-French-Maghrebian." The
"disorder" of which Derrida speaks, however, does not refer to the exodus
of Algerian Jews during the War of Independence, but relates to a history
when Algeria's colonial status quo was very much intact, and concerns the
question of *citizenship*. Though Derrida admits that citizenship is not an
identity in the way that cultural, linguistic, or historical commonalities
might confer on a community a sense of shared belonging, he nonetheless
insists that citizenship is not either a "superficial or superstructural predi-
cate floating on the surface of experience."[4] Moreover, its importance to a
sense of selfhood is all the more revealed when it turns out that citizenship
can be "precarious, recent, threatened," as was the case for the Jews of Algeria. Granted French citizenship by the *décret Crémieux* in 1870, Algerian
Jews were subsequently deprived of their citizenship by Vichy's *Statut des
juifs* of 1940, without reclaiming any other citizenship in the process. *"No
other,"* Derrida emphatically reminds us.

In *Monolingualism of the Other*, Derrida evokes memories of having lost
his French citizenship as a youth under the Vichy régime, during an Occupation in which Algeria, as Derrida points out, was in fact never occupied—
or at least not by the Germans. This was an entirely French affair—"a
Franco-French operation . . . an act of French Algeria in the absence of any
German occupation."[5] Thus, says Derrida, there is no alibi, no denial, no illusion possible. And while Derrida admits that his youthful self may not
have fully grasped what citizenship and its loss fully signified, he has no
doubt that this memory of exclusion is intimately related to the "disorder of
identity" that is part of his self-assignation as a Jewish-French-Maghrebian.

And for the former Jewish community of Algeria as well, Derrida suggests, whether it remembers, or with great effort strives to forget this privation of citizenship, this precarious experience of national belonging is nonetheless inscribed within its collective memory. The question Derrida poses is whether this "disorder of identity" could be said to "heighten the desire of memory" or to "drive the genealogical fantasy to despair"?[6]

*Monolingualism of the Other* is a multilayered text into which Derrida weaves philosophical and personal reflections on questions of language, identity, and memory. While Derrida is concerned not to reduce these reflections to his individual trajectory, he nonetheless insists that he could not have even broached them without engaging with his own "Judeo-Franco-Maghrebian genealogy." And when, in so doing, Derrida encounters a "disorder of identity," it is soon clear that he is not seeking from this genealogy a solution that would allow him to vindicate and reclaim the fullness of a Jewish-Algerian identity. As his translator Geoff Bennington has pointed out, if Derrida experiences this memory of exclusion under the Vichy Régime as a wound, and as the period that imprints upon him a certain "belonging" to Judaism, it makes Derrida equally impatient with what Bennington calls "gregarious identification" or the "militancy of belonging."[7] Nor is identity for Derrida in any event something that can be given, received, or attained; what he argues is at stake, rather, is what he calls the "interminable and indefinitely phantasmatic process of identification," the "identificatory modality" that is secured by and within language.[8]

Within this context, however, his reflections on his Jewish-Algerian origins *do* have a specific place and function. They invoke a past—and above all a *status*—that, while not defining of all modalities of belonging to which Derrida lays claim, he nonetheless affirms as a distinct "subset" (*sous-ensemble*). More acutely, reflections on this status pose for him the question of what modalities of identification *could* be available for Algeria's Jews given a collective inscription within a national culture that first defined them as "indigenous Jews," subsequently confirmed them as French citizens, and then negated that act of inclusion—all, as Derrida notes, within two generations. Algerian Jews "could not properly *identify themselves,* in the double sense of 'identifying oneself,' and 'identifying oneself with' the other."[9] Even had the ignominy of Vichy not left its traumatic mark, identifying with the other had proved in any case a fraught exercise historically. Neither French, Metropolitan, nor Catholic on the one hand, nor Arab nor Berber on the other, the place of Jews within colonial Algeria was inherently unstable, vulnerable to the forces of deracination or acculturation from which, as Derrida, poignantly remarks, "I undoubtedly never completely emerged."[10]

This instability is the subject of the remainder of this chapter, though I am concerned to locate its traces not primarily in personal testimonies but in what I perceive to be a new historiography of the Jews of Algeria. Indeed, Derrida and others have drawn upon this new historiography as they trace the historical coordinates of their personal and familial memories and attempt to give meaning to these.[11]

The history of the Jews of Algeria has been written over the past century and a half, so my claim is not that this is a repressed history now brought to light as France's culpability for colonial and collaborationist crimes has been progressively revealed. Instead, I want to suggest a link between history and memory, where this new historiography is serving as a vector of memory, not unlike the manner in which the new historiography of Vichy has been both cause and consequence of a renewed Franco-Jewish politics of memory and identity in the past two decades.[12] Admittedly, this vector potentially rallies a much smaller constituency, but the question nonetheless arises as to what might be the political stakes of any identity claims—however judiciously asserted—based on Jewish-Algerian memories.

To pursue my claim, I want to stake out the historiographical parameters of three crucial moments—the Crémieux Decree, Vichy, and the Algerian War—and to signal some of the controversies and questions they elicit about the history and memory of Algerian Jews in particular.

## THE "GIFT" OF CITIZENSHIP

In his contribution to *Les Lieux de mémoire,* Pierre Nora's ambitious project on French national memory, Pierre Birnbaum describes Adolphe Crémieux, minister in several governments in the mid-nineteenth century, as a French Jew who so "fully identified with the emancipatory goals of the Revolution" that he claimed to see embodied in the France of 1789 "a divine flame" that had since become the expression of Judaism itself.[13] Minister of Justice for the Government of National Defence, Crémieux was responsible for drafting legislation that, on October 24, 1870, conferred French citizenship on Algeria's Jews. By this measure, France would gain thirty-four and a half thousand new citizens, and, as historian Michel Abitbol has remarked, Algeria's Jews would "leave Algerian history to enter that of France."[14] This is not to say that Jews had not been recognized as *French* before this date: in order to deal with the status of Algeria's *indigènes,* that is to say Arabs, Berbers, and Jews, the 1865 *Senatus Consulte* had created the category of French *subjects,* distinct from citizens, who could apply for citizenship if they were willing to give up their so-called *statut personnel*, or personal status. This essentially entailed renouncing the authority of religious tribunals in matters such as marriage, divorce, and inheritance and agreeing to be subject to French civil law in these domains. Between 1865 and 1870, only 288 Algerian Jews out of 35,000 applied for citizenship under these conditions.[15] It should also be noted that an even smaller proportion of Muslims opted for this route to citizenship, and French insistence on the renunciation of Muslim personal status would scupper many reform measures until de Gaulle granted French citizenship to Muslims without this condition in 1946. The discrepancy between the minuscule number of demands for French citizenship by Jewish *indigènes* in these years, and their massive accession to full French citizenship, entailing the loss of personal status, in 1870, has recently led historians to pose a number of questions about the meaning to be ascribed to this momentous event. That the Crémieux Decree is a *lieu de mémoire* of Algerian Jewry is not in doubt; but the character of this memory is the subject of considerable contestation.

Derrida's appraisal, circumspect in many ways, is ultimately a negative one. He speaks of a process at the turn of the century whereby "assimilation . . . and acculturation—the feverish bid for a 'Frenchifying' which was also an *embourgeoisification*—were so frantic and so careless that the inspiration of Jewish culture seemed to succumb to an *asphyxia:* a state of apparent death, a ceasing of respiration, a fainting fit, a cessation of the pulse."[16] Derrida's image of a thriving indigenous culture stifled by the very instrument of its political emancipation is one echoed by a strand of this new historiography that describes the Crémieux Decree as *le décret de sinistre mémoire*.[17] Algerian Jews, it is argued, anticipate their loss of personal status as too high a price to pay, given the religious freedom they had previously enjoyed and especially in light of the already considerable erosion of traditional life that had occurred in the prior decades.[18] In this interpretation, the well-meaning Crémieux is nonetheless cast as the Trojan horse of jacobin assimilationism, who recognizes that the decree *must* be imposed since citizenship for Algerian Jews will not be achieved by their own voluntary candidacy. For historians like Michel Abitbol, for example, Crémieux's victory is only the culmination of a longer process by which Algerian Jews became targets of the crusading spirit of French Jews, who projected their own historical trajectory of emancipation onto their co-religionists. At least from 1845, Abitbol points out, key positions in Algeria's Jewish *consistoires* had been occupied by Metropolitan rabbis, and forms of social assimilation promoted by them. If by 1870, Algerian Jews accept reluctantly, or even in some cases with enthusiasm, an obligatory French citizenship, this is partly because they had internalized the "civilizing" aspirations that had originated with ardent Metropolitan advocates of a French-Jewish symbiosis.[19]

While the new historiography generally tends to accept Abitbol's thesis that the Crémieux Decree played a decisive role in the "dejudaization" of the Jews of Algeria, other factors are entered into consideration that inflect this supposition in significantly different directions. Jacques Taïeb proposes that the Crémieux Decree be seen as the "accelerator" or "catalyst" for a *relative* "decomposition" of Jewish identity in Algeria, rather than the primary cause of a profound dismantling. His argument is that the destabilizing forces of modernity had already impinged on the Jewish-Algerian community well before 1870, that "Westernization" and "Frenchifying" (*francisation*) had been under way for several decades—whether by dint of scholarization, changing demographic patterns, or the rise of new nontraditional elites. Moreover, it was precisely these processes that had created a *demand* for naturalization on the part of a significant sector of Algeria's Jewish community, expressed through numerous petitions and the appeals of community and religious leaders. In this interpretation, the Crémieux Decree is the quintessential symbol of its time, and its disregard for cultural particularism the ideological essence of the "republican pact" to which it owed its inspiration. In fact, Taïeb locates the detrimental consequences of the Crémieux Decree precisely here: in the fact that the assimilationist dogma of republican jacobinism in his words "disarmed Algerian Jews into thinking that the decree was henceforth an inviolable and irrevocable principle within the French conception of citizenship"—a belief that would be shattered by the Vichy experience.[20]

Whatever the ambivalences of its reception by Algerian Jews, the Crémieux Decree claims a crucial place in the vicissitudes of turn-of-the-century French anti-Semitism. Edouard Drumont devotes a whole section of *La France Juive* to Crémieux and the allegedly corrosive effects of the decree on an organic national culture. "Never," says Drumont, "has the Jew shown himself more odiously indifferent to everything which concerns *la Patrie*, more implacably preoccupied with himself and his race, than in the case of the decrees submitted by Crémieux for the emancipation of the Algerian Israelites."[21] Drumont, as Birnbaum has shown, used the Crémieux Decree as a spearhead for mobilizing the *political* anti-Semitism that would overlay traditional forms of French anti-Semitism and culminate in the Dreyfus Affair, where the threat posed by Jews was seen to extend to the very heart of the French state.[22] In Algeria this political anti-Semitism focused in particular on the electoral power of the Jewish vote and the claim that this tended to be exercised *en bloc* and on behalf of the moderate republican party, the

Opportunists. Not only did this arouse the predictable animosity of anti-republican parties, but, on the left of the political spectrum, Radicals reached for an anticapitalist rhetoric infused with anti-Semitic stereotypes to express their own rancour. As Charles-Robert Ageron, among others, has pointed out, well before the turn of the century "[a]nti-Jewishness had become the common denominator of the Algerian Left."[23] By the end of the century, and fueled by the Dreyfus Affair, a hostility that had manifested itself primarily in anti-Semitic publications and anti-Semitic leagues had taken to the streets: Algiers, Oran, and Constantine in particular, cities where the largest population of Jews lived, witnessed the sacking of Jewish shops, the pillaging of Jewish quarters, and physical attacks resulting in deaths and injuries. Drumont himself was given an ecstatic welcome on a visit to Algiers and in 1898 was elected a city deputy, while the well-known anti-Semite Max Régis was elected the city's mayor.

It is from this new historiography that an increasingly "thick description" of the specific character of turn-of-the-century Algerian anti-Semitism emerges. In his fascinating study of Bône during this period, David Prochaska explains the especially virulent anti-Semitism of the so-called *petits blancs*—the Algerian settlers of Spanish, Italian, and Maltese origin—as a "classic case of status anxiety," and scapegoating by these more economically disadvantaged colonizers. He also argues that the anti-semitic crisis of this period comprised more than a racial element, functioning also as a "lightning rod which collected and deflected, as much as it focused, a whole range of collective resentments"—especially settler antipathy toward a metropole that was proving itself incapable of satisfying the settler's simultaneous demands for greater autonomy and protection of privileges.[24] Wherever the historiographical attention focuses, it is clear that, far from merely mimicking a Metropolitan sensibility, Algeria's political anti-Semitism was a distinctive phenomenon—not something incidental to, but a constituent feature of, the colonial mentality, deeply embedded in the fear that granting citizenship rights to one group of *indigènes* had threatened the very foundations of the colonial status quo.[25]

Nowhere is this more evident than in recent historiographical interpretations of Muslim response to the Crémieux Decree. For some time, a historical orthodoxy has prevailed that asserts an angry Muslim response to the discriminatory implications of the Crémieux Decree, made manifest in the 1871 insurrection of Muslims in Kabylie, Aurès, and the Constantine region. Anti-Semites like Drumont appeared to take up the Muslim defense, citing the latter's combat in the Franco-Prussian War as an additional justification for their anger faced with the collective naturalization of Algeria's

Jews.[26] Not surprisingly, the anti-Semites expended their campaigning energies on efforts to repeal the Crémieux Decree, not on agitating for the extension of citizenship to the Muslim population.[27] However, in the light of
the still widely held contemporary belief that the Crémieux Decree drove a
wedge into the Jewish-Muslim coexistence, I would only signal the thesis espoused recently by several historians that historical evidence does not cor-
roborate this claim. Ageron, Richard Ayoun, and others have instead trawled
archival sources where testimonies from the period—including those by military personnel, dedicated anti-Semites, and Muslim activists—deny this
causal link between Jewish naturalization and the 1871 insurrection. In these
accounts, for example, Muslims either state their unwillingness to follow the
path of Jews and give up their personal status or see the decree as paving
the way for eventual Muslim enfranchisement. That this expectation would
be thwarted for another seventy-five years by *pied-noir* intransigence does
not diminish the significance of this "revisionist" thesis. What this thesis
maintains is that the myth of the insurrection's being provoked by the naturalization of the Jews was created *retrospectively,* and instrumentalized by
anti-Semites like Drumont in a deliberate attempt to arouse Muslim resentment toward the Jews in a classic divide-and-rule strategy.[28] Not only was
this attempt unsuccessful at the time, but it would also prove unsuccessful
when later wielded for the same purposes—notably during the Vichy period.


## VICHY'S ALGERIAN SYNDROME

On October 7, 1940, as part of the series of infamous measures known as
the *Statut des juifs,* the Crémieux Decree was abrogated. As Paxton and
Marrus note in their classic study, *Vichy France and the Jews,* one of the co-
signatories to this measure was Marcel Peyrouton, a former governor-
general of Algeria sympathetic to the European settlers, who became
Vichy's minister of the Interior in September 1940. In fact Paxton and Marrus contend that rather than Vichy's putting pressure on Algeria with respect to racial laws, the situation was the reverse. Not only did Algeria
apply with gusto the *Statut des juifs,* Algeria's Vichyists went beyond its pro-
visions in order to exclude Jewish primary and secondary pupils from attending schools.[29] In remembering this period, Derrida recalls first of all
the intense "Pétainization" of his school in 1940–1941, where though he
was top pupil, he was prevented from raising the morning flag because of
his Jewishness. By the first day of the school year in 1942, Derrida was ex-
pelled from school and sent home, joining 18,500 other children who fell

above the 14 percent quota of Jewish children allowed to attend school by Algeria's very own *numerus clausus*.[30]

While Derrida suggests that this memory of a "degradation" constitutes the traumatic kernel of the Algerian-Jewish experience, it seems to me that what is surely the greater wound in this collective memory—and for this reason the more repressed—is the "scandal" that this new historiography has increasingly emphasized: namely, the fact that it took eleven months for the Crémieux Decree to be reinstated *after* the Allied landing in North Africa in November 1942. Paxton and Marrus, André Kaspi, Michel Abitbol, and others reveal how Algeria's new rulers, under General Giraud's influence in particular, and now under the governor-generalship of Marcel Peyrouton (returned from duty as Vichy's former Interior minister!) dragged their feet on the question of abrogating the *Statut des juifs* and especially of reinstating the Crémieux Decree.[31] Once again, the defense summoned is that such an expeditious action would provoke Muslim anger at a time when their support and military participation was needed for the liberation campaign. Indeed, when in March 1943, faced with British and American pressure, Giraud begins the process of abolishing the racial laws, he abrogates the Crémieux Decree for a second time, citing a desire to eliminate all racial discrimination between Muslims and Jews.[32] Only following de Gaulle's arrival and ongoing international protest was the decree finally reinstated in October 1943.

Was there any basis this time to this putative Muslim animus? All signs in recent historiography point to the contrary. Paxton, Marrus, and Kaspi document how Muslims generally abstained from the anti-Jewish campaign led by Algeria's Vichyists, or, in the case of the reformist Muslim elite, even declared their solidarity with the Jews. A letter of November 1942, signed by a group of Muslim leaders, made the observation that

> [b]y putting down the Jew, one only brings him even closer together with the Moslem. It was thought that at the abrogation of the Crémieux decree, the Moslems would rejoice; but the latter can easily see the dubious worth of a citizenship that the granting authority can take away after seventy years enjoyment.[33]

Ferhat Abbas, Muslim reformist, and later head of the FLN's Provisional Government, announced to the Vichyists: "Your racism goes in every direction, today against the Jews, and always against the Arabs."[34] At the same time, some Muslim nationalists pressed Algeria's Jewish leadership to follow the logic of their persecuted situation by refusing any eventual reinstatement of their citizenship and instead joining the nationalist camp in a common struggle on behalf of an independent *Algerian* citizenship.[35] This overture was politely but firmly refused.

## FROM JEWS TO *PIEDS-NOIRS?*

As we know, the decision on the part of Algeria's Jews to face their future as French citizens did indeed have profound consequences. By the time the Algerian War of Independence breaks out, it is difficult to separate the reaction of Algeria's Jews from the rest of the *pied-noir* community. Writing in 1961, for example, in his lesser-known work *Les Français d'Algérie*, Pierre Nora observed:

> From the largest capitalist *colon* to the small Jewish tailor, from the descendants of old French families to Maltese workers, from the large merchant to the small *colon* of the interior, nationalist passion is at the same temperature. What unites psychologically all these categories is stronger than what separates them socially.[36]

This is echoed in a recent study of Algerian Jewry by Joëlle Allouche-Benayoun, who describes at length the social hierarchies to which this community was continually subject—even at the best of times. He then notes: "The crossing of the Mediterranean, *la nostalgie du pays perdu*, achieved in France what had never occurred in Algeria: the proximity of Algeria's Jews and the 'others,' all having become *les pieds noirs*, bonding together in the myth of a fraternal Algeria."[37]

This is where contemporary historiography concedes that much work remains to be done, though in the last few years, the specific nature of Algerian Jewish allegiance during the War of Independence has been further investigated.[38] In the main, recent historiography has shown that Jewish community organizations advocated and sustained a position of extreme moderation.[39] However, it has been argued that regionality and the degree of assimilation played a role in differentiating the Jewish response, with the Jews of Algiers adopting the more liberal posture, Constantine Jews tending toward an extremist stance, and Jews of the interior often siding with the FLN.[40] These claims need to be substantiated by concrete documentation and also mapped across the temporal dimension of the war that saw the more general *pieds-noirs* response evolve from confidence, to disquiet, to a feeling of being duped, and finally to despair.

The atypical Jewish response also merits attention. In a recent memoir, Daniel Timsit explains his pro-FLN sentiments as the logical outcome of his youthful involvement in the Algerian Communist Party commencing in 1944; he recalls joining the demonstration of Algerian nationalists on May 1, 1945, and caring for nationalist hunger strikers of the MTLD (precursor of the FLN) as a young hospital intern in 1950. Acknowledging that his radical itinerary was not representative of the larger Jewish community, he nonetheless maintains that those Algerian Jews who became sensitized to the nationalist cause through adherence to the Algerian Communist Party did so "en tant que Juifs algériens."[41] Timsit carried his convictions "jusqu'au bout," leaving the Communist Party when it condemned the 1954 uprising and joining the *maquis* in 1956 as a bomb-maker for the FLN network based in Algiers. This role induces much agonizing soul-searching in Timsit's memoir but doesn't fundamentally put into question his chosen political itinerary. Arrested and risking the death penalty, Timsit is convinced that he was saved from this fate by his family's influence and the discreet intervention of Jewish notables and he also attributes to his trial, and the emotions that it generated, a temporary rapprochment between the Jewish and Muslim community.

If Timsit's case is virtually unique, there is at the other end of the political spectrum the issue of a more numerous—even if still minor—participation of Jews in the OAS, a memory that is particularly taboo within a community that prefers to remember itself only as a victim of the dereliction that characterized France's colonization process.[42]

On a number of occasions throughout the war, the Jewish community was specifically addressed by the FLN and urged once again to link its future with the independence cause. The decision not to do so has been widely accepted as evidence that, whatever iniquities members of this community had endured in the course of their grueling apprenticeship as French citizens, this was nonetheless the fate they had chosen. Michel Abitbol asks whether this choice *could* have been otherwise, given a colonial situation that "had erected unbridgeable barriers between diverse religious ethnies that had each adopted different strategies *vis-à-vis* the colonial state, its 'codes' and policies."[43]

In a sense an answer to this question must also be sought in conjunction with the new historiography of Algerian nationalism. Here I can only mention in passing the work of Mohamed Harbi, André Nouschi, Benjamin Stora (himself an Algerian Jew), and others on the occlusion within Algerian memory of other strands of Algerian nationalism that played a crucial role in the formation of a national consciousness in the preindependence period.[44] What were the constituents of this consciousness apart from the desire for an independent nation-state? Charles-Robert Ageron has argued that, while religion was not ostensibly foregrounded by the FLN, a contradictory discourse on the role Islam would play in the new Algerian state was embedded in a number of FLN statements.[45] For many Algerian nationalists, Muslim identity was indeed one of the stakes of the independence struggle, and had been so in the longer history of Algerian nationalism—associated with Messali Hadj—to which the FLN was a mere newcomer. This was a sentiment that the radical, secular-oriented FLN leadership simply could not afford to ignore. Thus it was not at all clear either within the FLN—or, as Ageron suggests, to Algerian Jews as well—what place would be accorded religious minorities if this aspiration for a nation defined in terms of religion prevailed. After 1960, as the war intensified, the targeting by the FLN of synagogues, rabbis, community venues, and leading Jewish figures (like the philosopher Raymond Bénichou and the singer Raymond Leyris) clearly also sent messages to the Algerian Jewish community that appeals for their support of independence had now been superseded by more lethal means of persuasion. Algeria's Jews were among the first to leave the country, even before the mass exodus of summer 1962, and the question must be posed whether their precipitate departure was not in fact due to a collective premonition that their place in an independent Algeria was nowhere near as secure as the FLN statements had implied. This "trou de mémoire" is one that can only be excavated by the combined efforts of Jewish *and* Algerian historiography.[46]

I raised earlier the question of what might be the political stakes of any identity claims based on the rekindling of Jewish-Algerian memories and the new historiography that accompanies them. This is a question of considerable sensitivity in a situation where any reinterpretation of Algerian historiography has potentially far-reaching implications for an understanding of the sources of the country's present unspeakably violent conflict.[47]

A number of historians upon whom I've drawn deny that a nostalgia for roots lies behind the renewed affirmation of Judeo-Algerian specificity.[48] Yet this disclaimer sits uneasily alongside the observation that France is currently in the grip of a commemorative obsession "that has elevated patrimonial memory" to the status of a virtual obligation. Nora describes *la mémoire patrimoine* as memories rooted in specific loci of a particular region rather than in the narratives of the nation's past. This localized heritage, claimed as the cornerstone of one's singular identity, has allegedly reinforced the power of "sectoral identities" in the French body politic to the detriment of the republican aspiration to represent an inclusive collec-

tive identity.[49] Yet Nora's assumption that this memorial militancy "from below" also necessarily excludes those diasporic groups who cannot celebrate
the kind of palpable attachments—material or symbolic "sites"—valorized
by patrimonial memory, does not, as we've seen, apply to the expatriated
*pied-noir* community. On the contrary, precisely because Algeria is an absent site of patrimonial memory—a *non-lieu de mémoire*—remembrance is
all the more psychically charged, and runs the risk of succumbing to *nostalgérie,* to an enduring melancholia over the traumatic loss of an idealized
love object.[50] The tense and emotive circumstances of their departure may
consign the former Jews of Algeria to this modality of memory; however,
the specificity of their history and their location within the colonial context
also differentiates their *mémoire patrimoine* from that of their *pieds-noirs*
compatriots. I would suggest that the assertion of this distinction is one of
the stakes of current identity claims.

This interpretation is borne out in a striking manner by a unique ethnog-
raphy that anthropologist Joëlle Bahloul carried out in the 1980s among her
own Jewish-Algerian relatives, formerly residents of Sétif and since their
departure living in Marseilles and in the Paris metropolitan region.
Bahloul's interest lay primarily in showing, in Bachelardian fashion, how a
diasporic community is obliged to structure memory primarily in spatial
terms. The "uprooted memories" of a diasporic community, according to
Bahloul, must compensate for lack of access to their own *lieux de mémoire*
and the more "intangible relation to the past" that such physical distance
may impose, by summoning memories whose key locus is the very spatial
parameters from which the community is physically estranged. Surcharged
memories of places—especially domestic spaces—are, according to
Bahloul, "part of the syndrome of exile." They are an "embodiment of the
life cycle" and therefore an "embodiment of genealogy"—highly cathected
substitutes for the physical traces of lineage their bearers have been forced
to abandon. Their function is to "erase deracination by re-creating genealogical loci."[51] Bahloul's relatives, the Senoussi family, had preserved the
affective intensity of their symbolic connection to their Algerian homeland
by summoning a wealth of memories that crystallized around the Sétif residence occupied by this extended family and their Muslim neighbors. Individual and family narratives—the temporal dimension of memory—were
reconstructed around the experiences, rituals, and interactions that occurred within this domestic space and its immediate environs.

Within this "architecture of memory" (to use Bahloul's elegant term), a
subtle picture emerges of the character of Jewish-Muslim interaction over
a period of several decades that resonates in largely reinforcing ways with

the historiographical discourses I have earlier sketched. Most notably, rec-
ollections by both the Senoussi family and their Muslim neighbors invariably place emphasis on a legacy of co-residence "without animosity," and
any discord that is recalled is attributed to the provocations of French anti-
Semites rather than internally-induced racial tensions. As Bahloul notes:
"Jewish and Muslim voices concur on the theme that the Christians created
discord between the two dominated communities."[52] Even when Bahloul's
interlocutors recall conflicts between the two communities whose tensions
directly infiltrate the space of the Senoussi household—the Sétif pogrom of
1935, the latter stages of the War of Independence—the theme of "mutual
protection" prevails over any discussion of their discordant effects. At the
same time, Bahloul observes that if such memories paint a rather idyllic
portrait of harmonious coexistence on the part of two "outsider" communities, there is also an insistence on a "distinction without hostility" that
marked everyday rituals and interactions. And while many of these were
religiously determined and concerned boundaries marked by dietary, social,
and linguistic codes, Bahloul remarks on the eagerness displayed especially
in Jewish memories to emphasize such distinctions, "using a wealth of details" that reflects the narrators' drive to put behind them some of their indigenous Maghrebian traits and embrace Western modernity.[53] Perhaps in
this (very human) desire to have it both ways—the desire for "harmony
without anarchic mingling," in Bahloul's apt expression—such memories
serve to articulate both the historical reality of Jewish-Muslim existence *and*
promote the "genealogical fantasy" of which Derrida speaks.[54]

A question remains: why are claims of Jewish-Algerian specificity sur-
facing now—whether in historiography or popular memory—more than
three decades after an exodus to the metropole during which such distinctions were neither recognized nor sought? The fact that an assertion of
Judeo-Algerian identity is making its presence felt at this particular con-
juncture cannot be without significance. Undoubtedly, this relates to the
wider reconfiguration of French Judaism faced with the so-called crisis of
republican identity. But there are other contingencies to consider as well,
though these must be elucidated with some care. As Algeria's civil war—
described by one oppositionist as "une guerre *contre* les civils"[55] or war
*against* civilians—continues, former Algerian Jews have been prominent
amongst those expressing solidarity with Algeria's beleaguered democratic
forces (Derrida, Cixous, Jean Daniel to name but a few).[56] In 1999, Enrico
Macias joined forces with Algerian musicians and the popular singer Cheb
Mami and released a CD of malouf music entitled "Hommage to Cheikh
Raymond" (i.e., Leyris). For his part, Algeria's President Abdelaziz Boute-

flika recently paid tribute to the significant contribution the Jews of Constantine had made to the city's "common patrimony." In these gestures, however much they are geared to Algeria's contemporary crisis, there is in my view a surplus of signification that harks back to the long and complex vicissitudes of Jewish-Muslim coexistence in Algeria—some features of which I have tried schematically to outline.

Which is perhaps only to confirm the basic premise that historical memory is always in the service of present political needs; but one can only hope that its current deployment will help to advance the democratic outcome upon which Algeria's future so desperately depends.

## NOTES

This (modified) chapter is reprinted with permission from Nancy Wood, *Vectors of Memory: Legacies of Trauma in Postwar Europe* (Oxford: Berg, 1999). Unless otherwise stated, translations from the French are my own.

1. See José-Alain Fralon, "Enrico, paroles de paix," *Le Monde*, November 15, 1995. The verse form is not conducive to translation, but the gist is the following: "I left my country/I left my house/My life, my sad life/purposelessly drags on/I left my sun/I left my blue sea/Their memories are reawakened/long after my goodbye/Sun, sun of my lost country!/White villages that I loved/Girls that I once knew."

2. Fralon, "Enrico, paroles de paix."

3. Fralon, "Enrico, paroles de paix."

4. Jacques Derrida, *Monolingualism of the Other; or, The Prosthesis of Origin*, trans. Patrick Mensah (Stanford, Calif.: Stanford University Press, 1998), 15; originally published as *Le Monolinguism de l'autre* (Paris: Galilee, 1996).

5. Derrida, *Monolingualism of the Other*, 17.

6. Derrida, *Monolingualism of the Other*, 18.

7. See Geoff Bennington, "Curriculum Vitae," in *Jacques Derrida* (Chicago: University of Chicago Press, 1993), 326–27.

8. Derrida, *Monolingualism of the Other*, 28.

9. Derrida, *Monolingualism of the Other*, 52.

10. Derrida, *Monolingualism of the Other*, 53.

11. See, for example, Hélène Cixous's ruminations on her Jewish-Algerian past in "My Algeriance, in other words To Depart not to Arrive from Algeria," paper delivered at the conference "French and/in Algeria," Cornell University, October 1996, organized by Anne Berger. In this paper, Cixous argues that the war *was* "time's pivot," ordering all thought into the modes of before, during, and after. Cixous's father, a French army lieutenant on the Tunisian front in 1939, a doctor forbidden from practicing medicine by Vichy's racial laws, became a podiatrist to provide for his family. In Cixous's wry observation: "Vichy, which had forbidden him

the treatment of bodies, had nonetheless abandoned to him the corns of the feet"
(p. 12). Vichy, alleges Cixous, signified to the Jewish community of Algeria that it
had "sold its soul to France and for nothing . . ." (p. 6), the Crémieux Decree
proving to be, in Cixous's words, the "true *Gift*, an example of the gift-poison . . ."
(p. 9).

12. See my *Vectors of Memory: Legacies of Trauma in Postwar Europe* (Oxford:
Berg, 1999) for an analysis of Vichy historiography as a vector of memory.

13. For the English version of Birnbaum's original contribution to *Les Lieux de
mémoire*, see "Gregoire, Dreyfus, Drancy, and the Rue Copernic: Jews at the Heart
of French history," in Pierre Nora, ed., *Realms of Memory: The Construction of the
French Past, Vol. 1: Conflicts and Divisions*, trans. Arthur Goldhammer (New York:
Columbia University Press, 1996), 389.

14. "Quitter l'histoire de l'Algérie pour entrer dans celle de la France." Michel
Abitbol, "La citoyenneté imposée, du décret Crémieux à la guerre d'Algérie," in
Pierre Birnbaum, ed., *Histoire politique des Juifs de France entre universalisme et
particularisme* (Paris: Presses de la Fondation nationale des sciences politiques,
1990).

15. This figure is given by Richard Ayoun in "Le décret Crémieux et l'insurrection de 1871 en Algérie," *Revue d'histoire moderne et contemporaine*, vol. 35
(janvier–mars 1988): 61. In "My Algeriance," Cixous notes that her family was one
of the few to apply for citizenship under the *Senatus Consulte*.

16. Derrida, *The Monolingualism of the Other*, 53.

17. The term "decree of sinister memory" is drawn from an unattributed source
in the journal *L'Arche* and cited by Joëlle Allouche-Benayoun in "Une histoire d'intégration: Les Juifs d'Algérie et la France," *Les nouveaux cahiers*, no. 116 (printemps 1994): 32.

18. A number of historians emphasize that before French colonization, Jews had
the status of *dhimmi*—a status that applied to all non-Muslims under Muslim rule.
This implied both protection and subordination, religious freedom and forms of
cultural discrimination and humiliation. See Richard Ayoun's description of *dhimmi*
in "Une Présence Plurimillénaire," in *Les Juifs d'Algérie: Images et Textes* (Paris:
Editions du Scribe, 1987).

19. See Abitbol, "La Citoyenneté imposée"; Shmuel Trigano, "L'Avenir d'un
déracinement," in *Les Juifs d'Algérie: Images et Textes*.

20. Jacques Taïeb, "Tumulte autour d'un décret: Le décret Crémieux ou la première logique coloniale," *Les nouveaux cahiers*, no. 123 (winter 1995–1996). I borrow the term "dejudaization" from Taïeb, whose article also explicitly highlights the
negative interpretation of the effects of the decree as a "revisionist" turn within this
new historiography.

21. See Edouard Drumont, *La France Juive: Essai d'Histoire Contemporaine*,
tome 2, 20th ed. (Paris: C. Marpon and E. Flammerion, n.d.), 11. Drumont also expresses the hope that Algeria will be the launching pad for the anti-Semitic campaign of the metropole.

22. Pierre Birnbaum, "The Empire Abandoned: From the Crémieux Decree to the Blum-Violette Plan," *Anti-Semitism in France* (Oxford: Blackwell, 1992).

23. Charles-Robert Ageron, cited by David Prochaska, *Making Algeria French: Colonialism in Bône, 1870–1920* (Cambridge: Cambridge University Press, 1990).

24. See Prochaska, *Making Algeria French* and Pierre Hebey, *Alger 1898: La grande vague antijuive* (Paris: NiL editions, 1996).

25. Pierre Nora describes the Dreyfus Affair in France as only one aspect of a more general nationalist crisis, whereas in Algeria, ". . . anti-semitism typified the crisis, and represented a crucial—perhaps decisive—moment in the formation of the reprobate sensibility of French Algerians and in their contradictory self-perception." See Nora, *Les Français d'Algérie* (Paris: Julliard, 1961), 100–101.

26. Drumont, *La France Juive.* Drumont (p. 12) speaks of the Prussian admiration for the Arab contingent of France's forces, evoking the "fantasy-like effect" that "their savage cries, their joy at hearing gunpowder, and their manner of pouncing like tigers" had on the enemy.

27. Drumont does hint that the Government of National Defence might have rewarded these "heroic Arabs" with citizenship; but nowhere does this become a battlecry of his anti-Semitic platform.

28. This argument is elaborated in great detail by Richard Ayoun in "Le décret Crémieux." Ayoun's article includes documentation of official investigations into the insurrection by the Constantine and Algiers judicial authorities, as well as extended testimony about the uprising given in 1872 by a Muslim peasant. In light of the fact that this was the period of transfer of power over Algeria from the French military to a civilian government, Ayoun's conclusion is that the uprising was primarily caused by the anticipated loss of influence of the Muslim aristocracy once the *colons* gained political power. He argues that "before, during and after the 1871 insurrection, Muslim opinion concerning naturalization remained the same, regarding Jewish accession to full political rights with perfect indifference" (74).

29. See Michael Marrus and Robert O. Paxton, "A Special Case: Algeria," in *Vichy France and the Jews* (Stanford, Calif.: Stanford University Press, 1995), 191–97.

30. See Bennington, "Curriculum Vitae," and Derrida, *The Postcard: From Socrates to Freud and Beyond* (Chicago: Chicago University Press, 1987). In *The Postcard,* Derrida writes: "The only school official whose name I remember today: he has me come into his office: 'You are going to go home, my little friend, your parents will get a note.' At the moment I understood nothing, but since?" (86). Cixous, "My Algeriance," also recalls herself and her brother being sent home under the *numerus clausus.* Alternative schools were set up by many Jewish communities—Camus was recruited by his friend André Bénichou to teach excluded secondary pupils for a limited time.

31. See Marrus and Paxton, "A Special Case: Algeria"; Michel Ansky, *Les Juifs d'Algérie, du décret Crémieux à la Libération* (Paris: Editions du Centre, 1950); Michel Abitbol, *Les juifs d'Afrique du Nord sous Vichy* (Paris: Maisonneuve &

Larose, 1988); André Kaspi, *Les Juifs pendant l'Occupation* (Paris: Seuil, 1991); Joëlle Allouche-Benayoun and Doris Bensimon, *Les Juifs d'Algérie* (Paris: BHP, 1989). Concluding his detailed study of this period, Abitbol remarks: "In invading France and preparing the path for the installation of the Vichy regime, the Germans were at the origin of the application of the racial laws in the metropole and in North Africa. But three years later, it was Frenchmen—and Frenchmen free of any external constraint—who were singularly responsible for delaying the annulment of these laws" (174).

32. See Ansky, *Les Juifs d'Algérie,* who quotes from the *Oran Républicain* of March 15, 1943, Giraud's justification that "relations between Muslims and Israelites must be those of men required to complement each other economically, whether working in workshops or in the interior, without either having the edge on the other" (285).

33. Cited by Paxton and Marrus, "A Special Case: Algeria," 195.

34. Cited by Jean-Louis Planche, "Violence et Nationalismes en Algérie (1942–1945)," *Les Temps Modernes 5900* (octobre–novembre 1996): 125.

35. Planche, "Violence et Nationalismes en Algerie." Planche offers an important account of the radicalization of Algerian nationalist sentiment between 1942 and 1945. Planche shows that both the Vichyist government of Algeria and the authorities installed after the Allied landing were well aware of the intensification of nationalist activity during this period, highlighted in 1943 by the issuing of *the Manifeste du People algérienne,* which demanded an independent Algerian state. This desire not to fuel nationalist resentment was embraced by both camps as another reason for the delay in reinstating the Crémieux Decree.

36. Pierre Nora, *Les Français d'Algérie,* 47. Nora's observations on the relations between Jews and Muslims are sharp and critical of prejudices on both sides. He notes a Jewish attitude that invokes an endemic anti-Semitism among Algeria's Arab population, at the same time that it appeals to the long-standing capacity for peaceful coexistence between the two groups. This "apparent contradiction," maintains Nora, "defines perfectly the ambiguity of their situation" (137). He also offers a scathing description of Algeria as a country founded on "le colonialisme foncier et la présence militaire, d'opinion conservatrice, catholique, pétainiste, giraudiste, franquiste, mussolinienne et collaboratrice . . ." (140).

37. Joëlle Allouche-Benayoun, "Une histoire d'integration," 72.

38. See in particular, the journals *Les nouveaux cahiers* (especially no. 116) and *Archives Juives* (especially 29, no. 1, 1996), that also confirm the difficulty of researching this topic because of the military sensitivity of some archival material, and the reticence on the part of the community to speak about the war.

39. See in particular Jacques Lazarus, "Rapport sur la situation des Juifs en Algérie au début de de l'année 1958," *Archives Juives,* 29, no. 1 (1996). Lazarus was director of the *Comité juif algérien d'études sociales,* one of the main social organizations of Algeria's Jews. In this report, written during the War of Independence, Lazarus shows an acute awareness of Algeria's vulnerability to political anti-

Semitism. And while he emphasizes that "il n'y a de politique juive," at the same time he insists: "to be Jewish is also a political—and not only religious or social—phenomenon" (52). The report cites the warm relations of Jews and Arabs during the Vichy period, yet at the same time affirms the attachment of Algerian Jews to their French citizenship. Lazarus urges moderation and an attitude consistent with their identity as "Français, Juifs, républicains et libéraux."

40. See Daniel Timsit, *Algérie, récit anachronique I* (Paris: Editions Bouchene, 1999).

41. Timsit, *Algérie, récit anachronique I*, 21.

42. Doris Bensimon, "La Guerre et l'évolution de la communauté juive," in Jean-Pierre Roux, ed., *La guerre d'Algérie et les Français* (Paris: Fayard, 1990), and Richard Ayoun, "Les Juifs d'Algérie pendant la guerre d'indépendance (1954–1962)," *Archives Juives* 29, no. 1 (1996).

43. Abitbol, "La Citoyenneté imposée," 215.

44. There is an abundant literature on this topic, but see in particular Mohamed Harbi, *Le FLN: Mirage et réalité* (Paris: Jeune Afrique, 1980); André Nouschi, *L'Algérie amère* (Paris: Editions de la Maison des Sciences de l'Homme, 1996); Benjamin Stora, *La gangrène et l'oubli* (Paris: La Découverte, 1991); *Histoire de L'Algérie coloniale, 1830–1954* (Paris: La Découverte, 1994).

45. Charles-Robert Ageron, "Une guerre religieuse?," *Archives Juives* 29, no.1 (1996). See also Richard Ayoun, "Le décret Crémieux."

46. For example, the attitude of Ferhat Abbas was highly ambivalent on this question. Richard Ayoun in "Le décret Crémieux" quotes several statements where Abbas explicitly links the fate of Algerian Jews with the French, and refutes their future right of emigration in an independent Algerian state.

47. See, for example, Benjamin Stora, *L'Algérie en 1995: La guerre, l'histoire, la politique* (Paris: Editions Michalon, 1995), a book of essays that attempts to demonstrate the link between nationalist violence during the War of Independence and the violence of the contemporary conflict.

48. See, for example, Joëlle Allouche-Benayoun, "Une histoire d'intégration," who suggests that the main pole of this identity is a liberal and antiracist attitude, not a *pied-noir* nostalgia.

49. This diagnosis of France's politics of memory is elaborated in Pierre Nora, "L'ére de la commémoration," in *Les Lieux de mémoire, Vol. 3, Les France* (Paris: Gallimard, 1992), 977–1012.

50. For a careful consideration of these issues, see Joëlle Hureau, "La mémoire repatriée," in *La France en Guerre d'Algérie* (Paris: BDIC, 1992), and *La mémoire des Pieds-Noirs* (Paris: Olivier Orban, 1987).

51. See Joëlle Bahloul, *The Architecture of Memory: A Jewish-Muslim Household in Colonial Algeria 1937–1962* (Cambridge: Cambridge University Press, 1996), 115.

52. Bahloul, *The Architecture of Memory*, 119.

53. Bahloul, *The Architecture of Memory*, 83.

54. The theme of Jewish-Muslim coexistence is reiterated in the fascinating film *Le Grand Pardon* (Alexandre Arcady, France, 1981). A police thriller, the film traces the fortunes and misfortunes of the wealthy (and shady) Bettoun clan, Jewish-Algerians who were part of the 1962 exodus and now run a gambling empire in France. The clan's chief rival is a *pied-noir* of Spanish origin, though for some time the clan believe they are being undermined by an Algerian boss (linked to the FLN) who is out to settle old scores. The resolution of the plot turns on recognizing the ultimately trustworthy relations between Jews and Muslims and the duplicity of *pieds-noirs*. Thanks are due to Ginette Vincendeau for alerting me to this film.

55. The term was used by Saïd Sadi, leader of the Rassemblement culturel et démocratique (RCD), at a meeting at the Mutualité, Paris, February 1997.

56. See Derrida's address to a 1994 meeting organized by CISIA (Comité International de Soutien aux Intellectuels Algériens) entitled "Parti Pris Pour l'Algérie," published in *Les Temps Modernes,* January 1995, and translated into English by Boris Belay in "'Translating' Algeria," *parallax* 7, 1998. Derrida speaks of "an Algeria to which I have often come back and which in the end I know to have never really ceased inhabiting or bearing in my innermost, a love for Algeria to which, if not the love of a citizen, and thus the patriotic tie to a Nation-state, is none the less what makes it impossible to dissociate here the heart, the thinking, and the political position-taking . . ." (19). I don't mean to imply that the political allegiances of former Jewish Algerians are self-evident, nor that the evolving political situation in Algeria and fractious divisions within the Algerian opposition and among French intellectuals have not complicated solidarity to a point where it is difficult to make any confident generalizations. However, I do want to maintain that a certain "will to solidarity" among former Jews of Algeria has been a modest but visible dimension of support activity.

# PART IV

# MISCEGENATION, DEGENERATION, AND OTHER METROPOLITAN ANXIETIES

The three chapters in this final section approach the question of postcolonial hybridity. In different ways, each explores how questions of postcoloniality and race undermine normative expectations of not only racial purity but also traditional adult behavior in French civilization. In addition, each chapter shows how such norms are based in part upon the failure to acknowledge hybridity. Together, these chapters demonstrate to what extent France and *Francophonie* cannot be separated from each other.

In chapter 14, Lyn Thompson analyzes Rachilde's 1900 novel *La Jongleuse* from the standpoint of race and creolity. In doing so, it not only fundamentally transforms our view of this particular text, but also casts new light on notions of fin de siècle decadence. Thompson notes that most discussions of this novel have completely ignored the heroine's ambiguous racial identity, preferring instead to see it as a straightforward statement of decadence and liberated female sexual agency. In contrast, she argues that Eliante's behavior must be considered in the context of traditional images of nonwhite women as oversexed and immoral, and is thus much more stereotypical than empowering. The very notion of the creole as indolent and decadent thus forms a key aspect of French ideas of decadence in the late nineteenth century. At a time when ideas of racial purity were looming large for many French, the mysterious postcolonial hybridity represented by *La Jongleuse* called into question traditional views of both sexuality and *national* identity.

A very different kind of postcolonial hybridity is the subject of chapter 15 by Tyler Stovall. His study of relations between colonial men and French women during the Great War reveals a little-known aspect of both France's wartime and colonial histories. In studying the wide variety of these relationships Stovall emphasizes their unusual context: the first major presence of nonwhite men on French soil, as well as the significant absence of French men due to military mobilization. This transfer of a large colonized population to the metropole blurred the distinction between France and its empire, as efforts to keep colonial men separate gradually fell apart. At the same time, the effort to maintain a separate colonial sphere in the metropole created new norms of racial segregation. Stovall shows how the concern of French authorities to limit interracial relationships involved both fears of miscegenation at home and of weakening the prestige of white French women in the colonies, women who represented a kind of antithesis to the New Woman at home. The chapter considers interactions of race, gender, and class to paint a portrait of a nation forced to confront a radically new relationship with its colonial subjects.

Chapter 16 by Georges Van Den Abbeele, titled "The Children of Belgium," discusses questions of postcolonialism and *Francophonie* from a strikingly novel perspective, that of childhood in Belgium. The author asks why it is that Belgium's national identity has so often been symbolized by child symbols, from the *Manneken-Pis* to Tintin. Van Den Abbeele shows how this is closely related to Belgium's underdeveloped sense of national identity in general, a nation that is not only divided internally but has throughout its history been infantilized by its powerful neighbor, France. Belgium thus represents a postcolonial nation within Europe itself: everything from its sharp ethnolinguistic tensions to its conflicted attitudes toward the French, recall the relations between France and its former colonies. Even Belgium's own colonial history in the Congo seemed to be that of one child trying to rule another, as the tremendous popularity of the comic book *Tintin au Congo* makes clear. Van Den Abbeele ends his chapter with a discussion of the massive pedophile scandal that erupted in Belgium in 1996. Belgians of all persuasions reacted with horror, demonstrating that once again the figure of the child was a potent symbol of national identity.

The chapters in this last section deal with three different aspects of postcolonial hybridity and challenges to traditional morality: decadence, miscegenation, and infantilization. They show how canonical images of French civilization are based upon the suppression of its hybrid, racially impure aspects.

**(14)**

# DECADENCE/DEGENERATION/ CRÉOLITÉ: RACHILDE'S LA JONGLEUSE

## Lyn Thompson

In his 1892 diagnosis of modern European society, Max Nordau bleakly defines the fin de siècle as an era dominated by "a common . . . contempt for
traditional views of custom and morality . . . to all, it means the end of an
established order, which for thousands of years has satisfied logic, fettered
depravity, and in every art matured something of beauty."[1] Nordau's oft-
cited analysis of Degeneration was largely a critique of the fin de siècle
artistic and literary movements that seemed to take pride in this cultural decay, to encourage and applaud the perversion of traditional bourgeois
morality and conventions—in short, to celebrate the "Decadence" of European civilization. Published in 1900, Rachilde's La Jongleuse (The Juggler)
was but one in a long series of provocative novels by an author who had acquired quite a reputation for herself as a "pornographer," the "Queen of the
Decadents."[2] Indeed, this "quintessential writer of the Decadence"[3] provides clear evidence of what Nordau would call "contempt for traditional
views of custom and morality": the basic structure of gender role inversion
combined with "monstrous" sexual proclivities, established in her best-
known novel, Monsieur Vénus (1884), replicates itself through much of
Rachilde's work as a persistent affront to bourgeois sensibilities. In La Jongleuse, in which Melanie Hawthorne finds "the most complete expression"[4]
of these themes, Eliante Donalger is the aggressive woman who "picks up"
young medical student, Léon Reille, juggles ruthlessly with his affections,
and uses him solely in the service of her own narcissistic desires.

In recent years, the decadent transgressions imputed to Rachilde's novels—historically cited in order to be condemned as part of the "degeneration" of artistic and intellectual life at the fin de siècle—have been recuperated by contemporary theorists who have resurrected the work of this relatively marginal author as a locus of subversive potential. Melanie Hawthorne, for example, sees Rachilde as something of a visionary who promoted theories of social constructionism *avant la lettre*, and most of the critical commentary on Rachilde focuses precisely on her treatment of sexuality and gender, her portrayal of the stereotypical "femme fatale" as the subject rather than the object of desire. But this kind of one-track reading becomes quite problematic when one approaches *La Jongleuse*; issues of racial difference, exoticism, and Orientalism circulate throughout the text, yet remain conspicuously absent from the surrounding critical discourse. When Eliante's Orientalist affections have been mentioned, they are noted almost ornamentally, as nothing more than standard elements of Decadent decor.[5] The issue of Eliante's *créolité* is rarely approached, except parenthetically by Hawthorne as a "marked difference [that] sets her apart from the rest of society, and enables her to comment with detachment on Parisian high society."[6] Never addressed is the way in which Eliante herself exoticizes the islands of her heritage.

I would like to confront the critical silences surrounding *La Jongleuse* by exploring the complex infrastructure of racial anxiety, ambiguity, and attraction that underwrites the politics of sexuality at the narrative's surface. Just as the sexual and sensual excesses of Decadent literature are rooted in a sense of national lassitude and racial degeneration, the sexual deviance of Rachilde's heroine is a similarly motivated construct. Eliante, the quintessentially Decadent woman, is also the quintessential *créole*—the curious product of colonial mixture and racial contamination.

Eliante's perversity—her aggressive and autonomous desire—is revealed to be less an expression of triumphant subjectivity than a textbook characteristic of the stereotypical creole woman. The insecurity of national and cultural identities, exacerbated by the French defeat in the war of 1870, the crisis of the Commune, the dividing effects of the Dreyfus Affair, and continuing colonial conflict with Britain, mandated efforts to preserve the French nation, the white race, and the ideals of bourgeois life through the surveillance and control of various sites of perceived vulnerability, not the least of which was the woman's body. Since life in the colonies and contact with the racial Other was seen as a source of contagion, contaminating the white woman, and thus reproduction itself, female sexual deviance translated easily into potential racial deviance, by either actual mixture or mere proximity. The creole born to the primitive cultures of island colonies was seen as inherently degenerate, one racial step backwards between the white man and the black. Whereas a play of exoticism and racism, attraction and repulsion, characterized the representation of the French creole throughout the nineteenth century, with the physical and moral differences of the distant Other sometimes presenting an appealing alternative to the constraints of European modernity, the survival of the nation in the wake of fin de siècle turmoil depended upon the purity of the race and the vigilant maintenance of this exotic distance. The fascination with the Other from faraway lands, the horror of the Other that has come too close, and the anxiety that emerges when that distinction is blurred were integral to both the criminalization and the policing of deviant sexuality, in the context of turn-of-the-century colonial France, and in the text of *La Jongleuse* itself. In this context, Eliante's excesses, her weaknesses, and her rejection of society's rules and restrictions pose an immediate threat, not only to codes of gender, but to codes of national and racial difference, and simultaneously reveal, like symptoms of a disease, the contamination already inherent in her identity.

## THE WOMAN

At first read, the most striking events of the novel involve Eliante's ostensibly perverse behavior. From the more explicitly theatrical moments such as
the orgasm she experiences when she embraces her beloved Tunisian vase
and her juggling of knives, to the more intimate exchanges with Léon, it becomes clear that what we see of Eliante is precisely a performance. Eliante,
"comédienne," artfully plays the leading roles of seductive and mysterious
femme fatale, abused yet grieving widow, concerned and motherly aunt in
a series of staged encounters whose performative value is enhanced by their
juxtaposition with the more private dialogue that occurs through an
exchange of letters. "I am only a woman," she says, "nothing more and nothing less" (13).[7] Thus she affirms her assumption of various roles as only different aspects of the role of Woman—which here consists ultimately of
masquerade. This performance, at least, is freely chosen, and skillfully executed. "I am free to choose my hour and even to not want to at all" (17), she
declares, in response to Léon's demands. Eliante's claim to desire or to not
desire, her claim to subjectivity, coupled with an extraordinary display of
autonomous and self-sufficient sexuality, is the perversion so often attributed to Eliante—the offense that infuriates Léon, while simultaneously
arousing in him the almost irrepressible desire to violate her. This trans-
gressive female subjectivity is also the perversion of *La Jongleuse*, the site
of scandal for the Rachilde of 1900, and the site of praise for the Rachilde
re-read a century later.

Looking more carefully at the scenes themselves, at Léon's simultaneously "dazzled, delighted, indignant" (23) reactions to Eliante's self-
performance, we can discern another desire. Counteracting the seductive
effects of the woman's demonstrations is a medical discourse that attempts
to translate her bizarre behavior into a clinically classified illness. To Léon,
this woman is a mystery, an utterly ambiguous figure whose identity is always in question. He has trouble reading her when her complexion is that
of "a woman who is suffering . . . or who has had too much fun" (35) and
when she moves "like a schoolgirl who was frightened . . . or very much
amused" (41). In the face of such indeterminacy, Léon struggles between
feelings of attraction and repulsion, between the seduction of the Other and
the horror of its existence. His only recourse is to the safety of scientific observation. As a medical student, not yet an accomplished doctor fully educated into objectively professional detachment, Léon can be tempted,
thrilled, seduced, yet still occupy the symbolic position of the medical establishment, the *scientia sexualis* of Foucault's *History of Sexuality*. Léon's

role, as medical observer, is to examine, dissect, diagnose, and police
Eliante's unstable body; his desire, as a man, is to violate it. His gaze breaks
her down into more manageable fragments, fetishizing various body parts,
miniaturizing her into a "painted doll," "a toy," "a curious object," as he examines the "blue veins along [her] wrist," "with the eyes of an expert in the
art of discovering physical flaws" (10). In reaction to Eliante's declarations
of freedom, Léon "sneers":

> "I'm drawn to you by a different curiosity from the one that draws little
> snobs. I'm not amused by the manners of high society where one is bored.
> Here, Eliante, I'm going to confess to you my real curiosity, the idea of a fu-
> ture doctor of medicine. I think you have leprosy, I'm taking exact note of
> your malady, heart or head, and now I'll retire very properly."
> He was trying to joke, but he was beginning to want to bite her.
> Her resistance was too absurd. What did she want from him?(17)

Free indirect discourse aligns Léon's gaze with the objective viewpoint of
the omniscient narrator, and encourages the reader to assume a similar position of simultaneous observation, frustration, and desire. However trans-
gressive or progressive Eliante's behavior, it is consistently coded by the text
as pathological, abnormal, an illness to be diagnosed, a mystery that must
be solved.

## THE CREOLE

But the mystery of Eliante's sexuality is also a mystery of identity: Léon
asks the question himself, "Who can she be, that woman?" (6). The first
descriptions of Eliante counterpose the darkness of her attire with the
artificial whiteness of her face, "she was whiter with her makeup than any
other made-up woman" (3). The distinction between her body and her
clothing collapses, while the only exposed part of her skin assumes a false
appearance. Provoked by the "naked and black feet" and "black hands"
of this "black woman," Léon demands: "Prove to me that you are not a
negress!" As Eliante complies almost too quickly by removing her glove
(10), the enigma of sexuality driving the narrative quest becomes simultaneously an enigma of race. The "immense oriental stole" that covers
her, and the "Chinese system" by which she eats, further reinforce
Eliante's difference and allure by shrouding her in and identifying her
with the exotic. In his commentary on the events of their first meeting,
Léon confesses that she has left him with a "very pronounced taste for

*exoticism*" (30)—whether he is referring to Eliante as an object of his nascent exoticism or to Eliante's own exoticist leanings, is ambiguous, perhaps because, as we shall see, the creole woman, in this case, is *both* exotici*zed* and exotici*zing*.

Léon's double reactions and his constant bewilderment *make sense* because the category of *créolité* is itself unstable; the creole is fundamentally indeterminate and multiple. To begin on the level of terminology, in Judith Raiskin's words, "'Creole' generally refers to those of (some) European descent born in European colonies or in independent territories that once were colonies. However, depending on the time and the place of its use, the term can signify full European ancestry (implying a claim of 'unsullied' whiteness), mixed 'racial' ancestry resulting from colonialism (usually implying some European ancestry mixed with African, Amerindian, or other so-called racial groups, depending on the location), or syncretic cultural and linguistic practices (such as 'creole' music, food, or language)."[8] In its most abstract, the term can denote any number of racial, cultural, or linguistic mixtures with varying degrees of relative whiteness or blackness, but the fundamental difference remains: the creole is racially ambiguous, whether biologically, behaviorally, or both. Indeed, the one often implies the other, so that an identity based entirely on mere location of birth, once appropriated by various ideological conceptions of race and environment, acquires connotations of not only cultural, but physiological difference. It suddenly becomes possible for Eliante, the child of parents who were "so French they had perished in the 1870 war: the father of a saber cut, the mother of sorrow" (45), to be described as "hardly French," "a capricious creole who is always cold, a bird of paradise with feathers painted for other skies" (46). Whatever the implications of creole self-identification, from the perspective of the metropole, the creole was essentially a racial inferior, though subject to both positive and negative forms of racial differentiation. To the medical and scientific community, the white creole was degenerate, inevitably weakened by the "environmental contamination" of life in the colonies.[9] For the literary exoticist, on the other hand, the creole might present more of an alternative model, a symbol of potential escape to a primitive paradise free from the trappings of European modernity.

Rachilde's portrayal of degenerate *créolité* appears to be contrived entirely on the basis of such stereotypical dogma regarding the behavioral and physiological effects of colonial birth. Poised at the end of the nineteenth century, *La Jongleuse* belongs not only in the context of a general cultural discourse of race, but in a long history of exoticist representations of the creole in French literature. Passing through Bernardin de Saint-Pierre's idyllic pastoral depiction of Paul and Virginie's life on Île-de-France, and the mystery and duplicitousness of Balzac's "Fille aux yeux d'or," among others, we find the most thoroughly detailed yet symptomatically ambivalent treatment of *créolité* in the work of Charles Baudelaire. Through both his own poetry and his critique of Leconte de Lisle, a creole from Réunion, he creates an image of the lazy, listless, yet alluring creole, a being physically and intellectually languid yet, as such, the object of poetic desire and identification. In *Blank Darkness: Africanist Discourse in French*, Christopher Miller describes in detail the ambivalence at work in Baudelaire's depictions of blackness and *créolité* with explications of "A une dame créole," "Le cygne," and "La belle Dorothée." He emphasizes the poet's double experience of attraction and repulsion toward the creole lady, and the way in which even as Baudelaire seems to ennoble *la dame créole*, the very act of ennoblement or enfranchisement is itself a matter of condescension and degradation. Ultimately, "the substance of her nobility and freedom is dubious."[10] As we shall see, the extent to which Rachilde's creole falls into precisely the same position of dubious and ironic ennoblement is remarkable and only reinforces Maurice Barrès's earlier reference to the young author (in his preface to *Monsieur Vénus*) as "Mademoiselle Baudelaire."

The simultaneously elevated and degraded state of the creole as manipulated by Baudelaire in turn reflects a general perception of the effects of environment on racial purity in nineteenth-century France. According to the *Grand Larousse du XIXe siècle*, "one generally gives the name of *créole*, to an individual of white race who is born on the American continent or in the Antilles; but this word also designates more specifically those persons who are descendent from a white race, but born in the tropics, in Louisiana, Guyana, the Antilles, Brazil, and also Mauritius and Réunion."[11] Beyond this general definition, the nineteenth-century dictionary enters into great detail as to their physical and psychological characteristics, displacing much onto the Spanish, but retaining the notion of descendence from a broader white race:

> Creoles, in the old American colonies of Spain, formed the second class of citizens. Some were descendants of conquerors of the New World; others of the noble families of Spain; many possessed great riches, but nevertheless, the hot climate, a skittish jealousy of the metropolitan government that excluded them from public offices, *so weakened in them all vigor and all activity*, that almost all wasted their life in *voluptuous languor*, and abandoned themselves to degrading superstition. The interior traffic of each colony, as well as the commerce with other colonies and with Spain, was in the hands of the Chapetons; the creoles, plunged into *an incurable laziness*, contented themselves with the revenue from their parents' properties. . . .
>
> In the French and English Antilles, the creoles of white race have always enjoyed the same rights as metropolitans. Under a new sun and a new sky, the morals of old Europe, mixing with indigenous customs, transform and become corrupt, and thus is born this ensemble of faults and qualities that constitutes the character of creoles. (My italics)[12]

The *Larousse* continues in a *blason* of the creole body to describe their strong build, their dull skin, their expressive and proud gaze, their supple members, their rapid physical development, and their lively if simple imagination. Unfortunately, two principal factors join to counteract the advantage that creoles would otherwise have over children born in other climates: they are spoiled by the excessive tenderness and indulgence of their parents and are continually surrounded by slaves. Hence the stereotypical laziness of Baudelaire's creoles, a luxury shared by Rachilde's Eliante. Already the creole's languor and laziness resemble that of the metropolitan decadent—a racial degeneracy echoed symptomatically in physiological degradation.

From Léon's first glimpse of "the woman in black" she begins to sound painfully familiar. "She was so supple, she bent over so quickly that, suddenly, one guessed that she was younger, more animal. . . . Her frail black hands quickly got the better of the immense oriental stole; she draped herself with the few movements of a cat getting under the bedcovers, and very carefully veiled her lips, probably afraid of coughing" (5). She's quick, supple, animal-like, yet also frail, weak, prone to illness in the cold of Paris in the fall. "I'm suffering," she says, ". . . from spleen, because of the rain, because of the autumn" (9). She's bored, filled with Baudelairean *ennui*. Léon enters her round dining room to find a sensuously tropical atmosphere. "It was warm; green silk hangings trickled in wavy folds from the ceiling like weeping willow branches, shelves held crystalware in varied, and fluid shades, neither door, nor window was visible, and a thick carpet, as soft as grass, imprisoned the ankle" (11). While the greenery seems to suffocate and entrap Léon, Eliante feels more comfortable in her unnaturally warm surroundings, and offers to set his place for dinner.

> Not anticipating that I would have the pleasure of inviting you back, dear sir, only one place has been set. Allow me to double it. I don't like servants while I'm eating. How about you?
> This was said with somewhat heavy irony. He let her organize a second place setting without answering. (11)

The irony, of course, unknown to Léon at this point in the narrative, is that she is a creole, and creoles, by *nature*, must always have servants and slaves—according to the *Larousse*, it is because they have always been cared for and waited upon that they came to develop their fatal flaw, their ubiquitous *paresse*.

Eliante's stereotypical character is further reinforced by the *Grand Larousse*'s definition in a long paragraph devoted specifically to an almost anthropological description of the *femme créole*.

Rarely endowed with the severe harmony that constitutes beauty, their figure almost always offers a combination more seductive and more difficult to describe that one calls physiognomy. It is in the large spiritual eyes of creole women that one finds the rare contrast of sweet languor and piquant vivacity. They are mostly remarkable for their beauty and their hair, which is of an incomparable black, and for the smallness of their arched feet. . . .

Jealous as tigresses, they have an often excessive tenderness for their children. Dancing has such an attraction for these daughters of the sun that they give themselves up to it with fury, regardless of the heat of the climate and the weakness of their constitution. They are very sober; chocolate and sweets, café au lait above all, compose almost all of their nourishment.

The dictionary's generalities provide a fairly accurate portrait of the ostensibly unique and extraordinary Eliante Donalger. She serves bananas, truffles, and creams of various colors, and drinks only pure water from an unusually delicate glass. She treats Léon as her child, with "excessive tenderness." And in the final scene of the novel, she surrenders herself to a stormy flamenco, a dance of excess and liberation, taught to her by "Ninaude, the poor negress that was so dirty" (199) that brings her to the point

of physical exhaustion and a symbolic suicide that foreshadows her actual
end. "Eliante was smiling, no longer concerned with the earth. She was
dancing for herself, in a hell she knew well, and did not fear the obstacles"
(197).

The *Larousse* is very specific about the creole woman's experience of obstacles:

> The state of idleness in which they are raised, the almost continual difficulties
> of the climate in which they live, the blind complacencies of which they are
> perpetually the object, the effects of a vivid imagination, all of these develop
> in them an extremely nervous sensibility. In a fundamentally melancholic tem-
> perament, this sensibility increases their indolence even more, which is often
> joined by a great vivacity. It only takes one desire to return all the energy to
> their soul. Accustomed to desiring imperiously, they become irritated against
> obstacles, and once the obstacle is surmounted, their carefree attitude re-
> turns.

Idle, yet vivacious, nervous, yet filled with desire, domineering,
imperious—all of these qualities might be attributed to Eliante, yet are
most often cited as aspects of her personality that contribute to her unusual strength of subjectivity, her claim to power as a woman reversing
the traditional paradigm of male dominance. In this case, it becomes
clear that her double nature and her claim to desire signify beyond the
realm of sexuality and gender. "I am only a woman, nothing more . . .
nothing less," she claims, yet Léon knows better: "it's terrible, your Chinese system. Vanilla, ginger, Indian pepper! That's enough to set a harem
ablaze . . . including the eunuchs! And you claim that you're only a
woman? Indeed!" (13–14). Indeed, Eliante is more than just a woman.
She is very specifically a *creole* woman. The powerful perversity of
Rachilde's heroine emerges not from a fountain of white bourgeois feminist determination, but from a particular racial deviance. The text's normative medical discourse works with Eliante's explicitly stereotypical
profile to align sexual independence with sexual deviance, and to link this
sexual deviance with a specific racial origin. Eliante has a different *nature*, which in turn explains her *behavior*, "a bird of paradise with feathers painted for other skies she wasn't born to look after children or care
for old men, that was obvious" (45). Later in the text, a conversation between Léon and Missie, her much-derided suffragette niece,[13] explicitly
links Eliante's mysterious racial identity with her mysterious behavior.
Missie, also trained in medicine, moves directly from a comment about

her aunt's "funny habits" to a statement about "these creoles," then declares that "Neither my uncle, nor I, nor anyone, we'll never know what she really is . . . Eliante is a pathological case, she's a nervous woman, superstitious, a little mad, but she isn't ill in the true sense of the word" (115–17). In one all-encompassing statement, Missie pinpoints the stereotypical nature of her aunt's abnormality. Eliante fits the profiles of a fin de siècle hysteric and tropical witch but is *pathological* only insofar as would be congruent with her *créolité*. She isn't ill in the true sense of the word, only in the sense of a *constructed* equivalence between illness and racial difference.

## A PASSING FETISH

The stereotype of the creole as embodied by Eliante encompasses more than just her physical and behavioral difference. The laziness, animality, aggressivity, and nervousness attributed to her nature are compounded by a desire to overcome this condition, a desire to be pure, to be uncontaminated. From within the context of fin de siècle Paris, Eliante recognizes her cultural mixture as degeneracy, and wants nothing more than to be a properly clean, pale, white French lady. This projected desire, a standard European presumption about creoles, manifests itself throughout the narrative in three principal forms: an abjection of blackness, a fetishization of whiteness, and an exoticization of the islands. As a creole, Eliante is neither perfectly Other, nor perfectly same, neither black, nor completely white. The juggling of the novel's title thus references more than the sexually dominant juggling of men (115), which is only a symptom of her racialized "nature" as a creole; first and foremost, Eliante juggles the multiple sides of her own identity. A mystery to the very French Léon, she is also a mystery to herself.

Because her parents were "so French they had perished in the 1870 war" (45), Eliante was sent to boarding school and then to a convent before being "rescued" by the marine officer who became her husband. All the while, she was cared for by Ninaude, an "old negress" from Martinique, who was eventually banished from their Paris home by Eliante's niece for being "dirty and superstitious" (154). While the fact that Eliante kept a black servant reinforces her stereotypical *créolité*, her relationship with this mother figure exposes her own ambivalence with regard to this mixed identity. In a letter to Léon, she speaks of Ninaude, her "last family," with a slight twinge of nostalgia, and remembers her "negress" as the one who taught her both

the art of the love letter and the intricacies of Spanish dance—thus identifying Ninaude, and by extension the islands, as the source of her performative abilities. However, she also emphasizes that this black mother-figure
was "a bit dirty and always had splashes of sugar on her," had "flies running
all over her," and, as Eliante mentions several times, was also covered with
fleas. Ninaude sang songs that were also dirty, filled with words that even
Eliante would not repeat in her letter, and told dirty stories, "as filthy as her
madras."

Most significantly, she "smelled of *fetishism* (unusual odor; a mixture of musk, sweat, coconut oil and rum!)" (133–38). The curious use of the term "fetishism" here most likely refers to the "primitive religions" ascribed to colonized peoples by European anthropologists and philosophers, with the fetishist identified at the turn of the century, in Anne McClintock's words, as an "atavistic subrace within the human race," "visible, living evidence of evolutionary degeneration."[14] Furthermore, odors have long been associated with racial difference, and consequently, with sexuality. As Sander Gilman explains in *Difference and Pathology*, the smell of a body may signify sexual availability, pollution, or disease; the corrupting female, the black woman, can be identified by smell even before she is seen.[15] Ninaude's "unusual odor," thus recalls the "parfum exotique," the smells of savory fruit, tropical plants, and human skin that pervade the exoticized islands of Baudelaire's poetry, operating as a sign of both racial *and* sexual otherness.[16] The dirt, the insects, and the odors together constitute the abject pollution of the black mother that Eliante must disavow in order to establish her clean and proper subjective position. To be white is to be clean—French bourgeois ladies do not smell of coconut oil.

Significantly, the odor of her black servant, a signifier of racial inferiority, has contaminated Eliante herself, lingering as an immutable trace of her degenerate origin. First released when she removes her glove to prove her identity, the odor of her body counteracts the shocking whiteness of her skin with a "penetrating perfume, a peppery odor, acidic, of which one didn't have the name immediately on the tongue, if one savored it, a smell of island fruit" (10). The odor emanates from everything around her, permeating her boudoir, her salon, even her birth certificate, removed from a yellowed envelope to further prove that she is who she says she is (her full name: *Blanche* Eliante). It ultimately achieves a rancid intensity, the "inexplicable smell of negro oil . . . a wild animal smell," the "perfume of negro races, of cannibals!" (183, 187). Existing outside of and prior to the restricted domain of visual recognition, penetrating the senses and lingering beyond the moment of initial apprehension, the ephemeral odor exuded by Eliante's skin creates an air of ambiguity that haunts its bearer: something between an alluring perfume, applied to the body as an artificial covering, part of her costume, and a smell emitted from the body itself, acidic and raw—the residue of a disavowed identity, blood that she cannot wash away. Even when her visual appearance *might* succeed in *passing*, the tropical aroma of her body promptly reveals her deception, as she herself acknowledges: "the intoxicating scent of the perfumes should have let you know who I was before showing you the whiteness of my arms" (168).

Ironically, this air that Eliante has "inherited" reveals another inheritance, another type of fetishism at work: Eliante's fetishization of whiteness itself, of the genetic purity that has been all but effaced by her foreign birth. Eliante's costume, her too white makeup, and the excessive covering of her body, might thus be read as part of her performance of whiteness—the performance of gender allied with a performance of race. By shrouding herself in black, she foregrounds the whiteness of the skin that is revealed; when she drapes herself in white, she wears less makeup, but receives the whitening reflections of her attire. The text, however, draws attention to this false performance by emphasizing the indeterminacy and duality of her appearance.

> She cut up the partridges, her hands freed from their black sheaths, her torso snugly pressed into the scabbard of her dress, and only her white hands were clearly visible, seeming even more naked. She was decidedly made-up, very pale from either powder or complexion. Even her eyes, black and white, were hidden beneath the fur of her eyelashes. Nothing showed her to be a woman. She remained a large, painted doll, very interesting because it is perfectly natural for dolls to be artificial. (13)

The narrator specifies that her white hands *seemed* naked, leaving room for significant doubt. She is made-up, but the paleness of her skin might be attributed *either* to the makeup *or* to her complexion itself. Everything about her seems artificial, yet natural, thus, the conclusion that her artificiality itself is perfectly natural, part of her nature as a creole who would consistently be "aspiring-after-France."[17] In Eliante's case, because she is a creole, white but not quite, the illusory value of her whiteness is also in question. She clearly wants to be white, and to be perceived as white, yet from the point of view of the French observer, her imitation is always imperfect, her masquerade is always evident *as such*, and thus reveals her "true" foreign nature. She does not *pass*. Léon finds the whole attempt at pallor to be only a symptom of an inner dirtiness—"Perhaps you never take it off, that black dress, only, if you sleep in it, it is the better to show up the whiteness of your skin, and that's hardly clean, my darling" (131) —a dirtiness reinforced by the smells that contradict the sight of her shockingly white skin, which "flashed with whiteness," yet "exuded a penetrating perfume, a peppery, acidic odor" (10).

Eliante's consuming fetishism of whiteness becomes fully concretized in the form of her "impassioned" love object, a Tunisian vase that is similarly "pale with pleasure":

Among the strange knicknacks of Japanese complication or Chinese tortuous-
ness, there was one admirable objet d'art placed in the middle of the room on
a pedestal of old pink velvet, as if on an altar; an alabaster vase the height of a
man, so slim, so slender, so deliciously troubling with its young man's hips,
with such a human appearance—even if it only had the traditional form of an
amphora—that the viewer remained somewhat speechless. The foot, very narrow, smooth as a spear of hyacinth, surged up from a flat oval base, narrowed
as it rose, swelled and attained, at mid-body, the dimensions of two beautiful

young thighs hermetically joined, and tapered off towards the neck where, in the hollow of the throat, a collar of alabaster shone like a fold of plump flesh—and higher up, it opened out, spreading into a corolla of convulvulus, white, pure, pale, almost aromatic, since the white smooth material with a milky transparence had such lifelike sincerity. This neck spreading into a corolla made one think of an absent head, a head cut off or carried on shoulders other than those of the amphora. (18)

This "white, pure, pale," alabaster vase, made of a "white smooth material with a milky transparence," is shaped like a human body whose head is supplied by Eliante's own as she leans over the open neck to inhale its perfumes. Overcoming his initial repulsion, Léon makes a curiously accurate analysis of this perversity and accuses Eliante of worshipping herself through the vase. Indeed, it is the purity and the whiteness of the vase that Eliante fetishizes—the potentially pure white part of herself, perceived as lack and reimagined as a concrete object of desire ready for her possession. Significantly, this fetish, perceived as an unblemished and complete (it was cracked, but she healed it) compensation for her lack, itself appears as a headless body, already symbolically castrated. It is no small irony, either, that the very act with which she demonstrates her claim on whiteness, the simultaneously psychoanalytic and almost religious fetishization of the vase, is interpreted by Léon as the height of perversity, a sexual abomination. Even as she attempts to reinstate the whiteness that she lacks as a creole, the sexual deviance of her actions functions as a symptom of *créolité* itself.

While she emulates the whiteness of the French bourgeois woman and repeatedly emphasizes the abject nature of the degenerate native, Eliante distances herself from her island origin by exoticizing it, reconceiving this part of herself as an Other through clichéd images, the alluring stereotypes of creole life, as created by imperial eyes. In the hopes of being perceived as white, Eliante employs the condescending veneration characteristic of European exoticism as a means of mimicking white discourse and white stereotypes. "I'm a little wild, I have to seek adventure according to my capricious nature of a beast brought up on all fours. Creoles, sir, are not put in diapers and strapped up in swaddling clothes, they are left naked wandering on the ground in the very first days of infancy" (49). This ironic return to her creole origins operates as a fantasy, a romantic image of how things might be in the "hot islands." The same impulse that drives Eliante to a reverence of the Oriental instills in her the desire to reconstruct the broken bonds that tie her to a foreign birth; both are imagined as Others, spaces of freedom from the constraints of white French bourgeois culture with which she longs to identify: "The colonies! A warm island . . . lots of flowers and the sea purring around you. Palm trees, big palm trees, and permission to run naked on the sand. Léon, that's my dream, my own dream, to go and live in the colonies!" (71). With this statement of subjective desire, Eliante simultaneously expresses her independence and inscribes herself within a larger narrative of exoticism that regards the tropical colony as an idyllic alternative to European modernity—a haven of savage freedom. Her embrace of *créolité* and her nostalgia for the "dirty Ninaude" thus reveal less a true acceptance of her colonial heritage than an exoticization of it—an exoticism that functions as an attempt to align herself with the gaze of white Europe, yet which only succeeds in aligning her with the exotic itself. Her taste for the Other only contributes to Léon's fascination with her, and to the narrative's containment of her within the bounds of a defined degeneracy: "She had the naiveté of Ninaude because she was from the land of dreams" (154).

## THE DECADENT

Current criticism of the work of Rachilde has in some ways been a constant battle for justification. Why should we revisit the petty novels of an author who even in her own time was left in the shadows of her more famous contemporaries? Thus far, Rachilde's redemption has been achieved by an analytical emphasis on the sexual politics of her texts, almost to the exclusion of any other aspect of her work. "To write *La Jongleuse*," says Claude Dauphiné in the introduction to the French edition, "was for Rachilde to attempt one more time, by the ways of art, to bring to life a project, to proclaim that woman has the right to love in her own way and to remain the master of her own destiny."[18] But however much we might be tempted to agree with Melanie Hawthorne's contention that "instinctively grasping a medical and psychological truth that the turn-of-the-century world was only beginning to understand," Rachilde's Eliante was "the spokesperson, albeit an amateur one, for the theory of [the] social construction [of sexuality],"[19] we must also acknowledge that, particularly in the context of the fin de siècle, issues of gender and sexuality are inextricable from those of race. The "four great unities" of Foucault's *scientia sexualis*—the hystericization of women, the psychiatrization of perversions, the sexualization of children, and the socialization of procreation—were also the "four great lines of attack" for a "technology of life," a "biopower" that disciplined bodies and regulated populations,[20] preserving the purity and strength of the race through the surveillance and control of sexuality.

A rereading of *La Jongleuse*, therefore, should not stop at a celebration of Eliante's autonomous self-creation, but should more carefully scrutinize the mechanisms within the text that both allow for such a construction and contribute to the ultimate recontainment of her transgression within a normalizing narrative. Eliante's sexual aggresivity, her power over men, is a stereotypical characteristic, inextricable from her identity as a creole. As the eponymous juggler, she occupies the central position of the strong and independent heroine, a liberated woman, but does so only as a function of her degenerate racial and cultural origin: her autonomous sexuality and subjectivity are ironically granted only within the confines of a racial difference and inferiority that she in turn spends the entire narrative trying to overcome. In the end, if Eliante's double nature, her essentially duplicitous and enigmatic character, works as a commentary on the nature of Woman, as one might first assume, this commentary is less liberatory than feminist critics would like to believe. If Eliante is a model for the ideal woman, then Woman is conceived of here as fundamentally degenerate, a descendent of Baudelaire's artificial femme fatale whose presence is at once appealing and frightening, and whose identity is constructed entirely upon its staged performance: a creole whose very racial distinction matches that of the fin de siècle decadent—sensual, frail, languid, nervous, and prey to a constant crisis of identity.

By the publication of *La Jongleuse* in 1900, the height of the Decadent movement had already passed; interests were shifting, the New Woman was born, and the prospect of the new century began to inject a note of optimism into discourses of degenerating nations. Maurice Barrès had already begun to transform the racist preoccupations with national decay into the racism of nationalist regeneration, a return to roots, and an escape from self-destruction through the cult of the self. With the figure of the creole, Rachilde prolongs the life of Decadent literature, and revives the cult of the artificial by returning to its forefather, the Baudelaire whose theories inspired the Decadents of the 1880s—"What Decadent writers cherished the most in the work of this poet, was, in effect, that which had intensely shocked his contemporaries: the primacy of sensation, a taste for the bizarre and the horrible, the deliberate search for the artificial, and finally, a voluptuous abandon to spleen"[21]—but also the Baudelaire whose fascination with *créolité* made a significant contribution to the literature of French exoticism. As the embodiment and epitome of the artificial, the physically weak, imitative, and nervous, the creole Eliante *is* the decadent, Baudelairean femme fatale, now aging past her prime: always made-up, always acting, always false, always deceptive, yet as such, the emblem of a movement that celebrated the perversity of a sick and dying civilization. Is she really forty years old, as rumors report? Too old to be desired, too old to be of any use? Or is she only thirty-five as she claims, as she *proves* by displaying her birth certificate?

Eliante's identity crisis reaches its physical apotheosis in her final performance, a dance worthy of her encyclopedic counterpart, to which she abandons herself "with a fury." As she enters the salon in a thundering Spanish dance, she appears instantly double, degraded in spite of herself: "Made up in a coarse manner, this woman, whose body could belong to a girl, had a face strangely beautiful and old" (194). She is woman and child, old and

young, now completely overcome by her inherently nervous nature: "The dancer, whose naked little arms, a child's arms, were extended, whose hands were clenched nervously on castanets, bent over slowly, and her frail legs, her tiny feet enclosed in back satin, had a kind of shudder, an undulation of the skin, resembling the first tremble of fever" (194). Then she explodes into "the living and suffering poem of a body tormented by strange passions," her body simultaneously opening and closing with the furious rhythm of the music. The onlookers are amazed, "She has admirable teeth!" "Yes . . . one would think they were false!" Her body is laid bare in all its essence: "Eliante threw herself forward with a supple, enormous leap, and turned, the skirt lifted up to her eyes, all her black body beneath appeared in a leotard, but the leotard let the flesh show through, watershot, one would have said, with a kind of milky sweat, and one ended up seeing, very distinctly, the white flesh of the entire body the way one sees naked legs beneath stockings" (197). Eliante is naked, yet clothed, a black body with white flesh, oozing a milky sweat—is this the milk of her truly white skin? or is it rather the result of the rice powder, the white makeup melting with her sweat? Because she is a creole, the ambiguity remains unresolved; her decadent artificiality is revealed to be an inherent aspect of her degenerate *créolité*. The milky sweat literalizes this paradox and brings it to the surface as a physical essence: at once an eerily *artificial* fluid exuded from the pores of her flesh, and a strangely *natural* and palpable manifestation of her racialized desires.

## NOTES

1. Max Nordau, *Degeneration*, trans. George L. Mosse (Lincoln: University of Nebraska Press, 1993), 5. Prints in this chapter are by Gustave Alaux and appeared in the 1925 edition of *La Jongleuse* (Paris: J. Ferenczi). Reprinted by permission © 2003 Artists Rights Society (ARS), New York/ADAGP, Paris.

2. Claude Dauphiné, *Rachilde* (Paris: Mercure de France, 1991), 11.

3. Maryline Lukacher, *Maternal Fictions: Stendhal, Sand, Rachilde, and Bataille* (Durham, N.C.: Duke University Press, 1994), 109.

4. Melanie Hawthorne, "Rachilde," in *French Women Writers: A Bio-Bibliographical Source Book*, ed. Eva Martin Sartori and Dorothy Wynne Zimmerman (New York: Greenwood, 1991), 346–56.

5. For an exception to this rule, see Elizabeth Louise Constable, "Dis-Orienting Cultural Economies: Questioning the 'Orient' in Balzac, Flaubert, Barrès, and Rachilde," dissertation (Irvine: University of California, 1995).

6. Melanie Hawthorne, "Introduction," in *The Juggler* (New Brunswick, N.J.: Rutgers University Press, 1990), xii.

7. All citations from the primary text are taken from the English translation by Melanie Hawthorne.

8. Judith L. Raiskin, *Snow on the Cane Fields: Women's Writing and Creole Subjectivity* (Minneapolis: University of Minnesota Press, 1996), 3.

9. Raiskin, *Snow on the Cane Fields,* 181.

10. Christopher L. Miller, *Blank Darkness: Africanist Discourse in French* (Chicago: University of Chicago Press, 1985), 104.

11. Pierre Larousse, *Grand Dictionnaire universel du XIXe siècle* (Paris: Administration du Grand Dictionnaire universel, 1866–1878). My translation.

12. A scenario reminiscent of the metropolitan dandy—Baudelaire in particular, who was temporarily "exiled" to the colonies to live on his parents' money.

13. Rachilde consistently maintained her distance from popular feminism, promoting a philosophy of individual achievement over group movements. Missie is constantly ridiculed by Eliante for riding bicycles, studying medicine, and smoking. To Eliante, she is nothing more than a *garçon manqué* and does not know how to "be a woman."

14. Anne McClintock, *Imperial Leather: Race, Gender, and Sexuality in the Colonial Contest* (New York: Routledge, 1998), 182.

15. Sander Gilman, *Difference and Pathology: Stereotypes of Sexuality, Race, and Madness* (Ithaca, N.Y.: Cornell University Press, 1985), 114.

16. See in particular, "La vie antérieure," "Parfum exotique," "La Chevelure," "Sed non satiata," "L'invitation au voyage," "A une dame créole," "Le voyage," "La belle Dorothée," "Un hémisphère dans une chevelure," "L'invitation au voyage" (en prose). Ninaude's "musk, sweat, coconut oil, and rum" seems to echo this passage from "Un hémisphère dans une chevelure": "Dans l'ardent foyer de ta chevelure, je respire l'odeur du tabac mêlée à l'opium et au sucre; dans la nuit de ta chevelure, je vois resplendir l'infini de l'azur tropical; sur les rivages duvetés de ta chevelure, je m'enivre des odeurs combinées du goudron, du musc, et de l'huile de coco."

17. Here, Christopher Miller's comments on Baudelaire's "A une dame créole" and "La belle Dorothée" seem to apply equally well to *La Jongleuse*: "Together, they project a permanent state of exile and desire onto the black and creole mind, an 'aspiring-after-France' like that of Villault de Bellefond's natives of Guinea, an experience of the self as a lack and a difference. Across the gap between Europe and the black world, the traffic is imitation, parody, and desire for sameness. Illusions of progress are produced within that framework: nobility, status, redemption, freedom. But at the moment when the barrier seems to have been crossed, a term arises to reveal the projected, dependent, attributed status of the illusion" (124).

18. Claude Dauphiné, "Introduction," in *La Jongleuse* (Paris: Editions des femmes, 1983), 22.

19. Melanie Hawthorne, "The Social Construction of Sexuality in Three Novels by Rachilde," in *Les Genres de l'henaurme siècle: Papers from the Fourteenth An-*

*nual Colloquium in Nineteenth-Century French Studies*, ed. William Paulson (Ann Arbor: University of Michigan Press, 1989), 49–59.

20. Michel Foucault, *The History of Sexuality: An Introduction, Vol. I.*, trans. Robert Hurley (New York: Vintage, 1990), 145–47.

21. Jean Pierrot. *The Decadent Imagination, 1880–1900*, trans. Derek Coltman (Chicago: University of Chicago Press, 1981).

## 15

# LOVE, LABOR, AND RACE: COLONIAL MEN AND WHITE WOMEN IN FRANCE DURING THE GREAT WAR

*Tyler Stovall*

As in so many other areas of national life, World War I constituted a water-shed for race relations in France.[1] Before 1914 the interaction of most French men and women with people of color had been limited to contacts with members of small communities in Paris, Marseilles, and other cities, or more commonly indirect exposure via the popular press and colonial litera-ture and travel accounts. As a result, few people in France had ever seen or talked to anyone who was not white.[2] In contrast, during the war France im-ported well over half a million soldiers and laborers to work in its factories and farms, and fight and die in its trenches.[3] This wartime experiment in multiculturalism was undertaken reluctantly, and essentially revoked within a year after the end of the conflict. Nonetheless this brief but massive influx of nonwhites had a significant impact upon French society, first setting forth themes that would come to fruition after 1945. One very important issue concerned relations between men of color and French women.[4] Members of the two groups encountered each other in a variety of ways, ranging from glimpses on streets and in other public spaces to intimate relationships to marriage. Such contacts were extremely controversial, attacked by both French men and French public authorities, and the danger of love across the color line was a key reason for France's decision not to renew its use of non-white labor during the interwar years. By bringing a central colonial anxiety, miscegenation, to the metropole, however, such contacts forecast the out-lines of postcolonial conflicts in the late twentieth century.[5]

Spurred on largely by feminist theory and its debates with Marxism, analyses of race, class, and gender have proliferated in recent years.[6] Many scholars have considered the way these various levels of difference have interacted with each other, shaping modalities of oppression and resistance and creating multiple identities for both individuals and groups. In particular, studies of working women of color have indicated the multiple ways in which oppressed people approach their relationship to the dominant culture.[7] Too frequently, however, studies of race, class, and gender have tended to privilege one set of differences at the expense of the others. Yet the difference between relations of gender, race, and class is also a difference of conceptual frameworks, so that analyzing their interaction requires a "Rashomon"-like sensitivity to the many alternate ways of viewing a given situation or problem. For example, an individual may consider his or her racial identity paramount in some circumstances, but in others gender differences may take pride of place. Moreover, one set of social identities may change the ways one conceives another, so that men and women can perceive the very nature of class differently.[8] Moreover, conflicts over race, gender, and class all have their own separate histories and power dynamics, so that they cannot simply be reduced to a question of social difference.

In this chapter I hope to contribute to these discussions by analyzing a very specific instance of interactions between race, gender, and class. The two central groups involved here are colonial men of color and white French women, and I intend to consider the images each had of the other as well as their lived history together during the war. But French women and colonial men did not encounter each other in isolation. Also important were the reactions of white working-class French men and, especially, the agenda of the French state, which is to say that of the nation's white male elite. In spite of the frequently positive nature of the encounters between colonial men and French women, French authorities intervened vigorously, and to a large extent successfully, to limit any intimacy or even contact between the two groups. While this prohibitionist effort arose essentially out of fears that such intimacy would harm racial and gender hierarchies, both in the empire and at home, it also had important implications for class politics, splintering the working class along racial lines.

In particular, the contacts between white French women and colonial men took place in the context of two important shifts in French life during the war. One was the shifting boundaries of gender and the role of women. As Mary Louise Roberts has shown, for many French the war destabilized traditional gender categories, leading to fears of French women's loss of femininity and the emasculation of the nation as a role.[9] At the same time the war years also brought an increased prevalence of racial thinking in France, due not just to the presence of colonials but also to the heightened importance of nationalism and of biological concepts of the nation.[10] Official French concern over the possibilities of miscegenation during the war reflected and contributed to both these developments. In opposition to what would become known after the war as the New Woman, French leaders counterposed the image of the French woman settler in the colonies.[11] Her sexual and racial virtue would not only civilize the empire but also serve as a model for gender relations in the metropole.

In their efforts to prevent intimate interracial relations, French leaders would also implicitly set forth a newly racialized vision of national identity. French women and colonial men came into contact in a number of ways largely because racial boundaries were not established in the metropole to the same extent that they were in colonial societies. Consequently, during the war, French officials scrambled to put these boundaries into place, often drawing upon imperial models. It was impossible, however, simply to recreate colonial society in metropolitan France: for one thing, the class divide between wealthy white settlers and poor natives could not be reproduced in a nation with a large white working class and peasantry.[12] Given that official policy often placed colonial men (especially workers) and French women in the same social situations, the boundary between them could not be one of status, as in the colonies, but had to be racial. As would become clearer during the 1920s, the war helped reframe French identity along racial lines.[13]

## FRENCH IMAGES OF RACE AND GENDER

Those individuals who came from the empire to serve France as soldiers and workers during the war often found that the French had definite preconceived ideas about them. From Montesquieu's *Persian Letters* to the era of renewed imperial expansion in the late nineteenth century, French literature had manifested a strong fascination with the exotic. Pierre Loti's 1881 novel *Le Roman d'un Spahi* was tremendously influential in shaping popular images of Africa for a generation to come.[14] French newspapers, especially the mass circulation Parisian dailies of the late nineteenth century like *Le Petit Parisien*, also devoted much attention to the nation's overseas possessions, usually emphasizing their exoticism and French military prowess.[15] While a number of themes emerge from this literature, the most important ones center around savagery and moral weakness. The French viewed Africans as completely uncivilized, violent cannibals prone to animal-like behavior. During the war this stereotype translated into a belief that Africans would make good soldiers because of their supposed predilection for bloodletting. In particular, African soldiers in wartime France were often associated with decapitation, the belief being that they would go into berserker fits on the battlefield, using their sabres to chop off enemy heads with savage glee. One detachment of African soldiers found itself warmly greeted upon its arrival by French crowds shouting "Bravo riflemen! Cut off the heads of the Germans!"[16] If images of savagery proved a positive attribute for French colonial soldiers during World War I, moral weakness was a distinctly negative one for French colonial labor. The laziness of colonial subjects is a central theme of French exoticist literature, so much so that a central mission of empire was seen to be civilizing the natives by teaching them the values of hard work.[17] Sexual abandon, or lust in the tropics, complemented the image of the indolent colonial subject. The legendary sexual prowess of blacks was of course most developed, but Asian and Arab colonies also appeared in the French popular imagination as places where the libido knew no bounds.[18] The category of moral weakness covers many other sins, including drink, drugs, gambling, insubordination, and strikes, and all loomed large in both general representations of colonial subjects and official discussions of nonwhite workers in wartime France.[19]

But not all the savages were in Africa. Eugene Weber has demonstrated how peasants and others on the margins of society were often represented as savages in colonialist terms.[20] A parallel set of discourses applied to French women, especially working women. France in the late nineteenth century was a nation where the very concept of a working woman was seen as a social outrage, where the most powerful symbol of the woman who worked for wages was the prostitute.[21] Domestic servants, who comprised the largest single category of working women in France before the war, were routinely portrayed as lazy, childlike, and sexually immoral.[22] At least these women had the virtue of working in the home; those employed elsewhere, such as in the textile and garment industries, were even more likely to appear oversexed and undercivilized to bourgeois male observers. Moreover, women in general were often portrayed as hysterical and uncontrollable, a gender whose unrestrained passions could run riot in violent mobs and threaten the very foundations of society. The *pétroleuses* of the Paris Commune symbolized this image of women as barbarians at the gate.[23] As Kristin Ross put it in her introduction to Emile Zola's novel *The Ladies' Paradise*: "Once they have assembled themselves into a crowd, women, whether strikers or shoppers, revert to

a primitive state: 'public' woman is woman preyed upon by savage or violent impulses."[24]

French bourgeois stereotypes of nonwhite subjects and of working
women were not the same, of course; rather, colonialist and sexist discourse
employed similar structures of domination. However, there were also important differences that became clear when World War I brought these two
worlds together, differences that rendered associations between colonial
men and white women so threatening. One indication of this was the shifting image of *la Coloniale*, the French woman in the colonies, before the
war.[25] As will become clear later, although physically absent from wartime
France, the female colonial settler was ever present in the imaginations of
both French and colonial men, constantly contrasted with the real live
women of metropolitan France. Ann Stoler and other scholars of gender
and empire have analyzed the ways in which white women in European
colonies came to symbolize gentility and civilization, the domestication of
male settlers and the transmission of European culture overseas.[26] Yet this
was certainly not true of many French women colonial settlers in the nineteenth century. Instead, their popular image had much more in common
with that of French working women in general. The first large group of
French women to settle in the empire during the nineteenth century did so
as convicts, sent to prisons in French Guiana and New Caledonia as punishment for a variety of crimes. Also important were women, especially
prostitutes and sellers of foodstuffs, who followed the progress of colonial
regiments across Asia and Africa. A third category consisted of pioneers and
adventurers, women like Isabelle Eberhardt, who converted to
Islam and moved to Algeria in 1897, or Madame de la Souchère, who
founded an Indochinese rubber plantation in 1909. Far from corresponding
to ideas of middle-class gentility, such women fit into the image of the
colonies as an escape from bourgeois morality.[27]

By 1914, however, the image of the French woman in the colonies had
shifted significantly. In 1897 two Frenchmen founded an organization, the
French Society for Women's Emigration to the Colonies, to promote female
settlement in the empire. Its particular goal was to provide white spouses
for French male settlers, developing French family life overseas in order to
make life in the empire more secure and genteel. In response to widespread public criticism of their mission, the organizers emphasized the
intelligence and above all respectability of those women interested in relo-
cating to the colonies. During its first year of operation, the society received
inquiries from 400 to 500 women desiring to move to the empire to find
jobs, husbands, or simply a new way of life.[28] While this organization ceased

operations after only a few years, it helped create a new image of *la Colo-niale*, one stressing domesticity, gentility, and loyalty to bourgeois values.[29] Contrasting sharply with stereotypes of both nonwhites and working women as primitive and threatening, the ideal of the French woman over-seas would motivate much of the hostility to relations between the two groups in France during the war.

## COLONIAL MEN AND FRENCH WOMEN

France's decision to use colonial soldiers during the war in Europe was not undertaken lightly. The creation of indigenous armies in the nation's over-seas possessions was by no means a new development in 1914: the nation's imperial expansion rested to a large extent upon the military efforts of non-white soldiers.[30] Yet, for a people whose idea of the armed forces still rested upon the model of the Revolutionary citizen army, the prospect of a fight-ing force composed of colonial subjects gave some pause. Largely inspired by Charles Mangin's *La force noire*, the French government began con-scripting African soldiers in 1912.[31] Roughly 200,000 colonial soldiers served in France during the Great War, the overwhelming majority *tirailleurs sénégalais* from West Africa.[32] Led by French officers, soldiers from the empire were grouped by nationality in segregated units. These troops saw heavy fighting against the Germans on the Western Front: after ten Senegalese battalions were massacred in November 1914, colonial troops were reintroduced to the front lines in the summer of 1916. The *tirailleurs sénégalais* took part in a variety of important battles, including the Somme, the Aisne, and the Chemin des Dames. They suffered heavy casualties and in general achieved a solid, at times distinguished, military record.[33]

The Great War also had a dramatic and largely unforeseen impact on the composition of the French labor force, diversifying it to an extent unimag-inable a few years earlier, as millions of French men mobilized for military duty. Whereas French women had frequently worked for wages before 1914, they were primarily confined to segregated sectors of the economy, especially domestic service and textiles. With the onset of war, however, both the shortage of male labor and the growth of the munitions industry brought the first major introduction of women into the previously mascu-line preserve of heavy industry. Close to 700,000 women worked in the French armaments industry during the war, constituting roughly 25 percent of its entire labor force.[34] Women also replaced absent men in much agricultural labor, going so far at times as to pull plows themselves. However, women's labor power was not enough for the nation's wartime needs, so France turned to recruiting foreigners as well. France already had a history of receiving immigrants unmatched in Europe: in 1911 the census recorded over one million resident aliens on French soil. Most of these came from nations bordering France, and these patterns of immigration continued during the war. Over 300,000 Europeans, primarily Spaniards, Italians, and Greeks, worked in France between 1914 and 1918. Yet the real innovation was the importation of "exotic" labor from the French colonies and China.[35] By the end of 1915 the War Ministry was calling upon colonial officials in North Africa and Indochina to furnish labor for use in France, while at roughly the same time Lieutenant Colonel Georges Truptil undertook a state mission to China to arrange for the use of Chinese workers. The first contingents of nonwhite laborers arrived in 1915, and by the end of the war over 300,000 men from China and the empire had spent time employed on French farms and factories.[36]

The introduction of nonwhite laborers and soldiers into metropolitan France took place in a context of gender relations that was highly unusual in two respects. First, the drafting of millions of French men radically feminized wartime civilian life. Whole villages lost their adult male population, retaining only children and the elderly.[37] Thus in coming to France colonial men often found a society that seemed essentially female.[38] Second, French authorities only recruited nonwhite *men* from the empire, leaving women of color behind. The use of colonial women never seems to have been considered; at a time when occupational barriers to French women were breaking down, separate occupational spheres for nonwhite men and women remained in force. The reluctant use of French women in war industries, plus the refusal to bring in women from the empire, to a certain extent reversed the traditional colonial relations of race and gender. Government authorities thus managed to create the colonialist's worst nightmare on French soil.

In particular, French women and colonial men working in the munitions industry had much in common. Both groups were outsiders, people brought into job sectors previously reserved for skilled white men for the sake of the war effort. The overwhelming majority of both women and nonwhite munitions workers lacked skills or experience in dealing with heavy industry, and found the world of the large factory an alien, uncomfortable environment. Largely because of their low skill levels, colonial and female workers often found themselves working side by side in the same industrial departments.[39] These were invariably the sectors that offered the hardest

work under the worst conditions. The extremely high rate of industrial ac-
cidents among women munitions workers testified to the difficulty of their
labor, while a 1917 report from one explosives factory noted that French
men working the most disagreable jobs were being systematically replaced
by Vietnamese workers.[40] Along with harsh working conditions went low
pay. Throughout the course of the war the French government maintained
officially separate pay rates for men and women in the armaments industry,
with women earning between 16 and 40 percent less than men for the same
work. Colonial laborers signed contracts at the point of recruitment speci-
fying their wages, based on the official government pay scales. Since these
contracts did not allow for changes corresponding to inflation or the upward
trend of wartime wages, colonial workers gradually became the most poorly
paid in France. Moreover, both groups were frequently used by employers
to undermine traditions of shop-floor automony, in particular pushing for
greater productivity by speeding up the pace of work. Finally, nonwhite
men and French women were seen by many in French society, including
male workers, unions, employers, newspapers and other sources of public
opinion, and government officials, as unwelcome interlopers in the world of
heavy industry.[41] For a variety of reasons,[42] their presence there was accepted reluctantly, to be dispensed with as soon as the war ended.

   Such parallels only go so far, however. French women were after all
French, and if they had transgressed their proper societal roles by taking
employment in heavy industry they were still natives of the country where
they worked. Colonial men could not have been more alien to their surroundings.[43] Not only did many work in a very different environment, but
most were completely new to France, indeed Europe, rarely even speaking
the language. French women in the munitions industry chose to work
there, and if their wages were less than those of men, they were much
higher than salaries paid for traditional women's work. Although in theory
nonwhites came to France of their own accord, in reality they usually chose
to do so under duress, so that their history is essentially one of forced labor
migration.[44] In addition, whereas French women enjoyed the right to work
and reside where they wished (or could afford), colonial workers lived in
France under the aegis of the military, which assigned them jobs and usually kept them segregated in barracks as far removed from French civilians
as possible.[45]

   These differences extended to the impressions nonwhite men and
French women formed of each other upon contact. One important group
of white women encountered by colonial soldiers were the *marraines de
guerre*, women who out of a sense of patriotic duty wrote letters to soldiers

to bolster their morale.[46] Some corresponded with African *tirailleurs*, gradually forming epistolary friendships and at times inviting them to their homes when they went on leave. In general, the *marraines* gave colonial soldiers their best opportunities to become acquainted with French civilian life, and generally left them with their most positive impressions of France. As one veteran explained many years later,

> the African soldiers in France had their *marraines de guerre* too. They were not prostitutes. They were girls of good families who saw us and knew that we were [far from] our countries. [And they realized] we needed some affection and some money . . . to buy cigarettes with, to go to the movies, and so on.
>
> [And we met them] on the street or in cafés. A French girl saw you and felt very pleased by [your appearance]. And she said to you that she wanted to take you to her house to present you to her parents. And you got [an adopted] French family in that way.[47]

As Joe Lunn has noted of the veteran *tirailleurs* he interviewed, they generally viewed women in France more positively than both French men and French women in the colonies. Soldiers also had fond memories of the nurses who cared for them after battle.[48]

For colonial workers, the sight of working women was one of the strangest things they came across while in France. Relatively few French women lived in the empire at all, and those that did lived (or at least were supposed to live) on a very different plane from indigenous men and women. Therefore, the prospect of white women not only working, but working at the same jobs as them often came as a shock. For example, one worker from Madagascar employed in a factory in Toulouse wrote: "Would you believe that white women, who at home love to be served, here work as much as men? In the factories they are very numerous and work with the same ardor as the men."[49] Another wrote to a friend in Madagascar encouraging him to come to France to get a white woman, noting that whereas at home they are very haughty, in France they lick the feet of Madagascan workers. This inversion of traditional hierarchies was certainly not absolute; the regimentation of colonial labor imported colonial ideas of residential racial segregation to the metropole. In a sense, the contrast between segregated barracks life and on the job contact with French women probably made the latter phenomenon seem even more extraordinary.

If the reactions of nonwhite men revealed both amazement and affection, those of French women often betrayed an initially racist and hostile perspective, followed by a growing sense of tolerance and interest. While no records exist of the opinions of factory workers, other women did record their impressions. Louise Deletang, a Parisian seamstress, recorded in her diary an encounter with a Moroccan in the street. They did not speak to each other, but Deletang nonetheless noted his rough air and the fact that he was accompanied by French street toughs; she gave thanks that an up-right French policeman was there to send these hoodlums packing and save her from the malignant attitude of the *Mauricaud*.[50] Encounters with colonial soldiers were more common, since they were often more visible than workers. Lucie Cousturier described the racial panic expressed by the women of her small village when a regiment of African riflemen was stationed nearby:

> What would happen to us? wailed the farm wives, we could no longer let our chickens roam near these thieves, or let our clothes dry outside or our fruit ripen on the trees. We could no longer let our little girls run along the roads among these savages. We ourselves would no longer dare go out alone to mow our lawns or gather firewood. Just imagine if one were captured by these gorillas![51]

However, such fears soon proved groundless, and Cousturier herself gradually came to admire these soldiers, even volunteering to tutor them in French. Another French woman, writing about African American soldiers passing through her village, first noted the fears of many women (including cannibalism), then observed how the troops soon won over the local villagers. Her rather florid description ended by noting: "In the lanes along the flowery hedges, more than one group of colored American soldiers fraternize with our people, while the setting sun makes blue the neighboring hills, and gently the song of night is awakened."[52]

As this last sentence suggests, contacts between French women and non-white men during World War I at times took on a sexual dimension. Information about this comes primarily from two sources: the letters of colonial workers and soldiers to friends and relatives back home, and the reports of the French censors charged with their surveillance. The former boasted about such relations, while the latter worried about them. One Tunisian worker stationed in the town of Montereau wrote that "the city where we are stationed is full of women, and fornication here is as abundant as grains of sand. As for me, I have four women, two young girls and two widows. I am awash in sensuality."[53] Rabetanety, a Madgascan employed in the arsenal at Tarbes, claimed that "I have noted my great desire to continue to serve the Patrie, but in reality I find French women too beautiful and genteel, and I would be crushed if I had to leave them."[54] This fascination with

French women could lead at times to bizarre conclusions, as shown by a letter from Salah-ben-Malah, a Tunisian worker stationed in Saint-Nazaire:

> In this land called France there are no longer any men at all, there are only women, who are very numerous. They tell us that when we have finished our work in France and are about to return home, they will give each of us three women that we will be allowed to bring to Tunisia. The subsistence of these women will be provided by the State. This is a piece of news as firm and certain as stone.[55]

While some of these accounts may have been idle boasting meant to titillate faraway friends and relatives, sexual contacts between French women and nonwhite men clearly took place in wartime France. This is demonstrated by the concerns that French officials, both censors and supervisors of colonial worker and soldiers, expressed over these interactions. A September 1917 report from a French censor observed the frequency of intimate relations between the Indochinese workers of the Toulouse area and the local female population, pointing out that while many of these women were prostitutes, that was not uniformly the case.[56] Nonwhite men, both soldiers and workers, did certainly avail themselves of the services of French prostitutes. The war brought a tremendous increase in the amount of sex for sale in France, and colonial men were no more immune to this temptation than English or American soldiers.[57] Their letters frequently indicate the prevalence of this activity, even at times giving price rates.[58] However, interracial sexual contacts in wartime France went beyond commercial transactions. As one of the censors noted, "Our Indochinese receive in effect letters that indicate that their female correspondants belong sometimes to the most respectable society."[59]

In fact, the letters written by nonwhite men in France reveal a wide range of sexual behaviors, from fleeting encounters with both prostitutes or women who were willing but not professionals, to long-term attachments and occasionally marriage. Several *marraines de guerre* fell in love with their correspondents and proposed to them.[60] The best source we have on this issue is a series of reports dealing with Indochinese workers and soldiers in 1917 and 1918. Perhaps not surprisingly, the correspondence indicates that soldiers tended to be more fleeting in their affections, whereas workers, whose contacts with French women were much more extensive, were more likely to establish durable relationships. For example, Pham Van Khuong, an Indochinese army interpreter stationed in Versailles, corresponded frequently with a Mlle. Ninon of Toulouse, who repeatedly proclaimed her love for him. At the same time he received angry letters from another French woman, a former mistress whom he had promised to marry in spite of the fact that he already had a wife in Indochina.[61] In contrast, Ky Sum, an Indochinese worker in Angoulême wrote: "My dear parents, I would like to inform you that I have already found a girlfriend here. I enclose her photograph. She is a worker who is employed in the same factory as me. When I was sick she often visited me at the hospital, and that is why I cannot do without her now."[62] As this case clearly indicates, feelings of affection and commitment at times characterized these relationships. The letters of French women to their Indochinese lovers also display strong attachments. A certain Andrea from Tarbes wrote to Mai, a metal worker, that she had just had a child, who was "very cute, but rather white," and signed herself "his wife forever."[63] A December 1918 report noted the existence of sixty mixed race children in the area around the Saint-Medard gunpowder factory, one of the primary employers of Indochinese labor.[64] The letters indicate interest in marriage on the part of both Indochinese men and white women, and roughly two hundred of these took place during the war. Moreover, the families of French women often welcomed their lovers. One soldier described how his girlfriend's father, a captain in an artillery regiment, treated them to lunch every day and regularly gave him money for clothes. Members of the Gaudet family, wine growers from the Charente, wrote numerous letters to Do Van Thinh, who they called Jacques and referred to as their son-in-law.[65] Given the generally lamentable treatment of colonial workers in particular during the war, these relations with French women and sometimes entire families were often the most positive and comforting aspects of their stays in France.

Yet sexual relations between nonwhite men and French women also at times provoked antagonism and even bloodshed. French male workers and soldiers displayed hostility toward colonial workers for a number of reasons, including accusations that they lowered wages and worsened working conditions, a belief that their use enabled the government to draft more French workers and send them to the trenches, and sheer racial antipathy. Numerous instances of racial violence, ranging from individual assaults to full-scale race riots, took place in France during the war, and hostility of French men toward such liaisons often triggered it. A report concerning attacks upon Indochinese workers by French soldiers observed that "jealousy over women has generally been the cause of these aggressions."[66] During February 1918, tensions between Madagascan workers and French men in Toulouse caused several incidents, including a brief riot between armed factions. Emmanuel Rasafimanjary described how he and a friend were called "*sales nègres*" while strolling with two French women and commented that "such incidents are frequent, French men being very jealous of the favors shown the Madagascans by French women."[67]

For the most part, such violence was a masculine affair, pitting men of different races against each other. Yet during the spring of 1917 a few incidents of violence between French women and colonial men occurred that give a different perspective to relations between the two groups. French morale and determination to wage war underwent a major crisis in April and May of 1917, as mutinies broke out in the army and a wave of wildcat strikes began in French workshops. Women were at the forefront of the new strike movement, first in the clothing industry and then in the munitions factories. When women strikers appealed to their nonwhite colleagues on the job to join them, however, they usually met with a negative or uncomprehending response. Few colonial workers had ever heard of trade unions before coming to France, and French unions had made no significant efforts to organize them before the strikes broke out in 1917. At the same time, rumors spread that both nonwhite soldiers and workers were being used to break strikes. The socialist newspaper *Humanité* published an article in September 1917 repeating the false allegation that Indochinese soldiers had fired upon striking French women in Paris and Toulouse after French troops had refused to do so.[68] Such rumors often produced racial violence in which French women at times participated. Mixed groups of men and women both verbally and physically harassed several North Africans employed by the City of Paris during this period. One gardener watering a lawn was accosted by several women who asked him to join their strike; when he refused, they called him a "dirty Sidi come to France to eat the bread of French workers," and struck him in the face.[69] Such incidents were few, but they suggest that some militant French women were not only angered by the refusal of colonial workers to join them, but also felt a sense of betrayal based upon an assumption of common interests.

In contrast, one of the most striking aspects of the history of wartime interracial relations in France is the almost complete absence of accusations of rape. Crimes of sexual assaults often remain hidden from public scrutiny, and there were most likely incidents involving nonwhite men and white women that never came to light. What is interesting here, however, is the absence of such a discourse given the prevalence of white fears about interracial rape and the frequency of such accusations in situations where members of different races are brought together.[70] Certain allusions to the possibility of sexual assault do exist in official reports on colonial workers and soldiers. A June 1918 army report advised against using Africans for farm labor, noting that they would often be employed on farms where women lived alone. Victor Fitoussi, a Tunisian Jew employed in Dijon, claimed in a letter discussing tensions with Arabs that "In France there are many Algerian, Moroccan, and Tunisian Arabs who only take women by force."[71]

Yet nowhere in the official literature or the correspondence does one find overt accusations or legal proceedings involving the rape of French women by colonial men. While this is difficult to explain, two possible reasons for such a surprising omission suggest themselves. First, as the emphasis on prostitution demonstrates, many French officials considered at least some French women just as willing to engage in interracial sex as their colonial partners; where nonwhite men took the initiative, they were usually portrayed as seducers, not violent aggressors. Second, the supposedly rampant sexuality of colonial men was linked to indolence and corruption, not violence. Colonial men were themselves often portrayed as childlike and effeminate.[72] A 1917 report on Madagascans in France commented that "The Madagascan easily lets himself be guided by the European, whose superiority he implicitly recognizes," then went on to say: "The Madagascan rarely attains an advanced age. The facility for promiscuity which he abuses, even from childhood, is for him a cause of degeneration and abbreviates his days."[73] The nonwhite man might represent a sexual threat, but it was one of seduction and decadence rather than outright violence.

## MISCEGENATION AND THE STATE

The question of rape raises the much broader issue of how the authorities of the French state dealt with interracial sexual relations during the war. Just as the war increased the role of the state over national life in general, it gave public authorities significant control over both French women and nonwhite men. After July 1916 the French government made recruitment of women for the labor force official policy, channeling hundreds of thousands of them into jobs in the munitions, railway, and other vital industries. The French army had primary responsibility for colonial men, both soldiers and workers: it recruited them, brought them to France, deployed them to their tasks, housed and fed them, and when the time came, sent them back home. Most of the munitions factories where colonial men labored, and frequently came into contact with French women, were state-run enterprises. In general then, the opportunities for interracial sexual contact were largely a creation of the French government, a factor that intensified public authorities' concern about the phenomenon.

One particularly significant aspect of state intervention was censorship. Starting in March 1915 the French army began organizing the interdiction and supervision of mail sent between France and the front, or between France and foreign countries. Concerned with preventing the spread of any information prejudicial to the national war effort, the Postal Surveillance Commissions read massive numbers of letters, telegrams, and postcards, reproducing any that seemed in any way suspect. By the time colonial laborers arrived in mass in 1916, the basic outlines of this system were in place, and it took a special interest in monitoring correspondence between nonwhite men and their friends and relatives back home in the empire. The work of these censors is of great service to the historian, providing excerpts from hundreds of letters written by colonial workers and soldiers during the war. These reports are particularly useful because they constitute not only the testimony of people whose voices are usually absent from written documentation, but also furnish a guide to the interests and agendas of those hidden individuals watching over them, and of public authorities in general.[74]

For example, in April 1917 a report from the Postal Surveillance Commission in Tunis signaled the rising number of letters about relations between Tunisian men and French women in France. In particular, the report warned against the increasingly vulgar nature of these letters, signaling a lamentable decline in respect for white women. As one example of this trend, it reproduced portions of the following letter by Tayeb Gananchi, a Tunisian worker employed near Paris:

> If you wish I will send you a *wagon* of young *French girls*, because here we have large quantities at our disposal. A kilogram of *vaginas* is worth five cents, as is a pound of *breasts*. But the cost of a night spent with these beauties is much higher: they ask two francs, food being paid for by their parents. If you don't believe me, come with Salah Bacha Fredj Ben Amer and his brother Abdesselam and you will see with your own eyes: it is a true happiness. . . . [75]

This excerpt, and the fact that censors included it in a special section, "native relations with French women," indicates the importance this issue assumed in the perspective of the French state. Moreover, the choice of such a degrading letter, when the censors could easily have selected others that spoke of affection, love, and commitment, clearly demonstrates the official perspective on contacts between nonwhite men and French women. Finally, this excerpt is obviously chosen for its shock value, both for the censor's supervisors and for the censor himself, an official charged with the wearying task of reading massive amounts of frequently boring correspondance. In evaluating the censors' perspective on interracial sexual relations, the sheer prurient interest of pornography should not be underestimated.[76]

In fact, the interest of French censors and officials in this issue was so great that by late 1917 many monthly reports on colonial workers and soldiers included a special section on relations with French women. These sections, often two to three single-spaced pages in length, discussed overall trends in such relations, and included excerpts from letters by both colonial men and French women. Most of them indicated that such contacts were increasing, and spoke of this trend with great concern. Since these were officials primarily concerned with nonwhite men, they at times spoke of the danger that their charges would be corrupted by unfamiliar French customs. More frequently they charged that colonial men were seducing naive French women. The case of the aforementioned Pham Van Khuong was discussed in detail, portraying this individual as an Indochinese Lothario with women all over France. In cases where the woman's relatives demonstrated affection toward her nonwhite lover, this was interpreted as evidence, not of his integration into proper kinship structures, but rather his ability to seduce an entire French family. Commenting on contacts between colonial men and French women, one report noted: "We emphasize our chagrin at seeing unfortunate French women blunder into such evidently grotesque relationships."[77]

Ultimately, however, the central issue was the threat posed by such relationships to the imperial order in general, and the prestige of *la Coloniale* in particular. Time and time again officials expressed their concern that French women, whether prostitutes or not, who consorted with nonwhite men would destroy their respect for white women in general, and that their letters would spread this shift in attitude back to the colonies. Key here was the obsession of censors and public authorities with pornographic postcards. Images of nude French women were widely available in Paris and other French cities,[78] and they came as a revelation to men from the colonies, who frequently sent them to their friends back home. Such naughty, disrespectful images of course represented a direct threat to the proper standing of white women in the colonies. More generally, the prospect of nonwhite men looking at erotic French postcards inverted the colonial pattern of European men admiring salacious images of native women.[79] Censors kept detailed statistics on them: for example, the December 1917 report on Indochinese correspondence noted 253 *nudités*, and subcategorized their senders by workers and soldiers, as well residents of Tonkin, Cochin China, Annam, and Cambodia. The postcards issue was the most graphic symbol of the broader concern that sending colonial men to France would undermine their respect for imperial authority, especially as far as gender was concerned. As the report from Tunisia that criticized the crude attitude of Tunisian workers toward French women put it, "[these letters] have recently taken on a lewd character that is all the more regrettable in that it is likely to give French women a bad reputation in the native quarters of Tunisia."[80]

The authorities did what they could to prevent such contacts from taking place. Nonwhite workers and soldiers were at times punished with fines and imprisonment for consorting with local women. The sending of pornographic postcards was banned, and those discovered were seized by the censors. One Indochinese worker wrote a friend saying that French authorities had forbidden them from mailing such cards, and violations would be punished by a month in prison.[81] In March 1916 military authorities established segregated hospitals for Senegalese soldiers, with an entirely masculine personnel, and in general tried to prevent French female nurses from coming into contact with the Africans. *Marraines de guerre* were warned from becoming too fond of Senegalese soldiers, whom they characterized as coming from cultures with contempt for women. Authorities also intervened to try to prevent French women from marrying nonwhite soldiers and workers, and while not always successful did have some impact in reducing the number of permanent relationships. In general, by 1918 French authorities concerned with imperial recruits, both soldiers and workers, had made limiting their contacts with white women one of their highest priorities.

To the extent that they succeeded in this goal, it was not so much in preventing or even limiting individual interracial contacts, but rather in establishing the very idea of a color line in France, particularly one governing relations between members of the opposite sex. This represented not so much importing colonial norms of behavior as transforming them to fit a radically different social context. It meant establishing the idea that men and women who worked in the same factory should not become socially or sexually intimate, or that it was acceptable for French women to spend time with some soldiers but not others, due to differences of culture and race. Concepts of race prompted officials to prevent interracial sexual contacts, with the ultimate goal of preserving imperial sexual and racial hierarchies, yet in doing so they also began to sketch out a system of postcolonial racial boundaries.

At the same time, the key role of the image of *la Coloniale* offers a new perspective on tensions over conceptions of French womanhood, one exacerbated by their relationship to racial distinctions. The concern for the image of white women in the colonies (at a time when their actual presence there was still quite small) must be seen as a counterpoint to wartime anxieties about gender in the metropole. If pure French womanhood no longer existed at home, perhaps one could recreate it in the overseas empire. Like the colonial army, the colonial female settler represented the salvation of French civilization in an uncertain and threatening world. This concern for the propriety of white women in the colonies also represented the mirror image of the vaunted colonialist exoticism of the 1920s in France, so much of which centered around a fascination with the black female body.[82] Love may often find a way, but in wartime France that way was usually blocked by a complex web of social aspirations and anxieties that would provide a powerful legacy for the new century.

## NOTES

Funding for this article was provided by the Committee on Research of the University of California, Santa Cruz. I am indebted to several individuals for their helpful suggestions in reading drafts of this article, especially Gary Wilder, Winnie Woodhull, Georges Van Den Abbeele, Karen Offen, Laura L. Frader, David Barnes, Richard Roberts, Joel Bienen, Gabrielle Hecht, Ann Stoler, and Michael Vann.

1. The recent historiography of the Great War has been divided on whether or not the war was in fact such a watershed, with many arguing that it merely exemplified trends already well under way. While this was true in certain areas, notably avant-garde culture and gender relations, I would argue that in questions of race the conflict constituted a massive new fact. See for example Modris Eksteins, *Rites of Spring: The Great War and the birth of the Modern Age* (Boston: Houghton Mifflin, 1989); Stephen Kern, *The Culture of Time and Space 1880–1918* (Cambridge, Mass.: Harvard University Press, 1983); Richard Wall and Jay Winter, eds., *The Upheaval of War: Family, Work, and Welfare in Europe, 1914–1918* (Cambridge: Cambridge University Press, 1988).

2. See on this point William B. Cohen, *The French Encounter with Africans: White Responses to Blacks, 1530–1880* (Bloomington: Indiana University Press, 1980).

3. If one adds to this the people of color brought by the British and American armed forces to work and fight in France, one arrives at a figure of well over one million nonwhite men on French soil during the conflict.

4. On questions of race in France after World War II, see Maxim Silverman, *Deconstructing the Nation: Immigration, Racism and Citizenship in Modern France* (London: Routledge, 1992); Alec Hargreaves, *Immigration, "Race," and Ethnicity*

*in Contemporary France* (London: Routledge, 1995); Françoise Gaspard, *A Small City in France*, trans. Arthur Goldhammer (Cambridge, Mass.: Harvard University Press, 1995).

5. On interracial sex and miscegenation in a colonial context, see Robert Young, *Colonial Desire: Hybridity in Theory, Culture, and Race* (London: Routledge, 1991); Owen White, *Children of the French Empire: Miscegenation and Colonial Society in French West Africa, 1895–1960* (New York: Oxford University Press, 1999).

6. For a good overview of this literature, see Karen Brodkin Sacks, "Toward a Unified Theory of Class, Race, and Gender," *American Ethnologist* 16, no. 3 (August 1989).

7. See, for example, Patricia Zavella, *Women's Work and Chicano Families: Cannery Workers of the Santa Clara Valley* (Ithaca, N.Y.: Cornell University Press, 1987); Evelyn Nakano Glenn, *Issei, Nissei, War Bride: Three Generations of Japanese American Women in Domestic Service* (Philadelphia: Temple University Press, 1986); Angela Davis, *Women, Race, and Class* (New York: Random House, 1981); Rosalyn Terborg-Penn, "Black Women in Resistance: A Cross-Cultural Perspective," in Gary Y. Okihiro, ed., *In Resistance: Studies in African, Caribbean, and Afro-American History* (Amherst, Mass.: University of Massachusetts Press, 1986).

8. See Earl Lewis's discussion of the concept of multipositionality in "Invoking Concepts, Problematizing Identities: The Life of Charles N. Hunter and the Implication for the Study of Gender and Labor," *Labor History*, no. 34 (spring–summer 1993).

9. Mary Louise Roberts, *Civilization without Sexes: Reconstructing Gender in Postwar France, 1917–1927* (Chicago: University of Chicago Press, 1994). See also Susan Grayzel, "Mothers, *Marraines* and Prostitutes: Morale and Morality in First World War France," *The International History Review* 19, no. 1 (February 1997); Sian Reynolds, *France between the Wars: Gender and Politics* (London: Routledge, 1996).

10. Alice Conklin, *Mission to Civilize: The Republican Idea of Empire in France and West Africa, 1895–1930* (Stanford, Calif.: Stanford University Press, 1997); Ruth Harris, "The 'Child of the Barbarian': Rape, Race, and Nationalism in France during the First World War," *Past and Present*, no. 141 (November 1993); William Schneider, *Quality and Quantity: The Quest for Biological Regeneration in Twentieth-Century France* (Cambridge: Cambridge University Press, 1990).

11. There is now an impressive body of literature on the history of European women and empire in the nineteenth and twentieth centuries. See Nupur Chaudhuri and Margaret Strobel, eds., *Western Women and Imperialism: Complicity and Resistance* (Bloomington: Indiana University Press, 1992); Antoinette Burton, *The Burdens of History: British Feminism, Indian Women, and Imperial Culture* (Chapel Hill: University of North Carolina Press, 1994); Julia Clancy-Smith and Frances Gouda, *Domesticating the Empire: Race, Gender, and Family Life in French and Dutch Colonialism* (Charlottesville: University Press of Virginia, 1998).

12. As scholars have pointed out, the class boundaries so characteristic of colonial societies were not natural, but rather often resulted from attempts by colonial administrators to suppress the population of poor whites. See Ann Laura Stoler, "Sexual Affronts and Racial Frontiers: European Identities and the Cultural Politics of Exclusion in Colonial Southeast Asia," in Frederick Cooper and Ann Laura Stoler, *Tensions of Empire: Colonial Cultures in a Bourgeois World* (Berkeley: University of California Press, 1997); Michael G. Vann, "White City on the Red River: Race, Culture, and Power in Colonial Hanoi, 1872–1954," (Ph.D. dissertation, University of California, Santa Cruz, 1999).

13. This raises the question of whiteness and its relevance to French life in the early twentieth century, a question I explore elsewhere in greater depth. See Tyler Stovall, "The Remaking of the French Working Class: Whiteness and the Exclusion of Colonial Labor after World War I," unpublished paper presented to the Stanford French Studies group, April 2001.

14. Léon Fanoudh-Siefer, *Le mythe du nègre et de l'Afrique noire dans la littérature française* (Paris: C. Klincksieck, 1968); Ada Martinkus-Zemp, *Le blanc et le noir* (Paris: A.-G. Nizet, 1975); Pierre Jourda, *L'exotisme dans la littérature française depuis Chateaubriand*, 2 vols. (Paris: PUF, 1938, 1956).

15. William H. Schneider, *An Empire for the Masses* (Westport, Conn.: Greenwood Press, 1982), especially 36–124.

16. Cited in Charles John Balesi, *From Adversaries to Comrades-in-Arms: West Africans and the French Military, 1885–1918* (Waltham, Mass.: Crossroads Press, 1979), 116.

17. Frantz Fanon, *The Wretched of the Earth* (New York: Grove Press, 1963); Albert Sarraut, *La mise en valeur des colonies françaises* (Paris: Payot, 1923); Albert Memmi, *The Colonizer and the Colonized*, trans. Howard Greenfield (New York: Orion Press, 1965).

18. Edward Said, *Orientalism* (New York: Random House, 1979); Basil Guy, *The French Image of China before and after Voltaire* (Geneva: Institut Voltaire, 1963); Christopher Miller, *Blank Darkness: Africanist Discourse in French* (Chicago: University of Chicago Press, 1985); Penny Edwards, "Womanizing Indochina: Fiction, Nation, and Cohabitation in Colonial Cambodia, 1890–1930," in Clancy-Smith and Gouda, *Domesticating the Empire: Race, Gender, and Family Life in French and Dutch Colonialism*.

19. See for example the 27-page report on nonwhite labor written in 1916, which stereotypes nearly every group brought to France. "Note relative au recrutement de la main-d'oeuvre coloniale Nord-Africaine et Chinoise: Considérations Générales," aôut 16, 1916, Archives Nationales, series 94 AP 135.

20. Eugene Weber, *Peasants into Frenchmen* (Stanford, Calif.: Stanford University Press, 1976).

21. James F. McMillan, *Housewife or Harlot: The Place of Women in French Society 1870–1940* (New York: St. Martin's Press, 1981); Alain Corbin, *Les filles de noce: misère sexuelle et prostitution* (Paris: Aubier Montaigne, 1978); Joan Scott and

Louise Tilly, *Women, Work, and Family* (New York: 1978); Bonnie Smith, *Ladies of the Leisure Class: The Bourgeoises of Northern France in the 19th Century* (Princeton, N.J.: Princeton University Press, 1981).

22. Theresa McBride, *The Domestic Revolution: The Modernisation of Household Service in England and France, 1820–1920* (London: Croom Helm, 1976).

23. Gay Gullickson, *Unruly Women of Paris: Images of the Commune* (Ithaca, N.Y.: Cornell University Press, 1996).

24. Kristin Ross, "Introduction to Émile Zola," in *The Ladies' Paradise* (Berkeley: University of California, 1992), xviii.

25. The term *la Coloniale* was also used to characterize the French colonial army. As I will argue below, this similarity of terminology was telling, for during World War I both colonial troops and French women settlers in the empire came, in very different ways, to stand for the aid that the colonies could render to the metropole.

26. Ann L. Stoler, "Making Empire Respectable: The politics of race and sexual morality in 20th-century colonial cultures," *American Ethnologist* 16, no. 4 (November 1989); Stoler, *Race and the Education of Desire: Foucault's History of Sexuality and the Colonial Order of Things* (Durham, N.C.: Duke University Press, 1995); Margaret Strobel, "Gender and Race in the 19th and 20th century British Empire," in Renata Bridenthal et al., eds., *Becoming Visible: Women in European History* (Boston: Houghton Mifflin, 1987); Amirah Inglis, *The White Women's Protection Ordinance* ( London: Sussex University Press, 1975).

27. France Renucci, *Souvenirs de femmes au temps des colonies* (Paris: Balland, 1988); Yvonne Knibiehler and Régine Goutalier, *La femme au temps des colonies* (Paris: Stock, 1985). This image of course corresponds to what empire represented for many European men as well, as exemplified by Paul Gauguin's flight from bourgeois respectability in Paris to Tahiti. See Kenneth Ballhatchet, *Race, Class, and Sexuality under the Raj: Imperial Attitudes and Policies and Their Critics* (London: Weidenfeld and Nicolson, 1980).

28. Knibiehler and Goutalier, *La femme au temps des colonies*, 88–92.

29. It is also notable that French colonial authorities began to favor the settlement of white women in the empire during these years. See Alice Conklin, "Redefining 'Frenchness': Citizenship, Race Regeneration, and Imperial Motherhood in France and West Africa, 1914–1940," in Clancy-Smith and Gouda, *Domesticating the Empire: Race, Gender, and Family Life in French and Dutch Colonialism.*

30. For example, members of the *tirailleurs sénégalais* (founded in 1857) saw service in both Algeria and Morocco. Marc Michel, *L'Appel à l'Afrique: Contributions et réactions à l'effort de guerre en A.O.F. (1914–1919)* (Paris: Publications de la Sorbonne, 1982).

31. Charles Mangin, *La force noire* (Paris: Hachette, 1910).

32. For a useful comparison with the British experience in the use of imperial troops, see Philippa Levine, "Battle Colors: Race, Sex, and Colonial Soldiery in World War I," *Journal of Women's History* 9, no. 4 (winter).

33. There is some dispute about the traditional idea that the French used African troops as "cannon fodder" during World War I. Charles John Balesi has rejected this idea as a myth, arguing that African casualties were no higher than French ones in comparable circumstances. More recently, Joe Lunn has contended that African losses were three times higher than French losses. See Balesi, *From Adversaries to Comrades-in-Arms*; Myron Echenberg, *Colonial Conscripts: The Tirailleurs Sénégalais in French West Africa, 1850–1960* (Portsmouth, N.H.: Heinemann, 1991); Joe Lunn, *Memoirs of the Maelstrom: A Senegalese Oral History of the First World War* (Portsmouth, N.H.: Heinemann, 1999).

34. McMillan, *Housewife or Harlot*, 131–62; Françoise Thébaud, *La femme au temps de la guerre de 14* (Paris: Stock, 1986); Yvonne Delatour, "Le travail des femmes pendant la première guerre mondiale et ses conséquences sur l'évolution de leur rôle dans la société," *Francia*, vol. 2 (1974); Margaret H. Darrow, *French Women and the First World War: War Stories of the Home Front* (Oxford: Berg, 2000).

35. The fact that workers from China, an independent nation not part of the French empire, were lumped in with colonial subjects rather than European laborers reinforces the racialized character of France's use of colonial labor during the war.

36. John Horne, "Immigrant Workers in France during World War I," *French Historical Studies* 14, no. 1 (spring 1985); Jean Vidalenc, "La main d'oeuvre étrangère en france et la première guerre mondiale (1901–1926)," *Francia*, vol. 2 (1974); Bertrand Nogaro and Lucien Weil, *La Main-d'Oeuvre Étrangère et Coloniale pendant la Guerre* (Paris: PUF, 1926); Tyler Stovall, "Colour-blind France? Colonial Workers during the First World War," *Race and Class* 35, no. 2 (October–December 1993).

37. Jean-Jacques Becker, *Les français dans la grande guerre* (Paris: Éds. Robert Laffont, 1980).

38. This fits in with a broader polarization between a masculine front line and a feminine home front that arose during the war. See on this point Roberts, *Civilization without Sexes*, 21–32. That this was not literally true was demonstrated by, among other things, the hostile reaction of many French civilian men to the colonial newcomers.

39. Laura Lee Downs, "Women's Strikes and the Politics of Popular Egalitarianism in France, 1916–1918," in Lenard Berlanstein, ed., *Rethinking Labor History: Essays on Discourse and Class Analysis* (Urbana: University of Illinois Press, 1993); John Horne, *Labour at War: France and Britain, 1914–1918* (Oxford: Clarendon Press, 1991).

40. Archives Nationales Section Outre-Mer (hereafter ANSOM), SLOTFOM 10, carton 2, report of May 23, 1917.

41. See on this point Jean-Louis Robert, "Ouvriers et Mouvement ouvrier parisiens pendant la grande guerre et l'immédiate après-guerre," thèse, Doctorat d'État, Université de Paris-I, 1989, 9 vols.; vol. 2, "La segmentation ouvrière."

42. These included fears such labor would adversely affect their fertility, lower wage levels, or (in the case of antiwar activists) prolong the war. See Darrow, *French Women and the First World War,* 201–2.

43. It is nonetheless true that French women and colonial men shared the same nebulous status as people who were French subjects but not full French citizens. Moreover, just as women's labor in the war factories represented not so much the introduction as the redeployment of women in France's wage economy, so must one consider the use of colonial workers in the broader context of the exploitation of native labor in the colonies. If one rejects the division between France and its colonies in favor of a vision of Imperial France as an hierarchical but unified political formation, the parallels between white women and nonwhite men become more evident.

44. See Tyler Stovall, "Colour-blind France? Colonial Workers during the First World War," *Race and Class* 35, no. 2 (October–December 1993).

45. One of the primary reasons for this segregation was precisely the desire to avoid contacts between nonwhite men and French women.

46. On the *marraines de guerre,* see Grayzel, "Mothers, *Marraines* and Prostitutes"; Darrow, *French Women and the First World War,* 79–89.

47. Interview with Mbaye Khary Diagne, in Lunn, *Memoirs of the Maelstrom,* 173.

48. Interview with Mbaye Khary Diagne, 172–78.

49. Société historique de l'Armée de terre (hereafter SHAT), 7 N 997, "Rapport mensuel," July–August 1917.

50. Louise Delétang, *Journal d'une Ouvrière Parisienne pendant la Guerre* (Paris: Éds. Eugène Figuière, 1936), 50.

51. Lucie Cousturier, *Des inconnus chez moi* (Paris: Editions de la Sirène, 1920), 13.

52. "The Colored Americans in France," *The Crisis,* February 1919, 167–68.

53. SHAT, 7 N 1001, report of April 1917, letter of Mahmoud Ben Arrar.

54. SHAT, 7 N 997, Contrôle Postal Malgache, report of July–August, 1917.

55. SHAT, 1 N 1001, Rapport sur les opérations de la commission militaire de contrôle postal de Tunis, March 1918.

56. SHAT, 7 N 997, Contrôle Postal Indochinois, report of September 1917.

57. See on this point James F. McMillan, *Housewife or Harlot* (New York: St. Martin's Press, 1981), 101–9.

58. In August 1917, for example, the Indochinese army interpreter Dau cited a price of three francs. SHAT, 7 N 997, report of August 1917.

59. SHAT 7 N 997, Commission de Contrôle Postal, Marseilles, October 1917.

60. Lunn, *Memoirs of the Maelstrom,* 173.

61. SHAT 7 N 997, Contrôle Postal Indochinois, report of August 1917. The report noted that "severe sanctions would seem to be justified."

62. SHAT 7 N 997, Contrôle Postal Indochinois, letter from Ky Sum to Hong in Travinh.

63. SHAT 7 N 997, Commissión de Contrôle Postal de Marseille, report of December 1917.

64. Cited in Mireille Favre, "Un milieu porteur de modernisation: travailleurs et tirailleurs vietnamiens en France pendant la première guerre mondiale," thèse pour diplôme d'archiviste-paléographe, 2 vols., École nationale des Chartes, 1986, 535.

65. SHAT 7 N 997, reports of August–December 1917.

66. ANSOM, SLOTFOM 10, carton 2, "Rapport de l'Agent d'Administration Principal MASSEBEUF, Commandant Supérieur des Groupements de Travailleurs Indochinois, sur la situation matérielle et morale des indigènes de Saint-Médard-en-Jalles," May 28, 1917.

67. ANSOM, SLOTFOM 1, carton 8, "Contrôle Postal Malgâche," report of February 1918. See also Tyler Stovall, "The Color Line behind the Lines: Racial Violence in France during the Great War," *The American Historical Review* 103, no. 3 (1998).

68. *Humanité*, September 17, 1917, p. 1; ANSOM, SLOTFOM 10, carton 2, "ORDRE du Commandant du 16ème Indochinois," June 20, 1917.

69. ANSOM, DSM, carton 5, report of June 19, 1917.

70. Pamela Scully, "Rape, Race, and Colonial Culture: The Sexual Politics of Identity in the Nineteenth-Century Cape Colony, South Africa," *The American Historical Review* 100, no. 2 (April 1995); Hazel V. Carby, "'On the Threshold of Woman's Era': Lynching, Empire, and Sexuality in Black Feminist Theory," in Henry Louis Gates Jr., ed., *"Race," Writing, and Difference* (Chicago: University of Chicago Press, 1986).

71. SHAT, 7 N 1001, letter from C.Victor Fitoussi to Mme. Emma Boudarra, "Rapport sur les opérations postales, Tunis," March 1918.

72. Indochinese workers in particular were often portrayed as docile and feminine, thus well-suited to certain kinds of manual labor requiring dexterity and nimbleness. Favre, "Un milieu porteur de modernization," 46–47. On the broader view of colonized men as effeminate, see Mrinalini Sinha, *Colonial Masculinity: The "Manly Englishman" and the "Effeminate Bengali" in the Late Nineteenth Century* (Manchester: Manchester University Press, 1995).

73. SHAT, 7 N 997, Commission militaire de contrôle postal de Marseille, rapport mensuel, July–August 1917.

74. See the documents in SHAT 7 N 949, 10 N 63; also, G. Liens, "La Commission de censure et la Commission de contrôle postal à Marseille pendant la première guerre mondiale," *Revue d'Histoire moderne et contemporaine*, October–December 1971.

75. SHAT, 7 N 1001, letter from Tayeb Bananchi to Ali-el-Aiachi, April 1917.

76. The question of how archives are constituted and how that influences the writing of history has received much commentary recently. My point here is to suggest that certain archival materials are more attractive than others not just for political reasons but also having to do with their correspondance to the expectations

of the archivist. See, for example, Joan Scott, *Gender and the Politics of History* (New York: Columbia University Press, 1988); Natalie Davis, *Fiction in the Archives: Pardon Tales and their Tellers in Sixteenth Century France* (Stanford, Calif.: Stanford University Press, 1987).

77. SHAT, 7 N 997, "Liaisons," December 1917.

78. Paul Hammond, *French Undressing: Naughty Postcards from 1900 to 1920* (London: Jupiter Books, 1976).

79. Sarah Graham-Brown, *Images of Women: The Portrayal of Women in Photography of the Middle East, 1860–1950* (London: Quartet, 1988); Malek Alloula, *The Colonial Harem*, trans. Myrna and Wlad Godzich (Minneapolis: University of Minnesota Press, 1986).

80. SHAT, 7 N 1001, report of April 1917.

81. SHAT, 7 N 997, report of August 1917, letter of Son to Bien De.

82. Jody Blake, *Le tumulte noir: Modernist Art and Popular Entertainment in Jazz-Age Paris, 1900–1930* (University Park: Pennsylvania State University Press, 1999); Elizabeth Ezra, *The Colonial Unconscious: Race and Culture in Interwar France* (Ithaca, N.Y.: Cornell University Press, 2000); T. Denean Sharpley-Whiting, *Black Venus: Sexualized Savages, Primal Fears, and Primitive Narratives in French* (Durham, N.C.: Duke University Press, 1999); Petrine Archer-Straw, *Negrophilia: Avant-Garde Paris and Black Culture in the 1920s* (New York: Thames & Hudson, 2000).

# ⑯

# THE CHILDREN OF BELGIUM

*Georges Van Den Abbeele*

The subject of Belgium may seem somewhat odd in the context of Francophone studies and its general development as a kind of postcolonialism with a French accent. Not only is Belgium *not* a former colony of France, but it is of course itself a former colonial power, which under the rule of King Leopold II carried out one of the most harrowing and ruthless episodes in the colonialist exploitation of Central Africa. Moreover, discussions of contemporary Belgium tend to reduce all too quickly to the reportedly hopeless ethno-linguistic strife between Flemings and Walloons, highlighting the fact that Belgium is at best only *partially* a Francophone country.[1] Yet the social and historical conditions that generated this strife and the very being of this nation, whose modern existence dates from the (French) revolutions of 1789 and 1830, have everything to do with what Belgians perceive—positively *or* negatively—as the long-standing cultural and political hegemony of France. Indeed, the uncertain quality of Belgian identity has much to do with this derivative relation to France, an uncertainty not at all resolved by its current splintering into regional identities under the recent 1993 constitutional changes that have all but converted what was once a nation-state into a decentralized federation of autonomous regions and so-called "linguistic communities."[2]

A colleague who teaches at the University of Brussels reports how every year she asks her students to recite the Belgian national anthem, and every year they answer with the opening bars of *La Marseillaise*: "Allons, enfants de la patrie. . . ." Of course, the confusion is not abated by the actual Belgian anthem, whose very name, *La Brabançonne*, already betrays an affinity with the French national anthem. Multiple revisions and competing versions of the song (French and Flemish) have also contributed to its less than enthusiastic reception by the citizens of Belgium. The very first version of *La Brabançonne*, dating from 1830, nonetheless overtly displays its genealogical link with *La Marseillaise* right from the opening verse: "Dignes enfants de la Belgique [Worthy Children of Belgium]."[3]

But exactly whose "children" are these? Modern Belgium first appeared as a revolutionary entity, the États-Belgiques-Unis [United Belgian States], in 1789, as news of events in France was met in the old Hapsburg Netherlands by an open revolt against Austrian rule.[4] By 1795, however, this "Belgium" had been fully incorporated into the French Republic as its nine newest departments. The next twenty years saw the massive implantation of French political and legal reforms (such as the Napoleonic code of law) as well as cultural values (including, most importantly, the social prestige of the French language itself). By the time the Treaty of Vienna in 1815 decided to reunite these southern Netherlands with the United Provinces— which had been since the sixteenth century the dream of Dutch patriots whether in the independent North or the Hapsburg-controlled South— what was to become Belgium had become so identified with France that the redrawing of boundaries felt more like a violation of sorts, a violent sundering from the parent body within which its republican aspirations had found so cozy an abode. To top it all off, the final humiliation of Napoleonic grandeur had taken place in the very heart of Belgium, near the forever after famous town of Waterloo.

It took only until the next upheaval in Paris, the revolution of July 1830, for the Belgians to follow again the lead of their Gallic counterparts this time by rising up in arms and unfurling the French tricolor flag against what was now perceived as oppressive Dutch domination. The result was an international crisis amid Dutch fears of rampant insurrection and possible civil war, British worries about the secessionist Belgians reuniting with France, and the newly established July Monarchy in France anxious to avoid war with Holland and England while expressing strong sympathy for the Belgian cause (*and* while simultaneously concentrating its efforts on the imperialist conquest of Algeria just underway since June of 1830). The future of Belgium, including its exact geographic boundaries and form of government (constitutional monarchy) was to be decided not by the self-proclaimed provisional government in Brussels but by an international conference of the "great powers" held in London in November 1830. Despite pressure from Holland, Prussia, and even Russia to quell the rebellion and restore the house of Orange to power in the "southern Provinces," a unique compromise between Talleyrand and his British counterpart, Palmerston, proposed a new, independent Belgian state whose "neutrality" would be guaranteed by the British crown. And while this celebrated act of English generosity would become the stated reason for the United Kingdom's later involvement in the world wars of the twentieth century, its original purpose was quite precisely to assure itself and the rest of Europe that Belgium would never again become part of a France eager to export its republican values. At the same time, a British-style constitutional monarchy was imposed with a suitable king chosen from the ranks of the minor German princes: Leopold of Saxe-Coburg-Gotha, whose main virtue lay in his family ties to the royal houses of *both* France and England—indeed his nephew, Albert of Saxe-Coburg-Gotha, would become quite famous as the soon-to-be Queen Victoria's royal consort, "Prince Albert." It need only be mentioned in passing that the Belgian preference for the then Duke of Nemours, son of the new French king, Louis-Philippe, was ruled out of hand, thus forestalling a potential dynastic merging of Belgium with France. What is worth highlighting, though, is the precedent established here for "international cooperation" and diplomacy between the great powers of Europe to decide among themselves the fate of other countries, often without accepting or even consulting the desires of the populations of those countries. The form of the international conference to broker what are in fact the mutual interests of the great powers would become, of course, a major institution in fostering colonialist and neocolonialist expansion on a worldwide level. The London conference of 1830 would pave the way for other meetings like the infamous Berlin congress of 1884 at which the European powers felt at ease in carving up the map of Africa according to their mutually agreed-upon spheres of colonial influence.[5]

The result of such big power meddling is to underscore the weakness, vulnerability, and dependency of the affected nation, subjugated even in the very proclamation of its "independence." The "new" nation is thereby humbled and infantilized, appearing as a child among nations, one that still has to learn the "right lessons" in political, economic, and cultural self-governance before becoming a full partner on the stage of international affairs. The difficulties such small and weakened nations face, with their borders and institutions defined from the outside by more powerful nations, are well known and need not be rehearsed again here. More relevant to the concerns of this volume, those difficulties and weaknesses are readily attributed not to historical conditions but to the inherent or racial "character" of the nation's inhabitants. A concise rendition of this kind of ideological reduction can be found in Charles Baudelaire's vituperative remarks on the "general characteristics" of Belgium: "Homuncularity of Belgium. This Homunculus, the result of an alchemical operation by diplomacy, believes himself to be a man. The fatuousness of the infinitely little. The tyranny of the weak. Women. Children. Dogs. Belgium."[6] While Baudelaire correctly targets the artificiality of the construction ("an alchemical operation by diplomacy"), he tendentiously devalues the country by feminizing, infantilizing, and bestializing its inhabitants. Belgium is deluded in believing it belongs to the race of man when it is only a lesser human being, a "homunculus," perhaps not even human at all. On the other hand, belittled Belgium has historically elicited protective reactions, most notably from Great Britain during the Great War, when widespread English propaganda about Belgian babies killed or displaced by the fighting drummed up support for the war effort in the United Kingdom and eventually the United States and spurred the creation of relief organizations like the "Children of Flanders Rescue Committee" chaired by the noted American writer Edith Wharton.[7]

For Belgians too, diminution seems unofficially to have taken its place in the national iconography (necessarily factitious in a land whose newfound independence ironically revealed its utter lack of unifying traits, cutting across a disparate collection of provinces with no common language[8]). In particular, a plethora of child heroes from the impudently urinating "Manneken-Pis" (monumentalized as a fountain in downtown Brussels) to Charles de Coster's *Tyle Eulenspiegel* (a youthful trickster taken from German folk legend transmuted into the eponymous hero of this attempt at a national epic) to the ubiquitous figure of Tintin and others have come to emblematize the collective aspirations of this "petit pays." The Flemish word, *manneken*, literally "little man," far from bearing the mechanical or cosmetic connotations of its French/English derivative (mannequin), much less that of Baudelaire's homunculus, merely implies youth by its application of the enclitic of diminution, -en, to the word for man. It is not a word devoid of affection as its use by parents to their children actively attests. The *manneken* is a potential man, with the added value of being as yet unformed, innocent, and uncorrupted (virginal even) on the one hand; impishly contestatory of the status quo on the other, pissing on the feet of authority.[9]

In a similar vein, the major Belgian literary movement of the nineteenth century was called "Jeune Belgique," not because it set itself up against some "old" or "vieille Belgique" but because Belgium was still "young" as a nation and its literary tradition had yet to be invented.[10] Interestingly, this movement was principally composed of ethnically Flemish authors (Maurice Maeterlinck, Emile Verhaeren, Georges Rodenbach, etc.) writing in French and eager for recognition from Parisian literary elites, if not emigrating to the French capital itself to take up residence in what beckoned as the center of cultural value for them. This "assimilative" impulse represents a powerful current in Belgian culture since the 1830s. To be published in Paris remains a powerful sign of distinction for Belgian writers and intellectuals, even today. To pass for French is and has been for many the highest compliment, and the town of Menton on the French Riviera is the retirement community of choice for many Belgians.

Oddly, the first casualties of this desire for assimilation were the indigenous Walloon dialects of southern Belgium. If Belgium could not be part of France, at least its citizens should speak the prestige language of the anti-Dutch Revolution as well as any Frenchman. The school system, aided by textbooks to help eradicate "Belgicisms," encouraged a purist appreciation of the French language. Far from allowing any kind of creolization of the French language to set in, the Belgians systematically rooted out and destroyed all vestiges of their own regionalism. Ironically, the most respected, authoritative, and intimidating grammarian of modern French is the Belgian Maurice Grevisse, whose *Le bon usage* and its abbreviated counterpart, *Précis de la langue française*, remain today the indisputably standard reference works for correct French grammar not only in Belgium but in France itself and the entire Francophone world.[11]

Dialectically opposite this francophilic desire for assimilation is a francophobic obsession with rejecting and rebelling against what is seen as a form of foreign domination buttressed by a collaborationist ruling class, the "Franskiljon" or French-speaking Flemings, that has long espoused French "identity" to advance its own class interests. This tendency is also most deeply rooted in Flanders where it has been expressed through various forms of Flemish or so-called "Flamingant" nationalism.[12] Interestingly again, the most extreme "Flamingant" or anti-French sentiments have always been strongest in the westernmost part of Belgium (between the North Sea and the Schelde River), which (along with the northernmost part of France) comprised the territory ruled by the old Count of Flanders whose liege lord was none other than the king of France. Thus, what are now the Belgian provinces of East and West Flanders correspond to the *only* part of Belgium that traditionally belonged to France. All other lands east of the Schelde and now included in Belgium (Brabant, Hainaut, Liège; comprising over three-fourths of its current surface area) historically belonged to that uniquely medieval conglomerate known as the Holy Roman Empire. So that what is now the Francophone or Walloon part of Belgium never was part of France, except during the brief period of French Revolutionary and Napoleonic rule. A sign of sorts is to be found in classic Belgian literature of French expression, such as De Coster's novel, or cinema such as *Carnival in Flanders* (1935; directed by Jacques Feyder from a screenplay by Charles Spaak) where the violence of foreign oppression is referenced with regards to the Spanish "fury" of the sixteenth century. By way of contrast, what has come to be regarded as the Flemish national epic, Hendrik Conscience's *The Lion of Flanders* (1838) portrays the heroic resistance of Flemish burghers to *French* domination culminating in the so-called Battle of the Golden Spurs outside Kortrijk (Courtrai) in 1302, which saw the pride of French knighthood ignominiously cut to pieces after being drawn into a swamp where their heavy armor and chain mail proved to be their undoing. The affective nadir of these narratives inevitably involves violence against women and children, often with a child hero fighting back against insuperable odds either victoriously (as in the case of Tyle Eulenspiegel and Lamme Goedzak) or in heroic defeat. Conscience's version is especially inflammatory as French soldiers pillaging Bruges under the leadership of the evil Sieur de Châtillon break into an attic where a young boy desperately tries to defend his sister and aged mother with a pole-ax:

> He held up his weapon in a threatening attitude against the intruders, and his blue eyes flashed with the heroism of despair; while the muscles of his delicate cheeks were violently contracted to an expression at once terrible and ghastly. There he stood, like the miniature statue of some Grecian hero. . . .
>
> Recovered from their first surprise, the soldiers pushed rudely forward . . . ; serious opposition on the part of the boy they never for a moment contemplated. What, then, was their astonishment when, with his left foot planted firmly behind him, he fiercely brandished his ax, and defied them to come on.[13]

What follows is an especially brutal scene where the young boy is killed after successfully wounding a French soldier, followed by the rape and murder of the two women, who also desperately fight off the French but to no avail: "she sprang like a wild tigress on the soldier, twined her arms around him, and dug her nails, as if they had been claws, into his face, so that the blood streamed down his cheeks" (353). It is not hard to see how such passages could stir up Flemish passions, especially in a late nineteenth-century context where language difference was less a regional than a class difference as thousands of impoverished Flemish peasants went to work in Walloon coal mines under horrendous and humiliating conditions to feed the fortunes of the French-speaking bourgeoisie. Populist sentiment among Flemings was fed by an unusual and volatile mixture of worker activism and

Catholic orthodoxy until a firm sense of Flemish identity came to prevail over any particular allegiance to the nation-state of Belgium itself.[14]

The world wars with their repeated occupations of Belgium by Germany further intensified feelings of estrangement between what began to be called the two "linguistic communities." In the first world war, only a tiny slice of West Flanders remained under Belgian control but four years of muddy trench warfare around the Yser-valley towns of Ypres and Dixmüde left a lasting perception of uncomprehending Flemish conscripts being ordered into battle and to their deaths as cannon fodder by French-speaking officers. Again, a class difference perceived as a language (and ethnic) difference has lingered as a long-standing grievance to this day when ardent Flamingants still make what they call the "Yser pilgrimage" to commemorate their outrage— and this despite a historical record that impugns the validity of this myth.[15] By the time Belgium was again occupied by Germany during World War II, the collaborationist temptation was overwhelming as a way to undo Francophone domination once and for all. Not only did Flemish nationalists look to the German authorities for the creation of an autonomous Flemish state, but in Wallonia, the ultra-fascist Léon Degrelle also pushed for an independent state to be composed of southern Belgium and parts of northern France to revive the old Burgundian realm of the late Middle Ages.[16]

The topic has been fictively treated in recent years by Hugo Claus whose *The Sorrow of Belgium* (1983) is considered by many to be the greatest Belgian novel and best Dutch-language novel of the twentieth century, and the work is often compared favorably to that of Joyce or Proust. Flemish enthusiasm and pride has been subdued, however, by the somber revelation that the Nobel-nominated author resides in, of all places, southern France, an embarrassment Hugo Claus himself satirizes in his poem "Scoop."[17] *The Sorrow of Belgium* once again presents a child protagonist, the boy Louis Seynaeve, in a context of foreign occupation. The novel is set in the fictional town of Walle, which is transparent as Kortrijk (recalling the setting for Conscience's novel), less than five miles from the French border and only about twelve miles from the center of Lille (by far the closest city), yet Kortrijk is and has long been one of most zealously Flamingant towns, a tendency exemplified by the Seynaeve family portrayed in the novel.[18] The reality of World War II first enters the lives of the characters, not with the German Blitzkrieg but with the unwelcome incursion of French soldiers supposedly sent to help defend Belgium from Nazi aggression:

> The French are on our borders, just itching to get into Belgium. Ostensibly to forestall the Germans. . . . France has to protect her heart, and her heart lies

between Paris and Brussels. That's why the French are sure to come storming in on us one of these days with their tanks and their spahis and their filthy magazines. . . . Even on the first day [of the war], the French (who had been waiting for the chance since Napoleon) poured into our country.

They hung around Walle, none too eager to make a rush for the fortified line they were meant to establish on the River Dijle near Leuven, while the Belgians kept the Hun at bay. . . .

The French, their helmets askew, stinking of garlic and Pernod, assaulted Flemish widows and orphans, forced their way into our homes without knocking, demanded drink and women, yes, just as if we were still living in the Middle Ages.[19]

From the point of view of Walle's fictive inhabitants, the "war" ends when German troops finally arrive and restore order. The clear references to Conscience's novel mark the French "protective" incursion as a violation, in cultural as well as military terms: the multiracial presence of colonial troops (spahis), dreams of empire (Napoleon), pornography, excessive eating and drinking, slovenliness, cowardliness, fornication, forcible entry, and rape. Collaboration with the German occupation never looked so good, and Claus's novel through the coming-of-age eyes of its young protagonist mordantly reveals the depth and extent of this national temptation. As if this controversial archaeology were not enough, Claus adds salt to the wound by the Frenchified Flemish spoken by his most Flamingant characters. The purist Flemings cannot seem to avoid speaking what often appears as a mixed French–Dutch patois. Incidentally, this "indigenous" Flemish (like the Walloon dialect) has also disappeared before the strict school-enforced use of correct, official Dutch (known as *Algemeen Nederlands*), so that Belgium's official languages today are in fact two different *foreign* languages.[20] Recapturing the old *Vlaamse taal* of the 1940s is not the least of the novel's literary achievements even as this greatest of Flemish novels proceeds to nothing less than the unrepentant deconstruction of the core hypocrisies behind Flemish nationalism. Arch-discontents with French civilization, Flemish nationalists appear to be reactive in their ideology, driven by an anti-French sentiment without which the *Vlaamse beweging* could not exist: one character in Claus's novel defines the "height of Flemish nationalism" as "starving to death with a loaf of French bread under your arm" (597). Finally, it is important to note that the novel's title refers generally to the "Sorrow of *Belgium*" rather than that specific to Flanders, even though at no point does the action ever leave Flemish territory. Moreover, the specific expression "sorrow of Belgium" appears in the text applied to a young girl Louis sees while on a bus to a fascist rally, then to himself as a boy, before it becomes the title of the short story he publishes that launches his writing career and brings the plot to a close. "Le jour de gloire est arrivé," the narrator writes in French, citing this second line of *La Marseillaise*, as Louis leaves for a celebratory dinner (p. 596). In any case, Belgium per se (not Flanders, not Wallonia)—as an affect at least if not a nation-state—here again appears in the persona of a child.

While the contrast between assimilated Franskiljon and separatist Flamingant appears more extreme, a similar tension can also be registered in Wallonia and underscores in both regions an overdetermined relation to France not unlike what is found in many of its former colonies. French influence in Belgian affairs also remains quite remarkable and unusual. In 1996, the Francophone Belgian author Pierre Mertens published in Paris a novel highly satirical of the Belgian royal family.[21] In anger and outrage, the latter sued the Belgian author *and* the French publisher for libel in a *French* court of law. Unbelievably, the French court sided with the Belgian royals and required Mertens and Seuil to excise several of the more inflammatory pages from his novel, effectively censoring it. The ruling is all the more ironic if one recalls the long history of French literature, especially during the *ancien régime*, when many refractory books were safely published abroad (the Netherlands, in particular) to evade the hands of French censors. Yet, in the last decade of the twentieth century, what was fundamentally a Belgian censorship dispute was settled in a French court.

Another recent case of making strange bedfellows with the French can be found in that curious *entente* between the far-right parties of France and Belgium, i.e., Le Pen's National Front Party and the extreme Flamingant Vlaams Blok. Inside Belgium, the Vlaams Blok resists all things Francophone in the interests of the Flemish "nation," yet abroad it consistently makes common cause with the Front National in such bodies as the European Parliament.[22] And taking a tip from the Front National's mobilization of anti-immigrant sentiments, the Vlaams Blok in recent elections has softened its militant separatism to make the immigrant issue the cornerstone of its appeal to voters. The result has been a renewed success for the Vlaams Blok not only in Flanders but also in the Francophone districts of Brussels (in 1999, it became the capital's dominant Flemish party).[23] One might also wonder why the Vlaams Blok feels the need to maintain a French version of their "national website" if not to seek the solidarity of the French extreme right. Interestingly, Walloon separatism (which also exists, most typically as a call to (re)unite with France) also belies its right-wing basis with such proclamations as "Better French than Red" uttered by Louis Michel, president of the Walloon Liberal Party, in a 1996 interview with the French daily *Le Figaro*.[24]

No discussion of a Belgium understood in its diversely "postcolonial" relation to France can fail to recall that greatest example of both imitation and rivalrous divergence from France, namely the sordid history of the Belgian colonial adventure in Africa. The topic is enormous, of course, and I can only indicate a few touchstones here. The specter of a child-nation attempting to lord it over another people through an infantilizing ideology issued in the overt paternalism of Belgian colonial rule, which marks it quite distinctly from French assimilationist and English associationist policies. This paternalism was at first incarnated in the figure of King Leopold II who personally ruled the so-called Congo Free State as his own private domain before ultimately "willing" it over to the Belgian government on his deathbed.[25] Interestingly, the original 1884 accords of Leopold's front organization, the International Association of the Congo, granted "preferred rights" to France in case the association ever needed to sell off its possessions.[26] Throughout, the self-proclaimed "humanitarian" aim of the colonial enterprise in the Congo was to "save" the Congolese from a variety of perceived or imaginary threats, from the "Arab" slavetraders evoked by the morally outraged Leopold to the communist menace supposedly posed by Patrice Lamumba (and that motivated his CIA-orchestrated murder), in sum over time cynically to save the Congo from itself as one of Africa's most populous and resource-rich countries. At pains, however, to differentiate themselves from their Gallic brethren, the Belgians also avowed a refusal to create a privileged or assimilated elite as their excuse for in fact utterly neglecting the educational needs of the Congolese.[27] The result was the infamous "leadership vacuum" at the time of Congolese independence in 1960, and that country's consequent vulnerability to neocolonialist meddling by the United States and France as well as Belgium, particularly in sustaining the pernicious and ruinous rule of Mobutu until 1997.[28]

But again it is a literary work of sorts that most explicitly demonstrates the ideology of Belgian colonial administration as the child of a child. The work I have in mind is *Tintin au Congo*, the second in the long series of Tintin comic books written by Hergé (Georges Remi). First published in 1930, *Tintin au Congo* stages its child hero on a quest to save the Congo (once again!) this time from, of all people, Al Capone and his Chicago gangsters who wish to control the Congo's diamond trade (historically the reason for Antwerp's renewed wealth in the twentieth century). The Africans in the story are all too stereotypically portrayed as lazy, cowardly, childlike, and easily manipulable by the young boy and his little dog, Milou, who after saving the "poor" Congolese from the American threat, join in some big game hunting and find what can only be called "original" ways to kill elephants, rhinoceri, and buffalo before returning to Belgium and further adventures. The final two leaves of the album are the most absurd in their depiction of various Africans bemoaning Tintin's departure by exaggerated weeping and wailing as well as idolizing fetish statuettes of Tintin and Milou. Despite a history that implicates Tintin (and author Hergé) not only in racism but anti-Semitism as well, this child figure remains one of the most prevalent Belgian icons: the boy reporter whose very innocence and naïveté is the source of his often witty ability to overcome evil and adversity (much the way Belgium during the same period likes to think of itself as internationalist and championing the rights of the small and the weak).[29] Indeed, the cultural sway of Tintin has been so great as to achieve what no other child of Belgium has done, namely to become a virtual emblem of *French* as well as Belgian identity, to the point that Charles de Gaulle is said to have remarked to André Malraux that Tintin was his only "international rival."[30]

Finally, and sadly, I cannot close the discussion of this overdetermined image of the child as icon of a nation with very little else in the way of cohesive bonds without referring to the horrifyingly uncanny scandal of the Belgian children during the height of what was already a constitutional crisis in 1996 with the newly circumscribed autonomous regions all but ready to split the country apart. Tapping into this generalized anxiety, a best-selling novel described an apocalyptic scenario for a Franco-Flemish war that would turn Brussels into a Sarajevo-like battleground.[31] But rather than issuing in any such anticipated demise of Belgium along separatist lines, the reality ushered in by the truly horrific revelations of the Dutroux pedophile scandal in late 1996 inspired mass protests by Belgians of *all* classes, ethnicities, and language groups along with demands for a renewed responsibility (a "new political culture") in state functions (police, judiciary, etc.) that had all but decentralized themselves out of existence.[32]

The events began as a sordid enough crime story, a child abduction case in August 1996 that appeared successfully resolved when fourteen-year-old Laetitia Delhez was rescued and the perpetrator, Marc Dutroux, arrested all within a week. Further inquiries, however, revealed ever wider and increasingly more sinister scenarios that placed Dutroux at the center of other child kidnappings orchestrated by a shadowy pedophile ring responsible for an extensive traffic in young girls resulting in their prostitution, pornographic exploitation, and murder. The monstrosity of these crimes took on an entirely new and disturbing dimension when the bodies of two eight-year-olds, Julie Lejeune and Melisssa Russo, were found buried on a property owned by Dutroux, where they had apparently starved to death while Dutroux himself was already in police custody (on unrelated car theft charges). It further came out that the police had already previously searched the premises on more than one occasion, incredibly without discovering the captive girls. Police incompetence was doubled by judicial oversight, which had led to Dutroux's "conditional release" from prison back in 1992 after having served only three years of a thirteen-year sentence for pedophilia and statutory rape. The horror of such outrageous police, judicial, and ministerial incompetences that led to the needless death of Dutroux's captives led many to believe that the evil Dutroux and his growing list of accomplices were in actuality "protected" by various higher-ups, with suspicions going all the way to high-ranking magistrates, government ministers, and members of the royal family.

The crisis in confidence reached its head on October 14, 1996, when the *Cours de cassation* (the Belgian equivalent to the Supreme Court) acted to dismiss the justice leading the inquiry into the Dutroux case, Jean-Marc Connerotte, for his having been present at a spaghetti dinner among whose other guests were Sabine Dardenne and Laetitia Delhez, the only two survivors of Dutroux's kidnappings. From a legal and technical standpoint, Connerotte had according to Belgian law broken his magisterial imperative of impartiality by interacting socially with victims of a crime under his jurisdiction. Popular reaction to the *Cour de cassation*'s "spaghetti ruling" was furious, however, and corroborated the Belgian public's absolute loss of confidence in its state officials and institutions. For while Judge Connerotte may have been technically in error for attending the dinner, he was widely perceived to be one of the few officials with any credibility actively seeking to get to the bottom of this apparently bottomless scandal. The swiftness of the action against Conerotte also contrasted mightily with the bureaucratic slowness and incomprehensible ineptitude that marked the pursuit of Dutroux himself and his cohorts. Conditions equivalent to a general strike reigned in Belgium in the ensuing days with many factories and most public transportation services ground to a halt. On Sunday, October 20, some 320,000 demonstrators wearing white in tribute to the innocence of the child victims walked silently through the streets of Brussels in muted protest of the Belgian state's apparent inability to defend even the lives of its children. The sheer size of what came to be known as the "White March" (one-third of a million out of a total population of only nine million!) and impressive diversity (Flemings, Walloons, immigrants, Belgians from every class, background, language, and region) recalled the kinds of popular manifestations that marked the very birth of Belgium in 1789 and 1830.

And it was an appeal specifically to the entity of *Belgium* that the White March orchestrated, in contrast to the discourses of separatism and decentralization that had drawn its political class close to a perilous dismantling of the state, which the Dutroux crisis made painfully evident. The White March visibly manifested what polls had long and consistently demonstrated, namely that over 90 percent of Belgians (in Flanders as well as Wallonia) opposed any separation of the country.[33] Energizing the White March, moreover, was the fear of a massive conspiracy that threatened not only the children of Belgium but also the child that is the nation of Belgium itself. Belgian nationalism again found its affective trigger in the defense of a land that is not father or mother but defenseless child. But this time, the threat to the nation lay, firstly, in the horrendous abuse and death of *real* children not just their iconic representation. Second, the danger came not from some foreign or external aggressor (France, Germany, or whoever) but from *within* the little kingdom itself. Whence the scandal of the Dutroux scandal. And while the White March can thus be seen to represent at long last a determined loss of innocence in Belgian political process, it remains to be seen whether that surge of populist sentiment will translate into effective institutional changes.

There is, above all, a tremendous risk of misrecognition here. The danger to Belgium and its "children" should not simply be incarnated in the sole figure of Marc Dutroux no matter how heinous he or his shadowy accomplices and/or protectors may be. While the Belgian Parliament's officially constituted Commissions of Inquiry into the matter failed to reveal much more than low-level "protections" or malicious negligence on the part of those who were in a position to track Dutroux's crimes, what became self-evident was the inexcusable lack of coordination or even basic comunication between the officials and institutions involved, i.e., the various branches of the police, gendarmes, magistrates, and prosecutors in different locales. Such disarray is not an anomaly or exception, though. It is the sad result of decades of decentralizing legislation on the part of the Belgian state, legislation it should be noted urged along not only by the loud voices of separatism and "autonomy" but also less spectacularly but just as effectively by the forces of globalization and capitalist development. The lowering of national borders/trade barriers has long been high on the Belgian political agenda since World War II, and Brussels has been the nerve center of European cooperation since well before the EU and going back to the predecessor of the Common Market, the European Coal and Steel Community, which enlarged the Benelux trade agreements to include France and Germany.[34] The result of these developments has been the extraordinary wealth of contemporary Belgium, whose central location has allowed it to capitalize on the freed movement of goods and services across international borders. Ironically, this same period saw the erection of internal borders *within* Belgium such as the linguistic frontier or the legislative limits on what constitutes the Brussels metropolitan area (now autonomous region). The easing of restrictions on economic movement has come in tandem with a narrowing of the reach of many state and public institutions.[35] But this neoliberal paradise also has its vices, for the very same conditions that have enabled the commercial prosperity of Belgium have plagued that nation with stupendous increases in crime and corruption. The very same rules that permit free trading in licit goods over borders also facilitate illicit trafficking in arms, automobiles, drugs, . . . and human beings.[36] The entrapment and prostitution of third-world women in Belgium was an issue well before the Dutroux affair, yet failed to elicit significant popular or political reaction.[37] Before Dutroux's horrendous crimes, outrageous acts like the 1991 assassination of a government minister (Albert Cools) or the three-year rampage of the gang known as the "tueurs de Brabant" who terrorized shopping centers in central Belgium went ineffectively investigated and suspiciously unresolved, yet no great outcry emerged. Similar scandals can be found, of course, in other first-world nations (where prostitution or pedophile rings figure all too commonly as news items), not to mention the massive and shameful trafficking in human beings that occurs worldwide (first-world as well as third-world, "developed" nations as well as "developing" ones) with scarcely a whimper of concern.

Significantly, one of the foremost critiques of this traffic in human beings that marks the "new" Europe is the Belgian film, *The Promise* (directed by Jean-Pierre and Luc Dardenne). The film, released less than a year after the Dutroux affair, features once more the story of a young boy, Igor, who aids an "illegally immigrated" African woman in her struggle with his evil father, Roger, responsible among other matters for the death of her husband. The Dardenne brothers' *cinéma vérité* style unhesitatingly exposes the generalized racism and institutional corruption that supports and encourages the unconscionable activities of traffickers like Roger—or like Marc Dutroux.

Yet, in the fall of 2003, over seven years after his arrest, Marc Dutroux has still not been brought to trial as lawyers and forensic experts repeatedly petition for delays to help prepare what can only be the biggest court case in Belgian history. His pedophilic crimes as affectively toxic to Belgium as regicide was to the France of the *ancien régime*, one can only wonder what punishment could ever fit the sheer *démesure* of Dutroux's deeds. At the same time, the protracted anticipation of his trial and conviction reactively maintains the fragile identity of this little country as aggressed child, an identity as we have seen that was forged out of its deeply conflicted history with the civilization of France. And this French "connection" still readily comes right to the surface in renditions such as the following: "Throughout history, the people of the largest city in the Wallonian province of Belgium, known as Charleroi, had been forced to engage in countless struggles against French domination in order to preserve their way of life. Recently, the people of Charleroi and its surrounding towns have been faced with a new enemy. Marc Dutroux. . . ."[38] But if we are thus uncomfortably forced to conclude that the figure of Dutroux can perversely be said to be keeping the identity of Belgium alive, then understanding itself in terms other than a child victim of foreign—especially French—aggression might well be the only chance for Belgium to emerge as something other than a federation in fragments.


## NOTES

I wish to thank the following agencies for their support in undertaking the research for this study: National Endowment for the Humanities, University oif California Humanities Research Institute, Davis Humanities Institute, Oregeon Humanities Center, University of California at Davis Committee on Research.

1. But is this anomaly not one in appearance only? Are not *all* Francophone countries in point of fact only partially so, either because there was an indigenous language in conflict with the imposition of French (Africa, Southeast Asia) or a creole alternative to French (West Indies, Réunion) or a territorial cohabitation with a rival tongue (Canada, Switzerland)? Despite the role of the French language as the common denominator of the "Francophone" world, everywhere in that world French exists in a tension with some linguistic alternative.

2. For an overview of the changes, see Rolf Falter, "Belgium's Peculiar Way to Federalism," in *Nationalism in Belgium: Shifting Identities, 1780–1995*, ed. Kas Deprez and Louis Vos (New York: St. Martin's Press, 1998), 177–97; and *Tweedracht maakt macht. Wegwijs in het federale België* (Tielt: Lannoo, 1994). Also, see *Belgique: la force de la désunion*, ed. Alain Dieckhoff (Brussels: Editions Complexe, 1996).

3. On the history of *La Brabançonne*, see Anne Morelli, "La construction des symboles 'patriotiques' de la Belgique, de ses régions et de ses communautés," in *Les grands mythes de l'histoire de Belgique, de Flandre et de Wallonie*, ed. Anne Morelli (Brussels: Editions Vie Ouvrière, 1995), 191–202; and Francis Martens, "La Belgique en chantant," in *Belgique toujours grande et belle*, ed. Antoine Pickels and Jacques Sojcher (Brussels: Editions Complexe, 1998), 19–40.

4. The classic history of early Belgium remains Henri Pirenne's monumental seven-volume *Histoire de la Belgique* (Brussels: Lambertin, 1932). For a recent

treatment of the international climate surrounding Belgian independence, see Jo Ellen Kerksiek, *The Great Powers and the Peace of Europe: Britain, France, and the Belgian Revolution, 1830–1839*, Ph.D. dissertation (University of Kansas, 1993). On the mythology of foreign aggression as a cornerstone of Belgian nationalism, I highly recommend Jean Stengers, "Le mythe des dominations étrangères dans l'historiographie belge," *Revue belge de philologie et d'histoire* LIX (1981): 382–401.

5. Ironically, the Berlin Conference addressed a new Belgian situation, specifically that represented by Leopold II's claims on the Congo. See Adam Hochschild, *King Leopold's Ghost: A Story of Greed, Terror, and Heroism in Colonial Africa* (New York: Houghton Mifflin, 1998), 84–87.

6. Charles Baudelaire, *Pauvre Belgique, Oeuvres complètes*, ed. Marcel Ruff (Paris: Seuil, 1968), 685, ft. 226; my translation.

7. See Shari Benstock, *No Gifts from Chance: A Biography of Edith Wharton* (New York: Scribner's Sons, 1994), 307–44.

8. This diversity of Belgium, coupled with the circumstances of its independence, make the country a kind of intellectual scandal for theorists of nationalism such as Benedict Anderson (*Imagined Communities* [London: Verso, 1983]) or Ernest Gellner (*Nations and Nationalism* [Ithaca, N.Y.: Cornell University Press, 1983]), for whom nationhood is dependent upon a commonality of language if not ethincity. The problem is that studies of nationalism take the relative homogeneity and political consolidation of France, England, and Germany as the paradigm for a nation-state, relegating all others to the status of problematic exception. The reality of the world, however, would suggest otherwise, that most nations are highly heterogeneous and polyglot. And, it need scarcely be said, that the desire of the great European powers to impose their homogeneous concept of nationhood on the rest of the world remains at the heart of countless contemporary conflicts from Bosnia to the Middle East and the Indian subcontinent. For a counterargument with respect to Belgium, see my "No Joking Matter: the 'Other' Belgium," *Social Identities* 7, no. 4 (2001): 511–24.

9. The origins of the famous *Manneken-Pis* statue in Brussels are lost in legend, although the story I learned as a child is as good as any. According to this story, the Holy Roman Emperor and King of Spain, Charles V, was greeted during his entry into Brussels by a small boy urinating in front of his carriage. Rather than be angered or offended, the noble lord found humor in the episode and ordered a statue made of the boy in the form of a fountain.

10. On the history of this literary movement, see Raymond Trousson, *La légende de la Jeune Belgique* (Brussels: Académie de langue et de littérature française, 2000). It would be interesting to compare the dynamics of Jeune Belgique to similar movements in other Francophone milieus, such as the writers and thinkers surrounding the journal *Jeune Afrique*, or even *Présence africaine*. What is striking is the continuing importance of the French language and Parisian publishing venues even while an independentist ideology motivates the content of the writing.

11. Maurice Grevisse's *Le bon usage*, first published in 1936 by Editions Duculot in Gembloux, Belgium went into its thirteenth edition in 2001. The shorter *Pré-*

*cis de grammaire française* also published by Duculot is now in its thirtieth edition. Alongside Grevisse's monumental work for the cause of French purism, it is worth noting such publications as *Chasse aux belgicismes* by Joseph Hanse, Albert Doppagne, and Hélène Bourgeois-Gielen (Brussels: Fondation Charles Plisnier, 1971) that specifically targeted "incorrect," i.e., regional, expressions for elimination. Interestingly, such "negative" grammars also remain as a significant record *a contrario* of the linguistic legacy of the old Walloon dialects. Even more recently, and as a sign of the times, these same Belgicisms are being collected as part of the Walloon patrimony, such as Georges Lebouc's *Le belge dans tous ses états: dictionnaire de belgicismes, grammaire et prononciation* (Paris: Bonneton, 1998) or the Internet site, http://www. chez.com/belgicismes/dico.

12. It is not the least of ironies here that the French-speaking Flemings are called by the *Flemish* word "Franskiljon" while the *French* term "Flamingant" is applied to hard-core Flemish nationalists.

13. Hendrik Conscience, *De Leeuw van Vlaanderen*, ed. J. M. Devos (Amsterdam: L. J. Veen's Uitgeversmaatschappij, 1961), 164–65; English translation from *The Lion of Flanders* (New York: P. F. Collier & Son, n.d.), 350–51.

14. The literature on the historical development of the Flemish movement is vast, and given its political stakes, unsurprisingly rife with contestation and disputes. Good introductions in English can be found in Aristide Zolberg, "The Making of Flemings and Walloons: Belgium, 1830–1914," *Journal of Interdisciplinary History* 5, no. 2 (1974), 179–235; Carl Strikwerda, *A House Divided: Catholics, Socialists, and Flemish Nationalists in Nineteenth-Century Belgium* (Lanham, Md.: Rowman & Littlefield, 1997); and *The Flemish Movement: A Documentary History, 1780–1990*, ed. Theo Hermans (London: Athlone, 1992). There is at least one notable consistency worth noting in the context of an essay like this one: the repeated failure and relative weakness of various pan-Dutch movements (i.e., those making common cause between Flanders and the Netherlands) speaks loudly to the *reactive* dimension of the Flemish movement, driven by an anti-French rather than a pro-Dutch sentiment. See Jean Stengers, "Belgian National Sentiment," in *Modern Belgium*, ed. Marina Boudart, Michel Boudart, and René Bryssinck (Palo Alto, Calif.: Society for the Promotion of Science and Scholarship, 1990), 94–95.

15. Christine Van Everbroeck, "Une conscience née dans le feu": divergences à propos du pourcentage de victimes flamandes de la Première Guerre mondiale," in *Les grands mythes de l'histoire de Belgique, de Flandre et de Wallonie*, ed. Anne Morelli (Brussels: Editions Vie Ouvrière, 1995), 233–42.

16. Martin Conway, *Collaboration in Belgium: Léon Degrelle and the Rexist Movement, 1940–1944* (New Haven, Conn.: Yale University Press, 1993).

17. Hugo Claus, "Scoop," in *Belgique toujours grande et belle*, ed. Antoine Pickels and Jacques Sojcher (Brussels: Editions Complexe, 1998), 421.

18. The counterintuitive finding that border areas tend to be more strongly nationalist than those in a country's interior, their proximity to a foreign land triggering a stronger need to assert their national identity, is the fascinating discovery

made by Peter Sahlins in his *Boundaries: The Making of France and Spain in the Pyrenees* (Berkeley: University of California Press, 1989).

19. Hugo Claus, *Het Verdriet van België* (Amsterdam: De Bezige Bij, 1983), 300–304; *The Sorrow of Belgium*, trans. Arnold J. Pomerans (Harmondsworth, U.K.: Penguin, 1990), 239–45.

20. Three, if one counts the small Germanophone community to the East, legally on a par with the Flemish and Francophone linguistic communities since 1989. On the standardization of Flemish into Dutch, see Kas Deprez, "The Dutch Language in Flanders," in Hermans, *The Flemish Movement*, 416–29; and "The Language of the Flemings," in Deprez and Vos, *Nationalism in Belgium*, 96–109.

21. Pierre Mertens, *Une paix royale* (Paris: Seuil, 1995). I discuss the particularities of this case of transnational censorship in my "The Persecution of Writing: Revisiting Strauss and Censorship," *Diacritics* 27, no. 3 (summer 1997): 3–17.

22. See Jos Bouveroux, "Nationalism in Present-Day Flanders," in Deprez and Vos, *Nationalism in Belgium*, 209–18; and Hans-Georg Betz, *Radical Right-Wing Populism in Western Europe* (New York: St. Martin's Press, 1994), especially 19–21, 136–39.

23. Bouveroux, "Nationalism in Present-Day Flanders," 214.

24. *Le Figaro* (October 29, 1996); see discussion and reactions to Michel's statement in *La Libre Belgique* (October 30, 1996, p. 4). Interestingly, Louis Michel subsequently became prime minister in the current Belgian government headed by Guy Verhofstadt, the long-time leader of the Flemish liberal party, the *VLD*, so that the current Belgian "coalition" government is a coalition of neoliberals and separatists, none of whom have any interest in strengthening the central state. It should also be duly noted that, while both Michel and Verhofstadt are clearly on the political right, both remain staunch advocates of parliamentary democracy and are extremely anxious to distinguish themselves from the extreme right-wing and neofascist ideology of groups like the Vlaams Blok. At the same time, they readily albeit quietly borrow ideas and themes from the Vlaams Blok when it benefits their political or electoral agenda. The situation here again mirrors that of France where "mainstream" political leaders likewise take over certain Lepenist views while maintaining theor public distance from the Front National.

25. The best recent discussion of Leopold's rule in the Congo remains Adam Hochschild, *King Leopold's Ghost*.

26. A copy of this document can be found in Adolphe Lejeune-Choquet, *Histoire militaire du Congo* (Brussels: Maison d'édition Alfred Castaigne, 1906), 43.

27. Jean-Paul van Bellinghen, "Belgium and Africa," in *Modern Belgium*, ed. Marina Boudart, Michel Boudart, and René Bryssinck (Palo Alto, Calif.: Society for the Promotion of Science and Scholarship, 1990), 159.

28. In addition to his well-known friendships with successive French and American presidents, Mobutu also engaged in often grotesque imitation of various Belgian kings, in particular Leopold II's naming of landmarks after himself and rapacious diversion of state resources for personal luxuries such as a yacht and villa

on the French Riviera (see Hochschild, 304). Thierry Michel's documentary *Mobutu, King of Zaire* (35mm; Belgium, 1999) also has some remarkable footage of Mobutu imitating King Baudoin's dress and personal style. The Congolese imitation/rejection of Belgium would thus present a second-order mirroring of Belgium's similar relation to France.

29. Of all the revisionist entries in Anne Morelli's controversial collective volume, *Les grands myths de l'histoire de Belgique, de Flandre et de Wallonie*, the article that sustained the most outrage and fury was Joël Kotek's piece, "Tintin, un mythe belge de remplacement" (281–92), which clearly explicated the less than innocent profile of that comic book child at the hands of his Rexist-leaning creator. While the deconstruction of other Belgian myths could be begrudgingly tolerated, Tintin appeared sacrosanct by many, who strongly felt the cartoon icon should not be subjected to such critical scrutiny (from a personal conversation with Anne Morelli).

30. André Malraux, *Le Miroir des Limbes* (Paris: Gallimard, 1976), 629.

31. Jacques Neirynck, *Le siège de Bruxelles* (Paris: Desclée de Brouwer, 1996).

32. The most serious and sustained intellectual reflection on the Dutroux scandal is the collective volume, *L'affaire Dutroux: la Belgique malade de son système*, ed. Yves Cartuyvels et al. (Brussels: Editions Complexe, 1997). For a concise and even-handed overview of the complex series of events surrounding the revelations about Dutroux as well as the stunning number of scandals that have plagued Belgium in the last several decades, see Dirk Barrez, *Het land van de 1000 schandalen* (Zelik: Roularta, 1997). Also see Marcel Paquet, *Le fascisme blanc: mésaventures de la Belgique* (Paris: Editions de la différence, 1998) and Claude Moniquet, *Les dossiers noirs de la Belgique* (Neuilly-sur-Seine: Michel Lafon, 1999). A good introduction in English to the entire Dutroux affair can be found by Rachael Bell at the website www.crimelibrary.com/serial3/marcdutroux/html.

33. Alain Dieckhoff, "Présentation," in *Belgique: la force de la désunion* (Brussels: Editions Complexe, 1996), 16.

34. The earliest formulation of this internationalism as a specific form of Belgian nationalism appears in the works of Henri de Man: "Belgien als Europäisches Problem," (1942) in M. Brélaz, ed., *Henri de Man: le "Dossier Léopold III" et autres documents sur la période de la seconde guerre mondiale* (Geneva: Antipodes, 1989), 272–76; *Réflexions sur la paix* (Brussels: Toison d'Or, 1942); *Au delà du nationalisme* (Geneva: Cheval ailé, 1946). De Man repeatedly sees European unification as the key ironically to maintaining a strong and independent Belgium (as opposed to its fragmentation along ethnolinguistic lines). It is, of course, equally ironic that it was none other than his chief political rival, Paul-Henri Spaak, who most aggressively pursued De Man's theoretical vision of a Europe "beyond nationalism" into the practical reality of the various consortia and "common markets" (i.e., De Man's "Zollverein") that ultimately led to the advent of the European Union.

35. The one exception being the seemingly limitless growth in the *social* reach of political parties through their affiliated institutions (credit unions, insurance

providers, professional organizations, etc.), a process variously referred to as "particracy" or the "pillarization" of Belgian society. For an extensive discussion and critique, see Paquet, especially his chapter on "Particratie et fascisme blanc," in *Le fascisme blanc*, pp. 139–89 and *passim*.

36. That any one of these forms of criminal commerce can cross into any other is readily evidenced if we remember again that Julie and Melissa starved to death while Dutroux was in prison for his involvement in an automobile trafficking ring, parallel but not immediately related to his simultaneous deeds trafficking children.

37. One of the prime voices calling attention to the plight of foreign women forced to work as prostitutes in Belgium was the late King Baudoin himself, yet this protest once again remained solely on a moral level without translating into any effective political action or even analysis.

38. Rachael Bell, "Marc Dutroux: The Child-Killer Who Slipped through the System," (accessed at) www.crimelibrary.com/serial3/marcdutroux/index.html.

# FURTHER READING

## GENERAL

Apter, Emily. *Continental Drift: From National Characters to Virtual Subjects*. Chicago: University of Chicago Press, 1999.

Green, Mary Jean, et al., eds. *Postcolonial Subjects: Francophone Women Writers*. Minneapolis: University of Minnesota Press, 1996.

Haut Conseil de la Francophonie. *L'état de la francophonie dans le monde*. Paris: La Documentation française, 1986–2001. (Published every year or two, these official publications of the HCF provide the best statistical information on French language use throughout the world, who speaks it, how it is spoken, in what specific contexts, etc.)

Lebovics, Herman. *True France: The Wars Over Cultural Identity, 1900–1945*. Ithaca, N.Y.: Cornell University Press, 1992.

Lionnet, Françoise. *Postcolonial Representation: Women, Literature, Identity*. Ithaca, N.Y.: Cornell University Press, 1995.

Rosello, Mireille. *Declining the Stereotype: Ethnicity and Representation in French Cultures*. Hanover, N.H.: University Press of New England, 1998.

Sherzer, Dina, ed. *Cinema, Colonialism, Postcolonialism: Perspectives from the French and Francophone World*. Austin: University of Texas Press, 1996.

Stovall, Tyler. *France Since the Second World War*. Harlow, U.K.: Longman, 2002.

Walker, Keith. *Countermodernism and Francophone Literary Culture: The Game of Slipknot*. Durham, N.C.: Duke University Press, 1999.

## PART I: THE INTELLIGENTSIA AND NEW CONCEPTIONS OF FRENCH IDENTITY

Badiou, Alain. *Conditions*. Paris: Seuil, 1992.

Balibar, Etienne, and Immanuel Wallerstein. *Race, Nation, Class: Ambiguous Identities*. Translation of Etienne Balibar by Chris Turner. London: Verso, 1991.

Benton, Timothy. "Voyage d'Orient." In *Le Corbusier: Architect of the Century*. London: Arts Council of Great Britain, 1987.

Betts, Raymond. *France and Decolonization, 1900–1960*. Basingstoke, U.K.: Macmillan, 1991.

Braudel, Fernand. *The Identity of France*. 2 vols. Translated by Siân Reynolds. New York: Harper and Row, 1988–1990.

de Certeau, Michel. *Heterologies: Discourse on the Other*. Minneapolis: University of Minnesota Press, 1986.

———. *The Writing of History*. Translated by Tom Conley. Minneapolis: University of Minnesota Press, 1988.

———. *The Capture of Speech and Other Political Writings*. Translated by Tom Conley. Minneapolis: University of Minnesota Press, 1997.

———. *Culture in the Plural*. Translated by Tom Conley. Minneapolis: University of Minnesota Press, 1997.

Charle, Christophe. "Sentiment National et Nationalisme en France au XIX Siècle." *Bulletin de la Société d'Histoire Moderne et Contemporaine*, nos. 1–2 (1996): 22–27.

Debray, Régis. *Teachers, Writers, Celebrities*. London: New Left Books, 1981.

Deleuze, Gilles. *Foucault*. Translated by Séan Hand. Minneapolis: University of Minnesota Press, 1988.

Derrida, Jacques. *Monolingualism of the Other; or, The Prosthesis of Origin*. Translated by Patrick Mensah. Stanford, Calif.: Stanford University Press, 1998.

Diéguez, Manuel de. *Essai sur l'universalité de la France*. Paris: A. Michel, 1991.

Fierro-Domenech, Alfred. *Le Pré carré: Géographie historique de la France*. Paris: Robert Laffont, 1990.

Gaffney, John, ed. *France and Modernisation*. Aldershot, U.K.: Avebury, 1988.

Giard, Luce, ed. *Michel de Certeau: Cahiers pour un temps*. Paris: Centre Georges Pompidou, 1987.

Giard, Luce, Hervé Martin, and Jacques Revel, eds. *Histoire, mystique et politique: Michel de Certeau*. Grenoble: Jérôme Millon, 1991.

Hayward, Susan. *French National Cinema*. London: Routledge, 1993.

Hémon, Louis. *Maria Chapdelaine: A Tale of the Lake St. John Area*. Translated by W. H. Blake. New York: Modern Library, 1934.

Jourda, Pierre. *L'exotisme dans la littérature française depuis Chateaubriand*. 2 vols. Paris: PUF, 1938.

Judt, Tony. *Past Imperfect: French Intellectuals, 1944–1956*. Berkeley: University of California Press, 1992.

Julien, Charles André. *Une pensée anticoloniale: positions, 1914–1979*. Paris: Sindbad, 1979.

Khilnani, Sunil. *Arguing Revolution: The Intellectual Left in Postwar France*. New Haven, Conn.: Yale University Press, 1993.

Kuisel, Richard. *Seducing the French: The Dilemma of Americanization*. Berkeley: University of California Press, 1993.

Le Corbusier [Jeanneret, Charles-Edouard]. *The Decorative Art of Today*. Translated by James Dunnett. Cambridge, Mass.: MIT Press, 1987.

Lyotard, Jean-François. *Political Writings*. Edited and translated by Bill Readings. Minneapolis: University of Minnesota Press, 1993.

Morton, Patricia. *Hybrid Modernities: Architecture and Representation at the 1931 Colonial Exposition, Paris*. Cambridge, Mass.: MIT Press, 2000.

Noiriel, Gérard. *The French Melting Pot: Immigration, Citizenship, and National Identity*. Translated by Geoffroy de Laforcade. Minneapolis: University of Minesota Press, 1996.

Nora, Pierre, ed. *Realms of Memory: The Construction of the French Past*. 3 vols. Translated by Arthur Goldhammer. New York: Columbia University Press, 1996.

Paxton, Robert O. *Vichy France: Old Guard and New Order, 1940–1944*. New York: Knopf, 1972.

Porterfield, Todd. "The Obelisk at the Place de la Concorde." In *The Allure of Empire: Art in the Service of French Imperialism, 1798–1836*. Princeton, N.J.: Princeton University Press, 1998.

Rabinow, Paul. *French Modern: Norms and Forms of the Social Environment*. Cambridge, Mass.: MIT Press, 1989.

———. *French DNA: Trouble in Purgatory*. Chicago: University of Chicago Press, 1999.

Reader, Keith. *Intellectuals and the Left in France since 1968*. Basingstoke, U.K.: Macmillan, 1987.

Renan, Ernest. "What Is A Nation?" Translated by Martin Thom. In *Nation and Narration*, ed. Homi K. Bhabha. London: Routledge, 1990.

Rosanvallon, Pierre. *Le Sacre du citoyen: Histoire du suffrage universel en France*. Paris: Gallimard, 1992.

———. *Le Peuple introuvable: Histoire de la représentation démocratique en France*. Paris: Gallimard, 1998.

Ross, Kristin. *Fast Cars, Clean Bodies: Decolonization and the Reordering of French Culture*. Cambridge, Mass.: MIT Press, 1995.

———. *May '68 and Its Afterlives*. Chicago: University of Chicago Press, 2002.

Roth, Michael S. *Knowing and History: Appropriations of Hegel in Twentieth-Century France*. Ithaca, N.Y.: Cornell University Press, 1988.

Roudinesco, Elisabeth. *La bataille de cent ans: histoire de la psychanalyse en France*. 2 vols. Paris: Seuil, 1986 [Volume 2 only has been translated into English under the title, *Jacques Lacan & Co: A History of Psychoanalysis in France, 1925–1985*. Translated by Jeffrey Mehlmann. Chicago: University of Chicago Press, 1990].

Rousso, Henri. *The Vichy Syndrome: History and Memory in France since 1944.* Translated by Arthur Goldhammer. Cambridge, Mass.: Harvard University Press, 1991.

Sahlins, Peter. *Boundaries: The Making of France and Spain in the Pyrenees.* Berkeley: University of California Press, 1989.

Sarraut, Albert. *La mise en valeur des colonies françaises.* Paris: Payot, 1923.

Schneider, William. *An Empire for the Masses.* Westport, Conn.: Greenwood Press, 1982.

———. *Quality and Quantity: The Quest for Biological Regeneration in Twentieth-Century France.* Cambridge: Cambridge University Press, 1990.

Schor, Naomi. "The Crisis of French Universalism." *Yale French Studies* 100 (2001): 46–64.

Scott, Joan Wallach. *Only Paradoxes to Offer: French Feminists and the Rights of Man.* Cambridge, Mass.: Harvard University Press, 1996.

Silverman, Maxim. *Deconstructing the Nation: Immigration, Racism, and Citizenship in Modern France.* London: Routledge, 1992.

Terdiman, Richard. *Present Past: Modernity and the Memory Crisis.* Ithaca, N.Y.: Cornell University Press, 1993.

Touraine, Alain. *The May Movement: Revolt and Reform.* New York: Random House, 1971.

Vincendeau, Ginette. *The Companion to French Cinema.* London: British Film Institute, 1996.

———. "Melodramatic Realism: On Some French Women's Films in the 1930s." *Screen* 3 (summer 1989).

Wahnich, Sophie. *L'impossible citoyen: L'étranger dans le discours de la Révolution française.* Paris: Albin Michel, 1997.

Weber, Eugen. *Peasants into Frenchmen: The Modernization of Rural France.* Palo Alto, Calif.: Stanford University Press, 1976.

Williams, Allan. *Republic of Images: A History of French Filmmaking.* Cambridge, Mass.: Harvard University Press, 1992.

Wood, Nancy. *Vectors of Memory: Legacies of Trauma in Postwar Europe.* Oxford: Berg, 1999.

## PART II: BLACK DIASPORA AND *CREOLIZATION*

### Primary Works

Alexis, Jacques Stephen. *General Sun, My Brother.* Translated by Carrol F. Coates. Charlottesville: University Press of Virginia, 1999.

Bâ, Amadou Hampaté. *Jésus vu par un musulman.* Abidjan: Nouvelles Editions africaines, 1976.

———. *The Fortunes of Wangrin.* Translated by Aina Pavollini Taylor. Ibadan, Nigeria: New Horn Press, 1987.

———. *Kaidara*. Washington, D.C.: Three Continents Press, 1988.

———. *Amkoullel, l'enfant Peul: mémoires*. Paris: Agence de coopération culturelle et technique, 1991.

———. *Il n'y a pas de petite querelle: nouveaux contes de la savane*. Paris: Stock, 1999.

Bâ, Mariama. *So Long a Letter*. Translated by Modupé Bodé-Thomas. London: Heinemann, 1981.

Beti, Mongo. *Mission Accomplished*. Translated by Peter Green. New York: Macmillan, 1958.

———. *Mission to Kala*. Translated by Peter Green. London: Heinemann Educational, 1958.

———. *The Poor Christ of Bomba*. Translated by Gerald Moor. London: Heinemann, 1971.

———. *Perpetua and the Habit of Unhappiness*. Translated by John Reed and Clive Wake. London: Heinemann Educational, 1978.

———. *Lament for an African Pol*. Translated by Richard Bjornson. Washington, D.C.: Three Continents Press, 1985.

———. *The Story of the Madman*. Translated by Elizabeth Darnel. Charlottesville: University Press of Virginia, 2001.

Bugul, Ken. *The Abandoned Baobab: The Autobiography of a Senegalese Woman*. Translated by Marjolijn de Jager. Chicago: Lawrence Hill Books, 1991.

Casseus, Maurice. *Viejo*. Port-au-Prince: Editions "La Presse," 1934.

Césaire, Aimé. *A Season in the Congo*. Translated by Ralph Manheim. New York: Grove Press, 1968.

———. *The Tragedy of King Christophe; a play*. Translated by Ralph Manheim. New York: Grove Press, 1969.

———. *Cadastre*. Translated by Emile Snyder and Sanford Upson. New York: Third Press, 1973.

———. *The Collected Poetry*. Translated by Clayton Eshleman and Annette Smith. Berkeley: University of California Press, 1983.

———. *A Tempest: Based on Shakespeare's The Tempest: Adaptation for a Black Theatre*. Translated by Richard Miller. New York: G. Borchardt, 1985.

———. *Lost body*. Introduced and translated by Clayton Eshleman and Annette Smith. New York: G. Braziller, 1986.

———. *Lyric and dramatic poetry, 1946–1982*. Translated by Clayton Eshleman and Annette Smith. Charlottesville: University Press of Virginia, 1990.

———. *Notebook of a return to my native land*. Translated by Mireille Rosello and Annie Pritchard. Newcastle upon Tyne, U.K.: Bloodaxe Books, 1995.

Chamoiseau, Patrick. *Creole Folktales*. Translated by Linda Coverdale. New York: New Press, 1994.

———. *Ecrire en pays dominé*. Paris: Gallimard, 1997.

———. *School days*. Translated by Linda Coverdale. Lincoln: University of Nebraska Press, 1997.

———. *Solibo Magnificent*. Translated by Rose-Myriam Réjouis and Val Vinokurov. New York: Pantheon Books, 1997.

———. *Texaco*. Translated by Rose-Myriam Réjouis and Val Vinokurov. New York: Pantheon Books, 1997.

———. *Strange words*. Translated by Linda Coverdale. London: Granta Books, 1998.

———. *Childhood*. Translated by Carol Volk. Lincoln: University of Nebraska Press, 1999.

———. *Chronicle of the Seven Sorrows*. Translated by Linda Coverdale. Lincoln: University of Nebraska Press, 1999.

———. *Seven Dreams of Elmira: A Tale of Martinique: Being the Confessions of an Old Worker at the Saint-Etienne Distillery*. Translated by Mark Polizzotti. Cambridge, Mass.: Zoland Books, 1999.

Chamoiseau, Patrick, and Raphaël Confiant. *Lettres créoles: tracées antillaises et continentales de la littérature: Haïti, Guadeloupe, Martinique, Guyane, 1635–1975*. Paris: Hatier, 1991.

Condé, Maryse. *Heremakhonon*. Paris: 10/18, 1976. [Re-edited as *En attendant le bonheur*. Paris: Seghers, 1988]. English translation: *Heremakhonon: A Novel*. Translated by Richard Philcox. Washington, D.C.: Three Continents Press, 1982.

———. *Une saison à Rihata*. Paris: Robert Laffont, 1981.

———. *Ségou. Les murailles de la terre*, tome 1. Paris: Robert Laffont, 1984. English translation: *Segu: A Novel*. Translated by Barbara Bray. New York: Viking, 1987.

———. *Ségou. La terre en miettes*, tome 2. Paris: Robert Laffont, 1985. English translation: *The Children of Segu*. Translated by Linda Coverdale. New York: Ballantine, 1990.

———. *Moi, Tituba sorcière . . . Noire de Salem*. Paris: Histoire romanesque/ Mercure de France, English translation: *I, Tituba, Black Witch of Salem*. Translated by Richard Philcox. Charlottesville: University Press of Virginia, 1992.

———. *La Vie scélérate*. Paris: Seghers, 1987. English translation: *Tree of Life*. Translated by Victoria Reite. New York: Ballantine, 1992.

———. *Traversée de la Mangrove*. Paris: Mercure de France/ Folio, 1989/1995. English translation: *Crossing the Mangrove*. Translated by Richard Philcox. New York: Anchor Books/Doubleday, 1995.

———. *Les Derniers rois mages*. Paris: Mercure de France, 1992 [corrected edition, 1993]. English translation: *The Last of the African Kings*. Translated by Richard Philcox. Lincoln: University of Nebraska Press, 1997.

———. *La Colonie du nouveau monde*. Paris: Robert Laffont, 1993.

———. *La Migration des coeurs*. Paris: Robert Laffont, 1995. English translation: *Windward Heights*. Translated by Richard Philcox. London: Faber & Faber, 1998.

———. *Desirada*. Paris: Robert Laffont, 1996. English translation: *Desirada*. Translated by Richard Philcox. New York: Soho Press, 2000.

———. *Pays mêlé: nouvelles*. Paris: R. Laffont, 1997. English translation: *Land of many colors*. Translated by Nicole Ball. Lincoln: University of Nebraska Press, 1999.

———. *Le coeur à rire et à pleurer: contes vrais de mon enfance*. Paris: Robert Laffont, 1999. English translation: *Tales from the heart: true stories from my childhood*. Translated by Richard Philcox. New York: Soho, 2001.

———. *Célanire cou-coupé: roman fantastique*. Paris: R. Laffont, 2000.

———. *La belle créole: roman*. Paris: Mercure de France, 2001.

Confiant, Raphaël. *Eau de café*. Translated by James Ferguson. New York: Faber & Faber, 1999.

———. *Mamzelle Dragonfly*. Translated by Linda Coverdale. New York: Farrar, Straus & Giroux, 2000.

Damas, Léon-Gontran. *Graffiti*. Paris: P. Seghers, 1952.

———. *Black-Label*. Paris, Gallimard, 1956.

———. *African Songs of Love, War, Grief, and Abuse*. Translated by Miriam Koshland and Ulli Beie. Ibadan: Mbari Publications, 1961.

Dépestre, René. *A Rainbow for the Christian West*. Translated by Jack Hirschman. Fairfax, Calif.: Red Hill Press, 1972.

———. *Bonjour et adieu à la negritude*. Paris: R. Laffont, 1980.

———. *Vegetations of splendor*. Translated by Jack Hirschman. Chicago: Vanguard Books, 1980.

———. *Hadriana dans tous mes rêves*. Paris: Gallimard, 1988.

———. *The Festival of the Greasy Pole*. Translated by Carrol F. Coates. Charlottesville: University Press of Virginia, 1990.

———. *Anthologie personnelle: poésie*. Arles: Actes Sud, 1993.

Diop, Birago. *Tales of Amadou Koumba*. Translated by Dorothy S. Blair. London: Oxford University Press, 1966.

———. *Mémoires*. Paris: Présence Africaine, 1978.

———. *Mother Crocodile*. Translated by Rosa Guy. New York: Delacorte Press, 1981.

Diop, David. *Hammer Blows and Other Writings*. Translated by Simon Mpondo and Frank Jones. Bloomington: Indiana University Press, 1973.

Dorsinville, Roger. *Un homme en trois morceaux*. Paris: U.G.E., 1975.

Glissant, Édouard. *The Ripening*. Translated by Frances Frenaye. New York: G. Braziller, 1959.

———. *Malemort*. Paris: Editions du Seuil, 1975.

———. *The Indies*. Translated by Dominique O'Neill. Toronto: Éditions du GREF, 1992.

———. *Tout-monde*. Paris: Gallimard, 1993.

———. *Black Salt: Poems*. Translated by Betsy Wing. Ann Arbor: University of Michigan Press, 1998.

———. *Le monde incréé: poétrie*. Paris: Gallimard, 2000.

———. *The Fourth Century*. Translated by Betsy Wing. Lincoln: University of Nebraska Press, 2001.

Hibbert, Fernand. *Séna*. Port-au-Prince: Imprimerie de l'Abeille, 1905.

——. *Les Thazar*. Port-au-Prince: Imprimerie de l'Abeille, 1907.

Innocent, Antoine. *Mimola on l'Histoire d'une cassette*. Port-au-Prince: Imprimerie E. Malval, 1906.

Kane, Hamidou. *Ambiguous Adventure*. Translated by Katherine Woods. New York: Walker, 1963.

Laferrière, Dany. *Comment faire l'amour avec un nègre sans se fatiguer*. Montreal: VLB, 1985. English translation: *How to Make Love to a Negro*. Translated by David Homel. Toronto: Coach House Press, 1987.

——. *Cette grenade dans la main du jeune nègre, est-ce une arme ou un fruit*. Montréal: VLB, 1993. English translation: *Why Must a Black Writer Write About Sex?* Translated by David Homel. Toronto: Coach House Press, 1994.

Laye, Camara. *The Dark Child*. Translated by James Kirkup and Ernest Jones. New York: Farrar, Straus & Giroux, 1954.

——. *A Dream of Africa*. Translated by James Kirkup. London: Collins, 1968.

Lhérisson, Justin. *La Famille des Pitite-Caille*. Paris: Firmin-Didot, 1929.

Marcelin, Frédéric, *Thémistocle-Epaminondas Labasterre*. Paris: Ollendorff, 1901.

Oyono, Ferdinand. *Houseboy*. Translated by John Reed. London: Heinemann, 1966.

——. *The Old Man and the Medal*. Translated by John Reed. New York: Collier Books, 1971.

——. *Road to Europe*. Translated by Richard Bjornson. Washington, D.C.: Three Continents Press, 1989.

Price-Mars, Jean. *So Spoke the Uncle*. Translated by Magdaline W. Shannon. Washington, D.C.: Three Continents Press, 1983.

Roumain, Jacques. *La Montagne ensorcelée*. Port-au-Prince: Collection indigène, 1931.

——. *Gouverneurs de la Rosée*. Port-au-Prince: Collection indigène, 1944. English translation: *Masters of the Dew*. Translated by Langston Hughes and Mercer Cook. New York: Reynal & Hitchcock, 1947.

——. *Ebony wood/Bois-d'ébène: Poems*. The French text with a translation by Sidney Shapiro. New York: Interworld Press, 1972.

——. *When the Tom-Tom Beats: Selected Prose & Poems*. Translated by Joanne Fungaroli and Ronald Sauer. Washington, D.C.: Azul Editions, 1995.

Schwarz-Bart, André. *The Last of the Just*. Translated by Stephen Becker. New York: Atheneum, 1960.

——. *A Woman Named Solitude*. Translated by Ralph Mannheim. New York: Atheneum, 1973.

Schwarz-Bart, Simone. *Pluie et vent sur Télumée Miracle*. Paris: Seuil/ Points, no. 39, 1972/1995. English translation: *The Bridge of Beyond*. Translated by Barbara Bray. New York: Atheneum, 1974.

——. *Between Two Worlds*. Translated by Barbara Bray. Oxford: Heinemann, 1992.

——. *In Praise of Black Women*. Translated by Rose-Myriam Réjouis and Val Vinokurov. Madison: University of Wisconsin Press, 2001.

Sembene, Ousmane. *God's Bits of Wood*. Translated by Francis Price. Garden City, N.Y.: Doubleday, 1962.

———. *Xala*. Translated by Clive Wake. London: Heinemann, 1976.

———. *Black Docker*. Translated by Ros Schwartz. London: Heinemann, 1987.

Senghor, Léopold Sédar. *Prose and Poetry*. Selected and translated by John Reed and Clive Wake. London: Oxford University Press, 1965.

———. *Nocturnes*. Translated by John Reed and Clive Wake. London: Heinemann, 1969.

———. *The Foundations of "Africanité" or "Négritude" and "Arabité."* Translated by Mercer Cook. Paris: Présence Africaine, 1971.

———. *Poems of a Black Orpheus*. Translated by William Oxley. London: Menard Press, 1981.

———. *The Collected Poetry*. Translated by Melvin Dixon. Charlottesville: University Press of Virginia, 1991.

Sylvain, Georges. *Cric? Crac!: fables créoles*. Port-au-Prince: Fardin, 1901.

Thoby-Marcelin, Philippe, and Pierre Marcelin. *Le Crayon de Dieu*. Paris: La Table Ronde, 1952. English translation: *The Pencil of God*. Translated by Leonard Thomas. London: Victor Gollancz, 1956.

Zobel, Joseph. *La Rue cases-Nègres*. Paris: J. Froissart, 1950. English translation: *Black Shack Alley*. Translated by Keith Q. Warner. Washington, D.C.: Three Continents Press, 1980.

## Secondary Works

Adejunmobi, Moradewun. *J. J. Rabearivelo, Literature, and Lingua Franca in Colonial Madagascar*. New York: P. Lang, 1996.

Alexis, Stephen. *Black Liberator: The Life of Toussaint Louverture*. Translated by William Stirling. New York: Macmillan, 1949.

Bernabé, Jean, Patrick Chamoiseau, and Raphaël Confiant. *Eloge de la Créolité*. Paris: Gallimard, 1989.

Beti, Mongo. *Main basse sur le Cameroun; autopsie d'une décolonisation*. Paris: F. Maspero, 1972.

———. *La France contre l'Afrique: retour au Cameroun*. Paris: Éditions La Découverte, 1993.

Beti, Mongo, Odile Tobneret, et al. *Dictionnaire de la negritude*. Paris: L'Harmattan, 1989.

Blackburn, Robin. *The Overthrow of Colonial Slavery, 1776–1848*. London: Verso, 1988.

Césaire, Aimé. *Letter to Maurice Thorez*. Paris: Présence Africaine, 1957.

———. *Discourse on colonialism*. Translated by Joan Pinkham. New York: Monthly Review Press, 1972.

———. *Toussaint Louverture: La Révolution française et le problème colonial*. Paris: Présence Africaine, 1981.

Chipman, John. *French Power in Africa*. Oxford: Blackwell, 1989.

Cohen, William. *The French Encounter with Africans: White Response to Blacks, 1530–1880.* Bloomington: Indiana University Press, 1989.

Condé, Maryse. *La Parole des femmes: essai sur les romancières des Antilles de langue française.* Paris: L'Harmattan, 1979.

———. "Order, Disorder, Freedom, and the West Indian Writer." *Yale French Studies* 83 (1993): 121–35.

Condé, Maryse, ed. *L'Héritage de Caliban.* Pointe-à-Pitre: Éditions Jasor, 1992.

Condé, Maryse, and Madeleine Cottenet-Hage, eds. *Penser la créolité.* Paris: Karthala, 1995.

Conklin, Alice. *Mission to Civilize: The Republican Idea of Empire in France and West Africa, 1895–1930.* Stanford, Calif.: Stanford University Press, 1997.

Cooper, Anna J. *Slavery and the French Revolutionists (1788–1805).* Translated by Frances Richardson Keller. Lewiston, N.Y.: Edwin Mellen Press, n.d.

———. *A Voice from the South by a Black Woman of the South* (1892). Reissued in The Schomburg Library of Nineteenth-Century Black Women Writers. New York: Oxford University Press, 1988.

Dash, J. Michael. "The Marxist Counterpoint—Jacques Roumain: 1930s to 1940s." *Black Images* 2, no. 1 (spring 1973).

———. *Literature and Ideology in Haiti, 1915–1961.* Totowa, N.J.: Barnes & Noble, 1981.

———. *Haiti and the United States: National Stereotypes and the Literary Imagination.* Basingstoke, U.K.: Macmillan Press, 1988.

———. *Edouard Glissant.* Cambridge: Cambridge University Press, 1995.

———. *The Other America: Caribbean Literature in a New World Context.* Charlottesville: University Press of Virginia, 1998.

———. *Culture and Customs of Haiti.* Westport, Conn.: Greenwood Press, 2001.

Denis, Lorimer, and François Duvalier. *Le problème des classes à travers l'histoire d'Haïti.* Port-au-Prince: Collection Les Griots, 1959.

Depestre, René. *Pour la révolution, pour la poésie.* Montreal: Leméac, 1974.

———. *Le Métier à métisser.* Paris: Stock, 1998.

Diop, Cheikh Anta. *The African Origin of Civilization: Myth or Reality.* Translated by Mercer Cook. New York: L. Hill, 1974.

———. *The Cultural Unity of Black Africa: The Domains of Patriarchy and of Matriarchy in Classical Antiquity.* Chicago: Third World Press, 1978.

———. *Precolonial Black Africa: A Comparative Study of the Political and Social Systems of Europe and Black Africa from Antiquity to the Formation of Modern States.* Translated by Harold J. Salemson. Westport, Conn.: L. Hill, 1987.

———. *Civilization or Barbarism: An Authentic Anthropology.* Translated by Yaa-Lengi Meema Ngemi. Brooklyn, N.Y.: L. Hill, 1991.

———. *Towards the African Renaissance: Essays in African Culture & Development, 1946–1960.* Translated by Egbuna P. Modum. London: Karnak House, 1996.

———. *African Antiquity.* Paris: Présence Africaine, 1998.

Diop, Samba, ed. *Fictions africaines et postcolonialisme.* Paris: L'Harmattan, 2002.

Fanon, Frantz. *Black Skin, White Masks*. Translated by Charles Lam Markmann. New York: Grove Press, 1967.

———. *Toward the African Revolution*. Translated by Haakon Chevalier. New York: Monthly Review Press, 1967.

———. *The Wretched of the Earth*. Translated by Constance Farrington. New York: Grove Press, 1968.

Fanoudh-Siefer, Léon. *Le mythe du nègre et de l'Afrique noire dans la littérature française*. Paris: C. Klincksieck, 1968.

Fick, Carolyn E. *The Making of Haiti: The Saint Domingue Revolution from Below*. Knoxville: University of Tennessee Press, 1991.

Gabel, Leona C. *From Slavery to the Sorbonne and Beyond: The Life and Writings of Anna J. Cooper. Smith College Studies in History*, vol. XLIX. Northampton, Mass.: Department of History of Smith College, 1982.

Garrigus, John D. "White Jacobins/Black Jacobins: Bringing the Haitian and French Revolutions Together in the Classroom." *French Historical Studies* 23, no. 2 (spring 2000): 259–75.

Georgel, Chantal, Françoise Vergès, and Alain Vivien, eds. *L'Abolition de l'esclavage: Un combat pour les droits de l'homme*. Paris: Editions Complexe, 1998.

Gifford, Prosser, and William Roger Louis. *The Transfer of Power in Africa: Decolonization, 1940–1960*. New Haven, Conn.: Yale University Press, 1982.

Gilroy, Paul. *The Black Atlantic: Modernity and Double Consciousness*. Cambridge, Mass.: Harvard University Press, 1993.

Glissant, Edouard. *Monsieur Toussaint*. Translated by Joseph G. Foster and Barbara A. Franklin. Washington, D.C.: Three Continents Press, 1981.

———. *Caribbean Discourse: Selected Essays*. Translated by J. Michael Dash. Charlottesville: University Press of Virginia, 1989.

———. *Poetics of Relation*. Translated by Betsy Wing. Ann Arbor: University of Michigan Press, 1997.

———. *Traité du tout-monde*. Paris: Gallimard, 1997.

Guérin, Daniel. *The West Indies and Their Future*. London: Dennis Dobson, 1961.

Gyssels, Kathleen. *Filles de solitude, essais sur l'identité antillaise dans les (auto-) biographies de Simone et André Schwarz-Bart*. Paris: L'Harmattan, 1996.

Harrow, Kenneth, Jonathan Ngaté, and Clarisse Zimra. *Crisscrossing boundaries in African Literatures*. Washington, D.C.: Three Continents Press, 1991.

Irele, Abiola. *Literature and Ideology in Martinique: René Maran, Aime Césaire, Frantz Fanon*. Buffalo, Council on International Studies, State University of New York at Buffalo, 1971.

———. *The African Experience in Literature and Ideology*. London: Heinemann, 1981.

———. *The African Imagination: Literature in Africa and the Black Diaspora*. Oxford: Oxford University Press, 2001.

James, C. L. R. *The Black Jacobins: Toussaint L'Ouverture and the San Domingo Revolution*. 2d ed. New York: Random House, 1963.

———. "The Black Jacobins" (play). In *The C.L.R. James Reader*. Edited by Anna Grimshaw. Oxford: Blackwell, 1992.

——. *A History of Pan-African Revolt*. Rpt. Chicago: Charles H. Kerr, 1995.

Jonassaint, Jean. *Le Pouvoir des mots, les maux du pouvoir. Des romanciers haïtiens de l'exil*. Paris: Arcantère, 1986.

——. *Des romans de tradition haïtienne. Sur un récit tragique*. Paris: L'Harmattan, 2002.

Kadish, Doris Y. "The Black Terror: Women's Responses to Slave Revolts in Haïti." *The French Review* 68, no. 4 (March 1995): 668–80.

Kadish, Doris Y., and Françoise Massardier-Kenney, eds. *Translating Slavery: Gender and Race in French Women's Writing, 1783–1823*. Kent, Ohio: Kent State University Press, 1994.

Kesteloot, Lilyan. *Les Écrivains noirs de langue française: naissance d'une littérature*. Bruxelles: Édition de l'Institut de Sociologie, 1963 and Éditions de l'Université de Bruxelles, 1977. English translation: *Black Writers in French: A Literary History of Negritude*. Translated by Ellen Conroy Kennedy. Philadelphia: Temple University Press, 1974.

Malena, Anne. *The Negotiated Self: The Dynamics of Identity in Francophone Caribbean Narrative*. New York: Peter Lang, 1999.

Martinkus-Zemp, Ada. *Le blanc et le noir*. Paris: A.-G. Nizet, 1975.

Miller, Christopher L. *Blank Darkness: Africanist Discourse in French*. Chicago: University of Chicago Press, 1985.

Mudimbe V. Y. *The Invention of Africa: Gnosis, Philosophy, and the Order of Knowledge*. Bloomington: Indiana University Press, 1988.

——. *The Rift*. Translated by Marjolijn de Jager. Minneapolis: University of Minnesota Press, 1993.

——. *The Idea of Africa*. Bloomington: Indiana University Press, 1994.

Mudimbe V. Y., ed. *The Surreptitious Speech: Présence Africaine and the Politics of Otherness, 1947–1987*. Chicago: University of Chicago Press, 1992.

Ndiaye, Christiane, and J. Semujanga, eds. *De paroles en figures. Essais sur les littératures africaines et antillaises*. Montreal: L'Harmattan, 1996.

Ngate, Jonathan. *Francophone African Fiction: Reading a Literary Tradition*. Trenton, N.J.: Africa World Press, 1988.

Peabody, Sue. *'There Are No Slaves in France": The Political Culture of Race and Slavery in the Ancien Régime*. New York: Oxford University Press, 1996.

Pfaff, Françoise. *The Cinema of Ousmane Sembene, A Pioneer of African Film*. Westport, Conn.: Greenwood Press, 1984.

——. *Conversations with Maryse Condé*. Lincoln: University of Nebraska Press, 1996.

Praeger, Michele. *The Imaginary Caribbean and the Caribbean Imaginary*. Lincoln: University of Nebraska Press, 2003.

Raiskin, Judith L. *Snow on the Cane Fields: Women's Writing and Creole Subjectivity*. Minneapolis: University of Minnesota Press, 1996.

Rinne, Suzanne, and Joëlle Vitiello, eds. *Elles écrivent des Antilles . . . (Haïti, Guadeloupe, Martinique)*. Paris: L'Harmattan, 1997.

Robinson, Cedric. *Black Marxism. The Making of the Black Radical Tradition.* London: Zed Press, 1983.

Rosello, Mireille. *Littérature et identité créole aux Antilles.* Paris: Editions Karthala, 1992.

Roumain, Jacques. *Analyse schématique, 1932–1934.* Port-au-Prince: Editions idées nouvelles, idées prolétariennes, 1999.

Schmidt, Hans. *The United States Occupation of Haiti, 1915–1934.* New Brunswick, N.J.: Rutgers University Press, 1995.

Senghor, Léopold Sédar. *African Socialism: A Report to the Constitutive Congress of the Party of African Federation.* Translated by Mercer Cook. New York: American Society of African Culture, 1959.

———. *Négritude et humanisme.* Paris: Editions du Seuil, 1964.

———. *Négritude et civilisation de l'universel.* Paris: Seuil, 1977.

———. *Ce que je crois: négritude, francité et civilisation de l'universel.* Paris: B. Grasset, 1988.

Sharpley-Whiting, T. Denean. *Black Venus: Sexualized Savages, Primal Fears, and Primitive Narratives in French.* Durham, N.C.: Duke University Press, 1999.

———. *Frantz Fanon: Conflicts & Feminisms.* Lanham, Md.: Rowman & Littlefield, 1998.

———. *Negritude Women: Race Women, Race Consciousness, Race Literature.* Minneapolis: University of Minnesota Press, 2002.

Sharpley-Whiting, T. Denean, and Joy James, eds. *The Black Feminist Reader.* London: Blackwell, 2000.

Sharpley-Whiting, T. Denean, Lewis R. Gordon, and Renee T. White, eds. *Fanon: A Critical Reader.* London: Blackwell, 1996.

Stovall, Tyler. *Paris Noir: African Americans in the City of Light.* Boston: Houghton Mifflin, 1996.

———. "Histories of Race in France." *French Politics, Culture & Society* 18, no. 3 (fall 2000).

Wolcott, Derek. "A Letter to Chamoiseau." *What the Twilight Says: Essays.* New York: Farrar, Straus & Giroux, 1998.

## PART III: ORIENTALISM AND THE MAGHREBIAN PRESENCE IN POSTCOLONIAL FRANCE

### Primary Works

Audisio, Gabriel. *Jeunesse de la Méditerranée.* Paris: Gallimard, 1935.

———. *Algérie méditerranée. Feux vivants.* Limoges: Rougerie, 1957.

Begag, Azouz. *Le gone du Châaba: roman.* Paris: Seuil, 1986.

———. *Les chiens aussi.* Paris: Seuil, 1995.

———. *Dis oualla!: récit.* Paris: Fayard, 1997.

———. *Zenzela: roman.* Paris: Seuil, 1997.

———. *Quand on est mort, c'est pour toute la vie.* Paris: Gallimard jeunesse, 1998.

———. *Le passeport: roman.* Paris: Seuil, 2000.

Ben Jelloun, Tahar. *L'écrivain public: récit.* Paris: Editions du Seuil, 1983.

———. *The Sand Child.* Translated by Alan Sheridan. San Diego, Calif.: Harcourt Brace Jovanovich, 1987.

———. *Solitaire.* Translated by Gareth Stanton and Nick Hindley. London: Quartet, 1988.

———. *The Sacred Night.* Translated by Alan Sheridan. San Diego, Calif.: Harcourt Brace Jovanovich, 1989.

———. *With Downcast Eyes: A Novel.* Translated by Joachim Neugroschel. Boston: Little, Brown, 1993.

———. *State of Absence.* Translated by James Kirkup. London: Quartet Books, 1994.

———. *Corruption.* Translated by Carol Volk. New York: New Press, 1995.

———. *This Blinding Absence of Light.* Translated by Linda Coverdale. New York: New Press, 2002.

Bensmaïa, Réda. *The Year of Passages.* Translated by Tom Conley. Minneapolis: University of Minnesota Press, 1995.

Boudjedra, Rachid. *Journal palestinien.* Paris: Hachette, 1972.

———. *Topographie idéale pour une agression caractérisée.* Paris: Denoël, 1975.

———. *FIS de la haine.* Paris: Denoël, 1992.

———. *Lettres algériennes.* Paris: B. Grasset, 1995.

———. *The Repudiation.* Translated by Golda Lambrova. Colorado Springs, Colo.: Three Continents Press, 1995.

———. *La vie à l'endroit.* Paris: B. Grasset, 1997.

Charef, Mehdi, *Le Thé au harem d'Archi Ahmed.* Paris: Mercure de France, 1983. English translation: *Tea in the Harem.* Translated by Ed Emery. London: Serpent's Tail, 1989.

Chraïbi, Driss. *Heirs to the Past.* Translated by Len Ortzen. London: Heinemann Educational, 1972.

———. *The Butts.* Translated by Hugh A. Harter. Washington, D.C.: Three Continents Press, 1983.

———. *Mother Comes of Age.* Translated by Hugh A. Harter. Washington, D.C.: Three Continents Press, 1984.

———. *Flutes of Death.* Translated by Robin Roosevelt. Washington, D.C.: Three Continents Press, 1985.

———. *Mother Spring.* Translated by Hugh Harter. Washington, D.C.: Three Continents Press, 1989.

———. *Birth at Dawn.* Translated by Ann Woollcombe. Washington, D.C.: Three Continents Press, 1990.

———. *The Simple Past.* Translated by Hugh A. Harter. Washington, D.C.: Three Continents Press, 1990.

———. *Inspector Ali.* Translated by Lara McGlashan. Colorado Springs, Colo.: Three Continents Press, 1994.

———. *Muhammad: A Novel.* Translated by Nadia Benabid. Boulder, Colo.: Lynne Rienner, 1998.

———. *Vu, lu, entendu: mémoires.* Paris: Denoël, 1998.

Dib, Mohammed. *Algérie.* Paris: Seuil, 1952.

———. *Un été africain, roman.* Paris: Seuil, 1959.

———. *Le talisman, nouvelles.* Paris: Seuil, 1966.

———. *Dieu en Barbarie, roman.* Paris: Seuil, 1970.

———. *Habel: roman.* Paris: Seuil, 1977.

———. *Omneros.* Translated by Carol Lettieri and Paul Vangelisti. Los Angeles: Red Hill Press, 1978.

———. *Who Remembers the Sea.* Translated by Louis Tremaine. Washington, D.C.: Three Continents Press, 1985.

———. *O vive: poèmes.* Paris: Sindbad, 1987.

———. *Le Sommeil d'Eve: roman.* Paris: Sindbad , 1989.

———. *Neiges de marbre: roman.* Paris: Sindbad, 1990.

———. *L'infante maure: roman.* Paris: A. Michel, 1994.

———. *L'enfant-jazz: poèmes.* Paris: Editions de la Différence, 1998.

———. *Si Diable veut.* Paris: A. Michel, 1998.

———. *Le coeur insulaire: poèmes.* Paris: Différence, 2000.

———. *The Savage Night.* Translated by C. Dickson. Lincoln: University of Nebraska Press, 2001.

———. *Simorgh.* Paris: A. Michel, 2003.

Djaout, Tahar. *L'exproprié.* Alger: Société Nationale d'Edition et de Diffusion, 1981.

———. *Solstice barbelé: 1973–1975.* 2d ed. Sherbrooke: Naaman, 1983.

———. *Les rets de l'oiseleur: nouvelles.* Alger: Entreprise Nationale du Livre, 1984.

———. *L'invention du désert.* Paris: Seuil, 1987.

———. *The Last Summer of Reason: A Novel.* Translated by Marjolijn de Jager. St. Paul, Minn.: Ruminator Books, 2001.

———. *The Watchers: A Novel.* Translated by Marjolijn de Jager. St. Paul, Minn.: Ruminator Books, 2002.

Djebar, Assia. *The Mischief.* Translated by Frances Frenaye. London: Elek Books, 1958.

———. *Fantasia: An Algerian Cavalcade.* Translated by Dorothy Blair. London: Quartet, 1985.

———. *Women of Algiers in their Apartment.* Translated by Marjolijn de Jager. Charlottesville: University Press of Virginia, 1992.

———. *A Sister to Scheherazade.* Translated by Dorothy S. Blair. Portsmouth, N.H.: Heinemann, 1987.

———. *Far from Medina.* London: Quartet Books, 1994.

———. *Ces voix qui m'assiègent: en marge de ma francophonie.* Paris: A. Michel, 1999.

―――. *So Vast the Prison.* Translated by Betsy Wing. New York: Seven Stories Press, 1999.

―――. *Algerian White: A Narrative.* Translated by David Kelley and Marjolijn de Jager. New York: Seven Stories Press, 2000.

Kateb, Yacine. *Nedjma, A Novel.* Translated by Richard Howard. New York: G. Braziller, 1961.

―――. *Intelligence Powder.* Translated by Stephen J. Vogel. New York: Ubu Repertory Theater Publications, 1985.

―――. *Boucherie de l'espérance: oeuvres théâtrales.* Edited by Zebeida Chergui. Paris: Seuil, 1999.

Musette [Auguste Robinet]. *Cagayous. Ses meilleurs histories.* Edited by Gabriel Audisio. Paris: Gallimard, 1931.

Randau, Robert. *Les colons.* Paris: E. Sansot et Cie, 1907.

Skif, Hamid. *Nouvelles de la maison du silence.* Alger: Entreprise nationale du livre, 1986.

―――. *Poèmes d'El-Asnam et d'autres lieux.* Alger: Entreprise nationale du livre, 1986.

## Secondary Works

Abitbol, Michel. *Les juifs d'Afrique du Nord sous Vichy.* Paris: Maisonneuve & Larose, 1988.

Ageron, Charles Robert. *France coloniale ou parti colonial?* Paris: PUF, 1978.

Alloula, Malek. *The Colonial Harem.* Translated by Myrna and Wlad Godzich. Minneapolis: University of Minnesota Press, 1986.

Allouche-Benayoun, Joëlle. "Une histoire d'intégration: Les Juifs d'Algérie et la France." *Les nouveaux cahiers,* no. 116 (printemps 1994).

Allouche-Benayoun, Joëlle, and Doris Bensimon. *Les Juifs d'Algérie.* Paris: BHP, 1989.

Ansky, Michel. *Les Juifs d'Algérie, du décret Crémieux à la Libération.* Paris: Editions du Centre, 1950.

Ayoun, Richard. "Une Présence Plurimillénaire." *Les Juifs d'Algérie: Images et Textes.* Paris: Editions du Scribe, 1987.

―――. "Le décret Crémieux et l'insurrection de 1871 en Algérie." *Revue d'histoire moderne et contemporaine,* vol. 35 (janvier–mars 1988).

Bahloul, Joëlle. *The Architecture of Memory: A Jewish-Muslim Household in Colonial Algeria, 1937–1962.* Cambridge: Cambridge University Press, 1996.

Baroli, Marc. *La vie quotidienne des Français en Algérie, 1830–1914.* Paris: Hachette, 1967.

Begag, Azouz. *L'immigré et sa ville.* Lyon: Presses universitaires de Lyon, 1984.

―――. *North African Immigrants in France: The Socio-Spatial Representation of "Here" and "There."* Studies in European Culture & Society, Paper 2.

Loughborough, U.K.: European Research Centre, Loughborough University, 1990.

Behdad, Ali. *Belated Travelers: Orientalism in the Age of Colonial Dissolution.* Durham, N.C.: Duke University Press, 1994.

Ben Jelloun, Tahar. *French Hospitality: Racism and North African Immigrants.* New York: Columbia University Press, 1999.

Bertrand, Louis. *Le Sang des races.* Paris: Albin Michel, 1926 (first published, 1899).

Birnbaum, Pierre. "The Empire Abandoned: From the Crémieux Decree to the Blum-Violette Plan." In *Anti-Semitism in France.* Oxford: Blackwell, 1992.

Birnbaum, Pierre, ed. *Histoire politique des Juifs de France entre universalisme et particularisme.* Paris: Presses de la Fondation nationale des sciences politiques, 1990.

Bloom, Peter. "Beur Cinema and the Politics of Location: French Immigration Policies and the Naming of a Film Movement." *Social Identities* 5, no. 4: 469–87.

Boudjedra, Rachid. *Peindre l'Orient.* Cadeilhan: Zulma, 1996.

Bourdieu, Pierre. *Sociologie de l'Algérie.* Paris: Presses Universitaires de France, 1961.

Cesari, Jocelyne. *Etre Musulman en France: Associations, Militants et Mosquées.* Paris: Khartala, 1994.

Fanon, Frantz. *A Dying Colonialism.* Translated by Haakon Chevalier. New York: Grove Press, 1965.

Gafaiti, Hafid. *Kateb Yacine: un homme, une oeuvre, un pays.* Algiers: Laphomic, 1986.

———. *Boudjedra, ou, La passion de la modernité.* Paris: Denoël, 1987.

———. *Les femmes dans le roman algérien: histoire, discours et texte.* Paris: L'Harmattan, 1996.

Gafaiti, Hafid, ed. *Rachid Boudjedhra, une poétique de la subversion.* 2 vols. Paris: L'Harmattan, 1999–2000.

Graham-Brown, Sarah. *Images of Women: The Portrayal of Women in Photography of the Middle East, 1860–1950.* London: Quartet, 1988.

Harbi, Mohamed. *Le FLN: Mirage et réalité.* Paris: Jeune Afrique, 1980.

Hargreaves, Alec. *Immigration and Identity in Beur Fiction.* New York: Berg, 1991.

———. *Immigration, "Race," and Ethnicity in Contemporary France.* London: Routledge, 1995.

Hargreaves, Alec, and Michael J. Heffernan, eds. *French and Algerian Identities: From Colonial Times to the Present.* Lewiston, N.Y.: Edwin Mellen Press, 1993.

Hargreaves, Alec G., and Timothy G. Stenhouse. "The Gulf War and the Maghrebian Community in France." *The Maghreb Review*, vol. 17 (1992).

Hebey, Pierre. *Alger 1898: la grande vague antijuive.* Paris: NiL editions, 1996.

Hureau, Joëlle. *La mémoire des Pieds-Noirs.* Paris: Olivier Orban, 1987.

———. "La mémoire repatriée." In *La France en Guerre d'Algérie*. Paris: BDIC, 1992.

Ireland, Patrick R. *The Policy Challenge of Ethnic Diversity: Immigrant Politics in France and Switzerland*. Cambridge, Mass.: Harvard University Press, 1994.

Imache, Tassadit. *Une Fille sans histoire*. Paris: Calmann-Lévy, 1989.

Kepel, Gilles. *Les Banlieues de l'Islam*. Paris: Seuil, 1987.

Khellil, Mohand. *L'Intégration des Maghrébins en France*. Paris: Presses Universitaires de France, 1991.

Leconte, Daniel. *Les Pieds-Noirs: histoire et portrait d'une communauté*. Paris: Seuil, 1980.

Lorcin, Patricia M. E. *Imperial Identities: Stereotyping, Prejudice and Race in Colonial Algeria*. London: I. B. Tauris, 1995.

Lowe, Lisa. *Critical Terrains: French and British Orientalism*. Ithaca, N.Y.: Cornell University Press, 1991.

MacMaster, Neil. *Colonial Migrants and Racism: Algerians in France, 1900–1962*. New York: St. Martin's Press, 1997.

Marrus, Michael, and Robert O. Paxton. "A Special Case: Algeria." In *Vichy France and the Jews*. Stanford, Calif.: Stanford University Press, 1995.

Memmi, Albert. *The Colonizer and the Colonized*. Translated by Howard Greenfield. New York: Orion Press, 1965.

———. *Le Racisme*. Paris: Gallimard, 1982.

Milza, Olivier. *Les Français devant l'immigration*. Paris: Editions Complexes, 1989.

Moulin, Jean. *Enquête sur la France multiraciale*. Paris: Calmann-Lévy, 1985.

Nora, Pierre. *Les Français d'Algérie*. Paris: Julliard, 1961.

Nouschi, André. *L'Algérie amère*. Paris: Editions de la Maison des Sciences de l'Homme, 1996.

Prochaska, David. *Making Algeria French: Colonialism in Bône, 1870–1920*. Cambridge: Cambridge University Press, 1990.

Rosello, Mireille. *Postcolonial Hospitality: The Immigrant as Guest*. Stanford, Calif.: Stanford University Press, 2001.

Roux, Jean-Pierre, ed. *La guerre d'Algérie et les Français*. Paris: Fayard, 1990.

Stora, Benjamin. *La gangrène et l'oubli*. Paris: La Découverte, 1991.

———. *Histoire de L'Algérie coloniale, 1830–1954*. Paris: La Découverte, 1994.

———. *L'Algérie en 1995: La guerre, l'histoire, la politique*. Paris: Editions Michalon, 1995.

Tarr, Carrie. "Questions of Identity in Beur Cinema: From Tea in the Harem to Cheb." *Screen* 34, no. 4: 321–42.

Timsit, Daniel. *Algérie, récit anachronique I*. Paris: Editions Bouchene, 1999.

Tlemçani, Rachid. *State and Revolution in Algeria*. London: Zed, 1986.

Vogl, Mary. *Picturing the Maghreb: Literature, Photography, (Re)presentation*. Lanham, Md.: Rowman & Littlefield, 2003.

Woodhull, Winifred. *Transformations of the Maghreb: Feminism, Decolonization, and Literature*. Minneapolis: University of Minnesota Press, 1993.

## PART IV: MISCEGENATION, DEGENERATION, AND OTHER METROPOLITAN ANXIETIES

### Primary Works

Bouraoui, Hédi. *Bangkok Blues*. Ottawa: Editions du Vermillon, 1994.

Claus, Hugo. *The Sorrow of Belgium*. Translated by Arnold J. Pomerans. Harmondsworth, U.K.: Penguin, 1990.

Lê, Linda. *Slander*. Translated by Esther Allen. Lincoln: University of Nebraska Press, 1996.

———. *Les trois Parques*. Paris: C. Bourgois, 1997.

———. *Autres jeux avec le feu*. Paris: C. Bourgois, 2002.

Lefèbvre, Kim. *Métisse blanche*. Paris: Bernard Barrault, 1989.

———. *Retour à la saison des pluies*. Paris: Editions de l'aube, 1995.

Mertens, Pierre. *Une paix royale*. Paris: Seuil, 1995.

Neirynck, Jacques. *Le siège de Bruxelles*. Paris: Desclée de Brouwer, 1996.

Rachilde. *La Jongleuse*. Paris: Editions des femmes, 1983 (1900).

———. *The Juggler*. Translated by Melanie Hawthorne. New Brunswick, N.J.: Rutgers University Press, 1990.

### Secondary Works

Archer-Straw, Petrine. *Negrophilia: Avant-Garde Paris and Black Culture in the 1920s*. New York: Thames & Hudson, 2000.

Balesi, Charles John. *From Adversaries to Comrades-in-Arms: West Africans and the French Military, 1885–1918*. Waltham, Mass.: Crossroads Press, 1979.

Becker, Jean-Jacques. *Les français dans la grande guerre*. Paris: Robert Laffont, 1980.

Betz, Hans-Georg. *Radical Right-Wing Populism in Western Europe*. New York: St. Martin's Press, 1994.

Blake, Jody. *Le Tumulte Noir: Modernist Art and Popular Entertainment in Jazz-Age Paris, 1900–1930*. University Park: Pennsylvania State University Press, 1999.

Bongie, Chris. *Exotic Memories: Literature, Colonialism, and the Fin de Siècle*. Stanford, Calif.: Stanford University Press, 1991.

Carroll, David. *French Literary Fascism: Nationalism, Anti-Semitism, and the Ideology of Culture*. Princeton, N.J.: Princeton University Press, 1995.

Cartuyvels, Yves, et al., eds. *L'affaire Dutroux: la Belgique malade de son système*. Brussels: Editions Complexe, 1997.

Clancy-Smith, Julia, and Frances Gouda, eds. *Domesticating the Empire: Race, Gender, and Family Life in French and Dutch Colonialism*. Charlottesville: University Press of Virginia, 1998.

Conklin, Alice. "Redefining 'Frenchness': Citizenship, Race Regeneration, and Imperial Motherhood in France and West Africa, 1914–1940." In Julia Clancy-Smith and Frances Gouda, eds. *Domesticating the Empire: Race, Gender, and Family Life in French and Dutch Colonialism.* Charlottesville: University Press of Virginia, 1998.

Constable, Elizabeth. "Yellow Fevers: Women Writers, Decadence and Discourses of Degeneracy." *L'Esprit Créateur* 37, no. 3 (1997): 25–37.

Conway, Martin. *Collaboration in Belgium: Léon Degrelle and the Rexist Movement, 1940–1944.* New Haven, Conn.: Yale University Press, 1993.

Cooper, Frederick, and Ann Laura Stoler. *Tensions of Empire: Colonial Cultures in a Bourgeois World.* Berkeley: University of California Press, 1997.

Corbin, Alain. *Les filles de noce: misère sexuelle et prostitution.* Paris: Aubier Montaigne, 1978.

Cousturier, Lucie. *Des inconnus chez moi.* Paris: Editions de la Sirène, 1920.

Darrow, Margaret H. *French Women and the First World War: War Stories of the Home Front.* Oxford: Berg, 2000.

Delatour, Yvonne. "Le travail des femmes pendant la première guerre mondiale et ses conséquences sur l'évolution de leur rôle dans la société." *Francia,* vol. 2 (1974).

Delétang, Louise. *Journal d'une Ouvrière Parisienne pendant la Guerre.* Paris: Éds. Eugène Figuière, 1936.

Deprez, Kas, and Louis Vos, eds. *Nationalism in Belgium: Shifting Identities,, 1780–1995.* New York: St. Martin's Press, 1998.

Dieckhoff, Alain, ed. *Belgique: la force de la désunion.* Brussels: Editions Complexe, 1996.

Downs, Laura Lee. "Women's Strikes and the Politics of Popular Egalitarianism in France, 1916–1918." In Lenard Berlanstein, ed. *Rethinking Labor History: Essays on Discourse and Class Analysis.* Urbana: University of Illinois Press, 1993.

Echenberg, Myron. *Colonial Conscripts: The Tirailleurs Senegalais in French West Africa, 1850–1960.* Portsmouth, N.H.: Heinemann, 1991.

Edwards, Penny. "Womanizing Indochina: Fiction, Nation, and Cohabitation in Colonial Cambodia, 1890–1930." In Julia Clancy-Smith and Frances Gouda, eds. *Domesticating the Empire: Race, Gender, and Family Life in French and Dutch Colonialism.* Charlottesville: University Press of Virginia, 1998.

Ezra, Elizabeth. *The Colonial Unconscious: Race and Culture in Interwar France.* Ithaca, N.Y.: Cornell University Press, 2000.

Favell, Adrian. *Philosophies of Integration: Immigration and the Idea of Citizenship in France and Britain.* New York: St. Martin's Press, 1998.

Favre, Mireille. "Un milieu porteur de modernisation: travailleurs et tirailleurs vietnamiens en France pendant la première guerre mondiale." Thèse pour diplôme d'archiviste-paléographe. 2 vols. École nationale des Chartes, 1986.

Gafaiti, Hafid, ed. *Culures transnationales de la France.* Paris: L'Harmattan, 2001.

Gaspard, Françoise. *A Small City in France.* Translated by Arthur Goldhammer. Cambridge, Mass.: Harvard University Press, 1995.

Grayzel, Susan. "Mothers, *Marraines* and Prostitutes: Morale and Morality in First World War France." *The International History Review* 19, no. 1 (February 1997).

Gullickson, Gay. *Unruly Women of Paris: Images of the Commune*. Ithaca, N.Y.: Cornell University Press, 1996.

Hammond, Paul. *French Undressing: Naughty Postcards from 1900 to 1920*. London: Jupiter Books, 1976. '

Hargreaves, Alec. *Immigration, "Race," and Ethnicity in Contemporary France*. London: Routledge, 1995.

Harris, Ruth. "The 'Child of the Barbarian': Rape, Race, and Nationalism in France during the First World War." *Past and Present*, no. 141 (November 1993).

Hermans, Theo, ed. *The Flemish Movement: A Documentary History, 1780–1990*. London: Athlone, 1992.

Hochschild, Adam. *King Leopold's Ghost: A Story of Greed, Terror, and Heroism in Colonial Africa*. New York: Houghton Mifflin, 1998.

Horne, John. "Immigrant Workers in France during World War I." *French Historical Studies* 14, no. 1 (spring 1985).

Horne, John. *Labour at War: France and Britain, 1914–1918*. Oxford: Clarendon Press, 1991.

Knibiehler, Yvonne, and Régine Goutalier. *La femme au temps des colonies*. Paris: Stock, 1985.

Lionnet, Françoise. "'Logiques métisses': Cultural Appropriation and Postcolonial Representations." *College Literature* 19–20/3–1 (1992–1993): 100–120.

Lunn, Joe. *Memoirs of the Maelstrom: A Senegalese Oral History of the First World War*. Portsmouth, N.H.: Heinemann, 1999.

McMillan, James F. *Housewife or Harlot: The Place of Women in French Society 1870–1940*. New York: St. Martin's Press, 1981.

Moniquet, Claude. *Les dossiers noirs de la Belgique*. Neuilly-sur-Seine: Michel Lafon, 1999.

Morelli, Anne, ed. *Les grands mythes de l'histoire de Belgique, de Flandre et de Wallonie*. Brussels: Editions Vie Ouvrière, 1995.

Nogaro, Bertrand, and Lucien Weil. *La Main-d'Oeuvre Étrangère et Coloniale pendant la Guerre*. Paris: PUF, 1926.

Nordau, Max. *Degeneration* (1892). Translated by George L. Mosse. Lincoln: University of Nebraska Press, 1993.

Norindr, Panivong. *Phantasmatic Indochina: French Colonial Ideology in Architecture, Film, and Literature*. Durham, N.C.: Duke University Press, 1996.

Paquet, Marcel. *Le fascisme blanc: mésaventures de la Belgique*. Paris: Editions de la différence, 1998.

Pick, Daniel. *Faces of Degeneration: A European Disorder, c.1848–c.1918*. Cambridge: Cambridge University Press, 1989.

Pickels, Antoine, and Jacques Sojcher, eds. *Belgique toujours grande et belle*. Brussels: Editions Complexe, 1998.

Pierrot, Jean. *The Decadent Imagination, 1880–1900*. Translated by Derek Coltman. Chicago: University of Chicago Press, 1981.

Renucci, France. *Souvenirs de femmes au temps des colonies*. Paris: Balland, 1988.

Reynolds, Sian. *France between the Wars: Gender and Politics*. London: Routledge, 1996.

Robert, Jean-Louis. "Ouvriers et Mouvement ouvrier parisiens pendant la grande guerre et l'immédiate après-Guerre." Thèse, Doctorat d'État. 9 vols. Université de Paris-I, 1989.

Roberts, Mary Louise. *Civilization Without Sexes: Reconstructing Gender in Post-war France, 1917–1927*. Chicago: University of Chicago Press, 1994.

Smith, Bonnie. *Ladies of the Leisure Class: The Bourgeoises of Northern France in the 19th Century*. Princeton, N.J.: Princeton University Press, 1981.

Stengers, Jean. "Le mythe des dominations étrangères dans l'historiographie belge." *Revue belge de philologie et d'histoire* LIX (1981): 382–401.

Stoler, Ann. "Making Empire Respectable: The Politics of Race and Sexual Morality in 20th Century Colonial Cultures." *American Ethnologist* 16, no. 4 (November 1989).

———. *Imperial Monkey Business: Racial Supremacy in Social Darwinist Theory and Colonial Practice*, ed. Jan Breman. Amsterdam: VU University Press, 1990.

———. *Race and the Education of Desire: Foucault's History of Sexuality and the Colonial Order of Things*. Durham, N.C.: Duke University Press, 1995.

Stovall, Tyler. *The Rise of the Paris Red Belt*. Berkeley: University of California Press, 1990.

———. "Colour-blind France? Colonial Workers During the First World War." *Race and Class* 35, no. 2 (October–December 1993).

———. "The Color Line behind the Lines: Racial Violence in France during the Great War." *The American Historical Review* 103, no. 3 (1998).

Strikwerda, Carl. *A House Divided: Catholics, Socialists, and Flemish Nationalists in Nineteenth-Century Belgium*. Lanham, Md.: Rowman & Littlefield, 1997.

Swart, Koenraad W. *The Sense of Decadence in Nineteenth-Century France*. The Hague: Martinus Nijhoff, 1964.

Tadiar, Neferti. "The Dream-Work of Modernity: The Sentimental Education of Imperial France." *Boundary 2*, vol. 22, no. 1 (spring 1995).

Thébaud, Françoise. *La femme au temps de la guerre de 14*. Paris: Stock, 1986.

Trousson, Raymond. *La légende de la Jeune Belgique*. Brussels: Académie de langue et de littérature française, 2000.

Van Den Abbeele, Georges. "No Joking Matter: The 'Other' Belgium." *Social Identites* 7, no. 4 (2001): 511–24.

Vidalenc, Jean. "La main d'oeuvre étrangère en France et la première guerre mondiale (1901–1926)." *Francia*, vol. 2 (1974).

Weil, Patrick. *La France et ses étrangers*. Paris: Gallimard Folio, 1991.

White, Owen. *Children of the French Empire: Miscegenation and Colonial Society in French West Africa, 1895–1960*. New York: Oxford University Press, 1999.

Zolberg, Aristide. "The Making of Flemings and Walloons: Belgium, 1830–1914." *Journal of Interdisciplinary History* 5, no. 2 (1974): 179–235.

# INDEX

abolition, 129, 134–36
Académie française, 8–10, 16n8, 62
Acropolis, 50
Africa: colonization of, 325
Africans, 106–11, 129, 132, 176–79, 300, 332–33. *See also* Blacks
Algeria, 6, 199, 217, 247–48, 257–62
Algerian Jews. *See* Jews, Algerian
Algerians. *See* North Africans
Algerian War, 6, 187, 203–4, 238, 243; and Jews, 254, 264
anti-Semitism, 40n31, 194, 256–59, 264, 267n27, 268n36, 333
Arabs. *See* North Africans
architecture, 43, 50–51
art, 43–45, 48, 50–51, 136
assimilation, 4–9, 124, 106, 188, 198–99, 217–21
Baudelaire, Charles, 279–81, 291, 326
Belgium, 323–37; children, 326, 328, 330–35; cinema, 328, 336; colonialism, 323, 332; crime, 333–37, 342n36, 342n37; iconography of, 14, 333–35; identity,

14, 323, 336–37; language, 324, 327, 329, 339n11; and literature, 326–29, 332, 338n10; nationalism, 335, 338n8; relationship to France, 323–24, 327, 330–32, 337; trade, 335–36
Beurs. *See* North Africans
Bibliothèque Nationale, 138
blackness, 103–4, 116, 121–27, 178
blacks, 75, 116, 126, 131–38, 176, 180, 286; humanness of, 120–25, 192–93; in literature, 177–83; and Master-Slave dialectic, 119–21; reciprocal recognition with whites, 120, 127; self-consciousness, 122–26; stereotypes, 125–26, 183, 285; writers, 129–38, 147–65, 173–84

capitalism: in literature, 177–78
Carné, Marcel, 55
Casbah (Algiers), 55
Casseus, Maurice, 104, 173–84, 185n6
Catholicism, 329. *See also* religion
censorship, 311–13, 331

# ABOUT THE CONTRIBUTORS

**Janet Bergstrom** is a Professor in the Department of Film, TV, and Digital Media at the University of California–Los Angeles, and a founding editor of *Camera Obscura*. Her areas of research include feminism and film theory, émigré directors Lang, Murnau, and Renoir, and contemporary directors Chantal Akerman and Claire Denis. She published the anthology *Endless Night: Cinema and Psychoanalysis, Parallel Histories* (University of California Press, 1999), a voice-over commentary for Murnau's *Tabu* on DVD (Milestone/Image Entertainment 2002), and a 40-minute feature on Murnau's *4 Devils* for Fox's *Sunrise* DVD (2003).

**Hafid Gafaiti** is Jeanne Charnier-Qualia Professor of French and Francophone Studies at Texas Tech University. He has written extensively on contemporary Francophone literature, feminism, and cultural issues in a postcolonial setting. His most recent publications include *Rachid Boudjedra: Une poétique de la subversion: I. Autobiographie et Histoire* (L'Harmattan, 1999), *French Feminism Across the Disciplines* (Intertexts, 1998), and *Les femmes dans le roman algérien* (L'Harmattan, 1996). Currently, he is working on a book entitled *The Pact of Censorship* as well as two edited volumes: *Language and National Identity in Postcolonial Contexts* and *Problématiques Identitaires au Québec*. He is editor in chief of *Etudes Francophones et Comparées/Francophone and Comparative Studies*, published by L'Harmattan.

**Édouard Glissant** is distinguished Professor of French and Francophone Literature at the Graduate Center of the City University of New York. A novelist, poet, essayist, and literary critic, Glissant is one of the leading Francophone intellectuals of today and one of the founders of the *créolité* school of literary theory. He is in particular famous for his influential study of Caribbean diasporic identity, *Le Discours antillais* (Éditions du Seuil, 1981), translated into English under the title *Caribbean Discourse* by J. Michael Dash (University Press of Virginia, 1989).

**Donna Hunter** is Associate Professor of Art History at the University of California–Santa Cruz. She has published on French art and art history, in journals like *La révue de l'Art, Romantic Review*, and the *Oxford Art Journal*. She is currently working on a project concerning the visual culture of the Terror, concentrating on the work of Jacques-Louis David.

**Jean Jonassaint** teaches Francophone literatures in the Romance Studies Department of Duke University and serves on the editorial board of the journals *Études francophones* and *Nepantla: Views from South*. He is the author of *La Déchirure du (corps) texte et autres brèches* (1984), *Le Pouvoir des mots, les maux du pouvoir: Des romanciers haïtiens de l'exil* (1986), *Des romans de tradition haïtienne: Sur un récit tragique* (2002), and numerous articles focusing particularly on Francophone literatures.

**Valerie Kaussen** is Assistant Professor of French at the University of Missouri–Columbia. Her work focuses on the ways Caribbean identities are imaginatively mapped and how such mappings are enhanced or disrupted by the dynamics of global capitalism. Her current book project addresses representations of alternative modernities in Haitian twentieth-century fiction.

**Ethan Kleinberg** is Assistant Professor of History and Letters at Wesleyan University and Assistant Editor of *History and Theory*. His book *Generation Existential: The Reception of Martin Heidegger's Philosophy in France, 1927–1961* is forthcoming from Cornell University Press. His current research interests include European intellectual history, critical theory, educational structures, postcolonialism, and the reading and writing of history.

**Driss Maghraoui** is Assistant Professor of Modern Middle East, Islamic Civilization, World History, and French Colonial History at Al Akhawayn University in Ifrane, Morocco. He is completing a book on *Moroccan Colo-*

*nial Troops: History, Memory and the Culture of French Colonialism.* Maghraoui has a number of articles on the social and cultural history of colonial Morocco and North Africa. He is currently a Rice Foundation Visiting Assistant Professor in the History Department at Yale University.

**Patricia A. Morton** is Associate Professor of Architectural History and Theory at the University of California–Riverside. Her book on the 1931 Colonial Exposition in Paris, *Hybrid Modernities*, was published in 2000 by MIT Press and in Japan by Brücke in 2002. Her current research focuses on camp and "bad taste" in early postmodern architecture (1960–1975). She is editing a *Festschrift* in honor of Alan Colquhoun (Princeton Architectural Press), and a volume of essays on taste and popular culture in the 1960s (Blackwell Press). Professor Morton also writes on contemporary American and European architecture, gender, and postcolonial theory.

**Tyler Stovall** is Professor of History at the University of California–Berkeley, where he specializes in labor and urban history as well as the study of peoples of color in modern France. Major publications include *The Rise of the Paris Red Belt* (University of California Press, 1990), *Paris Noir: African Americans in the City of Light* (Houghton Mifflin, 1996), and *France Since the Second World War* (Longman, 2002). He is currently working on a social history of Caribbean migration to France.

**Richard Terdiman** is Professor of Literature and History of Consciousness at the University of California–Santa Cruz, where he teaches European literary and cultural history. He is the author of *Dialectics of Isolation: Self and Society in the French Novel from the Realists to Proust* (Yale University Press, 1976), *Discourse/Counter-Discourse: The Theory and Practice of Symbolic Resistance in Nineteenth-Century France* (Cornell University Press, 1985), and *Present Past: Modernity and the Memory Crisis* (Cornell University Press, 1993). Professor Terdiman is currently working on the pragmatics and politics of cultural theory and on the concept of time in modernity.

**Lyn Thompson** is a doctoral candidate in the Department of French at New York University. Her dissertation, "The Vicarious Voyage: Reading the Exotic in the Novels of Pierre Loti," combines narratological analysis with reception theory to examine the relationship between real and implied readers in the context of literary marketing, tourism, and colonialism in the fin de siècle.

**Georges Van Den Abbeele** is Director of the Davis Humanities Institute and Professor of French and Italian at the University of California–Davis. Author of *Travel as Metaphor: From Montaigne to Rousseau* (University of Minnesota Press, 1992) and a forthcoming volume, *Utopias of Difference: A Genealogy of the French Intellectual*, he is currently at work on theories of national identity with particular attention to the case of Belgium.

**Nancy Wood** is Dean of the School of Critical Studies at the California Institute of the Arts. She is the co-editor of *The Liberation of France: Image and Event* (Berg, 1995), and the author of *Vectors of Memory: Legacies of Trauma in Postwar Europe* (Berg, 1999).

**Winifred Woodhull** is Associate Professor of Literature at the University of California–San Diego. She is the author of *Transfigurations of the Maghreb: Feminism, Decolonization and Literature* (University of Minnesota Press, 1993) and has published widely on French avant-garde literature, literatures of immigration, and film.

**Ali Yedes** is Assistant Professor of French at Oberlin College. His published research addresses issues in North African, Beur, and Franco-Vietnamese literature. His *Camus l'Algérien* is forthcoming from L'Harmattan Press.